ORIGINS OF GENIUS

~ ORIGINS OF GENIUS ~

Darwinian Perspectives on Creativity

Dean Keith Simonton

New York   Oxford

OXFORD UNIVERSITY PRESS

1999

Oxford University Press

Oxford New York

Athens Auckland Bangkok Bogotá Buenos Aires Calcutta
Cape Town Chennai Dar es Salaam Delhi Florence Hong Kong Istanbul
Karachi Kuala Lumpur Madrid Melbourne Mexico City Mumbai
Nairobi Paris São Paulo Singapore Taipei Tokyo Toronto Warsaw

and associated companies in
Berlin Ibadan

Published by Oxford University Press, Inc.
198 Madison Avenue, New York, New York 10016
http://www.oup-usa.org

Oxford is a registered trademark of Oxford University Press

Library of Congress Cataloging-in-Publication Data
Simonton, Dean Keith.
Origins of genius:
Darwinian perspectives on creativity/
Dean Keith Simonton.
p. cm. Includes bibliographical references and index.
ISBN 0-19-512879-6
1. Genius. 2. Creative ability.
3. Darwin, Charles, 1809–1882. I. Title.
BF412.S58 1999 153.9'8 — dc21 98-45044

9 8 7 6 5 4 3 2 1
Printed in the United States of America
on acid-free paper

To all Darwinists

Contents

~

Preface

~

For nearly a quarter of a century, I have been conducting scientific inquiries into the nature and origins of creative genius. The subjects of these investigations have included thousands of eminent figures from most of the world's civilizations and key domains of creative activity: scientists and artists, philosophers and composers, poets and psychologists. During the course of my research, I have come to admire many outstanding exemplars of creativity. From European civilization, for instance, come such personal idols as Beethoven, Shakespeare, and Leonardo da Vinci. Nonetheless, because I am a behavioral scientist, my private list of heroes tends to be heavily weighted toward those who have made signal contributions to scientific knowledge. At the top of the roster are such notables as Galileo, Pascal, Newton, Faraday, Pasteur, and Einstein. But my all-time favorite is Charles Darwin. There are probably three main reasons for this choice.

First, Darwin had an unusually attractive and approachable personality, at least as revealed in his autobiography and correspondence. He had a rare combination of frankness, modesty, and persuasive self-confidence. Seriously dedicated to the hard work of science, Darwin also could enjoy the everyday world of family and community. He was arguably the most human of all scientific luminaries. He is certainly more accessible than Newton.

Second, all of his landmark contributions are accessible to educated lay readers—including me. One does not need special training, mathematical or otherwise, to read the *Origin of Species*, for example. Indeed, I can think of no scientific masterpiece that can boast such universal appeal. Newton's *Principia*, in contrast, is very tough going, even for physicists (who are now unschooled in its archaic mathematics). At the same time, Darwin did not compromise his scientific integrity or effectiveness in producing such a popular work. It is rich in logic and fact—features that render the work all the more thought provoking and convincing.

Third, and probably most important, no scientist, living or deceased, has more influenced my own thinking than has Charles Darwin. I may admire Einstein or Newton or Galileo, but their epoch-making ideas belong to someone else's discipline. In comparison, Darwin's powerful contributions have left their indelible imprints throughout the biological and behavioral sciences, psychology not excluded. Great psychologists as diverse as William James, Sigmund Freud, and B. F. Skinner have all acknowledged Darwin's penetrating influence. In fact, among the first behavioral scientists to feel the impact of Darwin's ideas was Francis Galton, whose 1869 *Hereditary Genius* is considered one of the landmarks in the scientific study of creative genius.

Which brings me to my purpose in writing this book: Not only do I admire Darwin as a creative genius par excellence, but in addition I believe that Darwin provided the secure foundations for a comprehensive theory of extraordinary creativity. For more than a decade now, I have been grappling with whether the diverse features of creative phenomena are best understood from a Darwinian perspective. This potential application is by no means new with me. I have many predecessors going as far back as Galton and James. Nevertheless, I believe the time has come to consolidate all of the diverse efforts at constructing a Darwinian theory of creative genius. Besides advancing our understanding of creativity, such a consolidation would also serve as a kind of homage to that scientist who most profoundly shaped my own thinking.

I would like to thank Joan Bossert and Philip Laughlin, my editors at Oxford, whose initial reactions to an early draft of this book were most encouraging. I am particularly grateful to Philip for his having obtained a balanced set of external reviewers. Two of these evaluators provided detailed critiques along with a willingness to be identified: Colin Martindale and Howard Gardner. In addition, Frank Sulloway provided numerous, detailed, and useful comments on what I had—quite mistakenly!—thought to be the final draft. Although none of these readers can be said to be sympathetic with everything in the final product, I hope that all will appreciate my attempts to accommodate their most significant criticisms. The book certainly has much fewer faults as a result of their input.

Charles Darwin did all of his research at home. He was therefore fortunate to have a family willing to provide him with that special environment he needed to read and write, contemplate and experiment. Because I also do virtually all of my own research at home, I must feel myself equally blessed. Specifically, I must explicitly thank my wife, Melody, and my daughter, Sabrina. Melody's role was especially crucial, and in all aspects of my life and work. I can think of no better way of honoring her contribution than to quote what Darwin said of his own wife:

> She has been my greatest blessing, and I can declare in my whole life I have never heard her utter one word which I had rather have been unsaid. She has never failed in the kindest sympathy towards me, and has borne with the utmost patience my frequent complaints. . . . I do not believe she has ever missed an opportunity of doing a kind action to anyone near her. I marvel at my good fortune that she, so infinitely my superior in every single moral quality, consented to be my wife. She has been my wise adviser and cheerful comforter throughout life, which without her would have been . . . a miserable one. . . . She has earned the love and admiration of every soul near her.

ORIGINS OF GENIUS

1

~

GENIUS
AND DARWIN

The Surprising Connections

~

Civilizations are often defined by the lives and works of their creative geniuses. The glory that was ancient Greece was built on the achievements of Homer, Pythagoras, Herodotus, Sophocles, Plato, Hippocrates, Phidias, and hundreds of other great creators. Modern European civilization was illuminated by the likes of Galileo, Descartes, Tolstoy, Rembrandt, and Mozart. The same story may be told of the world's other civilizations. The histories of Persia, India, China, and other high cultures are to a very large extent chronologically arranged biographies of notable creative minds. As Thomas Carlyle proclaimed in his famous 1841 essay *On Heroes*, "Universal History, the history of what man has accomplished in this world, is at bottom the History of the Great Men who have worked here." Among those he discussed at length as illustrations were Dante and Shakespeare, two of the greatest writers in any language.

So obvious is the debt civilizations owe these exceptional individuals that the appearance of such geniuses is often considered an indication of the creative health of a civilized culture. For example, this linking is evident in the 1944 *Configurations of Culture Growth* by Alfred Kroeber, an eminent cultural anthropologist. Wishing to gauge the emergence, growth, and stagnation of civilizations throughout the world, Kroeber could conceive of no better method than to assess the appearance of famous creators across a culture's history. A civilization enjoyed a golden age when it overflowed with first-rate creative minds, experienced a silver age when the creative activity descended to a less notable level, and suffered a dark age when creators became few and far between. Indeed, this association goes beyond the abstract operational definitions of behavioral scientists. What nation does not take pride when one of its writers or scientists is awarded the Nobel Prize?

Yet who are these creative luminaries? Where do they come from? When do they appear? What are they like? Can any one of us become a creative genius? Or is high-caliber creativity limited to the one in a million?

These questions are important. In fact, they provide the impetus behind my writing this book. But before I can even begin to address these issues, I must first define what we will take to mean "creative genius."

Creative Genius

Actually, I need to define two distinct even if overlapping terms: *genius* and *creativity*. I will begin with a look at the multiple ways that genius can be defined, identifying the definition that will prove most useful in this book. I will then turn to the task of defining creativity, another concept that can be defined in more than one way. By merging these definitions, we end up with the book's subject matter.

Genius

The word *genius* has a curious etymology. It dates from Roman times, when the word signified the guardian spirit of a particular individual or location. Because this spirit provided for the distinctiveness or uniqueness of the entity with which it was identified, it came to represent that which was special about the person, place, period, or other entity. Thus, we could speak of the "genius" of a culture or era or even people, such as the genius of Native American culture, the genius of the Elizabethan age, or the genius of the Arabic language. With respect to individuals, the term *genius* became descriptive of some natural talent, ability, or disposition, especially when it goes well beyond the norm. Hence, a person might have a genius for making the most apt remarks in socially difficult situations. In the extreme case, an individual might achieve fame for the realization of this special talent. As a consequence, famous composers, artists, writers, and scientists began to be called geniuses. Beethoven was a musical genius, Shakespeare a dramatic genius, Michelangelo an artistic genius, Newton a scientific genius, and so forth. Because the successful exercise of these special aptitudes seemed to imply an extraordinary degree of intellect or talent, the word *genius* also began to be used in the more generic fashion favored today—as someone who exhibits exceptional intellectual or creative power. The specific application of this power was less important than the possession of the capacity. It is for this reason that Samuel Johnson, the author of the first English dictionary, could claim that "the true Genius is a mind of large general powers, accidentally determined to some particular direction."

Behavioral scientists have recognized the significance of the term *genius* by attempting to provide it with a more exact meaning. If the concept has any scientific content, it should be possible to devise quantitative measures to evaluate it. These measures may then be used to gauge the magnitude of genius an individual can claim, or at least to identify those who most deserve the appellation. Such measures are of two kinds, namely, those who attempt to assess intelligence and those who try to estimate eminence.

Intelligence. At the beginning of this century, psychologists tried to build a more precise definition on the more generic meaning suggested by Samuel Johnson. This new conception was founded on the intelligence test. Alfred Binet had already devised a measure of intellectual ability, which others transformed into a measure of IQ, the intelligence quotient. People with average powers received scores of 100, and scores lower or higher than this baseline figure indicated whether an individual was below or above average in intellectual ability. Eventually, a number of psychologists, such as Lewis Terman at Stanford University and Leta Hollingworth at Columbia University, began identifying children as "geniuses" who obtained exceptionally high scores on these tests. The exact cutoff would vary from researcher to researcher, although it seems that the threshold IQ ranged somewhere between 130 and 140. The basic assumption was that someone with an IQ in this range or higher could boast the "mind of large general powers" that might be channeled successfully into almost any activity.

This high-IQ definition of genius became very popular not only among psychologists but among the general public besides. Parents of high-IQ children would learn to call their offspring "geniuses." There even exists a society named Mensa that consists solely of "geniuses" who have scored a bit better than 130 on some standard IQ test. Even so, this psychometric definition leaves much to be desired. As will become apparent later in this book, a high IQ by no means ensures that an individual will display any special talent or achievement beyond the rather restricted ability to score high on standardized tests. For instance, the *Guinness Book of Records* notes that Marilyn vos Savant holds the record with an IQ of 228, and yet she does not have the kind of accomplishments to her credit that we might predict from such an exceptional intellect. Rather than discovering the cure for cancer or even making a better mousetrap, her achievements thus far have been limited to writing the weekly column "Ask Marilyn," in which she responds to readers' questions that supposedly only a real brain can answer.

Even worse, those with accomplishments worthy of the designation "genius" do not always make the IQ cut. When Terman first used the IQ test to select a sample of child geniuses, he unknowingly excluded a special child whose IQ did not make the grade. Yet a few decades later that overlooked talent received the Nobel Prize in physics: William Shockley, the cocreator of the transistor. Ironically, not one of the more than 1,500 children who qualified according to his IQ criterion received so high an honor as adults. Clearly, a Nobel laureate has much greater claim to the term *genius* than those whose achievements did not win them such applause.

Eminence. The last statement brings us to an alternative definition—the one preferred for use throughout this book. This particular definition's origins go back over a century, to Francis Galton, whose 1869 classic, *Hereditary Genius*, defined genius in terms of enduring reputation. By this Galton meant "the opinion of contemporaries, revised by posterity . . . the reputation of a leader of opinion, of an originator, of a man to whom the world deliberately acknowledges itself largely indebted." Certainly, those men and women who receive Nobel Prizes are honored for this very reason. When Niels Bohr received the Nobel Prize for physics, when Marie Curie received one for chemistry, when Ivan Pavlov received one for medicine and physiology, and when Toni Morrison received one for literature, they were being acknowledged for their notable contributions to their respective domains, and hence to human culture as a whole.

The only qualification that we must impose on this attribution is that, as Galton noted, the "opinion of contemporaries" must be "revised by posterity." There do exist occasions when contemporary judgment errs according to the retrospective assessment of subsequent generations. Banting and Macleod, for example, shared a 1923 Nobel Prize for figuring out a way to isolate insulin, yet now the credit is given to Banting and his laboratory assistant Best, the original role of Macleod now being considered minimal at best. Nonetheless, empirical studies have amply demonstrated that there exists a strong consensus linking the judgments of contemporaries with the evaluations of posterity. Those who were most famous in their own times tend to be the most eminent decades, even centuries, later. Hence, Dante was being overly pessimistic when he claimed that "worldly renown is naught but a breath of wind, which now comes this way and now comes that, and changes name because it changes quarter." In fact, eminence relies not only on transhistorical stability but on cross-cultural consensus besides. Individual differences in distinction cut across national boundaries and transcend subcultures within nations. For example, differential fame of African Americans within that minority culture correlates very highly with the differential fame of those same luminaries within the majority European American culture.

This eminence definition of genius has four major advantages. First, it automatically avoids the problem of the so-called unrecognized genius. If an individual commands no reputation, and thus is unrecognized, then it is not possible for him or her to claim status as a genius. Indeed, the phrase *unrecognized genius* becomes an oxymoron. Second, the eminence definition comes closer to what genius means in everyday language. The word is commonly used to refer to those individuals whose impact on history is most widely recognized as broad and enduring. Third, this definition captures something of the notion of uniqueness that is present in the word's etymology. People do not claim fame because they do what everyone else does. On the contrary, they attain distinction because they accomplish that which sets them apart from the crowd. Every first-rate genius is necessarily *sui generis.* Fourth, because eminence varies immensely from person to person, the current definition allows us to speak of degrees of genius. For instance, the place of Beethoven in the history of European music amply exceeds that of his contemporary Anton Reicha. On that basis we can style Beethoven the superior genius. Only Bach and Mozart have reputations that rival Beethoven's in the world of classical music.

Of course, no definition is perfect. Fame is at times capricious. Eminence is sometimes bestowed without complete regard to actual achievement. As Shakespeare once put it, "some are born great, some achieve greatness, and some have greatness thrust upon 'em." Even so, the connection between overt accomplishments and ultimate distinction is not so whimsical as to render this operational definition invalid. It will be sufficient for our purposes to concur with Thomas Carlyle when he noted that "fame, we may understand, is no sure test of merit, but only a probability of such." That probability is especially high when we deal with those who attain distinction for creativity.

Creativity

Another contemporary of Beethoven, Napoleon, also earned the title of genius, in his case military genius. Indeed, by the eminence definition, Napoleon's genius may have far exceeded that of Beethoven. Winning decisive battles probably has far more impact than writing popular symphonies. However, in this book our interest will be in genius associated with creativity rather than that associated with leadership. This imposes the need to define what counts as creativity. Fortunately, this is a somewhat easier task. Psychologists have reached the conclusion that creativity must entail the following two separate components.

First, a creative idea or product must be original. Producing exact copies of someone else's paintings, or reproducing verbatim quotes from other people's poetry, or repeating scientific theories that others have already presented before the world—none of this can be considered original. Hence, not one of these activities is deemed creative. However, to provide a meaningful criterion, originality must be defined with respect to a particular sociocultural group. What may be original with respect to one culture may be old news to the members of some other culture. Thus, Galileo's discovery of sunspots counts as an original contribution to European civilization even though the Chinese had noted their existence for well over a thousand years.

Second, the original idea or product must prove adaptive in some sense. The exact nature of this criterion depends on the type of creativity being displayed. In terms of technology, for example, an invention must not only be new, but it must also work. A rocket made of cinder blocks may be original, but if it cannot get off the ground, the conception cannot be considered creative. A scientific theory, in contrast, must be logically coherent and factually correct to count as adaptive. A theory that is self-contradictory or that conflicts with the best established empirical findings may be original, but it cannot be considered creative. In the arts, finally, adaptiveness often entails the capacity to maintain interest through novel expression as well as through powerful emotional appeal. For instance, a symphony that lacks beautiful or exciting themes and that fails to make a deeper emotional connection with the audience will fail by the criterion of adaptiveness. Clearly, an original idea or product is judged as adaptive not by the originator but rather by the recipients. Accordingly, we have another reason for maintaining that creativity entails an interpersonal or sociocultural evaluation. Not only must others decide whether something seems original, but they are also the ultimate judges of whether that something appears workable.

Given the foregoing two-criterion definition of creativity, we are now ready to define more precisely what we mean by creative genius. Essentially, these are individuals credited with creative ideas or products that have left a large impression on a particular domain of intellectual or aesthetic activity. In other words, the creative genius attains eminence by leaving for posterity an impressive body of contributions that are both original and adaptive. In fact, empirical studies have repeatedly shown that the single most powerful predictor of eminence within any creative domain is the sheer number of influential products an individual has given the world. Mozart is considered a greater musical genius than Tartini in part because the former accounts for 30 times as much music in the classical repertoire as does the latter. Indeed, almost a fifth of all classical music performed in modern times was written by just three composers: Bach, Mozart, and Beethoven. Parallel points can be made with regard to scientific creativity. The most potent predictor of contemporary and posthumous fame is the number of citations a scientist receives from other scientists who publish in professional journals. In fact, those scientists who receive the most journal citations also have the highest odds of earning the Nobel Prize for contributions to their scientific discipline.

Notice that this definition of creative genius agrees with Galton's eminence criterion. These individuals are originators whose contributions are acknowledged by contemporary and future generations. These are people to whom others feel indebted. And this indebtedness can be illustrated in countless ways. It is shown when we walk through an art museum, attend a concert or opera, see a classic play, or read a great book. Homage is paid when the discoveries and inventions of the past are used to construct the miracles of today, whether they be drugs, telephones, computers, automobiles, bridges, jet airliners, or rockets. Of course, some of us display our indebtedness in more explicit fashion when we attempt to build on the achievements of a notable predecessor. As Newton advised, we can see farther than the rest if we stand on the shoulders of giants. If we wish to see farther into the origins of genius, the giant on whose shoulders we must stand may just be Galton's cousin, Charles Darwin.

Charles Darwin

Was Darwin a genius? If we had to give an answer based on the intelligence definition, the answer might be negative. Darwin admitted in his autobiography that he was considered "much slower in learning than my younger sister" and that his teachers and father viewed him "as a very ordinary boy, rather below the common standard in intellect." At school he found himself "singularly incapable of mastering any language." Nor did he mature into a particularly brilliant adult, as he revealed in the following self-assessment:

> I have no great quickness of apprehension or wit which is so remarkable in some clever men, for instance, Huxley. I am therefore a poor critic: a paper or book, when first read, generally excites my admiration, and it is only after considerable reflection that I perceive the weak points. My power to follow a long and purely abstract train of thought is very limited; and therefore I could never have succeeded with metaphysics or mathematics. My memory is extensive, yet hazy: it suffices to make me cautious by vaguely telling me that I have observed or read something opposed to the conclusion which I am drawing, or on the other hand in favour of it; and after a time I can generally recollect where to search for my authority.

Naturally, such modest remarks are hard to translate into a specific IQ score necessary for the application of the intelligence criterion. Nonetheless, one of Terman's graduate students at Stanford provided an estimate of

Darwin's IQ score based on his childhood and adolescent activities and achievements, including any clear signs of intellectual precocity. He weighed in with an IQ of only 135. Although this would be high enough to earn Darwin membership in Mensa, it would not have been sufficiently high to be included in Terman's primary sample of intellectually gifted children. Because such membership nominally demanded an IQ score of at least 140, Darwin might have joined a Nobel laureate among the rejects. Hence, by this definition Darwin would at best be considered a borderline genius.

Yet there can be no doubt that Darwin fits the Galtonian definition of creative genius. The magnitude of his influence on both the biological sciences and the world at large is unquestionable, made evident in a multitude of ways. For example, one ranking of "the 100 most influential persons in history" placed Darwin 17th, immediately after Moses! Darwin's 1859 volume *On the Origin of Species* has been identified as one of the "books that changed the world." And this same book, coupled with his *Descent of Man*, constituted a whole volume of the anthology *Great Books of the Western World*. Even a century after his death, hundreds of scientific journal articles appear each year that pay explicit homage to his powerful ideas. And thousands of books have been written on Darwin, his theories, and his empirical discoveries.

Perhaps the most striking evidence for Darwin's status is the fact that his name has become an eponym. An eponym is a word that originated in someone's proper name, such as is so often seen in place-names. Many creative geniuses have had their names expropriated in this fashion—another form of acknowledging our indebtedness. In the sciences, for example, there are laws attached to the names of Coulomb, Dalton, Fechner, Joule, Ohm, and Weber; temperature scales named after Celsius, Fahrenheit, and Kelvin; measurement units named after Ampère, Ångström, Bell, Faraday, Henry, Ørsted, and Watt; as well as miscellaneous elements, effects, concepts, theorems, processes, instruments, and even whole fields named after Boole, Curie, Descartes, Einstein, Fermi, Fourier, Galileo, Galvani, Gauss, Lamarck, Linnaeus, Lister, Mach, Maxwell, Mendel, Newton, Pasteur, Pavlov, Ptolemy, and Pythagoras. In Darwin's case, of course, the relevant additions to the list of eponyms are the adjective *Darwinian* and the noun *Darwinism*.

But what is Darwinism? Why is it so important? What did Darwin contribute that earns him eponymic status? To address this question, we must recognize that there actually exist two kinds of Darwinism, the primary and the secondary. The primary form comprises Darwin's theory of biological evolution, along with the many scientific developments extending from this theory to explain the diverse features of living organisms. The secondary form of Darwinism, in contrast, has to do with the explanation of other phenomena not directly related to biological evolution. Darwinian theory provides the basis for describing analogous processes that operate outside the sphere of biological evolution proper. This distinction between primary and secondary Darwinism is extremely important, because their scientific standings are not identical and the phenomena they treat are usually very different. Therefore, I must devote some time to outlining what these two forms entail.

Primary Darwinism

In essence, Darwin's *Origin of Species* was devoted to establishing a phenomenon and a process. The phenomenon was the evolution of life-forms. Darwin spent many pages trying to show how all biological species, both living and extinct, descended from common ancestral forms. Earlier species would not only change over time but they would also frequently undergo speciation, producing two or more species where previously there had been only one. One of the more effective illustrations is that of the extremely varied species of finches Darwin observed on the Galápagos Islands during his famed *Beagle* voyage. Although at first Darwin made no explicit effort to include *Homo sapiens* in this documentation, a dozen years later, in *Descent of Man*, he made it clear that he believed the human species had also evolved. Humans shared ancestors with the apes, who in turn had common origins in the early mammals—and so on down to the very beginnings of life on this planet.

The very idea of biological evolution was extremely controversial at the time. Most Europeans, and even most naturalists, believed that the biblical accounts of creation, as described in the first chapters of Genesis, were literally true. All species were created in one grand miracle by God, and for the most part species had been fixed in form since the creation, an event that had transpired as late as around 4000 B.C. To be sure, some naturalists would allow for catastrophic events, such as Noah's flood, that might have caused the extinction of some early life-forms and thus account for the previously unknown, fossilized animals that were being excavated. Even so, there was no reason to doubt the basic veracity of the creationist theory. Yet not only did Darwin struggle to undermine this prevailing view, his eventual inclusion of the human species in the evolutionary model struck at the very heart of the biblical story. God did not especially create Adam out of clay or create Eve out of Adam's rib, but rather all of us were descended from lowly apes and monkeys.

Of course, not everyone was adamantly opposed to the doctrine of evolution. Many were willing to weigh the evidence and arrive at their own conclusions. Gradually, Darwin was able to win over many of his most important contemporaries, such as T. H. Huxley, who joined him in propagating the revolutionary idea. Moreover, in some respects evolution had the zeitgeist on its side. Victorian England was obsessed with the idea of incessant progress, and evolution seemed to imply that the very origins of life involved an unrelenting progression from the less adaptive to the more adaptive and from the simple to the complex. Thus, human beings could be placed at the pinnacle of the evolutionary progression. And, taking things a step farther, some Darwinians would descry a similar progression taking place within our species, placing some races above others in some hypothetical hierarchy of humanity. For example, just such a racial ranking was advocated by Galton in his *Hereditary Genius*, in which he placed the Athenians above the British, and the British above the Africans.

Although the phenomenon of evolution was the most controversial feature of Darwin's contribution in his own day, evolution is now considered by almost all biological scientists to be an established fact rather than a speculative theory. Even the majority of the Christian faiths have come around to accepting the phenomenon, interpreting Genesis in a more figurative sense. Where there still remains room for scientific controversy, however, is in the Darwinian process by which evolution was said to take place. Put in a nutshell, the process may be characterized by the following six assertions.

1. There occurs spontaneous variation in life-forms within any given species. For example, the beaks of finches may be big or small, long or short. Of course, finches may vary on a host of other dimensions as well, such as coloration, overall size, wing design, digestive enzymes, and various instinctive behaviors involving courtship, nest building, and so forth.

2. These variable characteristics are to some extent subject to biological inheritance. That is, parents with certain traits tend to produce offspring with very similar traits. Like breeds like.

3. Some trait-variant life-forms are better adapted to the environment than others. For instance, some types of beaks may work best for small seeds, others for large seeds, and still others for insects or other classes of food. If small seeds are the predominant food source, a particular type of beak will become more adaptive.

4. The capacity of any species to reproduce their kind well outstrips the capacity of the environment to feed and shelter the potential progeny, which necessitates a "struggle for existence." The inspiration for this proposition came from the 1798 *Essay on the Principle of Population* by Thomas Malthus, who first discussed the negative consequences of humanity's aptitude for reproducing itself faster than it can feed itself.

5. Those variants that are more fit are more likely to survive and repro-

duce their kind. Those finches with beaks that best permit the exploitation of available food resources will have higher odds of surviving to maturity and of procreating through several breeding seasons. This is the critical Darwinian mechanism of natural selection.

6. With each successive generation, the more fit variants will gradually replace the less fit variants in a given population. The outcome is a population that maximally adapted to the resources of a particular environment. Over time what will emerge is an entirely new species.

Not only could this process explain the evolution of a species over geological time, but it could also account for the divergence of single species into two or more species—the phenomenon of speciation. Any complex environment contains a large variety of resources, such as different types of food or forms of shelter. Although an organism might endeavor to exploit all available resources, pursuing the strategy of a generalist, such an organism would find it difficult to compete with other organisms that have specialized in the exploitation of a subset of those resources—those that belong to what is now termed an "ecological niche." The result is the phenomenon of adaptive radiation. Naturally, one example of such speciation is the way that "Darwin's finches"—another eponym!—filled up the ecological niches created by the volcanic emergence of the Galápagos Islands. A more dramatic illustration is the manner in which the dinosaurs differentiated into their extremely varied forms: carnivores and herbivores, big and small, in a myriad of structural configurations, walking over the surface of the earth, swimming the planet's oceans, and winging their way through its skies.

Hence, although this Darwinian process of natural selection could explain many aspects of the phenomenon of evolution, it was a far cry from a complete system. Darwin himself was well aware of many of the difficulties in his theory, and he spent much of his life trying to make improvements in his theoretical system. Moreover, after Darwin's death others developed various aspects of his basic theory, expanding the explanatory power and sophistication of primary Darwinism. Three developments since the *Origin of Species* are worth special mention here: sexual selection, the "modern synthesis," and sociobiology. Besides documenting the tremendous explanatory power of Darwinian theory, we will come across ideas that may have potential for helping us understand Darwinian perspectives on the origins of creative genius.

Sexual selection. Darwin realized very early that not all traits organisms possess can be easily explained according to the principle of natural selection. Indeed, sometimes a species would exhibit certain structures or behaviors that seem to be outright maladaptive. The classic example is the long and brilliant plumage of the peacock. If this grand display of feathers were so adaptive, one would think the peahen would boast the same characteristic. Instead, her tail has an appearance presumably more conducive to survival in the wild. Darwin recognized that such exaggerated traits were probably the upshot of sexual selection. Once the peahens, for whatever reason, began to prefer the peacocks with more impressive displays, those that beat out the competition sired more offspring. Each generation of males would possess even more impressive tail feathers. To be sure, the process cannot continue indefinitely. Eventually, the selection pressure exerted by the need for survival—the finding of food and the avoidance of predation—will outweigh any gains acquired in the sexual prowess conferred by these feathery advertisements. An equilibrium will be reached where the push of sexual selection toward larger and more brilliant tails will be counterbalanced by the pull of natural selection toward tails less cumbersome and conspicuous. The current peacock epitomizes the point of the even trade-off.

It is important to note that these two counteracting forces are really two means to the same end. Those traits that enhance the individual's ability to reproduce its kind will be the ones that will become more prominent in the next generation. Natural selection will determine which variant will survive to sexual maturity; but under circumstances in which females can choose among males who must compete for mates, such survival may not suffice to ensure reproductive success. To obtain that goal, males may have to incur some costs to win the sexual competition. But, on the average, the benefits compensate for the costs.

The "modern synthesis." Darwin's initial theory encountered two difficulties that were even more fundamental. First, his theory did not specify precisely how the spontaneous variations came about. Second, his theory did not provide a mechanism for the inheritance of adaptive traits. These two problems are closely related. Before the advent of modern genetics, there existed a common belief in "blending" inheritance: the offspring would possess traits that would be some average of those of its parents. One consequence of such a form of inheritance would be that variation in any trait would diminish with each successive generation until all members of a species would exhibit the same inherent value. To be sure, there might survive variation due to environmental circumstances, but such variation would not be inheritable and thus not subject to natural selection. Another consequence of blending inheritance is that if by some fluke an individual happened to possess a highly adaptive trait that departed from the average, that characteristic would quickly become diluted once that individual mated with the rest of the population. Under such conditions, it is difficult to imagine how evolution could take place.

Although Darwin did not realize it, the solution to this problem had appeared within the decade that followed the *Origin of Species*. An obscure Austrian monk named Gregor Mendel had published the results of a series of breeding experiments with garden peas. These results established the basis of modern genetics. Mendel showed that various traits that character-ize different varieties of peas, such as the color of the flowers, were carried by discrete units of inheritance that we now call genes. Moreover, during sexual reproduction, the diverse units freely recombine to produce an incredible variety of possible variants. This helped solve the problem of where the spontaneous variations originate. Just as important, the traits do not blend, but rather they maintain their integrity from generation to gen-eration. Indeed, according to Mendel's discovery of the distinction between dominant and recessive traits, an individual who received a dominant gene from one parent and a recessive gene from another would only exhibit the trait carried by the dominant gene. In any case, it soon became evident that variation in a population would be maintained across consecutive genera-tions, unless selective forces operated to the contrary. Although Mendel's original laws of heredity were to undergo many transformations over the years, it soon became clear that genetics helped resolve the difficulties in Darwin's theory.

So primary Darwinism merged with Mendelism to produce a new "ism" known as neo-Darwinism, or the "modern synthesis." Besides the laws of heredity, this updated version of Darwin's theory incorporated the phe-nomenon of mutation into the mechanism of spontaneous variations. Not all variants that appear in a population represent straightforward recombi-nations of genes received from parents. Sometimes totally new genes will appear as well. Such haphazard additions are most often deleterious, and many mutant variations do not survive or reproduce their novel kind. Even so, mutations can provide a powerful resource for evolution on those rare occasions when the new trait is highly adaptive.

Neo-Darwinism gave primary Darwinism a new lease on intellectual life. It thereby became a rich theory that could be expanded in many directions. For example, with the discovery of DNA (deoxyribonucleic acid) and the emergence of molecular biology, both inheritance and mutation could be understood in more fundamental terms. The evolution of species could be investigated from the perspective of transformation in the makeup of the DNA molecules that contain the genetic information. An earlier, but just as potent, development was the emergence of the notion of population genet-ics, which holds that a species can be conceived as a population with a set of genes that have a particular frequency distribution that transfers from gen-eration to generation according to genetic laws. Evolution takes place when the frequencies of various genes change over time in a manner that departs from the laws of heredity. Such changes in gene frequencies may reflect the operation of selection pressures. Or they could reflect the influence of such phenomena as genetic drift, which occurs in small populations when each generation obtains a random sample of the genes in the preceding generation. The discipline of population genetics provides a highly rigorous way of treating these diverse evolutionary changes by specifying the relevant processes in mathematical terms. For instance, these methods could be used to determine the precise circumstances under which sexual selection would produce a "runaway process," in which traits become increasingly exaggerated and maladaptive. Hence, with the advent of population genetics, primary Darwinism advanced from a qualitative explanatory theory to a quantitative predictive theory. Darwinism thus enabled biology to join the ranks of other mathematical sciences, such as physics, chemistry, and economics.

Sociobiology. Some gaps in Darwinism's explanatory scope still remained, however. One of the more irksome problems had to do with altruism. The Darwinian process appeared to favor only selfish behavior. In the struggle for existence—in the competition for food, shelter, and mates—there seemed no room for true self-sacrifice. To be sure, there might be occasions in which animals might engage in behavior with the superficial appearance of altruism. For example, animals might cooperate in the search for food or defense of their territory. And they might engage in acts of reciprocity, where favors might be exchanged according to the principle of "I will scratch your back if you will scratch mine." But insofar as this reciprocal altruism directly benefits the individuals engaged, such behaviors cannot be considered bona fide altruism. At bottom, cooperation and reciprocation can still be seen as manifestations of underlying "selfish genes."

Nevertheless, apparent acts of genuine altruism do seem to exist in nature. The most conspicuous examples, perhaps, come from the complex worlds of the social insects, such as honeybees and ants. The workers in these societies forfeit the opportunity to reproduce themselves in order to raise offspring on behalf of their queen. Besides putting their lives at risk when foraging for food, these workers will often sacrifice their lives in defense of the colony. This altruistic heroism is perhaps most dramatic in bees, whose barbed stingers often oblige their owners to commit suicide by disembowelment when attacking would-be invaders. Although perhaps not so sensational, similar acts of authentic altruism are sometimes prominent in the world of other social animals, such as the primates—including, of course, the human species.

One early solution to this enigma was to introduce the doctrine of "group selection." Although altruistic behavior might be costly to the well-being of individual organisms, it was argued that those species with more altruists may be more apt to survive and reproduce when that species competes with others in the exploitation of a particular ecological niche. In other words, the unit of selection was neither the gene nor the organism but rather the entire group making up a species. Although this account was not without attractions or adherents, it fell short of a convincing explanation. Population genetics could easily demonstrate that group selection would favor the increased frequency of altruistic genes only under the rarest of circumstances. Indeed, within any given population there will always exist selection pressures in favor of selfish individuals willing to take advantage of their altruistic conspecifics. Eventually, the genes carried by these "cheaters" will overwhelm those of the altruists. Hence, the very existence of altruistic proclivities would seem to be most perilous.

The real breakthrough came with the recognition that it was not the individuals that were being selected, but rather it was the genes. Not only could those genes reside in more than one individual, but also related individuals shared more genes than did unrelated individuals, and the higher the degree of relationship the larger the expected proportion of shared genes. Therefore, a gene that promoted altruistic behavior on behalf of close relatives could indeed survive and proliferate in a population. Individuals might even sacrifice their own reproductive success for the sake of related individuals with whom they shared enough genes. This possibility is most apparent in ants and bees. Owing to a peculiarity in the reproductive systems of these hymenopterans, a daughter is so highly related to her mother that considerable adaptive advantage can accrue to those genes that encourage the subordination of the daughters' reproductive interests to those of their queen. So the daughters become sterile workers who labor on behalf of the queen mother, helping the latter maximize the production of more sterile daughters. Thus, the apparently altruistic behavior remains selfish from the standpoint of the genes that support this subordination of individual interests to that of the colony. It is inclusive fitness, not individual fitness per se, that is being maintained—maintained through the process of kin selection.

Although the specific details differ, this same concept of inclusive fitness proved useful in explaining the appearance of altruistic behavior in other species, including mammals. For instance, the first member of a prairie dog colony to spot a predator will bark a quick warning to others rather than quietly disappear within the security of the colony's underground tunnels system. This seemingly unselfish behavior makes more sense when we learn that the individual is acting to maximize inclusive fitness. After all, the members of any given colony are likely to be very closely related. As a consequence, the modest risk incurred by the individual in possibly attracting the predator's attention is adequately compensated by the higher odds that other members of the colony who carry the same genes will be able to seek safety in time.

Once it became obvious that paradoxical behaviors like altruism could be explicated in terms of standard evolutionary theory, researchers endeavored to explain a great many social behaviors in strict Darwinian terms. The upshot was the emergence of the discipline of sociobiology, a research program most strongly associated with the zoologist Edward O. Wilson. Of course, the theorizing of sociobiologists was not always welcomed by other scientists, especially in the social sciences. It seemed like a classic instance of intellectual imperialism in which the theories of one discipline are imposed on the phenomena of quite another discipline. Moreover, some sociobiological explanations seemed not only reductionistic and deterministic but potentially sexist and racist besides. Sometimes sociobiologists seemed to defend the status quo, however inequitable, with assertions that such social injustices ensued from the evolutionary foundations of human nature.

Nonetheless, I think it remains fair to say that once we have time to weed out the good from the bad applications of sociobiological theory, the achievements of this form of Darwinism will be better appreciated. At the very least, sociobiology illustrates how very powerful were Darwin's original insights. More than a century after his death, his theory of evolution by natural selection can still inspire new attempts to expand its explanatory scope and accuracy.

Secondary Darwinism

After the advent of the "modern synthesis," primary Darwinism emerged triumphant in the scientific community. As its explanatory and predictive power became increasingly obvious, the same basic ideas soon began to be applied successfully to other phenomena besides organic evolution. These applications represent the emergence of secondary Darwinism. In these derivative extensions there was seldom a need to demonstrate the existence of a phenomenon analogous to evolution. On the contrary, these secondary applications usually begin with some occurrence of growth, change, or development assumed as empirical fact. As a consequence, the key goal of these secondary forms was to show that these evolutionlike phenomena represent environmental adaptations that are acquired through a Darwinian process of variation and selection.

To give a clearer idea of the nature of secondary Darwinism, I will offer brief examples of the most prominent applications. These illustrations fall into three categories according to the nature of the phenomena explained: the biological, the behavioral, and the cultural.

Biological phenomena. One of the most successful applications of secondary Darwinism is the immunological theory of antibody production. According to this theory, special cells (B lymphocytes) are constantly engaged in the random recombination of the various components of the antibodies that may successfully combat an antigen, such as a virus. When an antigen actually invades, a selection process takes place whereby those antibody combinations that best attack the intruder are selected at the expense of those that offer no defense. In a short time, the useful antibodies can be mass-produced until the immune system emerges victorious. This Darwinian procedure means that the system can guard against the evolution of new disease agents. This capacity is most critical, for the rate at which such agents can evolve is far more rapid than that of larger organisms such as the human being. Therefore, if humans and other large organisms with long life cycles had to acquire all the antibodies through organic evolution, they would probably face extinction. In a sense, every time we come down with a common cold, an eternal battle is being staged between a primary Darwinian process that yields ever more virulent antigens and a secondary Darwinian process that tries to counter with the most effective antibodies.

Another biological illustration involves the growth and development of complex nervous systems, such as the human brain. In central nervous systems of any complexity, there may be billions of neurons, each with thousands of synapses that support untold numbers of neuronal connections. It is inconceivable that the intricate neuronal circuitry can be completely specified in the genetic code. Therefore, much of the detailed structure of the brain must emerge developmentally, by some kind of interaction between genetic specification and environmental stimulation. Many neuroscientists have described this developmental process as entailing an essentially variation-selection procedure. In fact, these theorists have explicitly identified the hypothesized process as entailing "Darwinism of the synapses" or "neural Darwinism." Although the particulars of the supposed mechanism depend on the theorist, the basic principle is the same. There first occurs an undisciplined "blooming" of neuronal connections—far in excess of what is required for efficient information processing. Next, this profusion of potential neural networks is followed by a "pruning" of connections that fail to prove useful according to subsequent sensory experience. As one advocate put it, the brain is a "Darwin machine" that endeavors to "make lots of random variants by brute bashing about, then select[ing] the good ones." Such a flexible, Darwinian process permits the development of a nervous system maximally adapted to its experiential world.

Behavioral phenomena. It is one of the miracles of organic evolution that the primary Darwinian mechanism should discover two secondary Darwinian mechanisms for improving an individual's immunological and neurological systems. But these are not the only illustrations of secondary processes evolving out of the primary process. Another example comes from the realm of an organism's behavior. Obviously, one of the central means of adapting to the environment is to respond to it—to search for food, locate shelter, flee from predators, find mates, and so forth. Each organism possesses a whole repertoire of such behaviors dedicated to maximizing its adaptive fitness. For many species, the bulk of this behavioral repertoire may be provided by the primary Darwinian process of organic evolution. That is, the behaviors represent instinctive motor patterns that were the genetic gifts of many generations of evolutionary variation and selection. So essential is the evolution of these adaptive instincts that Darwin allotted an entire chapter of the *Origin of Species* to explaining their emergence.

Yet for those species with sufficiently complex nervous systems, the largest portion of the behavioral repertoire is acquired through direct experience with the world. Moreover, this learning process itself may be largely Darwinian. The most prominent proponent of this view was the psychologist B. F. Skinner, who devoted his life to outlining the principles of what he called "operant conditioning." Furthermore, he explicitly identified this learning process as functioning in the same way as Darwin's theory of evolution by natural selection. Each organism begins with a diverse assortment of rudimentary motor patterns that can be combined and recombined in an unlimited number of ways to produce more complex behaviors. The organism is thus capable of generating behavioral variations that provide the basis for environmental selection. Behavioral variants that produce positive consequences are retained, whereas those producing negative consequences are extinguished. In Skinnerian parlance, the organism emits "operants" that are then subjected to "reinforcement contingencies." To study this phenomenon scientifically, behaviorists would typically place a food-deprived rat or pigeon in what came to be known as a "Skinner box." To these conditions the creature would produce a wide variety of responses, most of which would prove futile; but eventually, by trial and error, the rat might press down a lever or the pigeon peck at a disk, and suddenly a food pellet would appear. With continued conditioning, the irrelevant actions vanish, and solely the appropriate operants remain. The animal is now optimally adapted to its environment, its behavioral repertoire shaped by the circumstances in which the organism must thrive and procreate.

Using this learning paradigm, Skinner and his followers were able to demonstrate that extremely complex behaviors could be established by this Darwinian procedure. Pigeons have been trained to use mirrors, play tunes on the piano, compete against each other at Ping-Pong, and engage in symbolic communication. Moreover, behaviorists have taken operant conditioning outside the laboratory in an attempt to show its utility in solving applied problems (through such applications as learning machines, token economies, and behavioral therapy). Skinner has used operant conditioning as a general explanatory framework for understanding the acquisition and use of language. Even more interesting, given the subject matter of this book, Skinner has attempted to explain creative behavior as another example of a conditioned operant. Although he only speculated on the possibility, some empirical research suggests that creativity may respond positively to reinforcement, at least under the proper circumstances. Hence, this instance of secondary Darwinian theory can claim tremendous explanatory scope.

Cultural phenomena. The adaptations acquired through organic evolution are retained in the population gene pool. There they can be readily passed down from generation to generation as a form of "received wisdom." In contrast, the adaptations acquired through operant conditioning are retained in the individual's memory. That means that the individual's death signifies a loss of that accumulated fitness. Therefore, it would seem more efficient to devise some means by which the skills and knowledge learned by one generation can be passed down to the next. The latter could then skip the trial-and-error process of their progenitors. Indeed, each generation could advance further than the previous generation, building on prior achievements to attain adaptive accomplishments ever more impressive.

The most obvious way of effecting this end is for the members of each successive generation to imitate the adaptive behaviors of their parents or other elders. The appearance of such "monkey see, monkey do" transferal of acquired expertise illustrates on a single level culture as an alternative means of retaining selected variants. If members of a species form social groups, with sophisticated means of communication—especially language—then the dissemination of adaptations can also occur by direct instruction, whether by parents, teachers, peers, or experts. Indeed, in literate civilizations that have produced books, the transfer of expertise can even skip generations. The European Renaissance was partly stimulated by the rediscovery of the classical Greek creators whose works had been lost to Western civilization since the decline of the Roman Empire.

Many researchers have suggested that cultures evolve just as species do, and that the mechanism underlying cultural evolution is closely analogous to that seen in organic evolution. Where the evolution of life-forms entails the selection of genetic variations, the evolution of cultures involves the selection of variations in acquired behaviors or beliefs. The units of selection in the former instance are genes, whereas the units in the latter case have been called "memes." This word derives from the Greek root for imitation; it thus represents the unit of imitation just as the gene stands for the unit of inheritance. According to Richard Dawkins, memes may include "tunes, ideas, catchphrases, clothes fashions, ways of making pots or building arches." Moreover, "just as genes propagate themselves in the gene pool by leaping from body via sperms or eggs, so memes propagate themselves in leaping from body to body via a process which, in the broad sense, can be called imitation." In addition, cultural evolution may exhibit many features found in organic evolution, such as analogs of random variation, genetic drift, and sexual selection.

Admittedly, there also exist striking contrasts between these two forms of evolution. For example, the transfer of adaptations in organic evolution usually occurs from parents to offspring, whereas the transfer in cultural evolution may take place between any two individuals. Indeed, the generational transmission may even be reversed, as when children find themselves teaching their embarrassed parents how to use the family computer. Furthermore, for organic evolution the genes are passed from genotype to genotype, ignoring whatever adaptations individuals may have learned during their lifetimes. For cultural evolution, in contrast, the memes go from phenotype to phenotype, bypassing the genotype altogether—but thereby speeding up the rate by which a population can adapt to environmental conditions.

These and many other differences notwithstanding, the similarities between the two evolutionary phenomena are close enough to inspire valuable theoretical and empirical analyses. For instance, the population-genetics methods that have proven so useful in the study of organic evolution have been fruitfully applied to the study of cultural evolution. In fact, these mathematical analyses have permitted the creation of "dual-inheritance" theories that treat organic and cultural evolution simultaneously. This is an important intellectual advance, for all human beings are ultimately the product of the interplay of two long evolutionary histories, one determining a person's genetic constitution, the other governing that person's cultural heritage. These dual-inheritance theories also illustrate how the distinction I introduced between primary and secondary Darwinism can sometimes break down. In such systems, the variation-selection process operates at two interacting levels, so that genes and memes undergo coevolution. Yet the very possibility of such a synthesis of the two types dramatically demonstrates how very powerful were Darwin's initial insights.

Darwinian Genius

What makes Darwinism so attractive to so many scientists is its parsimony. Extremely complex, varied, and even unusual phenomena can be explicated in terms of a simple variation-selection mechanism. The richly diverse forms of life on this planet, the adaptive flexibility of the immunological and neurological systems, the unlimited elaborations of learned behaviors, and the remarkable variability of human cultures and societies—

all these and more have been granted Darwinian interpretations. To be sure, not everyone is sympathetic to Darwinian theories. From the very onset critics felt that an intelligent universe filled with purpose had been replaced by a chaotic world without a set direction. The infinite wisdom of an all-powerful but caring Creator gave way to billions of hapless little creatures, each struggling to survive and reproduce by seemingly senseless trial and error. If primary Darwinism evokes so much complaint, secondary Darwinism cannot be expected to do much better. Critics of B. F. Skinner maintained that the behaviors that most distinguish humans from the brutes were precisely those that could not be explained by operant conditioning.

Even so, when a Darwinian explanation is found not to prove valuable in understanding a certain phenomenon, it often happens that the fault lies in which Darwinian mechanism was selected, not in Darwinism per se. Variation-selection processes occur at multiple levels, and so the investigator must be ever careful to adopt the proper level of operation. For instance, there exist many human social behaviors that may not comply with sociobiological interpretations because those behaviors have a cultural etiology. Yet insofar as cultural evolution is itself shaped by a Darwinian process, a valid explanation may finally emerge when the analysis is switched to populations of memes rather than genes. Similarly, although the Skinnerian conditioning paradigm stressed the variation and selection of behaviors, it is manifest that for complex cognitive systems, such as possessed by human beings, the Darwinian process more often operates internally. Before an individual acts in a novel situation, cognitive representations of alternative responses can be first generated and then tested against mental models of the external world. Finally, the researcher must always be wary of assuming that all secondary processes operate in precisely the same way as the primary process. As already noted, numerous functional differences divide organic and cultural evolution, and these differences must be accommodated for any scientifically useful account.

Once these precautions are taken, however, Darwinian theories can provide extremely potent explanations for a great many natural phenomena. Among those phenomena is human creative genius. Indeed, there is something quite natural about such a theoretical application. The very definitions of creativity and genius seem almost to beg for a Darwinian perspective. If creativity is defined as the output of ideas that are both original and adaptive, then the creative act may approximate a variation-selection process. The creator must generate many different novelties from which are selected those that satisfy some intellectual or aesthetic criteria. Those creative individuals who have produced an unusual number of original and adaptive ideas will then attain eminence, and thus be counted among the geniuses. An eminent creator, or genius, is someone who has contributed to subsequent generations an impressive body of achievements. Stated in terms of cultural evolution, the creative genius is a person who has produced a large assortment of memes to posterity. Creative geniuses exhibit extraordinary "reproductive success" through their "productive success."

Why, for example, do we call William Shakespeare a literary genius? The reason is obvious when we consider the Bard's legacy. Probably only the Bible is more likely to be found in English-speaking homes than is a volume containing the complete works of Shakespeare. His sonnets and other poems are still included in anthologies of great literature and are even recited as marriage oaths. His plays continue to be produced throughout the world, and in all the world's major languages. Indeed, his dramatic creations can be found on record, CD, videotape, and in full-length feature films. They have also been adapted or transformed in an astonishing variety of ways, such as in Akira Kurosawa's take on *King Lear* in his movie *Ran*, the updating of *Romeo and Juliet* in Leonard Bernstein's musical *West Side Story*, or the remake of *Hamlet* found in Tom Stoppard's *Rosencrantz and Guildenstern Are Dead*. Various other renditions of his dramas can be found in cartoons, comic books, and children's storybooks as well as in tone poems, songs, modern dance and ballet compositions, puppet shows, and kabuki theater. More operas are based on Shakespeare than on any other author; a partial list of composers who have written Shakespearean operas includes such names as Adam, Barber, Bellini, Berlioz, Britten, Bruch, Goldmark, Gounod, Halévy, Holst, Nicolai, Purcell, Rossini, Smetana, Vaughan Williams, Verdi, Wagner, and Wolf-Ferrari. Tourists still visit Hamlet's castle in Denmark and the (fictitious) tomb of Romeo and Juliet in Italy—not to mention all of the pilgrimages made to Shakespeare's home in Stratford-upon-Avon.

Moreover, it is not just the poems and plays that define his legacy to human culture. English is the second most widely spoken language in the world, and no other individual has contributed more to the richness of that language than Shakespeare. Hundreds of words and expressions that have now become part of everyday speech first appeared on his writing desk. Assassination, birthplace, critical, droplet, equivocal, fashionable, go-between, hostile, invitation, lament, majestic, ode, pious, quarrelsome, retirement, shooting star, transcendence, useless, vulnerable, watchdog, and zany—these are just a smattering of the many words first coined by his genius. And such expressions as "All the world's a stage," "caviar to the general," "the dogs of war," "eaten me out of house and home," "household words," "a lean and hungry look," "the milk of human kindness," "one fell swoop," "the primrose path," "strange bedfellows," "wild-goose chase," and "the world's mine oyster" have become so commonplace that some grammar checkers in word-processing software will tag many of these as clichés.

Furthermore, these gems of expression have inspired their counterparts in the main languages of the world, enriching each tongue with new terms, images, and metaphors. No wonder, then, that near the beginning of this century the Chinese poet Liu Boduan could write an "Ode to Shakespeare" that claimed "Three hundred years have passed 'twixt then and now, Yet all the world looks to that mountain's brow!" Liu's praise confirms what Ben Jonson said of his illustrious contemporary: "He was not of an age but for all time." If Jonson's prediction holds, then there still should live memes descended from the Bard's pen when the last lights of civilization expire.

Naturally, it was the same enduring nature of his legacy that obliged us to call Charles Darwin a creative genius. This legacy is acknowledged by the eponym that has attached his name to so much theoretical and empirical research in the biological and behavioral sciences. In the remainder of this book, I endeavor to carry this legacy forward into the very phenomenon that Darwin himself represents. For I believe that Darwinian theories can help us better appreciate the nature of creative genius. Indeed, I will argue during this book's course that such theoretical models enhance our understanding of Charles Darwin himself, whom we may take as an incontrovertible exemplar of genius-grade creativity. In a certain sense, I will sketch out Darwin's psychobiography, one conceptually Darwinist rather than psychoanalytic.

To make my case, each chapter will examine a different aspect of the phenomenon. Chapter 2 concentrates on the thought processes responsible for creative ideas, thus setting the stage for all subsequent discussion. Chapter 3 then covers the characteristics of creative individuals that enable them to generate those ideas. Chapter 4 continues the focus on the creator but this time scrutinizes the basis for the development of creative talent. Chapter 5 switches the unit of analysis from the creative genius to the products on which his or her reputation is based. In contrast, chapter 6 shifts the analytical unit in the opposite direction, to the groups, cultures, or civilizations in which the creative geniuses emerge. The final chapter reviews and evaluates what I consider the landmarks of our Darwinian tour of creativity.

I must stress that this panoramic view will not be totally uncritical, despite my professed enthusiasm for Darwinian principles. Theoretical interpretations can be bad as well as good. One of my goals is to examine the strengths and weaknesses of Darwinian accounts of exceptional creativity. The famous evolutionary biologist Theodosius Dobzhansky once made the often-quoted claim that "nothing in biology makes sense except in the light of evolution." We seek to know the extent to which a similar remark may be applied to the origins of genius.

2

~

COGNITION

How Does the Brain Create?

~

Darwin's seminal ideas had an impact on epistemology, the philosophical enterprise devoted to comprehending the nature and origins of knowledge. The Darwinian theory of knowledge is called "evolutionary epistemology." As the name implies, this discipline attempts to comprehend the foundations and status of knowledge in evolutionary terms. Actually, as there are two kinds of Darwinism, so are there two types of evolutionary epistemology.

On the one hand, the theory of organic evolution can provide a basis for explaining the specific nature of the human mind. Presumably, the brain exists in its present state as the result of adaptation, like any other adaptation, and its structure and function may have been shaped by generations of natural and sexual selection. Indeed, the very nature of what constitutes "common sense" may have roots in our ancestors' needs to survive and reproduce. At the same time, any quirks and flaws in the human information-processing apparatus may be ascribed to the fact that certain intellectual skills may have contributed nothing to the reproductive fitness of ancestral *Homo sapiens*. In either case, primary Darwinism is being used to understand the human brain as a knowledge-making organ. Because the philosopher Immanuel Kant argued that human knowledge is shaped by innate categories of thought, Konrad Lorenz, the Nobel Prize-winning ethologist, has identified this first form of evolutionary epistemology as the "biologizing of Kant." This intellectual movement has become especially conspicuous in recent years, as is evident in Steven Pinker's 1997 book *How the Mind Works*.

On the other hand, evolutionary epistemology may assume the guise of secondary Darwinism. In this case the theory of evolution by natural selection provides a generic metaphor for understanding how organisms acquire knowledge. Although such analogical reasoning can prove hazardous, there is a certain aptness about this particular application. After all, to some extent inherited adaptations can be viewed as implicit forms of knowledge about the world. For instance, digestive enzymes reflect a knowledge about certain chemical processes, just as the wings of birds reflect a knowledge about inescapable aerodynamical laws. Similarly, learned behaviors that are acquired through operant conditioning constitute adaptations that are shaped by environmental consequences through a variation-selection procedure. And these operants, too, reflect implicit knowledge about cause-effect relationships in the world, such as the link between pecking at a disk and receiving a food pellet in a Skinner box. Hence, it seems easy to go the additional step and claim that all knowledge has its origins in some variety of variation-selection process. In the sciences, for example, the philosopher Karl Popper has observed: "The growth of our knowledge is the result of a process closely resembling what Darwin called 'natural selection'; that is, *the natural selection of hypotheses*: our knowledge consists, at every moment, of those hypotheses which have shown their (comparative) fitness by surviving so far in their struggle for existence; a competitive struggle which eliminates those hypotheses which are unfit." One of the most outstanding proponents of this secondary type of evolutionary epistemology is the psychologist Donald T. Campbell. More important for our current purposes, Campbell argued that the creative process itself can best be construed in Darwinian terms. In particular, he maintained that creativity involves the following three conditions:

1. There exists some process that generates *variations*. Just as biological evolution must begin with numerous genetic recombinations and mutations, so must creativity begin with the production of many diverse ideational variants.

2. These variations are subjected to some consistent *selection* mechanism. For biological evolution the fitness of variants is decided by natural or sexual selection. In the case of human creativity, the selectors are more likely to be cognitive or cultural in nature.

3. There is some *retention* procedure that preserves and reproduces the variations so selected. Where natural evolution retains and propagates the best genes through biological inheritance, the mental evolution

that produces creative ideas requires a memory system, plus an ability to communicate the stored ideas to others.

In line with Darwinian thought, Campbell claimed that this variational procedure at some point becomes essentially *blind*. By this qualifier Campbell did not insist that the variations be absolutely random, although they may be. He held only that the mind eventually reaches the point where it has no a priori basis for knowing which ideational variations will prove most effective. Neither prior experiences nor current environmental circumstances will provide sufficient clues about how to restrict the range of choices, nor does there exist any rationale for assigning useful priorities to the various alternatives. As a consequence, the process is reduced to a basically trial-and-error procedure, whether through cognitive rumination or behavioral experimentation. It is for this reason that Campbell chose to identify creativity as a process of "blind-variation and selective-retention."

The rest of this chapter will be devoted to assessing the plausibility of this Darwinian model of the creative process. I begin by examining what creators themselves have said about creativity. From there I will review the experimental research that bears on this question. Then I discuss what we might infer from computer programs designed to emulate the creative process. The chapter concludes with an overall evaluation of the variation-selection model.

Biographical Illustrations

Many notable creators have explicitly claimed that their creativity appears best described by a process akin to a variation-selection procedure. For example, Paul Valéry, the French poet and essayist, claimed that "it takes two to invent anything. The one makes up combinations; the other chooses, recognizes what he wishes and what is important to him in the mass of the things which the former has imparted to him." John Dryden, the English playwright and poet, conveyed a similar idea with more vivid imagery when he described the composition of a play as beginning "when it was only a confused mass of thoughts, tumbling over one another in the dark; when the fancy was yet in its first work, moving the sleeping images of things towards the light, there to be distinguished, and then either chosen or rejected by the judgment."

Nor are such claims confined to artistic creators, for similar reports come from scientific creators, suggesting that the creative process is the same for both artists and scientists. For instance, Michael Faraday, the great chemist and physicist, noted that "the world little knows how any thoughts and theories which have passed through the mind of a scientific investigator have been crushed in silence and secrecy by his own severe criticism and adverse examinations; that in the most successful instances not a tenth of the suggestions, the hopes, the wishes, the preliminatory conclusions have been realised." Likewise, the Nobel Prize-winning chemist Linus Pauling advised that the successful scientist must "have lots of ideas and throw away the bad ones. . . . [Y]ou aren't going to have good ideas unless you have lots of ideas and some sort of principle of selection." Charles Darwin himself confessed in his autobiography that "I cannot remember a single first-formed hypothesis which had not after a time to be given up or greatly modified." Hence, behind the clean logic and solid documentation of a scientific publication may hide a far more tentative history of trial-and-error.

Below I take advantage of the biographical reports of illustrious creators to fathom this process further. In particular, I will examine the role of associative richness, mental imagery, intuitive cognition, and serendipitous discovery.

Associative Richness

In organic evolution, variations are constantly created by the recombination of genes. In creativity, on the other hand, variations must be created by the recombination of ideas. This ability to engage in ideational permutations requires more than simply the capacity to retrieve concepts and images from memory. Also required is the ability to link these ideas by rather unusual pathways. This component was noted by the Austrian physicist Ernst Mach in a paper published more than a century ago. Although Mach allowed the advantages of possessing "a powerfully developed mechanical memory, which recalls vividly and faithfully old situations," he insisted that "more is required for the development of inventions." In particular, "more extensive chains of images are necessary here, the excitation by mutual contact of widely different trains of ideas, a more powerful, more manifold, and richer connection of the contents of memory." If the memory cannot support this associative chaos, there can be no creative imagination at all.

Mach was discussing scientific creativity, but the same may be said of any form of creative genius. For example, the eminent psychologist William James described "the highest order of minds" in this way: "Instead of thoughts of concrete things patiently following one another in a beaten track of habitual suggestion, we have the most abrupt cross-cuts and transitions from one idea to another, the most rarefied abstractions and discriminations, the most unheard of combination of elements, the subtlest associations of analogy; in a word, we seem suddenly introduced into a seething cauldron of ideas, where everything is fizzling and bobbling about in a state of bewildering activity, where partnerships can be joined or loosened in an instant, treadmill routine is unknown, and the unexpected seems only law." Henri Poincaré described this process in a more picturesque manner when he recounted an episode in which he suffered insomnia as a consequence of an evening cup of coffee. "Ideas rose in crowds; I felt them collide until pairs interlocked, so to speak, making a stable combination. By the next morning I had established the existence of a class of Fuchsian functions." Poincaré compared these colliding images to "the hooked atoms of Epicurus" that jiggle and bump "like the molecules of gas in the kinematic theory of gases" so that "their mutual impacts may produce new combinations." This choice of words is most provocative, for it implies a high level of randomness in the way that concepts and images are interconnected. The creative mind here seems capable of generating truly blind variations, as required by Campbell's Darwinian model.

Mental Imagery

Poincaré's description illustrates another common feature of creative thought: the frequent use of vivid or unusual imagery. Max Planck, the physics Nobel laureate, explicitly affirmed that creative scientists "must have a vivid intuitive imagination, for new ideas are not generated by deduction, but by an artistically creative imagination." And Albert Einstein held that "imagination is more important than knowledge" in the creation of new scientific ideas. This imaginative capacity can take many forms.

Einstein himself reported that "combinatory play seems to be the essential feature in productive thought." Furthermore, "the psychical entities which seem to serve as elements in [this] thought are certain signs and more or less clear images which can be 'voluntarily' reproduced and combined." These cognitive "elements are . . . of visual and some of muscular type." Although "the desire to arrive finally at logically connected concepts is the emotional basis of this rather vague play with the above mentioned elements," the combinatory play takes place "before there is any connection with logical construction in words or other kinds of signs which can be communicated to others." "The words or the language, as they are written or spoken, do not seem to play any role in my mechanism of thought." Indeed, "conventional words or other signs have to be sought for laboriously only in a secondary stage, when the mentioned associative play is sufficiently established and can be reproduced at will." The French mathematician Jacques Hadamard concurred when he described his own creative imagination, adding that "as to words, they remain absolutely absent from my mind until I come to the moment of communicating the results in written or oral form."

Because words and logic may come into play late in the mental process, the creative genius often finds it difficult to translate the images into a form accessible to others. Darwin repeatedly complained to his colleagues about the extreme difficulties he encountered trying to put his ideas down on paper, however unambiguous and self-evident they were to him. Galton observed his similar frustration:

> It is a serious drawback to me in writing, and still more in explaining myself, that I do not so easily think in words as otherwise. It often happens that after being hard at work, and having arrived at results that are perfectly clear and satisfactory to myself, when I try to express them in language I feel that I must begin by putting myself upon quite another intellectual plane. I have to translate my thoughts into a language that does not run very evenly with them. I therefore waste a vast deal of time in seeking for appropriate words and phrases, and am conscious, when required to speak on a sudden, of being often very obscure through mere verbal maladroitness, and not through want of clearness of perception. That is one of the small annoyances of my life.

Curiously, Galton admitted that words would sometimes appear in his creative thought, but when this auditory imagery took place it would not conform to standard linguistic expression. On the contrary, Galton's mind would experience nonsense words running by "as the notes of a song might accompany thought." Other creators have also reported unusual verbal associations, such as puns. Because these capricious associations are governed by superfluous sound patterns rather than logical linkages, they boast a superior capacity to originate new and inherently blind connections between otherwise isolated concepts.

When the average person on the street thinks about vivid and unusual imagery, dreams are what most often come to mind. There do exist biographical accounts of creative ideas occurring during this altered state of consciousness. The most often cited illustration is the insight that led Friedrich August Kekulé to decipher the ring structure of benzene. As someone who once aspired to become an architect, Kekulé was a great visualizer and dreamer. Earlier he had already dreamt of atoms in playful recombinations, but on this evening, "I turned my chair to the fire and dozed. Again the atoms were gambolling before my eyes. This time the smaller groups kept modestly to the background. My mental eye, rendered more acute by repeated visions of the kind, could now distinguish larger structures, of manifold conformation; long rows, sometimes more closely fitted together; all twining and twisting in snake-like motion. But look! What was that? One of the snakes had seized hold of its own tail, and the form whirled mockingly before my eyes. As if by a flash of lightning I awoke." Although there has been some doubt cast on the veracity of this story, the notion that creativity can emerge from dreamlike imagery has independent support from another quarter.

Psychiatrist Albert Rothenberg has systematically probed the relationship between creative thought and dream phenomena. His investigations were based partly on more than 1,670 hours of structured interviews with 57 highly creative artists and scientists, including recipients of the Nobel and Pulitzer Prizes, the National Book Award, and other prestigious honors. These interviews often took place while the subject was right in the middle of some creative project. By combining his interview data with retrospective studies of the products and introspections of other creators, Rothenberg identified two processes that bear a close relationship to dreams.

The first dreamlike process is called "homospatial thinking." This involves "actively conceiving two or more discrete entities occupying the same space, a conception leading to the articulation of new identities." In other words, two or more images are superimposed in the mind's eye, and by a cognitive fusion a novel image results. Although homospatial thinking applies to images of any modality, its operation is most obvious in visual imagery. Rothenberg presents an ample number of examples drawn from the visual arts. Leonardo da Vinci, Paul Klee, Oskar Kokoschka, Henry Moore, Claes Oldenberg, and others all provide illustrations. For instance, in Klee's 1927 *Physiognomic Lightning* the chief features of a man's face are delineated by a bolt of lightning, an integrated image ensuing from two heterogeneous elements. Later, Klee even documented the steps by which he conceived this painting, and the procedure was patently homospatial.

The second dreamlike process is called "Janusian thinking." This entails "actively conceiving two or more opposite or antithetical ideas, images, or concepts simultaneously." The term comes from the Roman god Janus, who had two faces simultaneously looking in opposite directions. Rothenberg found that his distinguished creators resorted to this paradoxical maneuver quite often in the act of producing original insights. In addition, he finds numerous illustrations of this trick in the historical record. For example, Rothenberg showed how Janusian thinking helped Einstein to arrive at the general theory of relativity. Einstein realized that an observer who jumped off a rooftop would not, in his immediate vicinity, find any evidence of a gravitational field. This apparent absence arises even though gravitation causes the observer's accelerating plunge. Rothenberg found another illustration in Niels Bohr's conception of the principle of complementarity. The very claim that light is both a particle and a wave is inextricably Janusian. Moreover, according to one of Bohr's sons, this Nobel laureate had elevated Janusian thinking to a basic technique of scientific discovery: "One of the favorite maxims of my father was the distinction between the two sorts of truths, profound truths recognized by the fact that the opposite is also a profound truth, in contrast to trivialities where opposites are obviously absurd."

Homospatial and Janusian thinking, when combined with other forms of imagination, provide the creative genius with the ability to generate exceptionally original ideational variants. Indeed, some of these imagery processes appear capable of producing the blind variations suggested by a Darwinian model of creativity. It is hard to conceive of a process more blind than one that deliberately thrusts together opposites in the hope of discovering some meaning far more novel and profound.

Intuitive Cognition

I must hasten to emphasize that not all ideational variants arise through such dramatic means. Indeed, viable recombinations of ideas may emerge even when there appears to be no imagery at all! For instance, when 64 eminent scientists were interviewed about their mental processes, a large proportion reported the frequent occurrence of "imageless thought," especially just before a breakthrough idea. Representative statements include: "I just seem to vegetate; something is going on, I don't know what it is"; "I often know intuitively what the answer is, and then I have to work it out to show it"; "You feel it in your guts."

Hadamard, the mathematician, even argued that much of the process by which new ideas emerge must take place at unconscious levels. In particular, he claimed that mathematical creativity requires the discovery of unusual but fruitful combinations of ideas. To find such novel variations, it is "necessary to construct the very numerous possible combinations." But "it cannot be avoided that this first operation take place, to a certain extent, at random, so that the role of chance is hardly doubtful in this first step of the mental process." Even so, "we see that the intervention of chance occurs inside the unconscious: for most of these combinations—more exactly, all those which are useless—remain unknown to us." Thus, Hadamard was asserting that the variation process was blind in two different senses. First, to a certain degree, the production of ideational recombinations occurs at least in part by some largely random or chance process. Second, the conscious mind may not be aware of the combinations produced until some variant arises that passes some selection criterion. So much of the variation procedure transpires unseen.

Poincaré, also a French mathematician, has described this process in more detail. In general, creative individuals begin with a problem, for which they attempt to find a solution. This is the phase of conscious preparation. When creators discover that a solution is not immediately forthcoming—when they find they are "hitting their heads against a brick wall"—they eventually give up, turning to other more fruitful activities, whether to creating other products or to the everyday chores of work and life. The creators thereby enter an incubation period with respect to the initial problem. Then without warning, creative persons may experience a sudden illumination. For instance, Poincaré offered the following observation: "I turned my attention to the study of some arithmetical questions apparently without much success and without a suspicion of any connection with my preceding researches. Disgusted with my failure, I went to spend a few days at the seaside, and thought of something else. One morning, walking on the bluff, the idea came to me, with just the same characteristics of brevity, suddenness and immediate certainty, that the arithmetic transformations of indeterminate ternary quadratic forms were identical with those of non-Euclidean geometry." Poincaré took this unexpected inspiration as a "a manifest sign of long, unconscious prior work." He concurs with Hadamard in holding that much of the ideational recombinations take place below the threshold of consciousness. In fact, "the sterile combinations do not even present themselves to the mind of the inventor. Never in the field of his consciousness do combinations appear that are not really useful, except some that he rejects but which have to some extent the characteristics of useful combinations."

Poincaré even explicitly identifies the intuitive process as fundamentally blind: "Among the great numbers of combinations blindly formed by the subliminal self, almost all are without interest and without utility; but just for that reason they are also without effect upon the esthetic sensibility. Consciousness will never know them; only certain ones are harmonious, and, consequently, at once useful and beautiful." To be sure, Poincaré admitted that sometimes "a sudden illumination seizes upon the mind of the mathematician . . . that . . . does not stand the test of verification; well, we almost always notice that this false idea, had it been true, would have gratified our natural feeling for mathematical elegance."

Finally, Poincaré uses the atomistic imagery quoted earlier to venture the following conjecture about the progression from preparation to incubation to illumination.

> The role of the preliminary conscious work . . . is evidently to mobilize certain of these atoms, to unhook them from the wall and put them in swing. We think we have done no good, because we have moved these elements a thousand different ways in seeking to assemble them, and have found no satisfactory aggregate. But, after this shaking up imposed upon them by our will, these atoms do not return to their primitive rest. They freely continue to dance. . . . The mobilized atoms are . . . not any atoms whatsoever; they are those from which we might reasonably expect the desired solution. Then the mobilized atoms undergo impacts which make them enter into combinations among themselves or with other atoms at rest which they struck against in

their course. . . . However it may be, the only combinations that have a chance of forming are those where at least one of the elements is one of those atoms freely chosen by our will. Now, it is evidently among these that is found what I called the good combination.

Hence, in the preparation period creators establish some of the material that is going to enter into the variational procedure. In the incubation period these and related ideas are freely varied at unconscious levels of mental processing. When an acceptable combination appears, the outcome is thrust into consciousness during the illumination period. Of course, this is just the beginning of another variation-selection stage. Not all original ideas that appear in consciousness will survive verification, and of those that do survive, only a few will prove so fruitful to be worthy of extensive elaboration and development.

In any case, Hadamard and Poincaré viewed the incubation as an operation in which unconscious mental processes are spontaneously generating ideational recombinations. However, the actual mechanism may be less active than this. For instance, Darwin's younger contemporary Herbert Spencer—the evolutionist who introduced the term *survival of the fittest*—once offered the following speculation: "While thought continues to be forced down certain wrong turnings which had originally been taken, the search is in vain; but with the cessation of strain the true association of ideas has an opportunity of asserting itself. . . . [Q]uiet contemplation of the problem from time to time, allows those proclivities of thought which have probably been caused unawares by experiences, to make themselves felt, and to guide the mind to the right conclusion." In other words, during the incubation phase, the mind is incessantly bombarded by a diversity of stimuli. Indeed, the longer the incubation, the more different circumstances the creators will find themselves in—whether at work, at home, or on vacation—and hence the greater the variety of such essentially random stimulation. By chance, some of these external inputs may set the chain of associations off in a direction more likely to lead to a solution. Because this sensory bombardment will often take place at relatively subliminal levels of awareness, the subjective experience under Spencer's mechanism would likely be indistinguishable from that produced by the Hadamard-Poincaré process. Moreover, this alternative mechanism would still entail an intuitive variation-selection procedure. Instead of internal associations being selected for their utility, haphazard sensory influx is undergoing selection, the most fecund exciting the associative response that leads to an adaptive intellectual variant.

I return later to this issue when I examine the experimental literature. But first I need to turn to the last form of biographical evidence.

Serendipitous Discovery

Let us go back to Poincaré's remark about the "brevity, suddenness and immediate certainty" with which the solution to a problem appeared to him. Many other creators have reported similarly unexpected and dramatic episodes of illumination. The first recorded historical example is the famous episode in which Archimedes suddenly discovered the solution to a problem upon settling himself into a bathtub. Needing to find a way to measure the volume of an irregular solid—a recently crafted gold crown for the king—Archimedes realized that the water displaced by his body was exactly equal to the volume of his body that was submerged. Reportedly, he became so immediately excited by the realization that he ran outside into the streets screaming "Eureka," the Greek for "I have found it!" These eureka experiences are often so striking that the episodes become permanently engraved in the creator's memory. Charles Darwin recorded in his autobiography the moment when he arrived at his epochal solution to the problem of the origin of species: "I can remember the very spot in the road, whilst in my carriage, when to my joy the solution occurred to me."

Now there is one type of illumination event that occupies a special place in the Darwinian theory of creativity—the phenomenon of serendipity. This term originated in a letter by the author Horace Walpole, who derived the word from a fairy tale called "The Three Princes of Serendip," whose protagonists "were always making discoveries, by *accident* or sagacity, of things which they were not in quest of." This happy invention was revived by physiologist Walter Cannon in an essay entitled "The Role of Chance in Discovery." There he documented the numerous occasions when major contributions seem more attributable to accident than to genius. A similar point was made by physicist Ernst Mach in his article "On the Part Played by Accident in Invention and Discovery," albeit without providing such a convenient term for this phenomenon. Since these classic contributions, many books have been written on the subject, and the list of examples has become very long. Some of the most frequently cited cases include: European discovery of the New World (Columbus, in 1492), discovery of the interference of light (Grimaldi, in 1663), discovery of animal electricity (Galvani, in 1781), creation of laughing gas anesthesia (Davy, in 1798), discovery of electromagnetism (Ørsted, in 1820), discovery of ozone (Schönbein, in 1839), invention of synthetic coal-tar dyes (Perkin, in 1856), invention of dynamite (Nobel, in 1866), invention of the phonograph (Edison, in 1877), development of vaccination (Pasteur, in 1878), discovery of X rays (Röntgen, in 1895), discovery of natural radioactivity (Becquerel, in 1896), innovation of classical conditioning (Pavlov, in 1902), discovery of penicillin (Fleming, in 1928), invention of Teflon (Plunkett, in 1938), and invention of Velcro (de

Maestral, in 1948). Although we often think of serendipity as a phenomenon that occurs in the sciences, instances do in fact take place in the arts as well. For example, Henry James, the fiction writer, revealed in his preface to *The Spoils of Poynton* how his story grew from "mere floating particles in the stream of talk" during a casual dinner conversation. Hence, the phenomenon of serendipity is far more universal than is generally thought.

Upon closer examination, it becomes clear that serendipity may take a number of different forms. These forms vary according to the relative amount of "chance" involved as well as to the degree of intentionality underlying the discovery. To appreciate the potential contrasts, consider the following five cases.

Case 1: A person attempts to solve a problem and repeatedly fails. After incubating the question for some time, the person chances upon a fairly common circumstance that immediately inspires the solution. In this case, it is simply a matter of time before the required event will happen, and hence, to a certain degree the "accidental" input is inevitable. For example, when Gutenberg tried to solve the problem of how to mass-produce Bibles, he had worked out the notion of reusable type but had not yet figured out a workable device by which to make an imprint. It was during the wine harvest that he suddenly realized that the wine press provided the mechanical prototype for the printing press. He had found what he was looking for once the sequence of events had put him in the right place at the right time. There can be no doubt that all the other pieces of the puzzle were assembled, and the final piece would soon appear in the normal course of events.

Case 2: An individual attempts to solve a particular problem, but the solution requires a truly fortuitous event or sequence of events to be realized. The discovery in this case can be considered truly lucky, for it might not have happened at all. Charles Goodyear's discovery of vulcanization is a prime example. India rubber had the unfortunate characteristic of changing flexibility with the ambient temperature. It would become hard and brittle in cold weather, pliant but sticky in hot weather—which severely limited its utility as a production material. Because it was already known that sulfur would remove the adhesiveness, Goodyear began to experiment with this mixture. One day he accidentally dropped some of this mixture on a hot stove, and thereby discovered the secret. Presumably, without this highly fortunate mistake Goodyear might never have found the solution.

Case 3: Someone works on a problem and manages to find a solution. But in the process of making the intended discovery, the individual stumbles upon a totally unanticipated finding. For instance, when James Clerk Maxwell developed his electromagnetic theory, his original goal was not to explain light. But when he used his equations to calculate the speed of electromagnetic waves, he was surprised to discover the figure equaled the known velocity of light. Similarly, Paul Dirac's initial purpose behind creating his quantum-mechanical model of the electron was to make provision for relativity theory. Yet the existence of a hitherto unknown particle, the positron, just popped out of his equations. Physics was thus led to the entirely novel realm of antimatter. Unlike the cases of Gutenberg and Goodyear, Maxwell and Dirac discovered more than they had intended.

Case 4: A person is attempting to solve a given problem and has not yet succeeded (and may never do so). But along the way, the person chances across an unexpected discovery, such as a solution to an entirely different problem. The goal of Columbus was to find an alternative route to the Far East, but he ended up discovering the New World, albeit it was not at once obvious that he had done so. Observe that case 4 takes the lack of intentionality one step beyond case 3. The intended discovery is never made, while an unintended discovery is made in its stead. Serendipitous events like these play an important role in the theory of scientific revolutions proposed by Thomas Kuhn. In particular, Kuhn argues that the appearance of anomalies is what gradually undermines the confidence of a scientific community in a current theoretical paradigm. These findings may involve disconfirmed predictions or the discovery of unexpected phenomena. After a sufficient number of such anomalous results accumulate, the community enters a crisis stage that paves the way for the emergence of a new paradigm that displaces the old.

Case 5: Sometimes an individual is not looking for anything in particular, or at best is operating under only the vaguest of hunches. Perhaps the person is just "monkeying around" or "seeing what happens if"—that is, engaged in curious exploration or playful tinkering. By a stroke of blind luck, the individual stumbles upon an original but useful idea. This last case involves the highest degree of chance and the least degree of intentionality. It was an act of blind curiosity that motivated Antoni van Leeuwenhoek to direct his high-powered microscope at diverse substances and thus to discover a whole world of bacteria, protozoa, spermatozoa, and other fantastic organisms. His curiosity could tell him only that the findings might be interesting, and they fulfilled his expectations. Likewise, when Galileo pointed his newly improved telescope toward the heavens, he had no idea of what he would find. But what he saw was beyond what anyone at that time could possibly imagine—sunspots, lunar craters, Venusian phases, Jovian moons, Saturnian rings, and a host of other curiosities. Suddenly there appeared a vast array of anomalous discoveries that would destroy forever the Aristotelian and Ptolemaic cosmology that had dominated science since antiquity.

Some scholars would like to separate the first two cases from the last three. When individuals solve a problem they set out to solve, it is called "pseudoserendipity," no matter how much luck may have participated in the favorable outcome. On the other hand, whenever people come across an unexpected discovery, as in cases 3 to 5, the result is said to involve true serendipity. This distinction fits the folktale from which the word was born, and it seems more in accord with a Darwinian theory of creativity. Indeed, a number of scholars have suggested that true serendipity more closely approximates the genetic mutations of organic evolution. In the first two cases, the creator meant to make a particular discovery and eventually did so. The only surprise was the specific means by which the desired end was attained. But in the last three cases, ideational variants emerged that were totally unanticipated, even less intended. These useful and adaptive variations are thus truly blind in the sense implied by Campbell's theory. Moreover, like a chance mutation in organic evolution, these serendipitous ideas may radically alter the course of cultural evolution, obliging it to pursue unforeseen paths.

Although this Darwinian distinction between the pseudo- and true serendipity makes sense, too much can be made of the contrast as well. In some respects, the underlying thought processes may be very similar. After all, the same individuals who make unintended discoveries are often those who make intended discoveries, and the role of chance sensory input may be much the same. Some people have the capacity to take advantage of the opportunities provided by their experiential world, while others fail to do so. As Ernst Mach pointed out, many lucky discoveries "were seen numbers of times before they were noticed." Fleming was certainly not the first to see a bacterial culture ruined by mold, but he was evidently the first to notice the significance of this observation. This suggests that creative geniuses may enjoy a special openness to the potential implications of the innumerable stimuli that impinge daily upon their brains. Charles Darwin himself provides a good example of what may be lacking in those of us who seem not to have Fortune on our side. When Darwin had to specify what he considered his single best mental attribute, he claimed, "I think that I am superior to the common run of men in noticing things which easily escape attention." This exceptional capacity was confirmed by Darwin's son Francis, who was often his father's scientific collaborator. Francis took special note of his father's

> instinct for arresting exceptions: it was as though he were charged with theorizing power ready to flow into any channel on the slightest disturbance, so that no fact, however small, could avoid releasing a stream of theory, and thus the fact became magnified into importance. In this way it naturally happened that many untenable theories occurred to him; but fortunately his richness of imagination was equalled by his power of judging and condemning the thoughts that

occurred to him. He was just to his theories, and did not condemn them unheard; and so it happened that he was willing to test what would seem to most people not at all worth testing. These rather wild trials he called "fool's experiments," and enjoyed extremely.

Francis provided a curious example of one of these experiments: After noticing that the leaves of a certain plant seemed sensitive to table vibrations, Darwin asked his son to play his bassoon close to the plant, to determine if it might perceive sound! Francis's father was here displaying "his wish to test the most improbable ideas." Yet by conducting such experiments, Charles Darwin was sending open invitations to Fortune in the hope that something serendipitous would be sent his way. Sometimes she complied, and when she did, Darwin always took note.

Experimental Investigations

If the foregoing biographical reports represented the sole evidence for a Darwinian theory of creativity, the latter would be in a very sorry state indeed. After all, introspections into higher mental processes are fraught with all sorts of inherent difficulties, and memories about past events can undergo considerable distortion with the passage of time. Indeed, I must confess that it is quite possible to find notable creators offering descriptions of the creative process that run quite counter to what the preceding accounts seemed to imply. A case in point is "The Philosophy of Composition," an essay in which Edgar Allan Poe recounted the creation of his classic poem "The Raven." Because the essay appeared only one year after the poem's own publication, Poe's description certainly enjoys the advantage of being close to the events described. Yet in this account Poe said, "It was my design to render it manifest that no one point in its composition is referable either to accident or intuition—that the work proceeded, step by step, to its completion with the precision and rigid consequence of a mathematical problem." He then went on to show how logic dictated every single choice, from the optimal number of words right down to single words and images. Poe makes the whole creative process so straightforward, even mundane, that there seems little latitude for the kind of chaotic and unpredictable thinking discussed earlier.

Of course, Poe's report could be dismissed as just a piece of propaganda. He was engaged in attacking the prevailing Romantic notions of his day. As he put them, "Most writers—poets in especial—prefer having it understood that they compose by a species of fine frenzy—an ecstatic intuition." Moreover, Poe somewhat prided himself on his analytical skills, a trait that shows itself quite vividly in his detective stories, such in as "The Purloined Letter."

Nevertheless, if his testimony is dismissed as biased reporting, then why should not the same judgment be passed on all the biographical evidence that has been handed down to us? Certainly there is reason to believe that others have distorted the stories behind their creation to better fit the Romantic view of the creative process. Samuel Coleridge, for instance, reported how his poem "Kubla Khan" originated in an opium-induced stupor—a nice touch given the great vogue of this drug at that time. But scrutiny of his drafts shows that Coleridge probably made up this episode. Hence, rejection of any given bit of biographical evidence can cut both ways.

Rather than debate this matter further, it may behoove us to look elsewhere to see if there exist other, more scientific sources of evidence that endorse the Darwinian view. Here I review a diverse assortment of laboratory experiments that deal with pertinent aspects of the creative process. Although the participants in these experiments are more likely to be college students than established creators, the studies at least avoid the problems associated with using introspections and anecdotes. The specific experiments concern insight, imagery, and intuition.

Insight

Creativity is often identified with the process of insight. In fact, the term insight is sometimes used interchangeably with the moment of illumination in the creative process. Insight has also attracted a considerable amount of experimental research. The earlier Gestalt psychologists were especially interested in the phenomenon, and much of the subsequent research is founded on those pioneering inquiries. Although the bulk of the studies use human beings as experimental subjects, some studies have examined insight in animals. Let us review the latter inquiries before turning our attention to the former.

Animal studies. Because insight seems to be such a supreme mental ability, it may appear strange to look for insight in nonhuman organisms. Indeed, if not every human being enjoys the capacity for insight, it may seem absurd to study the phenomenon in animals. However, because Darwinism implies that there exists some degree of evolutionary continuity between humans and other animals, there should appear mental processes analogous to insight in our closest phylogenetic relatives. One likely prospect is the chimpanzee, an organism whose cognitive skills are remarkably close to those of *Homo sapiens*. One of the classic Gestalt studies of insight, in fact, was conducted by Wolfgang Köhler, using chimps. Köhler wished to show that the solution of problems required a perceptual process, one that entailed a sudden and novel reorganization of experience—the sudden insight. To make his case, he would present a chimp with an urgent but difficult problem: how to reach a banana that was set deliberately beyond arm's reach. Successful solutions required the chimp to put together a long pole from two short poles or to pile boxes on which the chimp could stand. In the typical experiment, the animal would try the most obvious tactics until it became apparent that nothing in its standard repertoire of behaviors would allow it to attain the goal. The chimp would then enter an incubation period, after which it would exhibit an apparent eureka experience. The necessary behaviors would then quickly follow until the banana was at hand. Because finding a solution required the organization of a novel sequence of behaviors, and because the solution came so suddenly, the chimpanzee can be said to have displayed insight. Outwardly, at least, there does not appear to be much of a difference between the manner in which the animals and Archimedes solved their problems.

The Gestaltists believed that such insightful behavior allows the organism to bypass trial-and-error learning. But this conclusion goes well beyond the evidence. Critics were quick to point out that the various behaviors that the animals had to assemble to solve the problem were already part of their repertoire. The chimps had previously learned to put the sticks together and to pile boxes. Moreover, the chimps surely could have used this basic input as part of an internal process of trial and error. Remember what creative individuals have said about the importance of generating lots of ideational variants—what Einstein called "combinatory play." Certainly, chimpanzees have the brains to engage in the same process, even if at a more limited level. If so, the mechanism underlying insight would still be Darwinian. Creative chimps would be manipulating representations of their behavioral world until they found a combination that satisfied the constraints of the problem situation, such as the height and distance of the hanging banana.

Actually, there already exists a highly successful explanation of Köhler's results completely within the framework of Skinner's operant conditioning paradigm. And, as pointed out in chapter 1, this learning paradigm is explicitly Darwinian in nature. The proponent of this theory is Robert Epstein, a close collaborator of B. F. Skinner's. Together they had launched a simulation project in which they attempted "to get pigeons to do some of the complex and mysterious things people do." At first, these behavioral simulations did not depart far from usual learning studies. The pigeons would simply undergo reinforcement for certain behaviors until the desired operants were established. But a serendipitous finding emerged that opened a whole new avenue of inquiry. Often when a pigeon was placed in a new situation in which previously learned behaviors did not apply, it would spontaneously generate new behaviors that were intriguing combinations of acquired behaviors. This led Epstein to examine the possibility that the insightful solutions displayed by Köhler's chimps might be exhibited by pigeons as well.

The experimental simulation required that the pigeon learn three behaviors. First, the pigeon learned it would receive food when it successfully pushed a box toward a green spot located at random positions on the floor of the Skinner box. Second, the pigeon learned it could obtain food by pecking at an object—made to look like a little banana—suspended from the top of the chamber. However, it also learned that the food would be delivered only if the pigeon's feet were standing on something. Jumping and flying at the toy banana accomplished nothing. Third, the pigeon learned how stepping on a box to peck at the banana was permissible, and the position of the banana-box combination was freely varied about the cage. After acquiring this behavioral repertoire, the pigeon was confronted with a novel situation: A banana was suspended out of reach, with the box located in another part of the chamber. None of the pigeon's learned behaviors will solve the problem, although the right combination will do the trick. So what did the pigeon do? It behaved in a manner virtually indistinguishable from Köhler's chimps. "At first the pigeon looked confused. It stretched toward the banana, looked back and forth from the banana to the box, and so on. Then, quite suddenly, it began to push the box toward the banana, sighting the banana as it pushed. Each pigeon stopped pushing when the box was beneath the banana and then immediately climbed and pecked." Significantly, pigeons that did not acquire the full behavioral repertoire either failed to solve the problem or solved it only through trial and error (depending on which operants had been learned). This replicates what has been found in chimpanzee studies as well. Chimps will show insight only when they have learned all the behavioral components required of the solution.

A critic might consider Epstein's simulation of insight more cute than convincing. But, on the contrary, Epstein has established the theoretical plausibility of this model in three important ways. First, he has carefully studied the behavioral processes that underlie the insight phenomenon in order to comprehend precisely how it works. For example, he has advanced the "principle of resurgence," which states, "When, in a given situation, a behavior that was previously successful is no longer successful, behavior that was previously successful in similar situations tends to recur." Thus, the organism begins to generate behavioral variants based on all those past circumstances that might bear some relation to the current problem. Second, Epstein has cast his explanation in more formal terms, producing equations that provide the basis for computer simulations. These equations describe how the probability of the appearance of various behaviors changes over the course of the organism's interactions with the environment. In other words, the model describes the manner in which the organism achieves increased adaptive fit by generating and testing behavioral variants. Third and last, Epstein did not rest content with applying his "generativity theory" to pigeons. He has applied the same paradigm to human subjects trying to solve a classic insight problem. The computer simulation predicts the behavior of humans just as well as it does for animals. As a consequence, insofar as creativity requires insightful behavior, Epstein's theory can be considered a viable Darwinian model of the creative process. Certainly the model incorporates a mechanism by which animals can generate behaviors that are both original and adaptive.

Human studies. The insight problem that Epstein successfully modeled using his generativity theory was the famous two-string problem. The participant in the experiment enters the laboratory and sees two strings hanging from the ceiling. The subject is told that the object is to tie the two strings together. In the vicinity are a number of objects that may be used to solve the problem, including a pair of pliers. The subject soon learns the task is more difficult than first meets the eye. The relationship between the distance between the strings and their length is such that one cannot simply grab the end of one string, walk over to where the second string hangs, grab that second end, and complete the task. Try as he or she might, the other string always remains frustratingly beyond reach. The solution requires the subject to use the pliers in an unusual fashion—to create a pendulum. Once the pliers are tied to the end of one string, and that string is set in oscillation, it is an easy matter for the subject to walk over to the second string, pull its end toward the first string, and grab the pliers as they swing toward the subject. The rest is simple.

Many subjects experience severe difficulty solving this problem, and research has unearthed some of the factors that enhance the odds of successful solution. One factor concerns the nature of the objects available to tackle the task. To use a pair of pliers as a weight requires the subject to perceive that tool in a different manner, as merely a mass suitable for making a pendulum. But if the available objects include a plumb bob, the probability of a solution increases dramatically. Another factor is even more provocative: The subject may respond to "hints." In one experimental condition the experimenter would casually walk by one of the strings, brush it "accidentally" with his shoulder, and thus set it in motion. Shortly after this clue the subject was much more likely to solve the problem. It is interesting to note that when subjects were asked how they arrived at the necessary insight, they would often fail to report the hint as the precipitating factor—the impact of the cue would be subliminal or unconscious.

This is but one example of the kind of problem studied in the rich literature on insightful problem solving. Although the details vary, the findings are generally comparable. When an individual first confronts a novel problem, the most obvious responses may utterly fail. To succeed, the various features of the problem must be reformulated in a different and often highly

unusual fashion. As a consequence, the problem solver may enter an incubation period, in which the mind must open up to various possibilities.
During this interval the individual is exposed to all sorts of extraneous
input. Some of this input is external (everyday events as well as work on
other projects), and other input is internal (retrieved memories, chains of
associative thought). But whatever the specific source, this bombardment is
constantly "priming," or exciting, different aspects of the mnemonic and
semantic networks surrounding a given problem. This largely random
influx of priming stimuli produces a series of alternative formulations,
some more fruitful than others, but with only one leading the individual
down the correct path to solution. In other words, during incubation the
mind is engaged in an inadvertent blind-variation process. The process is
"blind" because the order in which the new conceptions appear is determined by factors pretty much irrelevant to the problem. Indeed, it is the
very extraneous nature of this input that is so essential to the solution. Subjects get stumped on insight problems because the most obvious ways of
thinking about them prove abortive.

Because much of this haphazard input takes place at unconscious levels
of information processing, the problem solver might not be cognizant of
the stimulus that led to the successful solution. Like for the subjects in the
two-strings problem, the solution may be partly intuitive. As noted earlier,
this lack of awareness fits with the observations of notable creators themselves. For instance, Carl Friedrich Gauss, the reknowned mathematician,
once recorded that, after years of failing to solve a problem, "finally, two
days ago, I succeeded, not on account of my painful efforts, but by the grace
of God. Like a sudden flash of lightning, the riddle happened to be solved. I
myself cannot say what was the conducting thread which connected what I
previously knew with what made my success possible." Presumably, it was
some arbitrary event that inspired following the appropriate pathways to
the requisite insight. In the long interim between the posing of the problem
and the solution, Gauss's mind could do no more than generate unconsciously and blindly ideas that led nowhere.

One last point must be made with regard to incubation: This period may
facilitate solution finding by more than one means. Usually when people fail
to solve a problem, their level of arousal increases—they experience excitement and frustration. Such heightened emotion tends to constrict the width
of attention. In addition, higher arousal tends to make high-probability
associations even more probable and low-probability associations less so.
Given that the solution requires the ability to look at the problem in an original way, the individual must attain a more relaxed state to allow the low-
probability associations a reasonable chance to emerge. Hence, during the
incubation period arousal may be lowered enough to make the person more

able to take advantage of the sometimes subtle cues offered by the surrounding environment. In other words, the low-arousal state is more conducive to the Darwinian process needed to arrive at an insightful solution.

Imagery

Although I believe the experimental research on insight lends support to a Darwinian view of the creative process, the case is somewhat weakened by the nature of the problems normally found in such research. The typical insight problem has a well-defined answer. In fact, the connection between the problem and the solution is quite logical once the "trick" is known. Real creativity, however, does not begin with the knowledge that there even exists a true answer, and thus the phenomenon is far more open-ended. Recent attempts to develop the "creative cognition approach" have increasingly recognized this contrast, leading many investigators to ask that subjects generate truly original ideas. From the perspective of this book, the most interesting of these studies is the experimental research on the role of imagery in the production of creative ideas.

An excellent example is the work associated with the "Geneplore" model recently advanced by Ron Finke, Tom Ward, and Steve Smith. Although not explicitly formulated in Darwinian terms, the connection with a variation-selection framework is quite apparent. The very term *Geneplore* stands for "generate and explore." The authors see the creative process as consisting of the generation of combinations, followed by the exploration of their possibilities. In other words, the first stage entails a variation process in which new arrangements of mental imagery are freely generated; the second stage involves a selection process in which certain novelties are chosen for further development.

In the experimental research on the geneplore model, the connection with a variation-selection process becomes even more obvious. Subjects were given shapes or forms—lines, circles, triangles, letters, spheres, cubes, rings, hooks, etc.—from which they had to create objects with recognizable functions (e.g., furniture, appliances, tools and utensils, weapons, or toys). The products of this inventive activity were then evaluated by judges for their creativity. Some of the inventions arrived at were truly ingenious, including a hip exerciser, a shoestring unlacer, and a hamburger maker. More interesting still was how the creativity of the inventions would depend on the experimental conditions. In some conditions subjects themselves could select the shapes for the imaginative constructions, whereas in other conditions the subjects were simply given a random selection of forms. In yet another manipulation subjects themselves could choose the category of object they had to invent or the category would be selected randomly by the experimenter. The researchers showed that subjects arrived at the most innovative solutions when both the object parts that they had to work with and the category of object they had to invent were randomly selected from the larger pool of possibilities. The best creativity tends to be serendipitous rather than deliberate. One could hardly obtain a more blind basis for launching the combinatory process. By beginning with the totally unexpected, the participants in these experiments were forced to stretch their creativity to the highest degree.

This conclusion receives endorsement from experiments that have an entirely different theoretical foundation. Earlier I mentioned the work of Rothenberg on homospatial and Janusian thinking. Although the bulk of his research on these forms of imagery depended on interviews and other nonexperimental data, Rothenberg has also examined these processes in the laboratory. Of special interest are his investigations of homospatial thought. He and a colleague began by making up a set of visual stimuli that involved the superimposition of visual images. The superimpositions included all sorts of unrelated subject matter. For example, one contained a photograph of an empty French four-poster bed placed in a period room superimposed over a group of soldiers in combat who were taking cover behind a tank. These highly incongruous homospatial images were then shown to writers and to artists, the latter including individuals selected in a national competition by faculty at the Yale School of Art. The writers were instructed to create new metaphors inspired by the stimuli, whereas the artists were instructed to make pastel drawings. In comparison with the control group (e.g., subjects who saw the images only separately), individuals exposed to these visual juxtapositions of unrelated images generated more creative products, as judged by independent raters.

These are provocative results, for they suggest that creative imagery is excited by sensory input that is random or at least unusual. In fact, artists often report engaging in activities that might stimulate their visual imagination after a similar fashion. For instance, the surrealist painter and sculptor Max Ernst described how he so used the artistic technique of frottage: "I was struck by the obsession that showed to my excited gaze the floor-boards upon which a thousand scrubbings had deepened the grooves. . . . [I]n order to aid my meditative and hallucinatory faculties, I made from the boards a series of drawings by placing on them, at random, sheets of paper which I undertook to rub with black lead. In gazing attentively at the drawings thus obtained . . . I was surprised by the sudden intensification of my visionary capacities and by the hallucinatory succession of contradictory images superimposed, one upon the other." In this passage Ernst even makes explicit reference to homospatial imagery.

Together the above experiments underline the creative utility of mental imagery, while at the same time showing how the creative imagination seems to operate according to Darwinian principles. Not only must the mind be capable of engaging in wild combinatory play, but in addition this play often appears to be encouraged by the random juxtapositions of visual stimuli. Such stimuli optimally elicit cognitive mutations.

Intuition

The notion that much of the business of creativity can be ascribed to intuition is very old. We have already quoted the opinions of Poincaré and Hadamard on this subject. Many theorists have also placed considerable emphasis on the role the unconscious plays in the creative process. The most notable example is the attempts of Sigmund Freud and subsequent psychoanalysts to explain creativity in terms of primary-process thought. This mode of thinking is largely subconscious, highly primitive, even infantile, and rich in irrational associations. Indeed, the primary process was held responsible by psychoanalysts for the highly creative imagery and symbolism experienced in dreams. Although experimental research on intuitive processes has been going on for some time, it is perhaps only since the advent of modern cognitive psychology that genuine headway has been made. Certain of these findings suggest that unconscious mental processes may be a good source of ideational variants that would have a low probability of being produced by conscious mental processes. The following five conclusions deserve special attention:

1. Current research on implicit learning and memory suggests that the human mind can acquire a vast set of expectations in the absence of any awareness of the basis for those expectations. For example, experiments on artificial grammars show that individuals can judge the difference between permissible and impermissible symbol strings without being able to specify the corresponding grammatical rule. Psychologists have known for some time that classical and operant conditioning can sometimes occur in the absence of awareness, but results such as these indicate that unconscious expectations can be even more sophisticated.

2. Unconscious associations can greatly influence the course of thought in the absence of any conscious intervention. Indeed, the activation of a given part of a memory network can ramify to other portions of the network, activating associations that are sometimes only very remotely connected with the initial impetus. This unconscious process of "spreading activation" can play a major part in getting the mind to isolate components of a problem's solution that might otherwise be missed by directed, conscious thought.

3. The unconscious material in the mind is often stored in multiple ways, including in manners that are unusual, if not illogical. For

example, words are associated not only according to denotative meanings but also according to sound qualities and emotional connotations. Hence, in the tip-of-the-tongue phenomenon, individuals trying to retrieve a particular word will often extract from memory words that sound similar with respect to specific phonemes and the number of syllables. This permits the activation of associative material to follow several different paths simultaneously in a variety of "parallel processing."

4. Experimental research indicates that unconscious mental operations may be particularly useful to the solution of problems that require creative insight. For instance, cognitive psychologists sometimes study problem-solving processes using "protocol analysis," in which subjects are asked "to think aloud" while working on a given problem. Although this experimental instruction may not affect the performance of subjects working on more everyday problems, the imposition of such a condition does noticeably undermine performance when the subjects are trying to solve insight problems. Thinking aloud by necessity obliges the subject to rely exclusively on conscious mental processes in circumstances when unconscious processes are more likely to overcome the misperceptions and implicit constraints that obstruct finding the solution.

5. Unconscious mental processes can even support "feeling of knowing" states that are comparable to the unjustified "hunches" that are so often reported by creative individuals. Although these feelings are by no means infallible, and may often err, they can provide support for pursuing avenues that might be bypassed otherwise. In fact, experimental research has shown that even when hunches are incorrect, they often bear an associative link to the correct answer. These bad guesses show that a subject is "getting warmer" long before reaching the right solution to the problem. These results also indicate that the unconscious mind can generate ideational variants, thrusting into consciousness those that exhibit superior prospects of success.

The foregoing characteristics of intuition suggest a curious parallel between the emergence of creative ideas in the mind and the evolution of new life-forms in the organic world. When Darwin contemplated some of the possible objections to evolutionary theory, he realized that among the most crucial was the lack of well-documented lineages in the paleontological record. Instead, there were countless "missing links," or what Darwin called "transitional varieties." Even today, with the fossil evidence tremendously expanded, these gaps in the evolutionary record are the rule rather than the exception. In *Origin of Species*, Darwin dealt with this problem by arguing that these transitional species would probably be represented by very small populations. Moreover, such populations may not endure very long before facing extinction. After all, these transitional varieties would most likely be less well adapted than the forms that evolved from them. For example, species that can actually fly may quickly win the struggle for existence against species that can only glide or flutter. Hence, the paleontological record is dominated primarily by the successful varieties, only an occasional transitional form surviving to the present. This process is quite similar to that of the creative mind. Intuition is spontaneously generating all sorts of ideational combinations, but most of these are transitional ideas that fail to enter consciousness. Only a few ideational variants—either the solution itself or ideas that have some close associative connection—will emerge from the unconscious mind. As a consequence, the creator's memory retains only the highlights of the sequence of mental events that led to the solution. Solely the consciously deliberated ideas will become a part of the mind's "fossil record." The result is numerous cognitive missing links. The creative insight then so often emerges de novo, like Minerva from the head of Zeus.

Finally, it is important to recognize that the unconscious mind is not a single unit but rather an often loosely connected collection of sometimes rather distinct processes. For instance, some strongly practiced skills have become so automatic that there is no longer any cognitive need to attend to their execution. Other unconscious processes are assigned to the recognition of faces, the mastery of language, and the acquisition of emotional meanings. Some of these processes are potentially accessible to consciousness, and others not. Moreover, some of these processes are carried out in the more advanced portions of the brain, whereas others are apparently located in more primitive parts of the nervous system. The significant point is that the workings of the conscious mind represent only a small fragment of the total activity carried on by the mind at a particular time. Consequently, the unconscious mind is probably more capable of generating the blind variations required by a Darwinian theory of creativity. That is not to say that all ideational variants have intuitive origins. I have already noted how unusual imagery may also provide a valuable source of intellectual recombinations. Yet intuition just might provide the single most potent resource for the creative genius.

Computer Simulations

Modern cognitive science has relied ever more on computers as a means of developing a theory of the mind. In fact, to a very large degree computer models of mental processes have replaced mathematical models as the preferred approach to building comprehensive and precise theory. For the most part, unfortunately, these computational models deal with rather basic cognitive processes that appear far removed from what are required to achieve creative thoughts. Nonetheless, there have been a number of attempts to model the operations that can produce original ideas. These can be grouped into two distinct categories. The first set of models are founded on principles that seem totally antithetical to a Darwinian position. The second set, in contrast, consists of models that are explicitly Darwinian.

Discovery Programs

Earlier I mentioned Poe's claim that the composition of "The Raven" involved nothing more than the step-by-step application of a conscious, rigorous, and inevitable logic. Many cognitive scientists who study human problem-solving behavior would concur. Foremost among these advocates of the conscious and deliberate application of logic is Herbert Simon, a Nobel laureate. Simon has attempted to demystify the creative process by arguing that even the renowned achievements of so-called geniuses can easily be ascribed to far more basic mechanisms. For example, he has claimed that Mendeleyev's origination of the Periodic Law of the Elements required nothing more advanced than what is "required to handle patterned letter sequences." In fact, the bulk of Simon's work has concentrated on scientific discovery, which Simon believes follows logical principles that may be applied by anyone. To help make his case, Simon has conducted some informal experiments in which naive subjects were presented with a problem whose solution won renown for some past scientist. For instance, Simon reported, "On eight occasions I have sat down at lunch with colleagues who are good applied mathematicians and said to them: 'I have a problem that you can perhaps help me with. I have some very nice data that can be fitted very accurately for large values of the independent variable by an exponential function, but for small values they fit a linear function accurately. Can you suggest a smooth function that will give me a good fit through the whole range?'" Of the eight lunch companions, five found an answer within a couple of minutes or less. None suspected what Simon was up to, nor did any realize the historic nature of the problem given them. Still, those five anonymous individuals had independently arrived at Planck's formula for blackbody radiation. In another mini-experiment a mere graduate student in chemical engineering was able to derive the Balmer formula for the hydrogen spectrum. Moreover, this subject was asked to think aloud while solving the problem, and therefore protocol analysis could be applied to learn the search processes that led to the discovery. The thought processes were comparable to those revealed in Balmer's surviving documents. And those processes seemed to involve nothing more than straightforward logical reasoning.

These informal results have been confirmed in a more formal laboratory experiment. Subjects drawn mostly from a student population were presented raw data for five cases on two variables, s and q. The specific scores were: 36 and 88, 67.25 and 224.7, 93 and 365.3, 141.75 and 687, and 483.8 and 4,332.1, respectively. The subjects were told that the experimenters were "interested in how a human being discovers a scientific law." Accordingly, each subject was to identify a precise functional relationship between s and q. Four out of 14 subjects tested found the correct relationship. Yet what these successful problem solvers accomplished was a rediscovery of the third law of planetary motion first formulated by Johannes Kepler! In fact, the subjects wrestled with data for all practical purposes the same as those used by Kepler. The five sets of observations regard the planets Mercury, Venus, Earth, Mars, and Jupiter. Here s is the distance from the sun in millions of miles and q is the period of revolution in earth days. According to Kepler's third law, the distance cubed is proportional to the period squared, or $s^3 = kq^2$, where k is a constant. Furthermore, the protocols indicated that the successful subjects used the same methods found in other problem-solving experiments. For instance, to find the relationship between two variables one needs to find functions for each of the variables that produce a constant ratio. In this case, one must find a function f_1 of the distance and another function f_2 of the period such that $f_1(s)/f_2(q)$ returns about the same quotient k across all observations.

The computer models. The supremely logical nature of these thought processes implies that a computer might be programmed to duplicate the discoveries of illustrious scientists. Herbert Simon and his colleagues have attempted to do just that, writing a large number of "discovery programs." These programs are often christened with names of famous creative individuals, such as OCCAM, BACON, GALILEO, GLAUBER, STAHL, FAHRENHEIT, BLACK, and DALTON. And these tags are not wholly incidental. For example, BACON specializes in the inductive method, yielding data-driven discoveries as advocated in Francis Bacon's *Novum Organum*; GLAUBER, of Glauber's salt fame, concentrates on discoveries in chemistry.

But even more important, these programs have shown the ability to rediscover scientific laws or principles that have made human scientists famous. GLAUBER can learn to distinguish acid and alkali. STAHL can identify elements as components of substances. DALTON can take the output from STAHL to generate structural formulas consistent with atomic theory. Yet it is BACON that is the powerhouse of discovery programs. BACON has discovered Kepler's third law of planetary motion, Black's law of temperature equilibrium, Ohm's law of current and resistance, Prout's hypothesis of atomic structure, the Gay-Lussac law of gaseous reaction, the Dulong-Petit law of atomic heats, and the derivation of atomic weights by Avogadro and Cannizzaro. Some programs even duplicate some of the fine details of the process by which a scientist made a given discovery. For instance, KEKADA models the heuristics that Hans Krebs used to get the urea cycle. The programmers fixed this concordance by comparing the computer's output with both the notebooks and the living testimony of Krebs himself.

The criticisms. If these discovery programs accurately represent the creative process, then the Darwinian model advanced by Donald Campbell would seem most implausible. Nonetheless, several critics have pointed out limitations to these programs that render them less convincing as models. To begin with, the programs do not always re-create the cognitive processes of creative scientists. For example, one critic compared the logical operations presumed in the programs with the processes revealed in the extensive notebooks left by the physicist Michael Faraday. Faraday's dynamic use of visual imagery had no counterpart in these computer models. Although some progress has been made in incorporating imagery into discovery programs, these innovations have a long way to go before they can accurately simulate the imaginative experiences reported by creative individuals. In addition, the laboratory notebooks of Faraday, like those of many other notable creators, exhibit considerable cross-talk between separate projects. Ideas or themes that originally appeared to help solve one problem have a way of stimulating developments with other problems. An instance cited earlier is Poincaré's seaside discovery of the link between indeterminate ternary quadratic forms and non-Euclidean geometry. Yet such ideational interchanges have no counterpart in any of the discovery programs, all of which are designed to work on only one project from start to finish.

Furthermore, unlike scientists in the real world, discovery programs must always be given the problem to solve rather than discovering the problems for themselves. And some have argued that problem finding may be a skill every bit as important as problem solving. As Einstein noted, "The formulation of a problem is often more essential than its solution, which may be merely a matter of mathematical or experimental skill. To raise new questions, new problems, to regard old problems from a new angle, requires creative imagination and marks real advances in science." Einstein practiced what he preached. His contemporary physicists were not really bothered about inconsistencies between Newtonian mechanics and Maxwell's equations for electromagnetism. Not only was Einstein perplexed by the discrepancies, but he discovered that to solve the problem he himself had invented required him to devise a revolutionary new physics, the theory of special relativity. Hence, so long as these discovery programs only tackle problems given to them by human beings, we can only suspect their capacity to provide a comprehensive explanation for scientific creativity.

Even worse, these discovery programs can only work by extensively simplifying the problems they are given. This simplification occurs at both input and output ends. At the input end, the programs are fed the data in a highly abstract, even sanitized form. Real scientists, in contrast, often operate with a much more complex array of information that can vary tremendously in precision and relevance. As a consequence, scientific discovery normally requires a more haphazard examination of various possibilities, and only far later will it become more obvious what data are essential and what are superfluous. At the output end, moreover, the discovery programs begin with a well-defined set of criteria of what counts as a successful solution. Scientific creativity in the actual world, in contrast, may have to contend with considerably more ambiguity on this score. Not only must the scientist assess the solution's adequacy on the basis of personal criteria—including more nebulous aesthetic factors—but in addition the scientist will have to convince other members of the scientific community who won't be applying the same criteria to the solution. A good illustration concerns the discovery that the elements exhibit periodicities in their chemical and physical properties. Although Herbert Simon claimed that this was an easy discovery to make, that claim can be made only if we ignore the context in which that discovery had to be evaluated. Shortly before Mendeleyev offered his solution, John Newlands presented his comparable law of octaves at a professional meeting. A distinguished scientist chairing the session waxed sarcastic, asking whether Newlands had also tried placing the elements in alphabetical order. Clearly, these two scientists disagreed dramatically on what qualified as a scientific discovery. So far, discovery problems cannot implement a complex search through the data space, and even less can they display flexibility in the application of criteria regarding valid output.

Besides a certain rigidity in data input and theory output, discovery programs are rather fixed in their "throughput." These rule-driven programs successfully solve given problems by applying a predetermined set of heuristic principles to the data provided. Trial-and-error procedures are minimized by assigning an a priori ordering to the operations that will be applied. When BACON rediscovered Kepler's third law, for example, it began with the linear relationship between the two variables. Since that failed the criterion of a proportional relationship, one of the variables was squared and the empirical test again applied. This iterative process continued until the cube of one variable was found to be proportional to the square of the other. Although in a certain sense this sequence of transformations and tests involved some trial and error, there was too much wisdom underlying the procedure to make it count as truly blind. Rather than randomly trying out all possible mathematical relationships, the hypothesized functions proceeded from the simple to the complex by successive powers.

The rigidity of this information-processing procedure raises two related issues. First, the hierarchical ordering of the data manipulations was obviously installed after the fact, and therefore one must wonder whether the programs were specifically tailored to fit the problems in a post hoc manner. For example, Hermann von Helmholtz, the illustrious physiologist and physicist, once admitted

> that I had only succeeded in solving such problems after many devious ways, by the gradually increasing generalisation of favourable examples, and by a series of fortunate guesses. I had to compare myself with an Alpine climber, who, not knowing the way, ascends slowly and with toil, and is often compelled to retrace his steps because his progress is stopped; sometimes by reasoning, and sometimes by accident, he hits upon traces of a fresh path, which again leads him a little further; and finally, when he has reached the goal, he finds to his annoyance a royal road on which he might have ridden up if he had been clever enough to find the right starting-point at the outset. In my memoirs I have, of course, not given the reader an account of my wanderings, but I have described the beaten path on which he can now reach the summit without trouble.

To what extent do these programs merely reflect the advantage of hindsight, taking the preordained "royal path" so as to bypass the trial and error inherent in the genuine creative process?

Second, the kinds of heuristic searches that work well for one problem will not work well for a completely different problem. It is for this reason that there does not exist a single discovery program, but rather many discovery programs, each containing a subset of heuristic principles designed to solve a specific class of problems. Because real scientists are confronted with multiple problems, they must possess a diversity of problem-solving techniques, without knowing which particular trick or set of tricks will get them where they want to go. Indeed, not only must scientists select among alternative heuristic principles, they also must choose among alternative problems, trying to guess which problems are most likely to be solved with the tools at hand.

It should not be surprising, therefore, that these programs have so far been limited to making mere rediscoveries. Hence, they should be called "rediscovery programs." So let us ask: What would it take to devise discovery programs that are truly worthy of the name? These programs would have to increase the diversity of mental modalities and operations available, including adding various kinds of imagery and free association to the logical operators already incorporated in the computer models. The programs would have to be able to work on several projects simultaneously, permitting the free exchange of ideas across problems. The programs would have to feature the capacity not only to select among problems at any moment but even to discover new problems. The programs would have to deal with much more messy data sets in which it is not always clear what is useful and what not. At the same time, the programs would need the ability to consider a wider diversity of criteria by which potential discoveries are judged, and allow these criteria to change over time according to feedback from other projects or the environment. Moreover, the programs would contain a huge set of heuristic principles, with only the vaguest information on which principles will best work for the various problems in queue.

I would argue that such a bona fide discovery program, with so many choices at its disposal at any particular moment, would have to depend very heavily on trial and error in maneuvering through the intricately interconnected problem spaces. Moreover, the greater the novelty and complexity of the problems under consideration, the stronger the role of that dependence. To a large degree, the highly creative scientist may have little option other than to sample blindly modalities, processes, operations, problems, criteria, heuristics, and the other components of the rich phenomenon of scientific discovery. In short, I believe that when genuine discovery programs appear, they will in all likelihood operate according to a Darwinian view of the creative mind.

Genetic Algorithms

Perhaps the discovery programs were doomed to fail because they operate under a computer model of the brain that is fundamentally at odds with the reality. These programs work by a sequential, step-by-step logic defined by a priori decision trees that specify the if-then statements to which there can be provided discrete yes-no answers. Of course, this is the modus operandi of the conventional digital computer, founded on Boolean algebra, which has made computers the only machines comparable to the human brain in terms of information-processing power. But that success does not mean that these traditional simulations offer an adequate representation of the central nervous system. When a computer system (BIG BLUE) finally beat the world chess champion (Gary Kasparov), it did not do so by emulating the operations of the chess genius. On the contrary, the human brain was simply overwhelmed by the "brute force" capabilities enjoyed by the phenomenally fast machine. The mind was not outthought but rather outcalculated.

Fortunately, recent advances in computer models of the mind have taken an entirely different approach. In particular, these new "connectionist" and "neural network" models operate in a far more diffuse and probabilistic manner. Such modern approaches, moreover, are more likely to function by Darwinian principles. From a multitude of potential interconnections are selected that subset that best satisfy some external criterion of performance. Although at present such models are designed to simulate relatively simple mental processes, some psychologists have already suggested that these models hold far more promise in the eventual simulation of the complex process of creativity. In particular, Colin Martindale has delineated the intimate conceptual relationships among (a) Campbell's blind-variation-and-selective-retention model of creativity, (b) connectionist, neural-network, and spin-glass models (in solid-state physics), (c) such creativity mechanisms as remote associations and primary process, and (d) individual differences in associative gradients, defocused attention, and arousal level. In essence, Martindale has sketched the route by which connectionist models may eventually be able to simulate creativity in the fashion that actually takes place in the human mind.

At present, however, the more fruitful approach has been to design explicitly Darwinian computer programs. These can then be used to test whether blind-variation-and-selective-retention models can indeed support the evolution of complex, organized structures from simple elements. For example, researchers have constructed computer models of organic evolution by natural selection. In these simulations the characteristics of a hypothetical organism are specified by strings of computer code. These genetic strands are placed in an electronic "soup" and given the opportunity to reproduce their kind, often with the addition of sporadic random mutations. Quickly a struggle for existence ensues that permits the influence of selection pressures. Accordingly, over time the creatures evolve—yielding progeny with new genetic instructions. Even more fascinating, novel evolutionary phenomena will often appear. For instance, certain mutants may develop into parasitic organisms, which will then display population oscillations with their hosts that are indistinguishable from those observed in the natural world. In addition, eventually there may emerge more complex processes, such as sexual reproduction, sexual selection, and kinship selection. These computer simulations of organic evolution provide proof that the Darwinian process can indeed provide an explanation for complex adaptation.

It is a short step from these simulations of primary Darwinism to applications of secondary Darwinism in action. The pioneer in this development was John Holland, who received the first American Ph.D. in computer science. Holland was inspired by R. A. Fisher's 1930 book *The Genetical Theory of Natural Selection*, the landmark contribution to the development of a mathematical theory of evolution. The result was the problem-solving strategy of the computer-driven genetic algorithm. Genetic-algorithm programs start with a population of randomly generated strings of ones and zeroes, such as 011010. These binary strings function the same way as a genetic code. That is, the strings define the traits of some entity or system, in this case a potential solution to a given problem. The trial solutions represented by this random collection of binary strings can then be tested to determine which come closest to solving the problem. The least successful strings are then deleted, while the most successful are allowed to reproduce. This reproduction occurs sexually. Specifically, each strand pairs off with another strand, and then each exchanges a portion of its strand with its mate (the exact point of crossover being itself randomly determined). For example, suppose that 001001 and 110100 represent two strands that survived the first round of selection. They may mate by splitting after the fourth bit, the first part of one strand joining with the second part of the other strand. The outcome would be 001000 and 110101. Furthermore, genetic mutations can be introduced by randomly changing one or two bits on a subset of strands. Once this new generation is produced, the corresponding trial solutions can again be tested against the criterion. The whole Darwinian process may repeat, cycle after cycle, until the criterion of success is fully attained.

Despite the utterly blind procedures for producing variations, genetic algorithms have proven to be quite effective problem solvers. They can now already solve real-world problems, such as planning fiber-optic telecommunication networks, designing gas and steam turbines, enhancing the efficiency of jet engines, making forecasts in currency trading, and improving oil exploration and mining operations. Moreover, the basic Darwinian approach could be taken a step further to generate much more complex problem-solving systems. One of Holland's students, John Koza, extended genetic algorithms to a higher level of creativity by conceiving the procedure of genetic programming. In this technique, whole components of programs are subjected to blind variation, and thus the Darwinian process operates at a higher level of structure. This approach has worked well with such problems as designing electrical circuits, solving algebraic equations, determining animal foraging behavior, and finding optimal game-playing strategies.

It is interesting to note that these Darwinian programs can even make rediscoveries, just as claimed by the discovery programs discussed earlier. For example, genetic programming also managed to arrive at Kepler's third law of planetary motion. In fact, during the course of the evolution of a solution process, the program first came across a less accurate statement of the relationship between planetary distance and time of revolution—the same solution Kepler himself had published a decade before arriving at the more precise law! Genetic algorithms have even re-created lines from William Shakespeare in only a few dozen variation-selection cycles. For instance, Hamlet's "Methinks it is like a weasel" will appear in 10 to 50 generations. In contrast, the probability of the line being produced randomly— by a monkey typing madly away at a typewriter—is 28^{-27}, a prohibitively minuscule likelihood. The Darwinian process may be blind, but its selectionist feature renders it cumulative, making it far superior to pure chance.

Nonetheless, these acts of creative duplication are less important than the fact that these techniques have generated creative ideas of their own. Besides solving difficult problems in science, engineering, mathematics, and economics, Darwinian methods have even created original art and composed bebop jazz melodies. Although evolutionary programs are a relatively recent development, they hold great future promise for allowing machines to come close to matching the creativity of humans. Moreover, unlike discovery programs, these programs have very little intelligence built into them. They are merely endowed with a method of blindly generating variations and a criterion for selecting the best variations to add to the next evolutionary cycle. The discovery programs can probably know no more than their programmers, whereas genetic algorithms can acquire an expertise that exceeds that of their programmers.

Admittedly, unlike the discovery programs, genetic algorithms and their descendants were not specifically designed to simulate the creative process of the human mind. Their roots were directly in primary Darwinism, not in the secondary Darwinism represented by Campbell's blind-variation-and-selective-retention model. Even so, it seems that these programs inadvertently come very close to reflecting the actual processes reported by creative individuals. For example, earlier I quoted William James as observing how creative minds do not have "thoughts of concrete things patiently following one another in a beaten track of habitual suggestion." On the contrary, their intellects exhibit "the most abrupt cross-cuts and transitions from one idea to another" as well as "the most unheard of combination of elements, the subtlest associations of analogy." In short, the creative mind displays "a seething cauldron of ideas, where everything is fizzling and bobbling about in a state of bewildering activity, where partnerships can be joined or loosened in an instant." This graphic description comes remarkably close to what takes place during the sexual reproduction of binary strings that occurs in genetic algorithms. These strings break apart at random places and recombine with the fragments of other strings, generating thereby novel genetic instructions. By the same token, the creative mind may contain a chaotic soup consisting of strings of vague thoughts and images.

These ideational strings, too, may split up at unexpected places and recombine until a new, more adaptive configuration appears. A great part of this combinatory play is involuntary and unguided, and hence, to a large degree, blind.

The operation of these genetic algorithms can also be compared with the research done on the creative imagination. Particularly provocative are comparisons with Rothenberg's work on Janusian and homospatial processes. For instance, in the experiments on homospatial thinking, the production of creative drawings was enhanced by viewing two unrelated images superimposed. The resulting drawings tended to combine and integrate forms that emerged from the juxtaposition of the shapes. The outcome is artistic creations that look like visual analogs of the crossover occuring both in the binary strands of genetic algorithms and in the chromosomes of organic evolution.

Hence, despite the fact that genetic algorithms were designed to manifest Darwinian creativity rather than simulate human creativity, they may actually provide a crude model of the latter process. To the extent that the creative mind engages in the spontaneous splitting and recombining of chains of thought, we can say that the intellect is operating according to an analogous mechanism. Indeed, it may even be fruitful to apply some of the findings from these computer programs to help us better appreciate some of the finer details of the creative process. For example, the research on genetic algorithms has found that recombination plays a far more important role than mutation. That is, randomly flipping bits on strings contributes relatively little to reaching a solution in comparison to the crossover of two "mating" binary strings to produce two new "offspring" strings. The advantage of the recombinatorial procedure is especially important, moreover, when selection has had the opportunity to operate for several generations. Even so, sometimes a particular combination of bits that disappeared early in the evolution of the strands will need to reappear if the optimal solution is to emerge. Yet the extinct binary sequence may not easily appear through recombination of the surviving sequences. In this case, mutation provides a vehicle for reintroducing into the population the required combinations. It is conceivable that creativity in human beings functions in an analogous fashion. Most creative ideas may emerge from simple recombinations of material of previously established utility. Only when the creator is stumped on a truly difficult problem will it be necessary to depend on some ideational mutation that can propel the mind toward the solution. This "shot out of the blue" may require a totally serendipitous event.

Before advancing to a general assessment of Campbell's model of creativity, I wish to mention one recent development that has introduced a fascinating twist to Darwinian computation strategies. Genetic algorithms simulate the variation processes of primary Darwinism, but the simulation proceeds electronically rather than biochemically. That is, the program operates on binary computer codes rather than DNA strands. But now that we have the biochemical wherewithal to manipulate DNA, it would seem feasible to use DNA to generate the blind variations. The result would be a molecular computation technique that could be used to solve conceptual and mathematical problems. Indeed, because a test tube full of DNA can encode huge amounts of information and simultaneously process that information, molecular computation should originate rapid answers to the most difficult questions. This alternative Darwinian strategy was actually implemented in the mid-1990s by Leonard Adleman, a computer scientist at the University of Southern California. By substituting biochemistry (DNA) for electronics (silicon), this approach can quickly provide solutions to otherwise computationally intractable puzzles (e.g., the classic "traveling salesman problem"). This novel development in computer science represents another way that the distinction between primary and secondary Darwinism sometimes becomes blurred. Here the very molecular substance that provides the variational material for all organic evolution has been co-opted as the basis for creative problem solving by an equally blind variation-and-selection procedure.

Evaluations

Judging from the foregoing discussion, Campbell's blind-variation-and-selective-retention model seems to have considerable merit. The model appears consistent with what geniuses themselves tell us about the creative process, and it seems compatible with experimental research on insight, imagery, and intuition. Although this model is inconsistent with the underlying assumptions of discovery programs, these programs may have to acquire a Darwinian basis if they are ever to replicate creative behavior in the real world. More important, current research on genetic algorithms and genetic programming shows that computer systems based on Darwinian principles have the expected capacity for creativity. Of course, none of this can be taken as conclusive proof that Campbell's model is correct. At this point, it is probably safer to offer the more modest conclusion that at least the model has yet to be proven utterly implausible. Additional experiments and simulations are probably necessary before more can be claimed.

Nonetheless, I should end this evaluation of the Darwinian model by addressing two related issues. The first concerns a matter of secondary Darwinism: Do the blind variations that figure so prominently in organic evolution really have their counterpart in the emergence of creative ideas? Or is this just another one of those disanalogies that so often plague secondary theories? The second question involves a matter of primary Darwinism: Assuming that Campbell's model is correct, how would organic evolution produce a brain capable of creativity?

Variational Blindness

Ever since the advent of Darwin's theory of natural selection, the concept of "blindness" has provoked controversy. Many critics could not tolerate the notion that the spontaneous variation that fed the evolutionary process was unguided by some intelligence. This criticism was especially prominent among those who believed that an all-wise and all-powerful Creator had provided a guiding hand behind the cornucopia of life-forms that populate the planet. Yet even many notable scientists had difficulty accepting the idea that the sophisticated adaptations seen in the world could have been produced by a chance mechanism. This disbelief did not vanish with the advent of the "modern synthesis," despite the provision of specific processes— genetic recombination and mutation—that would support the production of blind variations. Even a century after the publication of the *Origin of Species*, a significant number of scientists argue that the variational procedure displays more insight. The most recent example is the research on whether certain bacteria exhibit "directed mutations," in which the resulting mutants are biased toward successful adaptations. Although the consensus view is that this phenomenon probably does not occur, a minority still maintains that organic evolution need not be as blind as stated by Darwinian theory.

It goes without saying that if primary Darwinism must contend with this issue, secondary Darwinism is even more vulnerable to the same objection. Few psychologists would deny that creativity involves some type of variation process. Even the discovery programs function by a generate-and-test procedure. The question of debate, rather, is about the degree of blindness underlying the production of the ideational variations. The very concept of blindness seems to run counter to the fundamental nature of the human being as a goal-directed organism. And as humans go, the lives of creative geniuses overflow with plans, purposes, and aspirations. They are individuals obsessed with a mission, with a destiny, devoting their whole careers to the creation of marvelous works in their chosen domains. Moreover, the commonplace conception of genius seems to be antithetical to the notion of someone who works by trial and error. Genius holds the connotation of intelligence, and haphazard searches seem the very opposite of intelligent behavior. Indeed, someone who insisted on generating utterly random thoughts might even be thought to suffer from a maladaptive psychopathology.

Yet objections such as these only exhibit a misunderstanding of the Darwinian theory of creativity. To see how, let us begin with the question of the creator's reason, and then turn to the matter of the creator's will.

Creative rationality. It cannot be overly stressed that logic and reason must play a critical part in any Darwinian model. Often the criteria by which ideational variations are selected are logical and rational, especially in the sciences. Even in the arts, logic and reason may impose constraints on what variants are chosen for further development. A plot in a novel, a character in a play, a figure in a painting, or an architectural plan are often governed by rational rules about what is plausible or workable. Thus, the selection portion of the variation-selection process is usually far from blind. The real question, then, is the blindness of the variational procedure.

It would seem that a Darwinian model requires that ideational variations would be strictly blind in the sense of being completely random or unpredictable. Yet such an extreme claim would not even apply to organic evolution. Of the various sources of genetic variability in the external world, only mutation can be considered totally blind in the strictest sense. Indeed, it is for this very reason that mutations are far more likely to be deleterious than adaptive. Genetic recombination, on the other hand, is far less blind. After all, the genes that enter into the combinatory process are mostly those that have proven their adaptive utility in previous generations. The only major exception to this rule is recessive genes that carry certain maladaptive traits, and even these will be common in the gene pool only when they confer some advantage under certain circumstances (e.g., sickle-cell anemia in malaria-plagued environments). In addition, the genes do not always undergo completely independent assortment in a classic Mendelian fashion, for those contained on the same chromosome will be subject to the phenomenon of linkage. The closer the two genes are on a given chromosome, the higher the probability that they will be inherited together. Moreover, because there may exist selection pressure in favor of maintaining certain combinations of genes intact, some of these constraints on pure random recombination may reflect the acquired wisdom of selection having operated in previous generations. In population genetics, this constraining outcome is known as "linkage disequilibrium."

Thus, blindness should not be viewed in all-or-nothing terms; but rather as a characteristic that admits degrees ranging from total randomness (mutation) to complete a priori constraint (linkage), with many gradations between (the probability of crossover). The same continuity applies to the term *chance,* which is often taken as being equivalent to blindness in many Darwinian models. There exist degrees of "chanciness." If you stand right in front of a dart board, you can push the darts into the bull's-eye with a 100% chance of success. If you step far enough back that you must actually throw the darts, the probability may shrink to 98%, only an occasional slip leading a projectile astray. But each successive step leads to a reduced odds of a hit. There will be a distance at which the probability will be only 50%, another at which it will reduce to 10%, and so on, approaching the point where a bull's-eye would be a matter of pure luck, and yet another point where you would say that a hit is absolutely impossible, or 0% with certainty (namely, the target lies outside your maximum throwing range). The blindness of creative variations has the same underlying continuity. This continuity will become more evident when I scrutinize three radically different theories of creativity—the behavioral, the psychoanalytic, and the cognitive.

1. Let us return to Epstein's generativity theory. When a hungry pigeon first enters the experimental chamber, it scans the environment, seeking the stimuli that inform it about the operants most likely to activate the release of a food pellet. If it sees a box beneath a toy banana, it goes to the box, climbs it, pecks at the banana, and gets the reward; if it sees a box over to the side and a target somewhere on the floor, it pushes the box toward the target to receive the expected reinforcement. The odds of a bull's-eye in either case is 100%. However, if we alter the conditions ever so slightly—start modifying the shape, color, locations, or other features of the box, the target, the banana, or other discriminative stimuli—the pigeon will experience more difficulties. Not only will the likelihood of the appropriate operant be a function of some generalization gradient for the discriminative stimuli, but in addition alternative operants learned under comparable circumstances will begin to have higher probabilities of activation. Indeed, if the operant with the highest probability does not produce the anticipated effect, the pigeon has no other choice but to start descending down a hierarchy of diverse operants. Moreover, if none of these pass the test, the pigeon must begin trying out operants in various combinations in a more or less haphazard fashion. Eventually, one combination does the trick—pushing the box under the banana as if the latter were the floor target—and the pigeon experiences a moment of creative insight. The important point here is that no abrupt switch takes place from the rational application of old behaviors to the blind search for some new behaviors. Rather, there occurs a roughly continuous descent into ever more blind behavioral variations.

2. Freud introduced the distinction between primary and secondary thought processes. Secondary process is that of the conscious mind. It operates according to the "reality principle," and it is therefore rational, pragmatic, logical. Consequently, according to psychoanalytic theory, the creative imagination must have its locus elsewhere in the mind. That locus, as noted earlier, is in the primary process, which is far more primitive, even infantile. Ruled by fantasy, and by unconscious impulses (the "pleasure principle"), this part of the mind lacks the social and intellectual constraints of secondary process. Being more irrational, the associative material produced

is much more blind—wild, unpredictable, juxtapositional, incongruous.

Therefore, it is not surprising that psychoanalytic theory has often discussed creativity in terms of "regression in service of the ego." The creative individual must leave secondary-process thought to descend into primary-process thought in order to arrive at truly original ideational variants. Nonetheless, we must take care not to see this regressive process as a discrete all-or-none affair. There are degrees of regression into primary process, a point adequately demonstrated by Colin Martindale in a long series of experimental and content-analytical investigations (see chapter 5). Dreams provide a good example of the range. Sometimes we have dreams so realistic that when we wake up we find it hard to believe that the events did not really happen. Other times our dreams consist of such bizarre ideas, such strange juxtapositions of people and circumstances, that they seem to make no sense whatsoever (to the secondary-process mind).

The fact that regression exhibits degrees is important. To a great extent, successful creativity entails finding the right level of primary-process imagery. Too much, and the outcome is highly original but useless variants, such as the crazy thoughts of psychotics or people under the influence of hallucinogenic drugs. Too little, and the result is adaptive, but lacking in originality, as in everyday thinking. Somewhere in the middle is the happy medium in which the product of originality and adaptiveness is maximized, thereby optimizing the magnitude of creativity. Thus, the regressive process must descend to the proper level of associative blindness.

Epstein has pointed out an interesting connection between psychoanalytic regression and the principle of resurgence in his generativity theory. The resurgence of older, once-adaptive operants will essentially represent a process of behavioral regression. As Epstein put it, "Freud's concept of regression could be considered a special case of resurgence in which the behavior that recurs is infantile." "If you are turning a doorknob that has always turned easily, for example, and it fails to turn, any and perhaps all of the behaviors that have ever gotten you through doors are likely to appear: You may turn harder, pull up on the knob, kick the door, shout for help, and so on." Depending on how desperate you are, this regression may descend yet more. You might begin to swear, utter "open sesame," whimper, fantasize about being rescued, throw a tantrum, or engage in some other more childish activity. I think this conceptual link is significant, for according to the behavioral interpretation, the creator descends to a deeper level of primary process only after the more shallow levels of primary process have failed to solve the problem. In other words, so long as a solution is not found, the variants must become ever more blind with time. At the ultimate end point are the cognitions of psychotics, whose consistent failure to resolve life's problems has backed them into a corner of absurd beliefs and behaviors.

3. The research on human problem solving, such as that represented by Herbert Simon and his associates, also supports the conclusion that blindness has degrees rather than yes-no attributes. If asked to multiply 216 by 37 (without a calculator), you apply the arithmetic method learned in elementary school to get the answer. The solution is thus acquired by a straightforward algorithm that requires the intrusion of no blind guesswork. More difficult problems, in contrast, may require a heuristic search through an array of possible solutions. For instance, one of the difficulties faced by students learning integral calculus is that the antiderivative of a function cannot always be found by an algorithmic solution. There exist a great diversity of integration tools, not all of which will succeed. So the student must acquire some "rules of thumb" that will restrict the range of possibilities to that smaller subset that have the best chance at helping to arrive at a solution. These rules provide hints about which equations are best integrated by substitution, which by parts, and so forth. Even then, a certain amount of trial and error may be necessary before the function is successfully integrated. Matters get ever more complicated when the student begins to study differential equations. Not only is the range of integration techniques vastly enlarged, but in addition the student learns that some differential equations may not even feature definite solutions. The heuristics become far richer, trial and error more prominent, and the blindness of the search far more conspicuous. Indeed, in the mathematical sciences a researcher will often devote years of effort in trying to solve a single differential equation, and frequently never succeed in doing so. Newton, for example, was never able to solve the differential equations necessary to describe the orbit of the moon around the earth (i.e., the "three-body problem")—despite his being one of the greatest mathematical geniuses of all time.

The above illustration comes from mathematics, where the role of rationality would seem paramount. Needless to say, searching for solutions becomes ever more blind when dealing with forms of creativity that lack precise criteria for evaluating successful solutions. Contrary to Poe's claims, writing a poem cannot proceed with the logic of a mathematical proof. The poet must acknowledge that the factors contributing to a poem's aesthetic success are far too complex, vague, and transient to permit composition to be reduced to heuristic principles, even less algorithms. The same holds for other forms of creativity, such as music and art. Even the writing of a successful scientific journal article demands the satisfaction of a myriad independent and constantly varying requirements. Moreover, the more original, daring, revolutionary, or breakthrough the creative endeavor, the less guidance can be expected from the application of logical principles. The number of potential heuristics increases dramatically, and new rules of thumb may have to be tried and tested. Even the creator's conception of the problem must undergo a series of unanticipated transformations before settling on the representation that supports a viable solution. In brief, as the amount of creativity required increases, the blindness of the search procedures will proportionally increase.

Note that this continuity can also be cast in the language of Epstein's generativity theory. When no algorithm exists that will immediately solve a given problem, the creator must fall back on one or more heuristic principles that seem to have worked well for similar problems in the past. If these fail, the criteria must be relaxed to allow the resurgence of heuristics ever more remotely related to the intransigent problem. Furthermore, eventually the individual will have to resort to the unguided recombination of the diverse techniques and approaches acquired over a considerable range of situations. This progression, again, entails a descent into an increasingly Darwinian form of creativity. Because the blindness can vary continuously as a function of problem difficulty, we should not really speak of creativity as Darwinian or not Darwinian. Instead, it is more accurate to speak in terms of the relative importance of Darwinian processes in the origination of a creative solution to a specific problem.

This notion that Darwinian blindness represents a continuous dimension rather than a discrete quality is absolutely essential to our understanding of creative genius. As will become apparent in later chapters, different creative domains, as well as distinct forms of creativity within a given domain, contrast greatly in the extent to which cognitive variations must be blind. Sometimes blindness plays a major role, and other times its involvement is minimal. Nevertheless, according to a Darwinian perspective, no supreme genius can operate without at least some variational blindness during critical points in his or her career.

Creative volition. Long before the advent of Darwin's *Origin of Species*, his grandfather Erasmus Darwin had offered a theory of evolution in which purpose played a major role. Each life-form on this planet is driven by a "lust, hunger, and a desire for security," he argued. As a consequence, by some mysterious process each creature would willfully modify its organs and behaviors to enhance its adaptation to the ever-changing surroundings. A bit later, but still a half century before *Origin of Species*, Jean-Baptiste Lamarck elaborated a somewhat similar theory, one that has earned its own eponym. Strictly speaking, Lamarckism makes two rather restricted claims. First, the organs that make up any individual organism can undergo changes in size, shape, or other features according to the amount of use or disuse received during that individual's life. Second, according to the doctrine of acquired characters, the adaptations thus obtained during the life of the parents would be passed down to the offspring. However, through some misunderstanding, Lamarckism is often incorrectly taken to encompass a purposive component as well. According to this misconception, the giraffe got a long neck because it wished for just such an improvement to reach the leaves growing higher in the trees.

On the basis of this misunderstanding, the term *Lamarckian* is sometimes applied to creativity as well. Creative people are actively engaged in creating new ideas, and creativity is a purposive activity that assigns meaning to their lives. For example, it was certainly Charles Darwin's lifetime goal to reach a deeper understanding of the biological world. He did not flutter randomly from topic to topic; instead his entire career following the *Beagle* voyage exhibited a developmental progression. Darwin's various projects are interwoven as part of his grand quest. And this ever-evolving tapestry is embroidered throughout with certain persistent metaphors that Darwin used to make sense of the natural world (e.g., the evolution of species as a branching tree). In short, the evolution of ideas in Darwin's brain exudes purpose in a manner seemingly "Lamarckian" (in the loose sense) rather than Darwinian (in the secondary sense). However, such an assertion, besides misapplying Lamarck's name, fails to comprehend the potent but circumscribed function of volition in a Darwinian theory.

On the one hand, it is doubtful that anyone can be outstandingly creative without really wanting to be so. Volition permeates many aspects of the phenomenon. For instance, seldom does a person crack a difficult problem without first spending considerable time preparing the groundwork. Not only must the individual be willing to devote years of effort in the acquisition of the necessary knowledge and skills, but also the creator must have struggled with the particular problem, or at least with a closely related riddle. Even serendipitous discoveries are not bestowed on creators indiscriminately. On the contrary, the foundation usually must first be laid by a person who has made a considerable intellectual and emotional commitment to a relevant domain. In the often-quoted words of Pasteur, "chance favours only the prepared mind."

More important, perhaps, is the fact that creative individuals are obsessed with certain problems and will not rest until those problems find solutions. Even when they give up on a problem, creators essentially enter an incubation period in which the question always lurks in the back of the mind. Creators thus demonstrate a certain, large-scale, form of the "Zeigarnik effect," which is what happens when experimental subjects who are not allowed to finish some tasks are more likely to recall those than other tasks they successfully completed. Because creators' lives are replete with such incomplete tasks, they are incessantly on the lookout for cues about how those tasks might be completed. Moreover, there will intrude many false alarms and blind alleys. Accordingly, creators cannot give up easily and may spend years before coming across a successful resolution. Indeed, Howard

Gardner has suggested that a creator's major breakthroughs are usually separated by a full decade. Einstein had contemplated a paradox in physics for nearly ten years before he finally arrived at the solution in the form of his special theory of relativity; the more complete solution, the general theory of relativity, had to wait another decade to emerge. In the restrictive sense of maintaining the necessary long-term commitment, then, Einstein can be said to have willed his theory into existence. He persisted when most others would have quit.

Finally, we must not forget another necessity of creative genius. It is not sufficient to resolve an obsession. The answer must undergo testing, elaboration, development. Revision and amendment may be required, and disappointing setbacks overcome. The creator may have to run a gauntlet of criticism and collegial advice. All this hard work that connects the initial creative insight to a finished creative product must be executed. There is no room for the weak of will or faint of heart in this arduous business. So, again, volition plays a crucial role even in a Darwinian theory of creativity.

On the other hand, a Darwinian theory makes a distinction between willfully seeking solutions to problems and willing the appearance of those sought-for solutions. It is one matter to ask a question, quite another to find an answer. And it is the latter process that is far more likely to be Darwinian in nature. Recall how Helmholtz described his own trial-and-error problem-solving process. The economist and logician William S. Jevons generalized Helmholtz's realistic modesty to all scientists when he wrote, in his book *The Principles of Science*, that

> it would be an error to suppose that the great discoverer seizes at once upon the truth, or has any unerring method of divining it. In all probability the errors of the great mind exceed in number those of the less vigorous one. Fertility of imagination and abundance of guesses at truth are among the first requisites of discovery; but the erroneous guesses must be many times as numerous as those that prove well founded. The weakest analogies, the most whimsical notions, the most apparently absurd theories, may pass through the teeming brain, and no record remain of more than the hundredth part. . . . The truest theories involve suppositions which are inconceivable, and no limit can really be placed to the freedom of hypotheses.

If the creator could so easily will into existence novel and workable solutions to troublesome problems, we would be hard-pressed to explain the reports of historic creators. Very often they describe the sudden appearance of a solution without the slightest participation of the will. I have already mentioned Archimedes' moment of insight in the bathtub. In a similar class is Hadamard's affirmation that "one phenomenon is certain and I can vouch for its absolute certainty: the sudden and immediate appearance of a solution at the very moment of sudden awakening." In the same category, finally, I may assign this episode recorded by Poincaré: "Just at this time I left Caen, where I was then living, to go on a geologic excursion under the auspices of the school of mines. The changes of travel made me forget my mathematical work. Having reached Coutances, we entered an omnibus to go some place or other. At the moment when I put my foot on the step the idea came to me, without anything in my former thoughts seeming to have paved the way for it, that the transformations I had used to define the Fuchsian functions were identical with those of non-Euclidean geometry." So typical are reports like these that Margaret Boden concluded, "*The bath, the bed and the bus*: this trio summarizes what creative people have told us about how they came by their ideas." Indeed, so involuntary are these events that creators sometimes insist illuminations took place largely in opposition to volitional control. The poet William Blake, for example, once noted that "I have written this poem from immediate dictation, twelve or sometimes twenty or thirty lines at a time without premeditation, and even against my will." And the philosopher Friedrich Nietzsche described the moment of volition-free inspiration in these terms: "One can hardly reject completely the idea that one is the mere incarnation, or mouthpiece, or medium of some almighty power. The notion of revelation describes the condition quite simply; by which I mean that something profoundly convulsive and disturbing suddenly becomes visible and audible with indescribable definiteness and exactness. One hears—one does not seek . . . a thought flashes out like lightning, inevitably without hesitation—I have never had any choice about it. . . . Everything occurs quite without volition, as if in an eruption of freedom, independence, power and divinity." The highly romantic, overwrought nature of this expression should not cause us to dismiss the veracity of the underlying proposition. Acts of creativity are not necessarily acts of will. To the degree that volition is absent, the creative process must be viewed as a form of secondary Darwinism, not pseudo-Lamarckism.

Before proceeding to the question of primary Darwinism, I would like to touch on a matter raised by some of the preceding introspective reports. According to the testimony of creative geniuses, novel insights sometimes arise through an illumination that is as sudden and complete as it is involuntary. The moment of inspiration often seems to embody a "quantum leap" or "breakthrough" that departs significantly from all that has gone before. This unexpected discontinuity would seem to run counter to the historical continuity often thought to be characteristic of organic evolution. Species were supposed to evolve by almost imperceptible steps, not massive jumps. In fact, these revelations appear more comparable to the "punctuated-equilibrium" theory that Eldredge and Gould first advanced in 1972 as a direct challenge to Darwinian gradualism. According to this alternative, the most frequent condition of most species is stasis, in which generation follows generation without noticeable change. Then, in a manner not unlike the sudden illumination of the creative genius, the species rapidly transforms into one or more new species. After speciation, stasis takes over again, as the new species attain new equilibria with their environments. To understand better how punctuated equilibrium connects with a Darwinian theory of creativity, I should note two facts.

First, Darwin himself was not of the mind that continuity necessarily implied constancy of evolutionary change. Nor did Darwin maintain that change was an inevitable feature. In particular, he observed: "Many species once formed never undergo any further change . . . , and the periods during which species have undergone modification, though long as measured in years, have probably been short in comparison with the periods during which they retained the same form." Thus, the pace of evolution may vary from stagnation to almost explosive change. Darwin required only that even the most rapid changes would take many generations to transpire. Especially complex adaptations could not appear overnight; rather there needed to be time for the variation-selection process to operate.

Second, evolutionary biologists recognize that phyletic gradualism and punctuated equilibria may represent end points of a continuum. Some evolutionary lineages may show one extreme, other lineages the other, but most are probably distributed somewhere between. In addition, different traits within the same lineage may exhibit distinct patterns. For example, the size of an organ might change more or less gradually, while the structure of another organ might follow the course of punctuated equilibria. The reasons for these contrasts are varied. Catastrophic environmental or ecological transitions—such as sudden changes in sea level or climate—can certainly affect abrupt alterations in corresponding adaptations. But there are also occasions when a species may chance upon a revolutionary adaptation that enables the quick exploitation of an ecological niche previously unoccupied.

I believe that this same dimension underlies what we know of the creative process. At one extreme are the sudden illuminations in which a grand idea appears only after a long incubation period of subconscious exploration—the cognitive analog of evolutionary stasis. At the other extreme are ideas that develop very gradually from crude beginnings, eventually reaching the status of a work of genius. Judging from notebooks kept by great creators, including Darwin, the creative career usually consists of a chaotic mix of sudden inspirations and step-by-step refinements of initial, uncultivated ideas. The illuminations are more dramatic, and thus most often remembered (at least if they have later proven correct). But a creative career cannot subsist on revelations alone. On the contrary, the bulk of the ideas on which creators stake their fame is probably the consequence of a more gradual ideational evolution.

The very capriciousness of this cognitive mixture of the quick and the slow serves only to accentuate the Darwinian claim: The creative genius has no real volitional control over the emergence of ideas.

Evolutionary Origins

Thus far, the focus has been on secondary Darwinism. Does the creative process in human beings really operate in a fashion analogous to what supposedly happens in organic evolution? But the next issue takes us back to primary Darwinism. How can a Darwinian theory of organic evolution account for the emergence of the creativity in the first place?

The most obvious answer is to claim that creative behavior enhances a creature's adaptive fitness. In other words, the evolution of creative behavior may have been favored by natural selection. This possibility is readily apparent in Epstein's research on generativity theory. The pigeons in his experiments seem to be operating according to highly adaptive principles. If what to do in a given situation is self-evident, by all means do it. If not, try out all behaviors that have worked under comparable circumstances. If none of those do the trick, then generate various combinations of behaviors that have solved similar problems, until a behavioral combination is found that receives reinforcement. Thus, trial and error is a last resort, but it is a resource that must be available if the pigeon is to attain full mastery of its environmental niche.

Naturally, trial and error is an inefficient process. Much time and energy can be expended to little or no avail. For example, the kittens in Edward Thorndike's classic puzzle box thrashed about chaotically until they chanced upon the latch that allowed escape. Such behaviors appear less than intelligent. However, for organisms with a highly sophisticated cognitive apparatus, this Darwinian procedure can be rendered far more efficient. Higher intellects possess internal representations (or models) of their external world. These representations are abstract, but they contain the core features of the real world and thus can be used to test potential solutions with a freedom and speed often impossible in the physical environment. Moreover, the more complex minds are able to insert themselves as actors in their mental worlds, as when intelligent organisms display the capacity for planning behaviors in advance and then execute those behaviors precisely according to plan. Once Köhler's apes had figured out how to get the out-of-reach banana, they could often do so smoothly and quickly, just as if they had performed that trick before. But, of course, the chimps *had* already carried out the appropriate behaviors—in their heads. What appears to be behavioral foresight is actually cognitive hindsight.

Human beings take the chimpanzees' cognitive capacity even further. Besides being able to engage in behavioral variations using internal representations of the self, others, and the world, humans can transform the problem into media and modalities unavailable to even the most intelligent of the beasts. The visual givens of the problem might be translated into verbal representations, for example. Those with sufficient training, moreover, may transform the problem into mathematical or logical representations. The trial-and-error procedures can then be applied to these translations, and often with superior success. In fact, with the advent of modern computers, programs can be written that will perform the necessary manipulations automatically, just as we saw in the case of genetic algorithms and programming. Darwinian creativity then for the first time can occur outside an organic system, whether cell nucleus or complex intellect.

Thus, human creativity seems a highly adaptive behavior that should be favored by natural selection. Given that *Homo sapiens* appears to be the most successful single species on this planet, maybe this argument is too obvious. Humans have emerged as monarchs of the ecological mountain because they have exhibited a creativity unrivaled by even the most impressive intellectual competitors, such as chimpanzees and dolphins. This creativity has enabled our species to fill niches far more diverse than those occupied by any other organism.

The foregoing adaptationist account is certainly plausible. Yet its very plausibility may in fact undermine its credibility. The adaptiveness of creative behavior seems so transparently true that this account may represent nothing more than another of those "just so" stories that plague so many Darwinian explanations. Indeed, this explanation may be so glib as to raise more questions than it answers. Consider the following three issues:

1. Although the adaptive value of creative behavior is apparent when it comes to technological domains—activities having to do with obtaining food, obtaining shelter, and self-protection—it is less apparent that creativity has evolutionary utility in fields that make no direct contribution to reproductive fitness. Michelangelo may have fed, clothed, and sheltered himself by painting frescoes in chapels and carving chunks of marble, but he also died childless. The average sixteenth-century Tuscan farmer, not showing an ounce of originality but instead relying on the tried-and-true agricultural techniques passed down for generations, would certainly have claimed more fitness than this exalted genius. In fact, Michelangelo's creative genius may have actually detracted from his reproductive fitness. A similar conclusion may be drawn with respect to Newton, Descartes, Beethoven, and innumerable other creators who apparently left no biologi-

cal progeny. Indeed, as we will see in chapter 3, creative individuals often feature many characteristics that would seem to militate against attaining fitness in the sense of primary Darwinian selection.

2. A related issue is the existence of pronounced individual differences in the amount of creativity displayed. Creativity seems to be a trait most people wish they had more of. Yet only a relatively small percentage of the population appears to display creative behavior with any conspicuous regularity. And creativity of the highest order is more rare still. Moreover, as will be seen in chapter 5, the distribution of creativity may differ from that of other characteristics presumably selected for their adaptive value. Physical traits like height as well as mental traits like intelligence tend to be normally distributed. That is, the distributions are described by a symmetric, "bell-shaped" curve. The distribution of creative behavior, in contrast, exhibits an extremely asymmetrical curve, with a small proportion of the population exhibiting a disproportionate amount of the creativity. It is not clear how this elitist distribution might be reconciled with the assumption that creativity has adaptive value.

3. Besides these individual differences within a particular society at a specific point in time, creativity can vary appreciably from culture to culture and period to period. This fundamental fact was pointed out at the beginning of chapter 1 when I spoke of golden ages and dark ages. Does this mean that creative behavior has more adaptive value in some societies and eras in comparison with others? If so, perhaps creativity is indeed an operant that can be reinforced under some circumstances and extinguished under others. Alternatively, of course, someone might adopt Galton's position that such contrasts across space and time are the inevitable consequence of contrasts in the innate capacity of various biological populations to produce genius. Then the more "advanced races" in some supposed evolutionary progression would boast the superior creative capacity—a potential interpretation that I shall consider in chapter 6.

In light of the above enigmas, it is not immediately clear whether the primary Darwinian process of biological evolution can account for the appearance of the secondary Darwinian process of creative thought. Compare this problem with attempts to explain the origins of, say, the secondary mechanism of the immune system. In the latter case, the adaptive value is quite evident, the individual differences much less pronounced, and the variation across cultures and periods probably minimal. All of this is guaranteed, courtesy of the straightforward fact that organisms incapable of defending themselves against pathogens are rather easily (and often dramatically) removed from the gene pool. Natural selection in favor of a Darwinian immune system can seem cruel, but ultimately the results are kind.

There are a number of potential resolutions of this enigma. For example, creative genius might be the product of some form of group selection something along the lines of altruistic behavior. Alternatively, creativity might result by some coevolutionary process involving the complex interaction of natural and cultural selection. Some of these possibilities will be discussed in later chapters. But for now let it suffice to say that it is not an easy task to explain how the primary Darwinian process could give rise to the appearance of creative genius.

Although the evolutionary origins of creative genius present such a puzzle, that mystery should not lead us to reject the idea that creative thought is fundamentally Darwinian. In fact, creativity probably constitutes the most successful of all Darwinian processes, whether primary or secondary. That is, if the success of a Darwinian mechanism is judged by the diversity of creative forms it generates, the creative mind just may come out on top. For instance, one scholar inferred from patent statistics that human inventions are as diverse as all the species that currently inhabit the earth. Yet if you add to this list of technological accomplishments all scientific journal articles, all musical compositions, all artistic masterworks, and all literary creations, it may be argued that the creative mind represents the single most potent Darwinian force on this planet, if not the universe. In future generations, for good or ill, its supremacy may emerge unchallenged, as the products of human genius continue to expand their presence over every inch of this globe, and sometimes reach to the farthest corners of the solar system.

3

~

VARIATION

Is Genius Brilliant — or Mad?

~

An essential component of all Darwinian theories is variation. Neither primary nor secondary theories can function without assuming that the units of selection display some degree of inheritable or transferable variation. The variants are what feed the selection process, whether natural or sexual, immunological or sociocultural. In the absence of such variability, Darwinian evolution and development would screech to a halt. It should not surprise us, therefore, that the behavioral scientists most influenced by Charles Darwin's ideas have displayed a fascination with how human beings can differ in so many of their attributes. Francis Galton counts among the earliest and most prominent examples. Profoundly inspired by reading *Origin of Species*, Galton became convinced that individual differences are both substantial and consequential. For example, Galton's 1869 *Hereditary Genius* argues emphatically that individuals vary immensely in what he styled "natural ability," a character that includes "those qualities of intellect and disposition, which urge and qualify a man to perform acts that lead reputation. I do not mean capacity without zeal, nor zeal without capacity, nor even a combination of both of them, without an adequate power of doing a great deal of very laborious work. But I mean a nature which, when left to itself, will, urged by an inherent stimulus, climb the path that leads to eminence, and has strength to reach the summit—one which, if hindered or thwarted, will fret and strive until the hindrance is overcome." Galton added that "it is almost a contradiction in terms, to doubt that such men will generally become eminent," for "the men who achieve eminence, and those who are naturally capable, are, to a large extent, identical." On the other hand, individuals who lack natural ability will be incapable of rising above the vast crowd of nonentities.

This hypothesized association between individual differences in natural ability and a person's eventual societal distinction is central to the fundamental question of this book—what are the origins of genius? As discussed in chapter 1, Galton defined genius in terms of reputation. Geniuses are those who have earned a name in the annals of human civilization. Moreover, in the case of creative genius, we have already claimed that this broad influence can be best gauged in terms of the creation of concrete products. Just as adaptive fitness in organic evolution is assessed by reproductive success, fitness in sociocultural evolution can be judged by productive fertility. In support for this Darwinian linkage, I should make two empirical observations.

First, creative personalities exhibit tremendous variety in the number of products they offer the world. At one extreme are those "one-idea" creators who have gone down in history for a single contribution. Gregor Mendel provides perhaps the most conspicuous illustration, for his entire posthumous reputation is founded on his experiments on trait inheritance in garden peas. At the other extreme are those "multiple-idea" creators whose brains seem to overflow with brilliant contributions. Charles Darwin himself provides an exquisite illustration. Despite sometimes severe health problems, Darwin was able to generate 119 publications on a tremendous diversity of topics in geology, zoology, botany, ecology, and psychology. Even when Darwin's theory of evolution suffered some neglect before its rebirth under the auspices of the "modern synthesis," he was still widely recognized as one of the most brilliant scientists of his era. Notwithstanding the protests of the religious establishment, Darwin was buried in Westminster Abbey, not far from Newton, Faraday, and Lyell.

Second, individual differences in total lifetime output are indeed associated with the degree of eminence achieved. In fact, research has consistently shown that the most powerful single predictor of reputation among both contemporaries and future generations is the person's sum total of contributions. Furthermore, almost all other variables that may correlate with the difference in fame between individuals do so only because they affect the output of creative products. To be sure, the relationship between productivity and eminence is by no means perfect. For example, John Edward Gray, an English naturalist and approximate contemporary of Darwin, could boast 883 publications. This figure is almost eight times what Darwin produced, and more than a hundred times more prolific than Mendel's measly seven publications! Yet Gray's reputation matches neither Darwin's nor Mendel's. Later I will discuss the nature of these imperfections in the productivity-eminence association. The main point here is that exceptions such as these do not suffice to overthrow the fundamental conclusion: Total lifetime productivity provides the best behavioral indicator of creative genius.

Given this productivity-eminence criterion for genius, the obvious question is whether creative productivity is linked to other individual-difference variables. After all, human beings may vary in a wide range of cognitive, motivational, and personality dimensions. Galton's definition of natural ability includes three distinct dimensions—intellect, motivation, and persistence. Psychologists who investigate human variation in intellectual and dispositional variables could certainly list a host of additional possibilities. Moreover, there already exists a huge literature on the individual-difference variables that correlate most highly and most consistently with creative behavior. Although the findings are quite rich, the psychometric instruments diverse, and the theoretical underpinnings quite varied, I argue that a consistent pattern emerges. Specifically, the pattern underlying all research findings is what would be expected from a Darwinian concept of creative genius. In other words, creative individuals may be said to have a "Darwinian personality." By this I mean that creators tend to have the attributes necessary to generate the numerous and diverse ideational variants required by Campbell's Darwinian model of the creative process. Some character traits may enhance this capacity for generating variations, whereas other traits may inhibit this capacity. The Darwinian personality features more of the former, fewer of the latter, yielding a distinctive trait profile.

Yet it is critical to recognize that different domains of creativity require varying amounts of variation-generation capacity. In some endeavors, ideational variations are highly constrained, whereas in others the variations must be free. For example, scientific creativity, on the average, operates under greater constraint than does artistic creativity. The concepts and techniques that the scientist employs in combinatorial play are rather abstract, specialized, and divorced from everyday experience. Accordingly, the variation process will be rather compartmentalized for the scientific genius. The artist, in contrast, must allow the imagination more freedom, encompassing the ideas and feelings of everyday life and using a vocabulary of expression more intelligible to a wider audience. Thus, in searching for the profile of the Darwinian personality, we should make allowance for the greater prominence of that profile among artists than among scientists.

However, even this complication must be rendered more complex. From a Darwinian perspective, not all forms of scientific creativity are the same, nor are all types of artistic creativity identical. Within the sciences, for example, Thomas Kuhn advanced the distinction between normal and revolutionary scientists. The former conduct research within the confines of a received body of theory and method—the old paradigm—whereas the latter offer novel theoretical and methodological approaches—the new paradigm. Because the revolutionaries allow greater scope to their search for an original paradigmatic system, one might infer that they are more likely to display Darwinian characteristics than the practitioners of normal science. Likewise, the art world does not represent a homogeneous set of creators either. Certainly, one of the most critical contrasts apparent in literature, music, and the visual arts is the distinction between classical and romantic styles, the former exhibiting more orderly restraint and logical structure, the latter more freedom and impulsive emotionality. Presumably the classicists would be less Darwinian in disposition than the romanticists, at least on the average. It may even be that the personality profiles of artistic creators overlaps those of scientific creators. A revolutionary scientist may have a similarly Darwinian disposition to a classicist artist to gain optimal success as a generator of original ideas. In any case, in this chapter we must take care not to assume that all creators display equivalent personal attributes.

These precautions in mind, I now review the research findings relevant to two broad domains of individual-difference variables, namely, intellect and character. In each domain I shall scrutinize a tremendous diversity of variables associated with creative genius that are consistent with the hypothesized Darwinian personality. To the extent that this demonstration is successful, this chapter should reinforce the argument advanced in the previous chapter that creative thought is at root Darwinian.

Intellect

As pointed out in chapter 1, although psychologists have often defined genius in terms of exceptional intelligence, the actual empirical relationship between the two phenomena is more ambiguous. No doubt a certain minimal level of intelligence seems necessary to demonstrate significant levels of creative behavior. That is, there exists some threshold level of IQ below which it is virtually impossible to claim any distinctive level of creativity. Although the exact location of this threshold is not known, there is no well-documented case of an eminent creator having a below-average intelligence. Even so, a high level of intelligence by itself cannot guarantee that a person will display an impressive degree of creativity. There are plenty of people with high-IQs, for example, who do not seem any more creative than individuals with average or even low IQ scores. On the other hand, the possession of an extremely elevated intelligence does not automatically mean that a person is doomed *not* to be creative. Indeed, an exceptionally bright individual can potentially boast more creative brainpower than can a less brilliant person. Consequently, as intelligence increases beyond whatever the threshold level may be, the height of eminence possible to achieve increases as well, producing what is sometimes called a "triangular distribution." At the lower levels of intelligence, the maximum level of achieved eminence is not very high, whereas at higher levels of intelligence the maximum is higher, albeit there will also exist a considerable number of creators who rise just barely above the nonentities in the annals of history.

From a Darwinian perspective, this complex linkage should not be all that surprising. Intelligence involves the capacity for acquiring and applying knowledge. To generate ideational variations, a person must have a sufficient repertoire of ideas that can be subjected to some combinatorial procedure. The more powerful the intellect, the larger the potential size of that repertoire. Even so, having an impressive collection of information and skills does not by itself suffice to support the production of ideational recombinations. The information must be organized in the appropriate fashion. Remember the earlier discussion of genetic recombination. If all genes are contained in a very small number of chromosomes, linkage is going to severely restrict the independent assortment of the genetic material. In contrast, if the genes are distributed over a large number of chromosomes, the genetic variations will much more readily proliferate.

Thus, it is the structure of intelligence rather than intelligence per se that should be of the greatest importance in a Darwinian model of the creative genius. Below this point is elaborated by looking at two illustrations, namely, remote association and divergent thinking.

Remote Association

In 1962, Sarnoff Mednick proposed an influential associative theory of the creative process. This theory was based on the premise that creativity requires the ability to make rather remote associations between separate ideas. Highly creative individuals were said to have a flat hierarchy of associations in comparison with the steep hierarchy of associations of those deemed less creative. Figure 3.1 provides a hypothetical illustration of the two opposing types of associative hierarchies. As this figure shows, a flat associative hierarchy means that for any given stimulus, the creative person has a great many associations available, all with roughly equal probabilities of retrieval. Because such an individual can generate many associative variations, the odds are increased that he or she will find that one association that will make the necessary remote connection.

A concrete example can be devised that uses actual word frequencies calculated from a large sample of people. Let us first imagine a person with steep associative hierarchies who is given the two words *foot* and *command.*

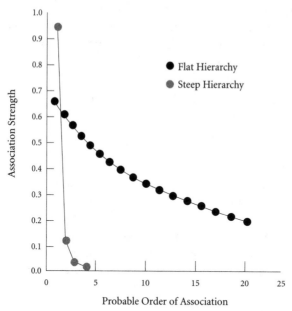

Figure 3.1 Steep and flat associative hierarchies according
to Mednick's theory of creativity.

The first word might quickly elicit such associates as "shoe, hand, toe, and leg," while the second word might rapidly evoke such associates as "order, army, obey, and officer." The individual would then fall silent, waiting for the next verbal stimulus. Because the two chains of association share not a single word in common, they fail to converge. Thus, "foot" and "command" remain unconnected in the person's mind. In contrast, an individual with a flat associative hierarchy might begin with the same initial associates, albeit with considerable alteration in order. More important, this second person might then append to "leg" the additional associates "soldier, ball, walks, amble, arm, sore, inch, rat, snow, person, physics, dog, mule, wall, shin, wash, hat, and end," plus trail "officer" with "performance, do, tell, shout, halt, voice, soldier, hat, polite, plea, book, salute, fulfill, obedience, war, and stern." In the second case, the two strings of thought actually contain not one but two associates in common, namely "soldier" and "hat." Hence, a person with a flat associative hierarchy will be far more likely to find an associative nexus between the two remote ideas of "foot" and "command." Actually, this illustration understates this ability, for it has relied on relatively commonplace associates according to standardized association tests. If we allow for the high probability that creative people will include rather idiosyncratic associations in their semantic networks, the odds of successful remote association becomes greater still.

Mednick's associative theory is quite provocative from the standpoint of Campbell's model of the creative process. Because flat associative hierarchies imply that the numerous alternative chains of associations feature comparable odds of activation, the search through the inventory of associative linkages will be largely unpredictable, perhaps even random. The flatter the associative hierarchy, the greater is the unpredictability or randomness of the exploration. Indeed, flat hierarchies would be quite susceptible to even the most subliminal of priming from external stimuli—effects that could haphazardly and transiently alter the comparative associative strengths of the available avenues of thought. Hence, highly flat hierarchies would tend to produce blind associative variations. Such mental explorations would be, in a word, Darwinian.

To give this associative theory some empirical grounding, Mednick devised the Remote Associates Test, or RAT. This instrument attempted to assess individual differences in the capacity to generate numerous associations. Each item on the RAT would list words to which the subject taking the test would have to pick another word that represented an associate of all the given words. To offer an easy example, "rat," "blue," and "cottage" would all share the associate "cheese." Because the common associate would not be a close associate of all the given stimulus words (e.g., "cat," "red," and "house"), the person would have to have access to a large number of associations to do well on the RAT. Although the test is not without its imperfections—most notably its use of a multiple-choice format that requires a single right answer—the RAT has done fairly well in validation studies. High scores on this instrument have been associated with higher levels of creativity. Just as important, scores on the RAT are associated with other attributes that should facilitate the variation process, such as the capacity for primary-process thought and synesthesia. The latter correlate is especially fascinating, because the ability for cross-modal associations would certainly yield associates far more remote than those confined to a single modality. One could hardly conceive an ideational junction more blind than one synesthetic!

Yet it remains fair to say that Mednick's associationist theory has more plausibility than the psychometric test used to provide an operational definition of the core concept of that theory. In fact, subsequent researchers have elaborated various aspects of Mednick's associationist theory to grant it greater explanatory power. For instance, many years ago I argued that this theory can help account for the importance of intuitive thought in creative individuals. As discussed in the preceding chapter, the autobiographical accounts of creators are replete with episodes of unconscious mental processing. According to this theory, there exists a correspondence between the strength of an association and cognitive and behavioral consequences. In particular, I proposed that the associative content of the mind may be stratified into four levels.

1. *Habitual associations* are those so automatic that they are elicited without conscious effort. For example, in most people the word *dog* will immediately evoke the response *cat*. These habitual responses are the first to emerge when a person generates associations to a particular stimulus.

2. *Cognitive associations* are those sufficiently well established to enter core awareness. Because such associates are conscious, they can be articulated and symbolized, and thus successfully communicated to others.

3. *Behavioral associations* are sufficiently strong to have repercussions for behavior but not strong enough to enter consciousness. As noted in chapter 2, there is ample evidence in studies of implicit knowledge that individuals can acquire expertise long before they become aware of what has been mastered. This information is therefore intuitive in nature.

4. *Attention associations* are sensory expectations too weak to support behavioral reactions, and yet strong enough to alert the mind to potential regularities in the environment. Associative material at this lowest level serves simply to orient attention toward sources of prospective knowledge.

This associative stratification was then integrated with Mednick's concept of associative hierarchies. At one end of an intellectual continuum are those individuals with steep hierarchies, that is, those whose minds hold largely a restricted supply of habitual and cognitive associations and an even more restricted reservoir of behavioral and attention associations. Because these people have so few total associations, they will have relatively few ways to connect between various concepts, and hence they will only rarely successfully link ideas by remote associates. At the other end of the continuum are those with flat hierarchies. Such individuals will have fewer habitual associations but will have more cognitive and, especially, behavioral and attention associations. Not only will their store of knowledge be more richly interconnected with various associative links, but in addition a large proportion of these associations will be intuitive in nature. As a consequence, they will probably more often report instances of intuitive hunches and imageless thought. There thus should be more instances of creative ideas emerging without the slightest hint about the chain of reasoning behind the discovery. In addition, minds with flat associative hierarchies are likely to more freely scan the environment for potential cues, and thereby they exhibit a greater propensity for making serendipitous discoveries. These individuals are likely to be more attentive to their surroundings.

It deserves emphasis that individuals with steep associative hierarchies can be every bit as intelligent as those with flat associative hierarchies. In the foregoing model, intelligence is determined by the total number of concepts forming associative networks. Therefore, two people can boast the same stock of conceptual material but differ immensely in the richness of associations linking their concepts. Individuals may be equal in intelligence while differing in how that intelligence is structured. In the above model, highly intelligent minds with steep associative hierarchies are styled "analytical geniuses," whereas those with flat hierarchies are styled "intuitive geniuses." Both may display genius-grade intellects, but only the intuitives are capable of thinking in a fully Darwinian fashion.

Figure 3.2 illustrates the theoretical contrast between the analytical and intuitive minds. Here the letters A through U represent concepts while the lines represent the associative linkages between those concepts. Both intellects hold the same number of concepts, but they differ greatly in the number of associations and in the strength of those associations. This contrast means that the intuitive genius will have more possible associative pathways connecting any two given concepts, with many of these pathways operating at unconscious levels of information processing. Given the large number of available routes and the relative associative weakness of any single path, the search for a connection between any two ideas will be more likely to be unpredictable, even random. In terms of Campbell's Darwinian model, ideational variations will be necessarily more blind. Note, too, that for the analytical genius there will exist a number of concepts that cannot be linked by any associative pathway whatsoever, no matter how long or tenuous. Individuals with this mental makeup may thus overlook ideational combinations that will be readily available to those with a richer associative network.

Naturally, analytical and intuitive geniuses are not types. Instead, they represent opposite ends of a continuum connecting those with the steepest associative hierarchies to those with the flattest hierarchies. Hence, certain kinds of creators will tend to fall at distinctive locations on this cognitive line. Artistic creators will be more prone to be intuitive, whereas scientific creators will tend to reside closer to the analytical end of the spectrum. Again, variable placement is likely to appear within each field. In particular, revolutionary scientists will be more intuitive than normal scientists, romantic artists more intuitive than the classical artists. Nonetheless, even the normal scientists should tend to be more intuitive than their noncreative colleagues.

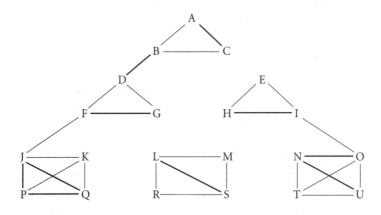

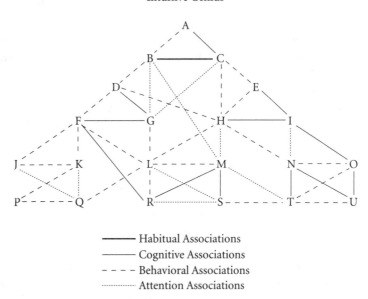

Figure 3.2 Hypothesized associative networks for analytical and intuitive geniuses according to the Simonton model.

Fortunately, there does exist empirical support for various predictions generated by this extension of the Mednick associationist theory. Particularly provocative is the evidence that successful creativity requires optimal placement along the intuitive-analytical dimension. In one study of scientific creativity using a free-association test, the generation of moderately atypical responses was more highly correlated with creativity than was either the production of commonplace associations or the production of extremely remote associations. The creative scientist must conceive original connections between ideas as long as those connections are not too strange. In contrast, as will be shown in chapter 5, the associative processes of artistic geniuses often must reach for the more bizarre associative links. Even so, even in artistic creativity there exists an optimum level of originality beyond which artists begin to lose their audiences.

Divergent Thinking

J. P. Guilford, one of the pioneers in the psychometric study of creativity, proposed a critical distinction between two kinds of thinking—convergent versus divergent. Convergent thought involves the convergence on a single correct response, such as is characteristic of most aptitude tests, like those that assess IQ. Divergent thought, in contrast, entails the capacity to generate many alternative responses, including alternatives of considerable variety and originality. Guilford and others have devised a large number of tests that purport to measure the capacity for divergent thinking. Typical is the Alternate Uses test, in which the subject must come up with many different ways of using a common object, such as a paper clip, toothpick, or brick.

The responses of the person taking the test can be scored on several dimensions, but three have received the most attention:

1. *Fluency* is the capacity to generate a large number of responses. In the Alternate Uses test, for example, an individual who thinks of a great many ways of using a paper clip would be scored as highly fluent on this task.
2. *Flexibility* is the capacity to generate responses that can be assigned to many different conceptual categories. In other words, this measure is a gauge of the ability to "change set" rather than always exploit the same function or property. For instance, a person who realizes that a toothpick can serve as a construction material or as something flammable is going to be more flexible than someone who thinks that a toothpick can only be used for picking at something.
3. *Originality* is the capacity to generate unusual but appropriate responses. Using a brick as a doorstop or paperweight is less novel than using broken bricks of different colors to create a wall mosaic.

Theoretically speaking, these three dimensions could be relatively independent of each other. For instance, a person who thought of dozens of uses for a brick would get a high score on fluency yet would get a low score on flexibility if all the uses entailed taking advantage of a single property, such as the brick's weight. Likewise, an individual might conceive of only a few uses for a paper clip, but all uses might be highly original. Nevertheless, scores on fluency, flexibility, and originality all display strong positive correlations, suggesting that they all measure the same underlying capacity for generating ideational variations. In particular, the more ideas a mind can produce, the higher the odds that those ideas will be original and varied. Flexibility and originality are both to a very large extent mere consequences of fluency. This is precisely what would be anticipated from the standpoint of a Darwinian theory of creativity.

Many investigators have tried to validate the various divergent-thinking tests against other criteria of creative performance. Although these validation studies have had some modicum of success, two main complications have emerged.

The first complication is that different forms of creativity tend to require contrasting proportions of divergent and convergent thinking. Just as was noted in the case of remote associations, scientific creativity needs a stronger dose of convergent thought, whereas artistic creativity is far more dependent on divergent thought. As before, these contrasts should reflect the degree to which a particular form of creativity depends on the production of blind variations. On the average, creative ideas in science have more a priori guidance than do those in the arts. The less divergent thinking required in a given domain of creativity, the less Darwinian it can be said to be.

The second complication is that generalized tests do not have as much predictive validity as tests more specifically tailored to a particular domain of creativity. It is difficult to predict creativity in music, for example, on the basis of how many uses the subject can imagine for a toothpick. A similar domain specificity has been found for word-association tests as well. Even so, from a Darwinian perspective we would not expect it to be otherwise. The variation process must operate on those concepts that belong to a specific discipline. Hence, tests of divergent thinking must be tailored to each domain. This constraint is somewhat analogous to what is seen in biological evolution: Short of a highly fortuitous coincidence in protein synthesis, abundant spontaneous variation in wing pigmentation will probably not aid a herbivorous insect species that needs to generate variations in digestive enzymes in order to counteract a new chemical defense adopted by its main food source.

From the Darwinian perspective, the research on divergent thinking has one major drawback: Because the precise cognitive mechanism for generating divergent ideas is not specified by any theory, it is not clear whether divergent thought entails any blind variation. This disadvantage stands in stark contrast to Mednick's theory, where it is easily seen how chains of association can quickly descend to the realm of nearly equiprobable associates (i.e., where the hierarchies become almost perfectly flat). Nonetheless, the associative theory itself may help resolve this question. The fluency, flexibility, and originality of divergent production may ultimately depend on an intellect in which concepts are richly interconnected by diverse associative linkages. As a consequence, divergent thinking of the highest caliber—especially as seen in artistic genius—would be contingent on a certain amount of decidedly blind variation. The empirical research using divergent-thinking measures seems to endorse this position. It typically happens that once the most obvious answers are given, the sequence descends to a series of highly unusual and unpredictable responses. Moreover, these latter responses are quite variable in quality, highly creative responses being mixed randomly with worthless responses. The emission of ideational variants thus becomes increasingly chaotic, as the mind regresses into increasingly Darwinian thought.

Character

Not all creativity tests concentrate on individual differences in the structure of a person's intelligence. Some gauge the individual's personality instead. The underlying assumption behind such assessments is that creativity is as much a dispositional characteristic as it is an intellectual trait. Each human being is a cluster of motives, traits, interests, and values, some of which are conducive to creativity, and some not. If the Darwinian viewpoint is correct, the characteristic personality profile of creators should not be arbitrary, but rather it should consolidate those personal attributes that are most conducive to the generation of ideational variations. Below I offer some evidence on behalf of this theoretical conjecture. I first examine the general profile and then turn to one additional trait that has the most profound implications for both primary and secondary Darwinian models of human creativity.

Personality

What is the typical creative genius like? According to the accumulated literature, creative geniuses are open to diverse experiences, display exceptional tolerance of ambiguity, seek out complexity and novelty, and can engage in defocused attention. They display a wide range of interests, including interests that extend beyond their immediate domain of creative activity. They are far more likely to be introverted than extroverted, and they may sometimes appear remote, withdrawn, and perhaps even antisocial. They also exhibit tremendous independence and autonomy, often refusing to conform to conventional norms—at times exhibiting a pronounced rebellious streak. They deeply love what they do, showing uncommon enthusiasm, energy, and commitment, usually appearing to friends and family as "workaholics." They are persistent in the face of obstacles and disappointments, but at the same time they are flexible enough to alter strategies and tactics when repeated failure so dictates.

Although no single creator will match this profile perfectly—for reasons discussed below—the foregoing personality sketch matches Darwin's own personality fairly closely. For example, in his autobiography he reports that "I had, as a very young boy, a strong taste for long solitary walks," in which he "often became quite absorbed." Later as an adult, he continued to engage in solitary activities, and he spent most of his career retired at his country home in Down rather than taking full advantage of all the social and professional stimulation available in London. Darwin also reported that early on he "had strong and diversified tastes, much zeal for whatever interested [him], and a keen pleasure in understanding any complex subject or thing." In fact, "independently of science, [he] was fond of reading books, and [he] used to sit for hours reading the historical plays of Shakespeare" as well as much other poetry. One book entitled *Wonders of the World* Darwin read often, and he claimed that it inspired in him "a wish to travel in remote countries, which was ultimately fulfilled by the voyage of the *Beagle*." Darwin always remained an omnivorous reader with a tremendous curiosity about diverse subjects. "His wide interest in branches of science that were not specially his own was remarkable," said his son Francis. Yet Darwin was not a mere cloistered bookworm. As a youth he loved horseback riding, hunting, fishing, and collecting all kinds of natural samples—enthusiasms that would prove most useful when he served as the *Beagle* naturalist. Thus, Darwin had the appearance of being rather well-rounded. Yet at the same time, he was persistent at any task he undertook. For instance, he devoted eight years to a monumental work on the cirripedes (barnacles), continuing his labors long after he found the work tiresome. His *Origin of Species* consumed even more time: He began accumulating notes on the subject in 1837, the theory assumed abstract form in 1842, a more complete essay was finished in 1844, and the final product emerged in 1859—22 years later. Darwin expressed his tenacity of purpose with the motto "It's dogged as does it." Finally, I might mention Darwin's unconventional attitudes about a wide range of matters, including his strong antipathy to slavery and his more generous attitudes toward the "inferior races" and the "lower classes." Darwin also entertained less than conforming attitudes toward the prevailing religious views of his time and station. Of course, when he finally ventured to replace the Genesis view of creation with his theory of evolution by natural selection, Darwin's religious iconoclasm became a cause célèbre.

But rather than show that the personality profile fits Darwin, it is more important to show how the character of the creative genius fits a Darwinian theory of creativity. To accomplish this task, we must recognize that these

traits actually form two separate clusters. One set of characteristics probably belongs most properly to primary Darwinism, whereas only the second
set pertains to secondary Darwinism.

Primary Darwinian traits. When Galton first introduced "natural ability"
as a construct to explain individual differences in eminence, he perceived it
in rather inclusive terms. The concept was inclusive, first of all, because it
encompassed a set of traits rather than just one—intellect, motivation, and
persistence. The concept was inclusive in a second sense as well, for natural
ability was hypothesized to underlie success in many different domains of
human achievement. It is for this reason that the book *Hereditary Genius*
treats not just famous creators and leaders but eminent divines and athletes
besides. Indeed, Galton might also have included celebrities in the performing arts, business, and maybe even organized crime. Behind the attainment
of greatness in any domain is a common cluster of attributes essential for
success. To be successful at any demanding profession requires intelligence,
enthusiasm, drive, persistence, commitment, and plain hard work. Moreover, these same traits may be considered extremely adaptive in a more general sense. It is hard to imagine the survival value of stupidity, apathy, pas-
sivity, inconstancy, irresolution, and laziness! Such a personality profile
would be as dysfunctional for a prehistoric hunter and gatherer as for a contemporary investment banker. In short, certain characteristics in the profile
of the creative genius are part of a generic recipe for success in life. Given
this universality, they are probably best considered among the human features favored by primary Darwinism. These traits are surely those that help
ensure the reproductive success of any individual who possesses them.

Secondary Darwinian traits. In contrast, other traits seem to provide
exactly what is necessary to fulfill the requirements of a variation-selection
model of the creative process, such as that put forward by Donald Campbell. As pointed out at the close of the preceding chapter, we have not yet
determined how to account for creative genius from the perspective of
organic evolution. Therefore, it is best to attach these characteristics to the
secondary class of Darwinian processes. This maneuver is especially necessary because it is not clear how some of these traits would be adaptive to a
particular organism. For example, wide interests might not be of much service if the pursuit of those interests consumes time that might be better
devoted to the development of some special expertise. Even worse, some of
these attributes might actually be maladaptive. What possible biological
utility can introversion have for a social animal such as *Homo sapiens*? Is a
lone wolf better off than the leader of the pack?

Once we assign these residual traits to secondary Darwinism, in contrast,
their functional value becomes clear. If the aim is to generate and retain
numerous and diverse ideational variants, we should predict that creativity

is more likely to appear in a person who has the following six characteristics:

1. Highly creative people harbor an impressive array of intellectual, cultural, and aesthetic interests. Individuals with broad interests, after all, are more likely to encounter concepts in multiple contexts, thereby enriching the associative linkages between various ideas in their heads. The result would be the flat associative gradients required by Mednick's theory, and hence the capacity for divergent thought demanded by Guilford's theory. The history of great creative ideas is replete with examples of people finding a solution to a major problem in one domain while engaged in "recreational reading" in an entirely different domain. Darwin reported that "fifteen months after I had begun my systematic inquiry [into the origins of species], I happened to read for amusement Malthus on *Population,* and being well prepared to appreciate the struggle for existence which everywhere goes on from long-continued observation of the habits of animals and plants, it at once struck me that under these circumstances favourable variations would tend to be preserved and unfavourable ones to be destroyed."

2. Highly creative individuals are widely open to novel, complex, and ambiguous stimuli in their surroundings. People receptive to a wide range of stimuli in the external world will necessarily be exposed to a broad spectrum of potential priming stimuli during the incubation phase of the creative process. The creative individual must remain always open to subtle cues in the environment that may prime just that missing chain of images or associations that eventually leads to the long-delayed solution of a particular problem. Indeed, as the occurrences of serendipity amply demonstrate, an unexpected input from the world may stimulate a train of thought that leads to totally unforeseen places.

3. Highly creative people are capable of defocused attention. As one creativity researcher put it, "the greater the attentional capacity, the more likely the combinatorial leap which is generally described as the hallmark of creativity." Defocused attention permits the mind to attend loosely to more than one idea or stimulus at the same time, even when these cognitions and perceptions bear no obvious relationship to each other. Yet certain combinations of these ideas may provide the basis for a creative insight. Most commonly, while creators are working on one problem, or even engaged in some irrelevant activity, they will be carrying around in the back of the mind or have "on the back burner" ideas belonging to seemingly different problems. The chance concurrence of these unconnected fragments then puts the missing pieces of the puzzle together. Such fortuitous coincidences, though rare, are

supremely blind, as demanded by Campbell's theory of creativity.

4. Highly creative individuals are unusually flexible both cognitively and behaviorally. For example, when a person cannot solve a problem immediately, it may not be an efficient strategy to doggedly insist on working on the problem until a solution is found. Rather, it may be more effective to incubate the puzzle for some time, taking advantage of any accidental stimulation provided in the interim. It is for this reason, as noted earlier, that eminent creators tend to work on several interrelated projects at once, jumping back and forth according to whatever happens to appear most promising at the moment. Darwin's own work habits are typical of what Howard Gruber aptly styled a "network of enterprises." As Darwin put it, "I have always had several quite distinct subjects in hand at the same time, [and] I keep from thirty to forty large portfolios, in cabinets with labelled shelves, into which I can at once put a detached reference or memorandum." Furthermore, sometimes a serendipitous event will hand-deliver an entirely new project. The gifted creators are those who are flexible enough to be opportunistic when Lady Luck thus knocks on the door. As B. F. Skinner expressed it, "a first principle not formally recognized by scientific methodologists: when you run onto something interesting, drop everything else and study it."

5. Highly creative people are introverted. Because the variation process is blind, and because so much of the variation-generation procedure must take place through long sequences of free association, creativity requires long hours of solitary contemplation. What William Wordsworth said of Newton would apply to any creative genius, namely that he was "a mind forever / Voyaging through strange seas of thought, alone." Hence, smoking a pipe in an armchair, taking a walk in the woods, engaging absentmindedly in some routine activity—these are the circumstances most supportive of Darwinian incubation. Experimental research has actually demonstrated rather conclusively that group problem-solving using more egalitarian "brainstorming" techniques usually yields dismal results in comparison with more solitary forms of problem solving. Individuals working alone will generate more and better ideas than will the same individuals working in a group. To be sure, sometimes interaction with other people, and especially with fellow creators, can sometimes stimulate the mind in new directions, promoting the discoveries that might otherwise remain out of reach. Nevertheless, for the most original geniuses, this social contact is always subordinate to the internal ruminations of their eternally preoccupied minds. Einstein once admitted: "I am a horse for a single harness, not cut out for tandem or

teamwork; for well I know that in order to attain any definite goal, it is imperative that *one* person do the thinking and the commanding."

6. Highly creative individuals are independent, autonomous, unconventional, and perhaps even iconoclastic. As a consequence, they will impose fewer a priori constraints on the scope of what they are willing to consider. Such people will be less prone to dismiss an idea as preposterous without first giving it a fair hearing. Many of the most original contributions to human civilization seemed absurd on first glance. Once when a world-class orchestra first rehearsed a new symphony, the musicians all laughed after playing the opening motif, and put down their instruments, believing that it was some practical joke. Had Beethoven had the same reaction when composing the piece, he would not have produced the Fifth Symphony, which is now believed to boast one of the most effective openings in the classical repertoire. Another lesson on this point is found in an episode in the early history of quantum theory. Once Wolfgang Pauli, the discoverer of electron spin, was presenting a new theory of elementary particles before a professional audience. Extended discussion followed, which Niels Bohr summarized to Pauli as follows. "We are all agreed that your theory is crazy. The question which divides us is whether it is crazy enough to have a chance of being correct. My own feeling is that it is not crazy enough." Because Bohr rejected conventional criteria of what counts as a good scientific theory, he was able to originate the complementarity principle and other radical ideas that revolutionized modern physics.

When I used Darwin to exemplify the creative genius, I admitted it is most unlikely that any given creator will fit the general profile perfectly, the theoretical foundation be what it may. There are three main reasons why these discrepancies may appear.

First, because there are so many personality traits associated with the capacity for creative thought, weaknesses in one trait may be compensated by exceptional strengths in one or more different traits. For example, someone who did not have very wide interests might still be exceptionally open to whatever novel experiences might come his or her way. Or, turning to the primary Darwinian traits, a relative weakness in intellectual power might be compensated by a superlative drive and determination. As observed in chapter 1, Darwin himself admitted that he was not the most brilliant naturalist of his day, but nonetheless he claimed compensatory virtues that would put him in the front ranks of world scientists. To be sure, these trade-offs can only be carried so far. Utterly lazy people who cannot force themselves to master the basic principles and skills of a creative domain are never going to rise above the status of amateurs or dilettantes.

Second, I have already emphasized the critical relevance of differences across domains of creative activity. Because scientific creativity is less Darwinian than artistic creativity, scientists will less likely fit the secondary profile than will artists. In the case of anticonformity, for instance, Kuhn has spoken of the "essential tension" that underlies all scientific creativity, for "very often the successful scientist must simultaneously display the characteristics of the traditionalist and of the iconoclast." And once more, within the sciences differences in traits can be expected between the normal and revolutionary scientists, the latter displaying more iconoclasm than the former. Similar qualifications apply to the other attributes that compose the general personality profile of creative genius.

Third, if individuals vary immensely in their creative power, they will also differ to the extent to which they will epitomize the Darwinian personality. Only the most prolific and profoundly original of creative geniuses would be expected to exhibit the full panoply of traits. In contrast, a creator who can claim but one, relatively minor contribution need not fit the profile at all. A one-idea person may not have engaged in any variation-selection process, and thus did not need the matrix of personality traits that support such Darwinian thought. For example, sometimes a person will introduce into a given discipline a concept or technique that is already well-established in another discipline. Such individuals may receive credit for the dissemination of knowledge, but their accomplishments may not have required great creative insight. Indeed, Mednick long ago recognized the possibility of a third type of association gradient besides those discussed earlier: Some individuals may have steep association gradients as seen in figure 3.1, but rather than generating the most obvious associates, all of their associations may be bizarre or unusual. According to Mednick's theory, although such individuals would not produce many ideas, the few they would generate would be highly original. Among the novelties produced may be one excellent idea on which to stake a claim to fame, diminutive though it be in comparison to the output of truly prolific creators.

The two factors of domain contrasts and individual differences are more or less unrelated to each other. You can be a great scientist or a mediocre one, an illustrious artist or an obscure one, and so forth. Accordingly, these two dimensions may jointly determine the odds of exhibiting a Darwinian personality in the manner depicted in figure 3.3. This shows the interrelation among the creative domain (e.g., artistic versus scientific), the magnitude of genius (e.g., level of productivity), and the degree to which a creator should display the Darwinian profile. On the average, scientific creators are

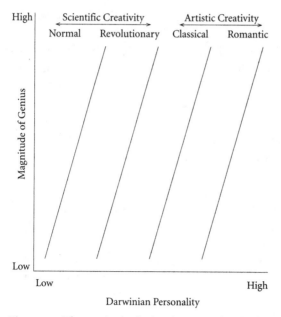

Figure 3.3 Theoretical relation between level of creative genius, domain of
creativity, and degree to which an individual should typify the
Darwinian personality.

likely to exhibit less of a Darwinian disposition than artistic creators. In
addition, there should appear contrasts among the scientists (normal versus
revolutionary) and the artists (classical versus romantic). Nevertheless,
within a particular creative domain, such as classical artists, the greater the
manifestation of genius, the more we would predict the appearance of the
secondary attributes of the Darwinian personality. Because of this within-
domain variation, there may appear some overlap across domains. The
greatest revolutionary in science may have a personality profile not all that
distinguishable from some lesser artist of a classicist inclination.

The foregoing complications should not obscure the central conclusion,
however. The general profile of the creative genius seems explicable in Darwinian terms, at least if we combine both primary and secondary processes.
Even so, it now comes time to admit that the above broad portrait of the
creative genius remains incomplete. A critical feature was deliberately omitted because it requires rather special treatment.

Psychopathology

Ever since the times of the ancient Greeks, genius has often been linked
with mental disturbance. Aristotle is said to have claimed, "Those who have
become eminent in philosophy, politics, poetry, and the arts have all had

tendencies toward melancholia." Similarly, Seneca held that "no great genius has ever existed without some touch of madness." In more recent times, the same link was still proclaimed. Thus, Shakespeare wrote, "The lunatic, the lover, and the poet / Are of imagination all compact." Nor has this viewpoint been confined to philosophers and dramatists. By the end of the nineteenth century, many behavioral scientists were espousing similar views. A notable example was the Italian criminologist Cesare Lombroso. In his 1891 classic *The Man of Genius*, Lombroso confidently asserted that genius was associated with "degenerative psychosis," especially that of the "epileptic group." Indeed, reputable psychiatrists would claim that genius was among the symptoms of an inferior genetic endowment. For instance, an 1895 article published in the *Journal of Nervous and Mental Disease* listed the four possible repercussions of a single congenital defect: "*First*, and most prominent in the order of frequency is an early death. *Second*, he may help swell the criminal ranks. *Third*, he may become mentally deranged and ultimately find his way into a hospital for the insane. *Fourth*, and least frequently, he startles the world by an invention or discovery in science or by an original composition of great merit in art, music or literature. He is then styled a genius." Psychologists as distinguished as Sigmund Freud and William James espoused comparable opinions. They might disagree on the details, such as the specific syndromes entailed, but they would concur that creativity and psychopathology bear an intimate relationship. The only dissonant voices in this overwhelming chorus are a handful of humanistic psychologists, such as Abraham Maslow, Carl Rogers, and Rollo May, who were so bold as to claim that creative individuals enjoyed better mental health than the rest of us. Yet however loud these dissidents might shout, they could hardly be heard through the grand chord of consensus.

A champion of Darwinist theories cannot help but feel a little discomfort with the received tradition. To begin with, the mad-genius association seems to fly in the face of primary Darwinian theory. Mental illness and emotional disturbance seem so antithetical to adaptive fitness that it appears impossible that either natural or sexual selection would favor the survival of pathological genes. If psychopathology fed creativity, how could there be any creativity at all? Furthermore, the notion of the mad genius appears inconsistent with some aspects of creativity, and thus would seem to undermine a secondary Darwinian theory of creativity. Specifically, creativity demands the origination of ideas that are *both* novel *and* adaptive. While madness might certainly generate novelty, it is not at all apparent that those novel notions would satisfy essential scientific or aesthetic criteria. The inhabitants of mental institutions are often the source of original ideas, but these ideas are not considered sane—rather, quite the contrary. Indeed, it is far from clear whether people with severe psychological disorders can

Table 3.1 ALLEGED PSYCHOPATHOLOGY AMONG EMINENT CREATORS

Schizophrenic disorders (and other cognitive psychoses)
Scientists: Tycho Brahe, Cantor, Copernicus, Descartes, Faraday, W. R. Hamilton, Kepler, Lagrange, Linnaeus, Newton, Pascal, Semmelweiss, Weierstrass, Horace Wells; *Thinkers:* Kant, Nietzsche, Swedenborg; *Writers:* Baudelaire, Lewis Carroll, Hawthorne, Hölderlin, S. Johnson, Pound, Rimbaud, Strindberg, Swift; *Artists:* Bosch, Cellini, Dürer, Goya, El Greco, Kandinsky, Leonardo da Vinci, Rembrandt, Toulouse-Lautrec; *Composers:* Donizetti, MacDowell, Felix Mendelssohn, Rimsky-Korsakov, Saint-Saëns.

Affective Disorders (depression, mania, or bipolar)
Scientists: Boltwood, Boltzmann, Carothers, C. Darwin, L. De Forest, J. F. W. Herschel, Julian Huxley, T. H. Huxley, Jung, Kammerer, J. R. von Mayer, V. Meyer, H. J. Muller, J. P. Müller, B. V. Schmidt, J. B. Watson; *Thinkers:* W. James, J. S. Mill, Rousseau, Schopenhauer; *Writers:* Balzac, Barrie, Berryman, Blake, Boswell, Van Wyck Brooks, Byron, Chatterton, Coleridge, William Collins, Conrad, Cowper, H. Crane, Dickens, T. Dreiser, R. Fergusson, F. Scott Fitzgerald, Frost, Goethe, G. Greene, Hemingway, Jarrell, Kafka, Charles Lamb, Jack London, Robert Lowell, Maupassant, O'Neill, Plath, Poe, Quiroga, Roethke, D. G. Rossetti, Saroyan, Schiller, Sexton, Shelley, C. Smart, T. Tasso, V. Woolf; *Artists:* Michelangelo, Modigliani, Pollock, Raphael, Rothko, R. Soyer, Van Gogh; *Composers:* Berlioz, Chopin, Elgar, Gershwin, Handel, Mahler, Rachmaninoff, Rossini, Schumann, Scriabin, Smetana, Tchaikovsky, Wolf.

Personality Disorders (including severe neuroses)
Scientists: Ampère, Cavendish, A. S. Couper, Diesel, Einstein, Frege, Freud, Galton, Heaviside, Huygens, Marconi, Mendel; *Thinkers:* J. Austin, Beccaria, Comte, Descartes, Hegel, Hobbes, Hume, Kierkegaard, B. Russell, Spencer, Voltaire, Wittgenstein; *Writers:* H. C. Andersen, E. B. Browning, R. Browning, Bunyan, Carlyle, Dickinson, Dostoyevsky, T. S. Eliot, Emerson, Flaubert, García Lorca, Gide, Allen Ginsberg, Gogol, Heine, G. M. Hopkins, A. Huxley, W. M. Inge, Melville, Pavese, Proust, S. Richardson, Rimbaud, Ruskin, Tennyson, Tocqueville, Tolstoy, Verlaine, Tennessee Williams, Zola; *Artists:* Borromini, Bramante, Caravaggio, Cézanne, Coco Chanel, Munch, Romney; *Composers:* Beethoven, Bruckner, Orlando de Lasso, Schubert, Wagner.

even make satisfactory judgments about what is right and wrong, true and false, beautiful and ugly.

Given these difficulties, I have two goals in this section. First, I will provide a brief review of the research results suggesting that some kind of relationship exists between psychopathology and genius. Second, I will give an overview of a recent theory proposed by Hans Eysenck, who has offered a foundation for that relationship from the standpoint of secondary Darwinism.

Empirical findings. It is easy to conjure up long lists of creative geniuses who have exhibited some guise of mental illness. Table 3.1 lists some of the more frequently cited examples. I must stress that few of these cases are founded on modern clinical diagnosis, and many are extremely conjectural. On the other hand, many other examples are quite secure. Some creators were actually placed in mental institutions, like Van Gogh and Schumann, while others either committed suicide, like Hemingway and Virginia Woolf, or became severe alcoholics, like Modigliani and Mussorgsky. Still others displayed symptoms of abnormality too conspicuous to be ignored, including the paranoia of Newton and the hysteria of Tchaikovsky.

Darwin's own pathology may fall in this category. He would often be prostrated by mysterious attacks of dizziness, heart palpitations, violent shivering, nausea, vomiting, and hysterical crying. These episodes were usually brought on by the mere act of conversing with people—revealing their psychosomatic origins. To avoid a recurrence, Darwin did everything possible to isolate himself from all but the briefest social interactions, even with his nearest relations. It is possible that Darwin suffered from the hyperventilation syndrome, which ensues from excessive arousal of the sympathetic nervous system. Whatever the correct diagnosis, there is no doubt that Darwin was emotionally and mentally unwell. His attacks would often incapacitate him to the point that he could not work at all. Even when the consequences were not so drastic, he avoided society to an unhealthy degree. Darwin himself confessed that he was "confined to a living grave."

At the very least, the names in table 3.1 suggest that people with mental disturbances *can* still attain distinction as creators. But do such lists imply any inference stronger than that? Probably not. There are thousands upon thousands of individuals who have gone down in history as creative geniuses. Hence, even if the incidence rate of psychopathology were far lower among such creators than in the general population, we should still be able to compile impressive lists of supposed mad geniuses. Thus, we cannot draw any conclusions without having the proper baselines or control groups. This methodological essential has been achieved in the following three sets of empirical investigations:

1. For nearly a century, behavioral scientists have conducted historiometric research on the likelihood that notable creators will exhibit some form of psychopathology. The bulk of these inquiries have claimed incidence rates higher than that found in the general population. The most recent historiometric inquiry on this subject is that reported by Arnold Ludwig in his 1995 book *The Price of Greatness*. After studying the lives of over a thousand eminent personalities, he showed that (a) the rate of mental disorder exceeded expectation and (b) a positive association exists between the presence of pathological

symptoms and the magnitude of achievement. Just as critical, he found considerable variation across different domains. In general, notable leaders displayed less evidence of disorder than did famous creators—something found by other historiometric inquiries as well. Moreover, among the various types of creative activities, illustrious scientists appeared more stable than did distinguished artists and authors. To offer specifics, whereas only 28% of the notables in the natural sciences experienced some sort of mental disorder, psychological problems plagued 60% of the composers, 73% of the visual artists, 74% of the playwrights, 77% of the fiction writers, and 87% of the poets. The last figure seems to endorse Thomas Macaulay's comment: "Perhaps no person can be a poet, or can even enjoy poetry, without a certain unsoundness of mind." It is interesting to note that Ludwig has more recently shown how parallel differentials hold within specific creative domains, depending on whether the emphasis is on logic, objectivity, and formalism or on intuition, subjectivity, and emotionalism. In painting, for example, only 22% of painters practicing a formal style exhibited some form of mental disorder, whereas this incidence rate increased to 52% for those painting in a symbolic style and to 75% for painters who expressed themselves in an emotive style. According to Ludwig, the data display the fractal characteristic of "self-similarity." The same pattern that separates leaders from creators, and then divides scientific creators from artistic creators, also permeates down various levels of resolution, culminating in the stylistic contrasts within a single creative domain, such as in painting.

2. Psychiatric research lends additional support to the hypothesis that outstanding creativity bears some relationship to psychopathology. Unlike the historiometric studies, these investigations examine samples of eminent contemporaries, using diagnostic criteria to establish the appearance of certain syndromes. These psychiatric inquiries have tended to focus on successful artists and writers, and within this group the inclination toward affective disorders (including bipolar or manic-depressive) is conspicuous, along with corresponding tendencies toward alcoholism, drug abuse, and suicide. Among the most prominent contributors to this research literature is Kay Jamison, who has persuasively argued for a firm linkage between affective disorders and the artistic temperament. Although some have criticized this research on methodological grounds, the findings are not at all discrepant with what has been found using more rigorous methods.

3. Like the psychiatric work, psychometric investigations apply their techniques to contemporary creators of note. An exquisite example is the research conducted at the Institute for Personality Assessment and

Research (IPAR) at the University of California at Berkeley. Eminent architects, writers, mathematicians, and other creators were invited to IPAR for intensive psychometric evaluation. Besides submitting to interviews and other assessments, the participants took a large inventory of standard psychometric tests, such as the Minnesota Multiphasic Personality Inventory (MMPI). Because these tests had norms based on general populations, standards of comparison were available. In addition, the IPAR researchers would invite less successful colleagues in the same creative domains to serve as matched controls. The IPAR studies again demonstrated that some degree of psychopathology is associated with creative achievement. The creative writers, for example, scored higher than normal on all the clinical subscales of the MMPI (namely, depression, hypomania, schizophrenia, paranoia, psychopathic deviation, hysteria, hypochondriasis, and psychaesthenia). Comparable findings have been reported by other researchers. Highly creative people show elevated scores on dimensions that indicate the presence of psychopathological symptoms. And elevated scores are especially common among those active as artistic creators. "What garlic is to salad, insanity is to art," said sculptor Augustus Saint-Gaudens.

To sum up, the historiometric, psychiatric, and psychometric literature converge on the same conclusion: The genius-madness link may be more than myth. Furthermore, the association between creativity and psychopathology is particularly prominent in those domains where the creative process must be the most Darwinian, as in poetry, fiction, and the visual arts—and especially in the most intuitive, subjective, and emotional styles of artistic expression. However, to comprehend better the relationship between psychopathology and creativity, two qualifications must be recognized.

First, although creative geniuses seem to exhibit above-average levels of psychopathological symptoms, these levels are seldom so high as to translate into total mental and emotional deterioration. Indeed, if they do suffer from such extreme degrees of disturbances, their creative careers terminate, whether by suicide or by complete intellectual or emotional incapacitation. Consequently, creative individuals tend to exhibit symptoms midway between those of the normal and abnormal personality. Dryden captured the fine distinction when he composed the often-quoted lines "Great Wits are sure to Madness near ally'd, / And thin Partitions do their Bounds divide."

Second, creative geniuses tend to possess other cognitive and emotional resources that help to channel and contain any potential psychopathology. Besides superior intelligence, eminent creators will possess considerable "ego-strength" and other traits of personal fortitude and self-discipline. These moderating attributes enable creators to exploit the strange ideas that fill their heads without allowing those ideas to take over the organization of their personality. Such traits also allow a person to engage in the full range of behaviors required for creative accomplishment. Albert Rothenberg has provided excellent examples in his psychiatric studies of the creative process in both schizophrenic and authentic poets. Unlike true poets, schizophrenic poets refuse to revise their initial drafts, revealing an inability to adopt a more objective perspective on their work. They are all inspiration without verification, variation without selection.

Unfortunately, although the link between psychopathology and creativity has been empirically determined, the precise causal foundation of the mad-genius syndrome has yet to be established. In fact, the number of potential causal explanations is actually rather large. For example, it could be that the achievement of eminence is profoundly stressful, and that the stress can sometimes provoke a mental breakdown. Under such a causal scenario, genius is only incidentally mad. Nonetheless, a distinguished researcher recently advanced a theory arguing that psychopathology may actually make a positive and direct contribution to the manifestation of creative genius.

Theoretical interpretation. Hans Eysenck was a pioneer in the empirical study of personality. Among his many contributions was the development of the Eysenck Personality Questionnaire, or EPQ. One subscale of this instrument has special pertinence for the question at hand, namely that which measures individual differences in psychoticism. At the low end of this dimension are those people who are socialized, conventional, and conformist but also empathic and even altruistic. Such low scorers are not only normal, but perfectly well adjusted for life in human society. At the high end of this dimension are those who are impulsive, egocentric, antisocial, impersonal, hostile, and aggressive, at times to a criminal degree, and who, at the higher extremities, display tendencies toward psychopathic, affective, and schizophrenic disorders. According to Eysenck, although high scores are associated with the appearance of pronounced psychopathology, moderately high scores are also linked with the manifestation of exceptional creativity. A considerable amount of psychometric research, in fact, supports this assertion.

Eysenck did not believe that the correlation between psychoticism and creativity is a mere empirical curiosity. On the contrary, Eysenck constructed a Darwinian theory that builds directly on the previous variation-selection models—he styled it the Campbell-Simonton theory. Eysenck began by recognizing the creator's need for an exceptional reservoir of remote associations that will provide a rich source of divergent responses.

He then reviewed an impressive number of empirical studies showing that psychoticism positively correlates with performance on word-association tests as well as on various measures of divergent thinking. Individuals scoring higher on psychoticism do indeed seem more capable of producing a large quantity of unusual ideas.

Furthermore, such intellects exhibit several cognitive quirks that make their thought processes depart from the norm—sometimes in a fashion that approximates the pathological. For instance, high scorers on psychoticism are more likely to engage in "allusive" or "overinclusive" thinking, in which the sharp distinctions between separate ideas are loosened, yielding overgeneralized concepts. They seem to lack the strong "filter mechanism" that keeps ideas within their usual conceptual boundaries. This cognitive deficiency is related to other peculiarities about the ways that high scorers process information. For example, higher psychoticism is associated with a weakened ability to inhibit environmental stimulation (i.e., reduced "negative priming" or "latent inhibition"). This means that their intellects are more subjected to the random influx of extraneous stimuli, which would in turn elicit incongruous associations. Of course, taken to the extreme, these same cognitive attributes will produce the kinds of symptoms that make life so difficult for the psychotic. But at less conspicuous levels, these same proclivities would permit the production of numerous ideas that are highly unexpected. People with just the right amount of psychoticism would be prone to have all sorts of seemingly irrelevant ideas pop into their heads almost randomly, and without control. Even if not meaningful in themselves, this chaotic influx of ideas can prime new chains of associations that lead to insights otherwise missed.

Indeed, some of these ideational variants will be bizarre enough to count as cognitive analogs of the genetic mutations in organic evolution. Consequently, the intellectual variations would satisfy the most controversial claim of Campbell's Darwinian theory of creativity—that the process operates with a certain degree of blindness. Some valuable proportion of the ideas that pass through the mind of a creative genius would be like "bolts out of the blue."

Eysenck's theoretical discussion concentrated on the cognitive implications of a certain degree of psychoticism. Nonetheless, the very nature of this dimension suggests two other ways that psychoticism may be associated with a high order of creativity:

1. The creative genius must impose few constraints on the range and freedom of thought. Conformity to conventional norms and attitudes will unduly restrict the number and diversity of ideational variations. Furthermore, during the selection phase of the variation-selection process, many original variants will be summarily dismissed

as inconsistent with some arbitrary but traditional standard and will thus never see the light of day. Hence, insofar as psychoticism is associated with independence, unconventionality, anticonformity, and iconoclasm, high scores on this dimension should enhance a person's ability to engage in Darwinian creativity. Like Henrik Ibsen's protagonist in *An Enemy of the People*—or the real-life example of Ignaz Semmelweiss confronting the medical establishment over the contagious nature of puerperal fever—the great innovator must be willing to take issue with the received tradition, even when it requires an epic battle against all the powers that be. It is no accident, for instance, that the greatest thinkers in the Western intellectual tradition tend to be those who refuse to conform to the contemporary philosophical zeitgeist, who advocate extreme positions, and who insist on combining those positions in highly unconventional ways.

2. The creative genius must often be willing to work hard and long on ambitious projects that verge on the unrealistic—a scientific magnum opus, an epic novel, a grandiose opera. To the extent that psychoticism is correlated with the appearance of manic affective disorders, individuals with this disposition will more likely be motivated to take on such lofty tasks. After all, during manic episodes creators would enjoy heightened levels of energy combined with intensified optimism about what they can accomplish. Indeed, the biographies of eminent creators often report periods in which they work on projects feverishly, and with little or no attention to life's pragmatics. Beethoven would often compose his masterpieces in an elevated state of "rapture." Once while Beethoven was working on the *Missa Solemnis*, his friend Schindler reported:

> I arrived at the master's home in Mödling. It was 4 o'clock in the afternoon. As soon as we entered we learned that in the morning both servants had gone away, and that there had been a quarrel after midnight which had disturbed all the neighbors, because as a consequence of a long vigil both had gone to sleep and the food that had been prepared had become unpalatable. In the livingroom, behind a locked door, we heard the master singing parts of the fugue in the Credo—singing, howling, stamping. After we had been listening a long time to this almost awful scene, and were about to go away, the door opened and Beethoven stood before us with distorted features, calculated to excite fear. He looked as if he had been in mortal combat with the whole host of contrapuntists, his everlasting enemies. His first utterances were confused, as if he had been disagreeably surprised at our having overheard him. Then he reached the day's happenings and with obvious restraint

he remarked "Pretty doings, these, everybody has run away and I haven't had anything to eat since yesternoon!"

Moving beyond the realm of mere anecdote, a detailed quantitative analysis in fact identified a conspicuous relationship between manic episodes and prolific output in the career of Robert Schumann, whose bouts with manic depression eventually led to his attempted suicide and institutionalization. The composer's creative effusions of 1840 and 1849, in particular, took place during manic highs.

After extensively illustrating the consequences of high psychoticism, I believe it is instructive to offer an example of a historical personality who would probably have scored extremely low on this dimension had the EPQ been available 150 years ago. The person is John Stearns Henslow, Darwin's botany professor at Cambridge, and the individual who nominated Darwin to serve as naturalist aboard the *Beagle*. Darwin recalled that Henslow's "knowledge was great in botany, entomology, chemistry, mineralogy, and geology," and "his judgment was excellent, and his whole mind well-balanced." Moreover, according to Darwin, "his moral qualities were in every way admirable. He was free from every tinge of vanity or other petty feeling." Darwin "never saw a man who thought so little about himself or his own concerns. His temper was imperturbably good, with the most winning and courteous manners . . . [and his] benevolence was unbounded." Yet Henslow was also "deeply religious, and so orthodox, that . . . he should be grieved if a single word of the Thirty-nine Articles were altered." Darwin also admitted that he did "not suppose that any one would say that he possessed much original genius." Indeed, it was actually Henslow who was first invited to serve aboard the *Beagle*, but he declined the opportunity to take so venturesome an action. One can only speculate how the history of evolution would have differed had Henslow been the naturalist to scramble over the Galápagos Islands. In fact, because Henslow could not advance beyond the restraints of his conservative spirit, he never was able to accept the bold evolutionary theory put forward by his most distinguished student.

Because Eysenck has provided extensive discussion of his theory, I cannot do full justice to his ideas here. Nor do I have the space to examine all the criticisms that might be inveighed against his theory. I will only direct the reader to his 1995 book *Genius: The Natural History of Creativity* and to a target article and ensuing commentary that appeared in a 1993 issue of *Psychological Inquiry*. Such additional readings will document the profound manner in which Eysenck connects his Darwinian theory with research on (a) individual differences in personality, (b) the cognitive processes underlying creativity, and (c) the genetic and environmental factors behind the emergence of creative genius. Eysenck himself admitted that his attempted integration may sometimes amply illustrate the phenomena of remote association and overinclusive thought. Nonetheless, the resulting synthesis is expansive, bold, creative—and explicitly Darwinian, in the secondary sense.

Evolution

As noted earlier, the personality profile of the creative genius contains certain features that seem inconsistent with what would be predicted according to the principles of organic evolution. Of all those features, it is creativity's affiliation with psychopathology that causes the most theoretical discomfort. Hence, the big question that comes to the fore is how to make the mad-genius relationship square with primary Darwinism. Whatever the assets of creativity, overt psychopathology does not appear to constitute adaptive behavior. So why would evolution favor its emergence?

One facile solution would be simply to deny that either madness or genius represent genetically transferable traits. The natural selection that drives organic evolution can only operate on *inheritable* variation among individuals. If both psychopathology and creativity are exclusively products of environmental influences, then there would be no necessity to look for circumstances that render these attributes adaptive. But this response will not do. There is already ample empirical evidence that both syndromes may exhibit a strong genetic foundation. Indeed, according to family pedigree studies, mental illness and exceptional achievement tend to appear in higher than normal frequencies in the same lineages.

Take, for example, a comprehensive Icelandic survey. Because the number of Icelanders does not get much beyond 200,000, and because immigration and emigration are relatively small, it is possible to trace genealogies for the bulk of its population. In addition, the mental hospital in Reykjavik can keep comprehensive records of mental disturbances among Icelandic citizens. These records were compared against luminaries who had made names for themselves as novelists, poets, painters, composers, and performers—according to *Who Is Who in Iceland*. It was thus possible to trace the genealogies of both achievement and insanity with a completeness unimaginable in gigantic and unstable populations like that of the United States. The family pedigrees were revealing. The relatives of schizophrenics were two to six times more likely to earn a place of creative distinction in Icelandic society. The incidence of insane relatives definitely exceeded what occurred in families whose members had not left their marks. Because compatible results have emerged in the survey of family pedigrees in other cultures, this co-occurrence cannot be a peculiarity of Icelandic culture. Illustrious creators do seem to originate from families in which mental disorders are rampant—at least in comparison to pedigrees that produce less outstanding minds.

There are many dramatic cases of these convergent pedigrees in the annals of human history. One especially fascinating example is the Huxley family. Thomas Henry—"T. H."—Huxley often suffered from depressive states, and his father had died in an asylum. Moreover, of T. H.'s seven siblings, only one sister could be considered relatively normal. T. H.'s own daughter, Marian, became extremely melancholic, lost her sanity, and died young. One of T. H.'s grandsons, Trevenen was also melancholic, and committed suicide. A second grandson, Julian, attempted suicide and suffered from depression. And a third, Aldous, experimented with hallucinogenic drugs and the occult. Several other temperamental disorders permeate the family history. Yet all of these disturbances notwithstanding, the Huxley family is distinguished for its output of first-rate creative minds. Sir Andrew Fielding Huxley, another grandson of T. H., shared the 1963 Nobel Prize for physiology or medicine. Sir Julian Huxley was a noted biologist who became secretary of the Zoological Society of London and the first director general of UNESCO. Aldous Huxley, though not knighted, became a famous author, most notably of the novel *Brave New World*. And, of interest to our discussion, two members with Huxley pedigree made critical contributions to the development and dissemination of Darwinian theory. In 1942, Sir Julian wrote *Evolution: The Modern Synthesis*, which helped establish the current version of the theory. In this he was following in his grandfather's footsteps, for T. H. was an early champion of the original theory of evolution by natural selection. So prominent and successful was his advocacy that T. H. earned the nickname "Darwin's bulldog."

The frequent appearance of such pedigrees implies that creativity and psychopathology feature a common genetic component. Hans Eysenck has actually proposed a sequential model that links these two individual-difference variables to underlying intellectual faculties (involving weakened cognitive inhibition), which is itself a consequence of a particular psychoneurological constitution (entailing hippocampal functioning and the neurotransmitters dopamine and serotonin). The latter, finally, is a function of genes that provide the basis for individual differences in the organization and operation of the nervous system. Eysenck's model is little more than a highly speculative sketch, but it at least provides a theoretical framework for understanding how there might exist a shared genetic foundation for the creative hits and crazy misses seen in such family pedigrees, as the Huxley line.

Whatever the fate of Eysenck's genetic model, the fact remains that individual differences in the capacity for genius and madness seem to share a hereditary component. This means that we cannot ignore the evolutionary consequence of having such genes in the population. If psychopathology is maladaptive, and if both psychopathology and creativity come with the genotype, it would seem that both behavioral phenomena would became increasingly rare. Depending on the selection pressures, creative genius might eventually disappear from the gene pool.

Curiously, one potential solution to this problem was offered in a 1964 *Nature* paper published by two distinguished evolutionists, Julian Huxley and Ernst Mayr, in collaboration with two psychiatrists who had special expertise in schizophrenia. After noting the strong evidence for the heritability of this common mental disorder, the authors observed that the gene for schizophrenia appears too frequently to be maintained by mutation alone. They accordingly examined the benefits and costs of possessing a genetic inclination toward schizophrenic disorder. For example, they discussed data showing that schizophrenics may be more physiologically robust than normal members of the population. The authors also suggested that the low fertility of schizophrenic males may be more than compensated by the high fertility of schizophrenic females. Therefore, Huxley, Mayr, and their coauthors concluded that the high incidence rate of schizophrenia could be "the result of a balance between its selectively favourable and unfavourable properties."

Unfortunately, these authors focused on the biological repercussions of mental disorder. It could just as well be argued that psychopathological symptoms may have certain social consequences that contribute to the survival value of the corresponding genes. This very possibility was put forward by Hammer and Zubin in 1968. They looked at psychopathology as a manifestation of a more general syndrome of what they styled "the cultural unpredictability of behavior." Some individuals in a population inherit a certain tendency to do the unanticipated according to societal norms and role expectations. Although psychopathology is one manifestation of this genetic inclination, it is not by any means the only one. The innate proclivity for unpredictability may take the form of creative genius, which can prove adaptive both to the individuals and to the culture that produces them. Whether this genetic endowment is positive or negative depends on certain cultural circumstances that channel the tendency in different directions. Hammer and Zubin directly compared this phenomenon with sickle-cell anemia. Although the gene for this ailment is disadvantageous in temperate environments, it acquires a selective advantage in tropical climates where people heterozygous on this trait can gain increased resistance to malaria. In a sense, the mental disorder of some humans is the price that society pays for the benefits of creative genius.

More recently, Geoffrey Miller has argued for the selective advantage of a genetic trait quite similar to cultural unpredictability. But his explanation was founded on the notion of "Machiavellian intelligence." According to the latter concept, human beings have had to evolve extremely complex cognitive and behavioral skills to survive the interpersonal politics of primate social systems. Such intricate systems require considerable acumen and dexterity to negotiate the elaborate web of cooperative and competitive activities that define an individual's place in the dominance hierarchies. Because a premium is placed on being able to "outsmart" rivals, the social primates have evolved a number of strategies that help prevent the disclosure of intentions. Among those strategies may be "proteanism"—the capacity to be unpredictable when necessary in a given social situation. Moreover, social proteanism would be useful in a variety of circumstances besides domestic politics. A warrior locked in mortal combat, for example, would certainly benefit if an enemy were unable to anticipate his next move.

One striking feature of Miller's theory of protean behavior is that it provides an evolutionary explanation for the emergence of a mechanism that can generate true randomness, the prerequisite for the production of genuinely unpredictable behavior. Many psychologists have claimed that human beings are incapable of producing unpredictable behaviors, but this only holds in highly artificial situations (e.g., when individuals are asked to write a sequence of random numbers). In contrast, this skill appears to be highly developed in social interactions in which there are painful costs to being successfully anticipated (e.g., business, sports, and games). Miller even made a specific connection between this intellectual capacity and Donald Campbell's blind-variation-and-selective-retention model. In doing so, Miller offered a primary Darwinian mechanism that would support the evolutionary emergence of the secondary Darwinian process of creativity.

The only feature missing from Miller's theory is an explicit treatment of psychopathology. However, it is not too far-fetched to conjecture that mental disorder may be the unfortunate consequence of inheriting too much proclivity for proteanism. Presumably, the optimal amount of protean behavior in the population would represent some equilibrium point between two maladaptive extremes on this trait—between psychosis and its opposite. At some point on the continuum between the optimally protean and the outright psychotic may then emerge the creative genius. This interpretation suggests that creativity need not have any special adaptive advantage from the standpoint of natural selection. Rather the creative genius may reside at the delicate neutral point between the highly fit protean intellect and the sadly unfit pathological mind. Perhaps only the greatest creators can stand at the very pivot between success and failure.

4

~

DEVELOPMENT

Are Geniuses Born—or Made?

~

You care for nothing but shooting, dogs, and rat-catching, and you will be a disgrace to yourself and all your family." Such was the prophesy of Darwin's father, who had lost all patience with his young son's inability to show direction and aptitude. Matters did not improve when Darwin entered his college years. He first enrolled at Edinburgh with the half-hearted intention of becoming a physician, like his father. Finding medical studies quite unattractive, Darwin proceeded to Cambridge at his father's urging, with the plan of becoming a minister. But that career goal, too, soon ran aground. After he earned an undistinguished bachelor's degree at age 22, he had no firm idea of what to do with himself. As is not surprising, when Darwin was invited to serve as the *Beagle* naturalist, his father was not inclined to give his consent. Rather than pursue a true profession, his son was apparently going to spend the next five years with only room and board as pay, and with no prospect of further advancement. His father made just one fateful concession, "If you can find any man of common-sense who advises you to go I will give my consent." Fortunately, Darwin's uncle was considered "one of the most sensible men in the world," and it was he who persuaded Darwin's father to relent. At this point, in the year 1831, Darwin's biography becomes history.

In modern terminology, I guess we would say that the young Darwin did not strike his father as particularly gifted or talented—except at wasting time and money. Had the senior Darwin wanted to, he certainly could have compared his son to Charles's young cousin, Francis Galton. Although more than a dozen years younger, Galton had already proven himself to be far more precocious. For example, several years earlier he had written the following letter to his sister:

MY DEAR ADÈLE,

I am 4 years old and I can read any English book. I can say all the Latin Substantives and Adjectives and active verbs besides 52 lines of Latin poetry. I can cast up any sum in addition and can multiply by 2, 3, 4, 5, 6, 7, 8, [9], 10, [11].

I can also say the pence table. I read French a little and I know the clock.

FRANCIS GALTON,
Febuary 15, 1827.

The numbers in brackets were those that Galton, in a display of second thoughts, erased from the letter; he used a knife to scratch out one number and, evidently finding this unsatisfactory, glued paper on top of the other number. Only one misspelling appears, the month that this letter was written (an error that some adults still make). There may even be a little brilliance hidden in the dating of this letter, which was written the day before his fifth birthday—as if young Francis were trying to extract the most possible credit for the precocity of a mere four year old.

In chapter 1, I mentioned how one of Lewis Terman's students had used biographical data about childhood and adolescent accomplishments to calculate Darwin's IQ. He scored 135. Using the same methodology, Terman himself estimated Galton's IQ as close to 200—or four standard deviations higher. Thus, in today's language, Galton would certainly be called a gifted or talented child, if not an unequivocal case of a child prodigy. Even so, Galton's ultimate achievements pale in comparison to those of his older cousin. By Galton's own criterion of genius, Darwin was the greater genius of the two. Only Charles Darwin belongs in that exclusive pantheon that includes Copernicus, Galileo, Newton, and Einstein. Wordsworth once said, "The Child is father of the Man." Yet that observation seems invalid here. The discrepant childhoods of Darwin and Galton do not predict the equally discrepant but inverted adulthoods.

This curious inconsistency in outcomes certainly raises the larger issue of talent development. What is the connection between the events of youth and the attainments of maturity? What are the factors responsible for the conversion of giftedness into genius? And, most critical, do Darwinian principles participate in any significant manner in the growth process? To address these questions properly requires that I first examine development from two contrary perspectives.

Nature and Nurture

Perhaps the most troublesome single debate in developmental psychology is the so-called nature-nurture issue. What are the relative contributions of genetic endowment versus early experience to the development of the human organism? This recurrent controversy has its natural counterpart in the phenomenon of genius. On the one side are those who would second John Dryden's assertion that "genius must be born, and never can be taught." Galton himself was initially in this camp. The reason Galton named his 1869 book *Hereditary Genius* was because he thought genius was precisely that—hereditary. If supreme natural ability drove the inevitable attainment of distinction, and if individual differences in natural ability are inherited from parents, then genius should run in families. A major portion of Galton's book, in fact, is expressly devoted to presenting long lists of eminent personalities who emerged from distinguished family lines. Indeed, his chapter headings read like a list of the ways one can attain a durable reputation: Statesmen, Judges, Commanders, Divines, Men of Science, Literary Men, Poets, Musicians, and Painters.

Naturally, in the "Men of Science" chapter, Galton gave the Darwin family its due. He noted that Charles Darwin (born 1809) was the grandson of Erasmus Darwin (born 1731), the poet and scientist who was an early advocate of evolutionary ideas. Galton also mentioned that Charles had a number of promising sons, although at the time the book was written Galton could not anticipate the scope of their achievement. Charles Darwin's immediate progeny included: Sir George Howard (born 1845), a distinguished mathematician and astronomer; Sir Francis (born 1848), a famous botanist; Leonard (born 1850), a noted engineer, economist, and eugenicist; and Sir Horace, (born 1851) an eminent civil engineer. Another illustrious Darwin necessarily omitted from *Hereditary Genius* was Charles's grandson through George, George Galton Darwin, who was a notable physicist. Less explicable is the exclusion of Charles Darwin's maternal grandfather, Josiah Wedgwood (born 1730), the potter who founded the Etruria factory that produced the celebrated "Wedgwood ware." Another descendent of Wedgwood's was Thomas Wedgwood (born 1771), an illustrious physicist and inventor. On the other hand, it was probably Victorian modesty that obliged Galton not to cite his own name in this pedigree, because he avoided doing so even in the 1892 edition that came out when he was quite famous himself. The most he would do was to say that he "could add the names of others of the family who, in a lesser but yet decided degree, have shown a taste for subjects of natural history." Galton and Charles Darwin were both grandsons of Erasmus Darwin, albeit through a different grandmother.

At first glance, the extensive lists of such lineages make a persuasive case on behalf of the innate genius thesis. Charles Darwin was himself quite convinced upon reading Galton's book, informing his cousin that "I do not think I ever in all my life read anything more interesting and original." In his autobiography Darwin further endorsed this genetic determinism when he admitted that he was "inclined to agree with Francis Galton in believing that education and environment produce only a small effect on the mind of anyone and that most of our qualities are innate." Yet although other researchers have replicated Galton's findings, Galton also quickly learned that other scientists would challenge his hereditarian stance. In his next book, *English Men of Science*, Galton yielded a little ground when he looked at some of the environmental factors that might contribute to the emergence of genius. In fact, the subtitle to this 1874 book is telling: "Their Nature and Nurture." Although these words are first associated together in Shakespeare's *Tempest*, it was Galton who introduced these terms into the language of behavioral science. As Galton explained, "the phrase 'nature and nurture' is a convenient jingle of words, for it separates under two distinct heads the innumerable elements of which personality is composed. Nature is all that a man brings with himself into the world; nurture is every influence from without that affects him after his birth."

Unfortunately for Galton, although he tried to integrate these two perspectives, later researchers increasingly tended to emphasize nurture over nature. Only recently has hereditarianism witnessed some revival in the face of the hegemony exercised by environmentalism. So let us first examine the nurture position before returning to the nature position.

Environmentalism

To comprehend the origins of genius from the perspective of a Darwinian environmentalism, I must begin by asking the same type of question examined in the preceding chapter. There the goal was to isolate those individual-difference variables that might facilitate a person's ability to engage in the creative process, as defined by Donald Campbell's variation-selection model. Similarly, certain kinds of environmental experiences may be more likely to enhance an individual's capacity for Darwinian creativity. Those experiences would presumably increase the number and diversity of ideational variations that could emanate from a creator's mind. These developmental experiences may facilitate this potential in two ways, the direct and the indirect. Direct developmental effects are those that expand the intellectual capacity for remote association and divergent thinking—the very cognitive processes that produce ideational variations. Indirect effects, on the other hand, are those that may encourage the development of the Darwinian personality that optimally supports engagement in the variational process.

Nevertheless, the search for both direct and indirect environmental factors must also take into consideration the domain of creative activity (see figure 3.3). If domains vary tremendously in the amount of Darwinian creativity required—from the minimal level of normal science to the maximal level of romantic art—then the developmental circumstances must differ in the same manner. The value of considering domain contrasts will become apparent when I scrutinize some of the factors that contribute to the development of creative talent. Below I examine the potentially nurturing consequences of enriched home environments, adversity and trauma, education, and marginality.

Enrichment. In chapter 1, I mentioned Lewis Terman's classic longitudinal study of over a thousand intellectually gifted children. Among the mounds of data he collected about these high-IQ children was information on the quality of their home environments. Their parents tended to have higher than average levels of formal education, and at least one parent tended to work at an intellectual profession, such as a doctor or lawyer. The homes of these bright children were also likely to contain private libraries well stocked with books of all kinds. Other studies of the gifted have found similar results. The parents highly value learning and supply their homes with intellectually and culturally stimulating magazines, games, and similar materials. Family outings will often include visits to museums, exhibits, galleries, libraries, and other places that stimulate intellectual development. Moreover, studies of eminent creators report similar findings of geniuses originating from such enriched family environments.

All early stimulation no doubt makes some contribution to intellectual development. Insofar as intelligence constitutes a primary Darwinian trait required for general success in any domain, such home environments can be said to contribute to the development of creative genius as well. Yet I have already pointed out that intelligence alone does not support creative genius. The knowledge in the brain must be organized in a structure that permits remote association and divergent thinking. As noted previously, few of Terman's children attained the highest levels of eminence, and those who did tended to achieve distinction in conventional occupations—professions in which creative ideas are not at a premium. The few who became notable for their creativity, moreover, were more likely to be scientists than artists. Therefore, the development of creative talent requires that the home feature enriching experiences that encourage the diversification of the intellect. The most diverse environments will be those of artistic creators, whereas the homes of scientific creators will fall somewhere between those of the artists and those of individuals who fail to display any pronounced levels of creativity.

There is already evidence for the existence of such a ranking of home environments. For example, one study examined U.S. male high school students who demonstrated special talent in either scientific or artistic creativity. Compared with a control group of students who demonstrated no particular talent, both groups of talented teenagers came from homes that were academically and intellectually superior. The parents were likely to be college educated, tended to engage in reading as a leisure-time activity, and were prone to offer models of creativity and interest in the student's chosen field. The parents were more likely than those of the control group to play a musical instrument, to engage in creative hobbies, and to visit art museums or galleries. Thus, the general pattern was a home environment that would provide rich stimulation for scientific and artistic talents alike.

However, in terms of environmental diversity, the homes of the young creative artists were more distinctive than those of the young creative scientists, the latter coming closer to what is normal for academically superior students, such as those studied by Terman. At the one end, a larger proportion of the parents of the artistic talents were born in a city, state, or country different from the one in which the family currently resided. The artistically talented teenagers were themselves more prone to have traveled to various parts of the country, as well as to have visited more distant locales. In addition, these same teenagers were more likely to have lived in more than one state during their childhood and adolescence. At the other end, a smaller proportion of the parents of the scientific talents were born in a foreign country, and a larger proportion were actually born in the city in which they were currently living. Moreover, the parents tended to have more conventional occupations and interests. For example, the young scientific creators were more likely "to have fathers who majored in business subjects in college, who play bridge as a hobby, and from whom the students had learned about sports." All in all, the data make it clear that the creative artists come from homes that have a greater likelihood of supporting the development of the mental capacities required for Darwinian creativity.

Adversity. Ironically, one of the reasons so few of Terman's gifted children grew up to become geniuses may be that they had it too good in childhood. The "Termites" were not only physically robust, but in addition most grew up in ideal homes of stable marriages and financial security. The English poet Dylan Thomas once warned: "There's only one thing that's worse than having an unhappy childhood, and that's having a too-happy childhood." Whatever the intellectual talents of Terman's children, their potential for genius may have been destroyed by a superfluity of happiness.

There is, in fact, empirical reason for believing that the development of genius may sometimes be enhanced by traumatic or adverse experiences in childhood and adolescence. For instance, eminent creators may display a disproportionate number of physical or sensory disabilities. Handicaps afflicted such diverse individuals as Thomas Edison, Homer, Aldous Huxley, Karl Jaspers, Frida Kahlo, Rudyard Kipling, Sean O'Casey, Joaquin Rodrigo, Charles Proteus Steinmetz, Henri Toulouse-Lautrec, Konstantin Tsiolkovsky, Carl Maria von Weber, and Stevie Wonder. Or, the disability will take the form of chronic illness in childhood or adolescence. Other times the adversity pertains more to the family circumstances. An example is the tendency for eminent personalities to come from homes that have experienced economic reversals or changes of fortune, even to the point of bankruptcy or impoverishment.

But the type of adversity that has attracted the most scientific research is early parental loss or orphanhood. This literature has found a tendency for geniuses of all kinds to have experienced the death of one or both parents at an early age. Table 4.1 provides some examples. Of course, without an adequate baseline for comparison, lists such as those in table 4.1 prove nothing. Nonetheless, several investigators have found the incidence rates of parental losses to be noticeably higher than what holds for the general population. Thus, one ambitious study of 699 eminent figures of world history discovered that 61% lost a parent before age 31, 52% before 26, and 45% before 21. Another study of 301 geniuses found that over one-fifth were plagued by orphanhood. A follow-up investigation, also based on famous people from all areas of accomplishment, discovered that nearly one-third had lost their fathers early on.

The orphanhood effect has been documented on more narrowly defined samples, too. Studies of large samples of scientists, for example, suggest that the incidence of orphanhood is indeed high; in one sample of 64 great scientists, 15% had lost a parent before age 10. Among eminent mathematicians, the percentages may be higher still: one-quarter had lost a parent before age 10 and nearly one-third before age 14. The results for creative writers are even more dramatic, for 55% were found to have lost a parent before age 15. Finally, an inquiry into British prime ministers found rates of parental loss of nearly 63%, a percentage far higher than any reasonable comparison group, such as those contemporaries who were English peers.

The effects of parental loss seems verifiable enough to have inspired investigators to propose explanations for how such traumatic events might contribute to the development of genius. Three environmentalist hypotheses are perhaps the most prominent. First, the trauma of parental loss produces a so-called bereavement syndrome, in which acts of achievement serve as emotional compensation. Second, such adverse events nurture the development of a personality robust enough to overcome the many obsta-

Table 4.1 INSTANCES OF PARENTAL LOSS IN
THE LIVES OF CREATIVE GENIUSES

Lost One or Both Parents in First Decade
Scientists: d'Alembert, I. Barrow, Berzelius, Boerhaave, Boyle, W. Bragg, Buffon, Carver, Cavendish, Copernicus, C. Darwin, Eddington, Flamsteed, A. Fleming, Fourier, Fulton, Haber, Haller, Helmont, Humboldt, J. Hutton, Huygens, Jenner, Kelvin, Kolmogorov, Kummer, Laënnec, Lavoisier, Lobachevski, Maxwell, Newton, Paracelsus, Pascal, Priestley, Quètelet, J. Rennie, Count Rumford, W. Smith, Steinmetz, Steno, Telford, Volta, C. T. R. Wilson; *Thinkers*: W. Blackstone, Confucius, Descartes, Hobbes, Hume, Leibniz, G. Marcel, Mencius, Montesquieu, Nietzsche, Rousseau, B. Russell, Shankara, P. Sarpi, Sartre, Shinran, Spinoza, Swedenborg, Voltaire; *Writers*: Baudelaire, Brontë sisters, Byron, Camus, Coleridge, Conrad, A. Cowley, W. Cowper, Dante, DeQuincey, Donne, Dumas *père*, Emerson, E. M. Forster, Gibbon, M. Gorky, brothers Grimm, Hawthorne, Hölderlin, Hu Shih, Ben Jonson, Keats, Lermontov, E. B. Lytton, Mallarmé, Maugham, G. Meredith, Molière, Montagu, Montaigne, Neruda, Poe, Propertius, Racine, Sainte-Beuve, Solzhenitsyn, Steele, Stendhal, Sterne, Swift, Thackeray, Tolstoy, Villon, Wordsworth, Zola; *Artists*: Canova, Delacroix, Diaghilev, D. W. Griffith, Fra Lippi, Masaccio, Michelangelo, Munch, Murillo, Raphael, S. Ray, Rubens; *Composers*: J. S. Bach, Corelli, Puccini, Scriabin, Sibelius, Wagner.

Lost One or Both Parents in Second Decade
Scientists: N. Abel, Ampère, J. Bruner, M. Curie, H. Davy, Durkheim, Galois, J. Gibbs, W. R. Hamilton, J. Henry, Hooke, Humboldt, Joule, A. Keith, Lamarck, Leeuwenhoek, Malinowski, Mendeleuev, Newcomb, B. Silliman, J. J. Thomson, Tsiolkovsky, An Wang, J. Watt, Weierstrass, E. Whitney, W. Wundt; *Thinkers*: Thomas Aquinas, Aristotle, Augustine, F. Bacon, Comenius, Croce, Erasmus, Frege, Hegel, Ibn Khaldún, Kant, Melanchthon, R. Niebuhr, Origin, Santayana, Schleiermacher, Schopenhauer, Zhu Xi; *Writers*: H. C. Andersen, Ariosto, Bellow, Bunyan, Calderón, Chateaubriand, J. F. Cooper, Dostoyevsky, Dreiser, G. Eliot, H. Fielding, Frost, Gide, Goldsmith, L. Hearn, Hugo, Malamud, Mann, Melville, Petrarch, Plutarch, D. Richardson, R. Sheridan, T. Tasso, Turgenev, Mark Twain, Vega Carpio, H. Walpole; *Artists*: Caravaggio, Claude Lorraine, J. L. David, Degas, Hiroshige, Spike Lee, Magritte, Whistler; *Composers*: Beethoven, Bruckner, F. Couperin, Handel, Liszt, Mussorgsky, Schoenberg, Schubert, Schumann, Tchaikovsky, von Weber.

cles and frustrations standing in the path of achievement. Third, parental loss and other forms of extreme adversity may set a young talent along a developmental trajectory that diverges from the conventional.

Each of these three interpretations has certain explanatory advantages and disadvantages. The bereavement-syndrome hypothesis has the asset of explaining the motivation for exceptional achievement in the first place. The robust-personality hypothesis, in contrast, presumes the existence of such a drive and concentrates instead on the essential role that persistence and determination play in the final realization of talent. The divergent-development hypothesis, finally, focuses on the notion that a highly traditional upbringing may encourage the growth of a conformist disposition, and thus ultimately thwart true innovation. All three accounts allow for creative genius as well as exceptional achievement in other domains, such as political leadership. All three can also incorporate various forms of adversity besides parental loss as part of the developmental process. And last, all three hypotheses allow for the possibility that the effects of early adversity might be too extreme, nipping the talent in the bud. This provision is crucial. Because juvenile delinquents and depressive or suicidal psychiatric patients may exhibit orphanhood rates similar to those of the eminent, it is clear that adversity can backfire. As one investigator noted, parental loss "can be an impetus for creative effort, a force for good, or it can have the effect of stunting personality growth and producing the concomitant antisocial acts, destruction of social relationships, and even the taking of one's own life."

From the standpoint of a Darwinian creativity theory, the divergent-development hypothesis may have the most explanatory power. One problem with the other two hypotheses is that they assume that the young talent is dramatically affected by the supposedly traumatic event. Yet in many cases this seems not to be the case. For example, Sir Isaac Newton's father died three months before his birth. Hence, young Newton could suffer no bereavement nor feel that he had some life challenge to overcome. Even when the timing seems more likely to produce effects, the expected trauma may not appear. For instance, although Darwin's autobiographical recollections go back to when he was four years old, his memory about his own encounter with parental loss was quite thin and cold. "My mother died . . . when I was a little over eight years old, and it is odd that I can remember hardly anything about her except her deathbed, her black velvet gown, and her curiously constructed work-table."

In comparison, the divergent-development interpretation does not presume that the effects of adversity are so sensational. Indeed, rather than one big trauma, a large number of rather small events might accomplish the same end, which is to set the talent on a developmental path that sets him or her apart from the rest of the crowd. So neither Newton nor Darwin needed to have felt the deaths of their parents in order to have experienced the consequences of being thrust along a divergent growth trajectory. In addition, this third hypothesis can more easily account for the fact that the incidence rates for trauma and adversity tend to vary according to the domain of creative achievement. Because various domains differ widely regarding the amount of Darwinian creativity they require, this variation should correspond to the extent to which talent development diverges from the norm. If artistic creativity is more Darwinian than scientific creativity, then development should be more divergent for the artists than for the scientists. This theoretical expectation is vindicated by research. For instance, the incidence of orphanhood for recipients of the Nobel Prize for literature is over eight times higher than that for winners of the Nobel Prize for physics.

The above points do not prove that the bereavement-syndrome and robust-personality hypotheses are completely wrong. It may even be that all three developmental processes work together in the nurturance of creative talent, the specific role of each varying from person to person according to the circumstances. Nonetheless, of the three explanations, the divergent-development hypothesis may have the greatest consistency with a Darwinian conception of the emergence of creative genius.

Education. Terman's intellectually gifted children were, if nothing else, highly accomplished students. Already in elementary school they were well in advance of their peers in academic achievement, and they continued to demonstrate scholastic prowess throughout their student years. Besides getting excellent grades and earning special honors, they attained high levels of formal education, including more than their share of doctorates and professional degrees. Terman's children not only did very well in school, but genuinely enjoyed school besides. It was the one place in their life where their talents could really shine. But if they were so proficient in school, college, and university, why didn't they achieve ever more successes once they launched their adulthood careers? Why doesn't graduating summa cum laude necessarily predict the later receipt of a Nobel Prize?

One Nobel laureate may have provided the beginning of the answer to this mystery. Albert Einstein once complained that "it is, in fact, nothing short of a miracle that the modern methods of instruction have not yet entirely strangled the holy curiosity of inquiry; for this delicate little plant, aside from stimulation, stands mostly in the need of freedom; without this it goes to wreck and ruin without fail. It is a very grave mistake to think that the enjoyment of seeing and searching can be promoted by means of coercion and a sense of duty." The tests that plague the school year were singled out for special condemnation. "One had to cram all this stuff into one's mind for the examinations, whether one liked it or not. This coercion had such a deterring effect on me that, after I passed the final examination, I found the consideration of any scientific problems distasteful to me for an entire year." Given Einstein's negative attitudes, his teachers were astonished when he became famous for his creative contributions to mathematical physics. For example, one university professor, Hermann Minkowski, admitted that his former pupil's achievements "came as a tremendous surprise . . . for in his student days Einstein had been a lazy dog. He never bothered about mathematics at all."

Nor would Darwin have disagreed with Einstein's negative opinions about school, as is evident from reading his autobiography. To provide but one illustration, Darwin complained that "during my second year at Edinburgh I attended Jameson's lectures on Geology and Zoology, but they were incredibly dull. The sole effect they produced on me was the determination never as long as I lived to read a book on Geology, or in any way to study the science." Fortunately, Darwin eventually overcame his repugnance: Had he not taken Lyell's *Principles of Geology* along with him on the *Beagle*, it is questionable whether he would have reached his insights about the origin of species.

But we have to be careful about condemning formal education on the basis of these personal testimonials. After all, many eminent creators were quite excellent students. Marie Sklodowska, later to assume the surname Curie, was two years ahead of her elementary school classmates in all subjects. She received a special gold medal when she graduated from the Russian lycée at age 16. Sigmund Freud was at the head of his class at the gymnasium, and graduated summa cum laude. J. Robert Oppenheimer graduated summa cum laude from Harvard with the highest honors ever awarded. So rather than play anecdote against anecdote, let us consider the following three empirical findings:

1. While the quality of scholastic performance may be modestly correlated with adulthood success in some domains, it bears no relation with achievement in other domains, especially in those areas requiring creativity. For example, one investigator scrutinized the undergraduate records of those elected as Fellows of the Royal Society. The academic performance of an FRS was usually undistinguished, and decidedly no better than a comparison group of scientists who were not so honored. Inquiries that examine a broader range of domains allow us to generalize this conclusion. Singular creativity may not correspond to earning high marks in school and college. This lack of correspondence between scholastic performance and creative achievement is particularly conspicuous in artistic creativity. Although D. H. Lawrence would eventually become a lauded British writer, in his secondary school composition class he ranked only 13th out of the 21 who took the course. Artistic creators are also more likely to have much more negative attitudes about their educational experiences in comparison with scientific creators.

2. Creative genius is not necessarily associated with attaining high levels of formal education. Certainly many great scientists—Newton and Darwin among them—managed to attain fame with no more than a bachelor's

degree, and many others—most notably Faraday—never even went to college. The irrelevance of advanced degrees in artistic endeavors is even more conspicuous. In the domain of creative writing, for example, Vera Brittain warned: "The idea that it is necessary to go to a university in order to become a successful writer, or even a man or woman of letters (which is by no means the same thing), is one of those phantasies that surround authorship." Indeed, empirical research has often found that achieved eminence as a creator is a curvilinear, inverted-U function of the level of formal education. That is, formal education first increases the probability of attaining creative success, but after an optimum point, additional formal education may actually lower the odds. The location of this peak varies according to the specific type of creativity. In particular, for creators in the arts and humanities, the optimum is reached in the last two years of undergraduate instruction, whereas for scientific creators the optimum may be delayed until the first couple of years of graduate school.

3. Although formal education thus seems to bear an ambivalent relationship to the development of creative talent, it must be stressed that those who later attained status as creators almost invariably engaged in the arduous process of self-education. Darwin disliked school and was quite content to be a mediocre student at the university; yet he was also deeply committed to self-education through extensive reading, scientific explorations of the English countryside, and conversations with established scientists. "I consider that all that I have learned of any value has been self-taught," Darwin once told his cousin Galton. In fact, one of the reasons creative talents often dislike school is that it can seem to interfere with their learning what they really want to know. When faced with the choice of reading a good book or studying for an exam, the extracurricular but still instructive diversion may win out. "I have never let my schooling interfere with my education," said Mark Twain. As should be of no surprise, one of the prime predictors of success in adulthood is being an omnivorous reader.

The foregoing empirical findings seem quite in line with the requirements of Darwinian creativity. To become a creative genius requires the acquisition of a certain minimum amount of knowledge and technique in the chosen domain. Therefore, *some* amount of formal training will certainly be helpful in talent development. Yet when taken to extremes, formal education can undermine the capacity for generating ideational variations. To obtain high marks in school often requires a high degree of conformity to conventional ways of looking at the world and people. Moreover, the increased specialization that becomes so conspicuous at higher levels of formal education can excessively narrow the range of perspectives that a person is able to entertain. Essentially, as the student progresses through the sequence of ever-higher degrees, the range of subjects, issues, theories, and techniques becomes ever more restricted. Such restriction will tend to confine the number and diversity of ideational variations that the individual can conceive. Hence, self-education may have the critical function of maintaining the necessary breadth in the face of the narrowing tendencies of formal education.

From a Darwinian perspective, moreover, it is telling that the development of scientific talent seems to be more intimately connected with academic training than is the development of artistic talent. As already observed many times, artistic creativity tends to lean more heavily on the blind-variation process than does scientific creativity, and thus the ill effects of formal education are more serious for artists than for scientists. However, the same theoretical argument would oblige us to make distinctions among artists and among scientists according to the degree to which the creative process is Darwinian. Hence, revolutionary scientists should tend to exhibit less academic success and accomplishment than normal scientists. Although no empirical study has looked at this possibility directly, there certainly seems to be ample anecdotal evidence on behalf of this conjecture.

Einstein, for example, earned his Ph.D. while working full-time at the Swiss patent office, and thus he could be said to have had no graduate education at all. Curiously, he earned his doctorate by submitting the least important of the papers he had finished in 1905. In contrast, the other papers—on Brownian motion, the photoelectric effect, and the special theory of relativity—he used to ensure his status as a scientific genius. Obviously, the pursuit of a Ph.D. was a mere sideshow in the development of his creative talent. Indeed, when Einstein first encountered difficulties getting the University of Zurich to approve the original version of his dissertation, his response was, "I shall not become a Ph.D. . . . . The whole comedy has become a bore to me." Happily, the complaint was that the paper was too short. So he played the cynical minimalist, added but one sentence, resubmitted the thesis, and became Dr. Einstein.

Marginality. There is one more peculiarity about Terman's sample of 1,500 gifted children that may help explain why so few attained the status of creative genius. The children came predominantly from majority-culture backgrounds. That is, they were overwhelmingly native-born, English-speaking, white, Anglo-Saxon, and Protestant. Yet this hegemony of the majority seems to run counter to the often-expressed view that creativity may be nurtured by the experience of being a "marginal" person. The sociologist Robert Park, for example, emphasized the significant place immigrants may have in cultural innovation: "One of the consequences of migration is to create a situation in which the same individual . . . finds himself striving to live in two diverse cultural groups." Consequently, "the 'cake of custom' is broken and the individual is freed for new enterprises and new associations." In a compatible vein, the historian Arnold Toynbee spoke of the "creative minority" who further human progress by their "withdrawal and return" relative to the majority culture.

The relevance of ethnic marginality in the development of talent to a Darwinian theory of creativity was made explicit by Donald Campbell. In his classic paper presenting his variation-selection model, he claimed that "persons who have been uprooted from traditional culture, or who have been thoroughly exposed to two or more cultures, seem to have an advantage in the range of hypotheses they are apt to consider, and through this means, in the frequency of creative innovation." The marginal person should display more associative richness, divergent thinking, and other cognitive processes that provide the foundation of ideational variations.

There exists some evidence, in fact, that ethnic marginality may make some contribution to the development of talent. For example, one study of eminent contemporaries found that around 19% were either first- or second-generation immigrants. In the United States alone, newcomers accounted for 44% of the eminent Americans. Indeed, their representation was seven times higher than of those Americans descended from families that had resided in the United States since shortly after the Revolution if not before.

But perhaps the history of the Jews in Western civilization provides the best-known illustration. One study in the 1970s found that although Jews made up only between 1% and 3% of the world's population, their presence in the lists of eminent creators exceeds statistical expectation by a factor of 10 or more. This distinction holds especially for such areas of creativity as mathematics, physics, chemistry, medicine, and economics. In fact, almost one out of five Nobel Prize recipients had come from Jewish backgrounds. This phenomenon probably has many sources, including the superior family environment often found in Jewish homes. Nevertheless, not the least of the developmental factors is the marginal position Jews have in Western culture. They are a Near Eastern people transplanted to a European culture, enabling them to bring the novel insights of the ethnic outsider. Moreover, Western Jews often exhibit high rates of bilingualism, frequently combining some European tongue with either Hebrew or Yiddish or both. Research has shown that intensive exposure to two or more different languages helps build the cognitive basis for creativity. After all, concepts will be coded in multiple ways, enriching the associative interconnections among various ideas. The process operating here is not unlike the possible role of hybridization in the generation of new biological species.

Although the emphasis of much of the empirical research has been on ethnic marginality, other forms of marginalization may also have a beneficial impact on talent development. Another possibility is religious marginality. In Great Britain, for example, many famous scientists and inventors did not belong to the established Church of England. Rather, they subscribed to one of the dissenting faiths. Joseph Priestley was a Nonconformist minister, John Dalton a Quaker, Michael Faraday a Sandemanian. Likewise in the United States, the per capita representation of Unitarians among notable scientists is well over 100 times greater than that of Methodists, Baptists, and Roman Catholics—the churches with the biggest memberships.

Finally, also of relevance is professional marginality. Arthur Koestler claimed in his *Act of Creation* that "all decisive advances in the history of scientific thought can be described in terms of mental cross-fertilization between different disciplines." Similarly, F. C. Bartlett, the cognitive psychologist, held that "it has often happened that critical stages for advance are reached when what has been called one body of knowledge can be brought into close and effective relationship with what has been treated as a different, and largely or wholly independent, scientific discipline." Such cross-fertilization of scientific domains is more likely to emerge from those who have switched fields. In fact, Thomas Kuhn, the historian of science, maintained that "almost always the men who achieve . . . fundamental inventions of a new paradigm have been either very young or very new to the field whose paradigm they change. . . . [T]hese are the men who, being little committed by prior practice to the traditional rules of normal science, are particularly likely to see that these rules no longer define a playable game and to conceive another set that can replace them." In support of these claims, one empirical study showed that the innovators in X-ray astronomy were likely to have been from fields marginal to the astronomical profession. A second investigation found a similar marginality effect concerning Alfred Wegener's theory of continental drift. In particular, the theory's opponents were usually well published in mainstream geology, whereas the main advocates often hailed from scientific disciplines outside the geosciences.

Because Darwin himself could be considered a professional outsider, these findings may help us appreciate the basis for his own scientific breakthroughs. Even so, from a Darwinian perspective, professional marginality has two features that distinguish its operation from ethnic marginality.

First, most of the cases of innovations by professional outsiders seem to involve the scientific enterprise. To be sure, examples can be given in the arts—such as the invention of mobiles by Calder, who had some training in engineering. Nonetheless, marginality of this kind seems to play a relatively minor role in the arts. The reason may be that scientists, unlike artists, tend to impose rather severe constraints on the production of ideational variants. Sometimes these a priori restrictions exclude the consideration of the very ideas that might have a reasonable chance of generating a solution to some enigma. Hence, it may require a total outsider to introduce a novel set of considerations. For example, paleontologists had grappled with the extinction of the dinosaurs ever since these behemoths first became apparent in the fossil record. However varied the speculations, the hypotheses stayed bound to terrestrial processes, such as climate changes or competition from early mammals. It took a nuclear physicist, Luis Alvarez, to propose that a 10-kilometer-wide asteroid, striking the earth at the end of the Cretaceous period, precipitated the catastrophic events that wiped out the dinosaurs.

Second, although ethnic marginality may be associated with highly prolific creators, professional marginality often seems linked to creators who had only one noteworthy idea. This difference may reflect a fundamental contrast in the developmental implications of these two forms of marginality. On the one hand, it is easy to conceive how early exposure to different cultures and languages might enhance the capacity for remote association and divergent thinking. On the other hand, the professional outsider may be doing nothing more than transplanting some established concept or technique from one discipline to another. If this is the case, then, as mentioned in the previous chapter, it is not essential that the outsider be engaged in generating ideational variations.

Even so, in this latter case we may still speak of creativity as being Darwinian, albeit at a different level of analysis. Instead of thinking in terms of a single mind producing blind variations of ideas, we can interpret the phenomenon in terms of a whole society producing blind variations of individuals. In other words, in any culture with sufficient occupational mobility, a certain number of people will be engaged in career changes. These changes may combine the expertise of different professions in a number of ways. A small proportion of these two-career individuals will be fortunate to have entered a field in which knowledge from their first career will contribute to their creative success in their second career.

Many others will not be so lucky. I say "lucky" because to a great extent the career switches may be blind, thus making the multiple-career combinations truly Darwinian at the individual level of analysis. Although most people do not change professions without the expectation of success in their next career, for some creators the choice may be wrong. Rather than a positive transfer of knowledge and expertise from one domain to another, the transfer may prove negative. The story of the German chemist Justus Liebig provides a needed antidote to enthusiasm over the potential fruitfulness of career changes. Liebig's creative achievements in pure organic chemistry earned him such acclaim that he was created a Baron. Yet when he later moved into applied agricultural chemistry, the results were extremely disappointing. Because his chemical fertilizers were based on false conceptions about plant nutrition, they failed miserably. Of course, Liebig would not have changed fields had he been able to anticipate the outcome. But his career switch was blind to its true prospects.

On the other hand, the story of another career change proves that the blindness can occur in the inverse direction. A person can change fields with no expectation of success and be proven wrong. When in the 1860s the French silk industry was being destroyed by some mysterious ailment, the chemist Dumas urged his former pupil Pasteur to work on the problem. The latter protested, "But I never worked with silkworms"; Dumas returned with the strange reassurance, "So much the better." Although the practical problem that Pasteur took on was much further removed from his field of expertise than was the case for Liebig, and despite the fact that Pasteur had much lower initial expectations of succeeding, it was Pasteur, not Liebig, who provided an example of successful professional marginality. Thus, Pasteur's career change was just as blind as Liebig's, but the Pasteur variant proved to have more adaptive fitness from the standpoint of the society at large.

Hereditarianism

The picture looks pretty bleak for the doctrine that genius is born and not made. A large number of environmental factors seem to nurture the cognitive and dispositional attributes required for Darwinian creativity. In particular, early experiences at home and school may facilitate the development of the capacity for generating ideational variations, and even instill the motivation and persistence necessary to exploit that capacity. Even Galton's family pedigrees might be explained away as evidence of nurture rather than nature. As will be discussed in chapter 6, creative potential also seems to be fostered by exposure to role models and mentors within one's chosen domain of creative activity. Therefore, achievement could run along certain family lines simply because of the greater availability of such environmental influences. Is it really necessary to explain the origins of the creative achievements of George, Francis, Leonard, and Horace Darwin when they all were exposed daily to a father who could serve as their model scientist and even scientific mentor?

Although Galton's hereditarianism appears defeated, Galton himself set the stage for a revival of a genetic theory of genius. He pioneered several techniques that would grow to become critical methods in the field of behavior genetics, including the use of twins to gauge the impact of heredity on individual differences. Let us begin by reviewing some of the key findings of this research, and then we can examine the implications for understanding the origins of genius.

Modern behavioral genetics. A great deal can be learned about human heredity by looking at twins. As is well known, twins come in two basic types, dizygotic (fraternal) and monozygotic (identical). The first share virtually identical environments but are no more similar genetically than other full siblings. The latter, in contrast, are genetically indistinguishable. To the extent that certain individual differences are genetically transferred, then, monozygotic twins should be much more similar than dizygotic twins. In fact, for a large inventory of cognitive and personality traits, monozygotic twins are extremely alike, whereas dizygotic twins are no more similar than other siblings. Particularly provocative are the results of studies examining monozygotic twins who were separated at infancy and raised in separate homes. These reared-apart identical twins share virtually no characteristics with their foster parents and siblings yet retain a supreme level of similarity to each other. Indeed, as these twins get older, and especially after they leave their foster homes, the resemblances increase, even when they have had no contact whatsoever with one another. Moreover, the genetically endowed similarities persist until old age. These solid findings prove that a substantial portion of a person's psychological constitution is determined by the genes received at the moment of conception. To be sure, the specific heredity coefficients vary from trait to trait. For cognitive characteristics, the degree of inheritance can be quite high, whereas for complex personality traits, such as religiosity, the genetic influence is lower. Yet somewhere between one-third and two-thirds of who we are seems attributable to our genetic endowment.

This remarkable but secure conclusion is joined by a second finding that is no less striking. Behavior geneticists have scrutinized the contributions made by environmental factors, taking special care to distinguish two kinds of such influences—the shared versus the nonshared. The shared environment is what all siblings experienced together because they all grew up in the same home with the same parents. The nonshared environment, on the other hand, is what is unique to each sibling. An excellent example is birth order: Only the firstborn has solely younger siblings, only the last-born has solely older siblings, and only the middle children have siblings both younger and older. The empirical research has convincingly demonstrated that for a great variety of individual-difference variables, it is the nonshared environment, not the shared, that is responsible for whatever cannot be attributed to heredity. It is for this reason that siblings turn out so different even when parents make every effort to raise all their children the same way. Cognitive and personality development is usually more contingent on what siblings do *not* have in common than on what siblings *do* share. The ineffectiveness of the shared environment also explains why identical twins reared apart are so similar to each other even when brought up in foster homes that feature quite contrasting life experiences and parenting styles.

In fact, some behavior geneticists have argued that parents play a very minimal role in the development of their children. Various socialization practices will simply have no consistent effect on how their children turn out. Because of the impact of the genes and the nonshared environment, a parenting technique that works well on one child might backfire on another. Only if the parents carefully tailor their interactions to meet the unique needs of each child can they hope to exert any developmental influence at all. Indeed, often it may be more appropriate to speak of children raising their parents than the other way around. For example, children may request toys and games that are consistent with their innate interests and talents and ignore gifts that they find boring despite encouragement given by well-meaning parents. Children try to shape their environment to comply with their inborn needs.

One final empirical lesson of behavior genetics deserves mention: On certain characteristics monozygotic twins are *too* similar relative to dizygotic twins. That is, a trait that shows practically no heritability in fraternal twins and other siblings might exhibit extremely high heritability for identical twins. This will happen when the trait in question requires the simultaneous presence of several separate traits, each of which is inherited independently. If one monozygotic twin inherits the entire collection, its twin will obviously do so as well. But it is extremely unlikely that two siblings originating from different zygotes would inherit all the requisite traits together.

David Lykken, a leading behavior geneticist, gave the example of "social potency." This trait involves "the self-perceived ability to influence, lead, or dominate others." Monozygotic twins, whether reared apart or together, closely match on this trait. Yet dizygotic twins are no more alike than any two randomly selected people from the population. Lykken speculated that this characteristic is not only polygenetic but in addition may require all the genes to participate if the trait is to appear at all. In particular, social potency "probably depends on some configuration of attractiveness, self-confidence, assertiveness, dominance—whatever the ingredients are of 'charisma.'" If one component is lacking, social potency cannot emerge as a character trait.

So distinctive is this form of inheritance that it has been given a special name: *emergenesis*. An individual-difference variable is emergenic when it consists of multiple genetic components, all of which must be inherited for the main character to appear at all. The confluence of these diverse but well-defined traits is what underlies a new, more comprehensive, emergent trait. The genotypic whole is greater than the mere sum of its genetic parts.

Genetic origins of genius. The preceding general conclusions, although derived from studies of everyday populations, have profound implications for our understanding of talent development. Most obviously, behavior genetics provides a firm basis for arguing that at least a portion of creative talent may indeed be innate. Presumably, talent in a particular domain depends on the possession of a particular set of cognitive abilities, interests, motives, and dispositions. To the degree that these are genetically endowed, it can be affirmed that the resulting talent is correspondingly inherited. Admittedly, some components of the required profile may have very low heritability, and thus these facets of genius may have to be nurtured by the environment. Nonetheless, it is likely that environmental nurturance can only go so far. If a person fails to inherit certain traits crucial to creative behavior—such as a sufficiently high intelligence—it is most improbable that even the most advantageous environment will succeed in making up the difference. Thus, genetic endowment may provide the necessary even if not sufficient conditions for the emergence of genius.

The behavior genetics research undermines the environmentalist position in yet another manner. A large hunk of the research on the childhood and adolescent antecedents of adulthood creativity assumes that shared environment has a powerful developmental impact. But if shared circumstances have minimal impact for most of the traits that define creative talent, all of this research may provide no support whatsoever for the nurture position. On the contrary, this environmentalist research may actually endorse the hereditarian view. After all, many in behavior genetics argue that several so-called environmental factors are more correctly placed in the column of genetic factors. This inversion of attribution can occur in two major ways:

First, because parents and children share genes in common, the parental genotype will result in a phenotype that will seem to influence the child's phenotype even though the latter is more accurately said to be a function of its own genotype, which is itself a direct function of the parental genotype. A concrete example will make this more clear. It may be that people who inherit a high degree of information-processing capacity—or native intelligence—will have a tremendous need for intellectual and cultural stimulation. They will accordingly buy books, subscribe to magazines, visit museums and galleries, engage in diverse hobbies, and do whatever else they need to maintain a mentally active life. Of course, they will also tend to choose mates who will closely match them in intellectual ability as well. Consequently, when individuals enjoying high natural ability decide to have children, they will more likely have offspring who will display a comparable need for intellectual and cultural stimulation. These progeny will take advantage of the opportunities available in the home. The environmentalist researcher then looks at this pattern and falsely concludes that it was the enriched environment that the parents offered their children which stimulated the latter's intellectual growth. This conclusion is false because it assumes that it was the home environment that produced their children's phenotype. Instead, the intellectual aptitude acquired by the progeny may reflect more strongly the underlying genotype, which just so happens to correlate strongly with the parental genotype with respect to native intelligence. Indeed, if the parents had not provided opportunities in the home for the desired stimulation, the children would probably seek out stimulation elsewhere—in the homes of friends, at school, at the public library, and so forth.

Second, a child with certain inborn talents may soon put pressure on the environment to make it conform more closely to feed those talents. Parents with sufficient resources will often respond accordingly, thereby producing an environment that conforms ever more closely to the child's gifts. To the outside observer it may appear as if the environment is influencing the child's development, but instead it is the child's genetic disposition that is influencing the home circumstances. The research literature on child prodigies is replete with examples of future geniuses who insist on pursuing specific enthusiasms even in the face of parental discouragement. A classic example is Blaise Pascal. Because his father wanted his son to learn Latin and Greek before undertaking mathematics, he had all books on the latter subject removed and even refrained from mentioning the subject as much as possible. However, with what little mathematical knowledge Blaise possessed, he was able to devise his own version of Euclidean geometry, inventing his own terms and theorems. He was not yet 12 years old. When his father discovered his son's secret activities, he realized that Blaise had a rare gift, and he adopted a more receptive attitude toward its further development. His son's inherent talent had won the day. By the time Blaise was 16 he had produced an original work on conic sections that provoked the envy of René Descartes, 27 years his senior. And by 19 Blaise Pascal had invented a calculating machine. Even greater scientific and mathematical achievements lay before him.

These two illustrations concerned the intellectual and cultural opportunities available in the home environment. An advocate of environmentalism might argue that the hereditarian viewpoint would have a hard time accounting for other developmental factors that seem obviously to involve nurture rather than nature. What about the developmental impact of early trauma and adversity, education, or marginality? How can these events possibly be ascribed to genetic endowment? Actually, a hypothetical connection can be conceived in every case. Take parental loss, for example. Parents who are more intelligent tend to delay reproduction until later in life, after their professional careers are established. In fact, data show that the parents of eminent personalities were older than is the norm when their illustrious progeny were born. Because the parents are much older, the odds will be greater that they might die when their offspring are in childhood or adolescence. The latter, of course, already inherited their parents' intellectual superiority, and so when they become more successful in life, their success may be falsely attributed to the traumatic experiences. I might add that although Darwin suffered parental loss at age eight, his mother was already in her 50s when she died, his parents having married in their mid-30s. Darwin himself put off family life until he had entered his 30s.

Similar arguments can be made to convert education and marginality into indicators of biological inheritance rather than determinants of development. In the first case, individuals with certain innate gifts may provide for those talents by purposively selecting the level and type of education most suitable for their cultivation. Hence, artistic talents may drop out of school sooner than scientific talents simply because the former discover much more quickly that fulfilling scholastic requirements has become irrelevant to the development of their gifts. In the case of ethnic marginality, a different process may be operating. For instance, it may be that those individuals who take the trouble to immigrate to a foreign land will tend to possess personal qualities that lead to success, such as intelligence, energy, motivation, and initiative. These advantageous traits are then passed down to their offspring. The causal basis is nature, but the superficial appearance is nurture. This was actually Galton's own explanation for any ethnic marginality effect.

I am not claiming that every putative environmental influence represents an exclusively genetic influence operating incognito. The claim is simply that it is not easy to tease out the relative contributions of nature and nurture. Developmental events and circumstances may not always be what they seem; what look like causes may actually be effects. An undetermined proportion of the so-called environmental determinants of talent development may be the mere consequences of underlying genetic processes. Doubts about the impact of nurture must be especially potent when the factors involve the shared rather than the nonshared environment. Although behavior genetics has identified some traits that are nourished by shared environmental influences, these are relatively rare, and none so far involve characteristics proven essential for creative genius. Consequently, we must be ever wary about claiming that certain home conditions encourage the emergence of creative talent.

However, we must be equally careful not to take the results of behavior genetics as endorsements of Galton's original hereditarianism. In some respects, contemporary research in behavior genetics has weakened that very theory as well. In particular, the phenomenon of emergenesis can undermine Galton's thesis that creative genius must run in family lineages.

If creativity consists of several critical components, all of which must be inherited before creativity can emerge, then it will be rather unlikely that creative genius can be passed down from parent to child. Nor will siblings exhibit any family resemblances in innate creative capacity—with the sole exception of monozygotic twins. Hence, creative giants may not necessarily arise from Galtonian pedigrees.

The concept of emergenesis is a relatively new idea in behavior genetics. Even so, there exists some empirical research suggesting that creativity may indeed constitute an emergenic trait. In addition, Lykken offered an interesting historical example—that of Carl Friedrich Gauss, the great mathematician. Gauss's father was a bricklayer, his mother a peasant, and Gauss's own son came nowhere close to matching his father's mathematical skills. Apparently, to become a Gauss requires a distinctive convergence of many abilities, interests, and values. If a single attribute is missing, you no longer have a Gauss. Curiously, Galton failed to discuss this discrepancy, and he even neglects to mention Gauss in *Hereditary Genius*. This omission is surprising, because Gauss had a telling influence on Galton's own work.

In fact, Galton's classic treatise contains other mysterious hints that emergenesis may account for the appearance of the most monumental genius. Many of the top-notch creative geniuses appear to have no family pedigree whatsoever. Consider the cases of Newton, Shakespeare, Beethoven, and Michelangelo. These four individuals epitomize the highest levels of creativity in the fields of science, literature, music, and art. Yet what sorts of pedigrees was Galton able to devise for such exalted geniuses? In the case of Newton, Galton devotes nearly two pages to discussing a highly speculative link with other relatives of far lesser distinction. Likewise, the best Galton could do for Shakespeare's pedigree is to dig up a lineage for Francis Bacon, a contemporary who some have unsuccessfully claimed to be the real author of the Bard's works. But Shakespeare himself has no pedigree. Beethoven created yet another anomaly for Galton's theory. Galton's only recourse was to repeat an old rumor that Beethoven was the illegitimate son of Frederick the Great of Prussia. Even if the rumor had foundation, it is hard to fathom how a merely competent flute player could provide the genetic foundation for Beethoven's immense musical powers. And with respect to Michelangelo's artistic lineage, Galton could find absolutely nothing at all. If height were inherited in the same fashion as these anomalous cases indicate, the tallest professional basketball players could have the shortest parents.

Emergenesis does more than merely create difficulties for Galton's simple genetic theory of talent development. It also introduces complications for understanding the evolution of creative genius from the perspective of primary Darwinism. In previous chapters I have tried to discern the selection pressures that might favor the appearance of genes for exceptional creativity. But if creativity is an emergenic trait consisting of a large number of independent traits that must be simultaneously present to produce a creative genius, then creativity can only undergo consistent selection when all the component genes exhibit a high degree of chromosomal linkage. If the traits are not easily inherited as a package—the most likely situation—then each of the separate genes making up the genotype of the creative genius must undergo its own individual evolution in the population. The greater the number of requisite genes, and the more varied the basis for reproductive fitness provided by those genes, the less the lucky conjunction of these genius-generating genes will be under the control of natural selection. In the extreme case, it might make little difference whether creative geniuses are at an advantage or a disadvantage in the struggle for existence. Darwin may have had seven children, and Galton zero, but this differential success may have had little impact on the relative frequencies of the various component traits in the gene pool.

This interpretation is consistent with Galton's contention that true genius is very rare. He estimated that only 1 out of every 4,000 individuals would qualify for this distinction—a very small percentage, roughly comparable to the proportion of people who would score 150 or higher on an IQ test. With only 0.025% having what it takes to be a genius, it hardly matters whether great creators are fertile or sterile. In comparison with the huge reservoir of genes available in the human population, the reproductive success of the creative genius would count for almost nothing. Hence, to the extent that exceptional creativity is highly emergenic, we need not even worry whether individual differences on this polygenetic characteristic are consistent with Darwin's theory of organic evolution. In a sense, Newton, Shakespeare, Beethoven, and Michelangelo were all freaks of nature. Such fortuitous freaks will always appear against heavy odds, regardless of their reproductive fitness.

Evolutionism

Earlier in this chapter I noted that Galton himself tried to reach an accommodation between the positions of nature and nurture. In the survey of eminent scientists presented in his 1874 *English Men of Science*, Galton went beyond the strictly genetic stance of his 1869 *Hereditary Genius*. In particular, he distributed a questionnaire among members of the Royal Society that asked them about various environmental circumstances that might have contributed to their scientific success. Among the conditions examined was birth order. Galton was, in fact, the first behavioral scientist to introduce this variable into research on talent development. Moreover, Galton reported the striking empirical finding that firstborns are overrepresented among illustrious scientists. This result is remarkable because the result seems contradicted by Galton's own family history, as well as by that of Charles Darwin. Galton was the last of nine children, Darwin the fifth of six. Yet Galton's own data indicate that he and his cousin had to rub shoulders primarily with firstborns.

Galton's finding has been replicated many times since 1874. For example, one study of 64 notable scientists found that fully 39 were firstborn, and another 13 were second-born. Furthermore, of the 25 who missed out on primacy of birth, 5 were oldest sons and 2 had an older sibling who had died in infancy or early childhood. Many of the rest were five or more years younger than their immediately older sibling. Typically, first borns represent 50% or more of the community of active scientists. The firstborns also surpass their later-born colleagues on various criteria of success. They are referred to more frequently in the scientific literature of their field. They receive higher creativity ratings at the hands of experts in their discipline. The firstborns even have a better chance of earning the Nobel Prize. Nor is this primogeniture effect restricted to science. In *A Study of British Genius* by Havelock Ellis, the same advantage was found for those who won an entry in *The Dictionary of National Biography*. Other studies demonstrated that the advantage holds for domains ranging from classical composers to politicans. One recent inquiry found that nearly half of all notable creators, leaders, and celebrities of the twentieth century were firstborn children.

Although the firstborn appears inevitably to come out on top, this is not always the case. Creative writers, for example, are more inclined to be later-born children, as are political revolutionaries. These exceptions would seem to cast into doubt any generalization about how birth order relates to creative genius. Yet this pessimistic conclusion would be very much mistaken. A child's ordinal placement in the family may have a powerful influence on personality development, including the nurturance of traits that determine creative behavior. As mentioned earlier, investigators in the area of behavior genetics have shown that the nonshared environment has much more impact on personality development than does the shared environment. And birth order constitutes nonshared environment par excellence.

Many researchers have tried to describe the developmental processes by which birth effects occur. But from the Darwinian perspective, the most provocative by far is the recent theory advanced by Frank Sulloway in his 1996 book *Born to Rebel: Birth Order, Family Dynamics, and Creative Lives.* What makes this theory so noteworthy is its explicit use of a Darwinian framework to explain why not everyone in Darwin's day was sympathetic to the doctrine of evolution by natural selection. In a sense, Sulloway used Darwinian concepts to explain the history of Darwinism. To pull off this feat, Sulloway was obliged to devise a complex theory that details how the development of creative talent is shaped by specific family circumstances, and especially by ordinal position.

Given that Sulloway required a hefty volume to expound and document his evolutionary theory, I do no more than provide a bare outline here. Again, the interested reader can always consult *Born to Rebel* to get a deeper understanding of this rich theory.

Openness and Birth Order

Frank Sulloway is a historian of science who has had a long fascination with Darwin and Darwinism. One fact about the early history of Darwin's theory greatly impressed him, namely that the *Origin of Species* provoked considerable controversy upon its publication, even among scientists. Ideally, the truth or falsity of a scientific idea is decided by fact and logic, but such rational considerations often played a minimal role in the case of Darwin's theory. Indeed, some of the most notable scientists of Darwin's time immediately blasted these newfangled ideas. These staunch opponents included Louis Agassiz, widely viewed as the greatest living naturalist; Adam Sedgwick, the distinguished geologist and Darwin's former teacher at Cambridge; and Pierre Flourens, the famous experimental physiologist and perpetual secretary of the French Academy of Sciences. To offer specifics, Agassiz branded Darwin's theory as "a scientific mistake, untrue in its facts, unscientific in its method, and mischievous in its tendency." Likewise, Sedgwick accused Darwin of deserting "the true method of induction," producing "a dish of rank materialism cleverly cooked and served up." And Flourens needed to write a whole book to inveigh against Darwin's *Origin*: "What metaphysical jargon clumsily hurled into natural history! What pretentious and empty language! What childish and out-of-date personifications!"

To be sure, Darwin's revolutionary theory had its early adherents as well. When T. H. Huxley first grasped the *Origin*'s core thesis, he at once propounded: "How extremely stupid not to have thought of that!" Even so, what struck Sulloway is how little the arguments focused on scientific issues per se. The controversy seemed more a conflict of personalities than of data or deduction. After scrutinizing more closely the participants in this vitriolic debate, Sulloway suggested that the differential response to Darwin's ideas may reflect individual differences in openness to experience. Those who have this openness are more favorably disposed to revolutionary ideas, whereas those who lack this openness are inclined to attack such ideas, doing what they can to conserve tradition or the status quo.

Given the impact of this personality trait, the next question is where individual differences in openness come from. How much of it is nature? How much nurture? Reviewing the behavioral genetic research regarding this character, Sulloway noted that around 30% or 40% of the variation may be ascribed to genetic endowment. Shared family environment accounts for an additional 5% of the individual differences. And, finally, the nonshared environment may explain seven times as much variance as the shared environment: fully 35%, or about as much as the genes. Sulloway then asked what aspect of the nonshared environment figures most prominently in the development of an open personality. After an extensive consideration of many possible influences, he concluded that birth order may represent the single most critical factor. The eldest children are more prone to identify strongly with parents and other authority figures. This identification with parental and societal authority is normally associated with being conforming and conventional, a tendency that makes the eldest children more disposed to be defensive about challenges to traditional ways of viewing the world. In short, the firstborn is less likely to exhibit openness to revolutionary ideas. Sulloway was thus led to the proposition that a scientist's ordinal position in the family may have been a significant developmental factor in determining who accepted and who rejected Darwin's theory.

In making this developmental connection, however, Sulloway was careful to distinguish between biological and functional birth order. The first category concerns the actual order that a child was brought into the world. Because of various extraneous circumstances, biological birth order has very little developmental interest. Siblings may die, and new siblings be adopted or acquired through remarriages. So what really matters is functional birth order, which pertains to what a person actually experienced growing up. If the firstborn sibling of a second-born child dies in infancy, the latter child becomes a functional firstborn. This distinction is crucial for using birth order to predict openness to scientific revolutions. Agassiz, for example, was biologically the fifth-born child of his parents (with three younger siblings). But none of his older siblings survived infancy, converting him into a functional firstborn.

If Sulloway had decided that biological birth order were more critical than functional birth order, then he would have to look for purely physiological causes for the effect of ordinal position. Perhaps he would have had to investigate the changes that might take place in the intrauterine environment in successive pregnancies. In contrast, the decision to focus on functional birth order located the causal process in the distinctive social environment occupied by each successive child. Given this locus, the issue is to discern the family dynamics underlying ordinal position. One of most brilliant aspects of Sulloway's theory is that he looks for those dynamics where many would least expect it—in the fundamental principles of Darwinian evolution.

Sibling Rivalries and Family Niches

Survival of the fittest—such is one of the cardinal concepts in Darwinian theory, primary or secondary. As Darwin deduced from the cruel realities of Malthusian population growth, not all offspring will survive to reproduce. Offspring without superior adaptive fitness will fail to make a contribution to the next generation's gene pool. We tend to conceive of the struggle for existence as taking place in the population of sexually mature adults. We conjure up images of adults competing for scarce food, shelter, and mates, some winning and others losing. Sometimes these images can include aggressive, even vicious and cruel behaviors—as in Tennyson's "Nature, red in tooth and claw"—but the struggle takes place among adults who have the wherewithal to contend on roughly equal ground. Yet the reality of evolution is that it sometimes inspires competition between the big and the small, the strong and the weak. And one place where this unequal contest can occur is the family.

To illustrate this point, Sulloway describes the phenomenon of siblicide. In the ovoviviparous sand shark, for example, the young engage in a life-or-death struggle in the usually protective confines of their mother's oviducts. The young eat each other until only one well-fed shark has emerged supreme. Albeit not nearly so dramatically, siblicide occurs frequently among birds as well. Typically, the eldest nestling, which is almost always the biggest and the strongest, will either peck a younger sibling until it bleeds to death or push it out of the nest to succumb to starvation or exposure. Almost always, the victim of this ugly competition is the youngest, the last of the brood to have hatched from its egg. In the more benign cases, this atrociously vicious form of sibling rivalry is only triggered when the eldest's body weight drops to a level that threatens its future fitness. In the more grim instances, the siblicide is inevitable. The parents produce a brood expecting only one to survive to maturity. The parental strategy apparently is to let "sibling selection" decide which of the offspring is most fit to compete in the world beyond the nest.

Although sibling rivalries certainly do not operate at this intensity among *Homo sapiens*, our species does exhibit more subtle forms. Each child must compete for parental attention and resources, and certain children have advantages over the others. The firstborn certainly has the biggest edge. The firstborn will have had the first shot at parental affection and investment, and will usually retain a privileged status so long as the child lives up to parental expectations. Furthermore, the firstborn will normally be more mature mentally and bigger physically relative to the later-born siblings. What firstborns cannot win by outsmarting the later-borns they can gain by physical intimidation. In a sense, the eldest have both brain and brawn on their side.

The firstborns are thus ensconced in a special family niche that their younger siblings can only envy. This means that later-borns must find some other niche that will allow them to win the parental involvement that they need for their own development. Trying to imitate what the eldest is doing will seldom gain the youngest much advantage. The eldest has already pre-empted the most privileged spot and will not take kindly to requests to share that position. Also, later-borns are not as able to act as a surrogate parent, which is typically part of the firstborn niche. Accordingly, the later-borns must employ some alternative strategy. According to Sulloway, the younger siblings must optimize their adaptive fitness by exhibiting Darwin's "principle of divergence." Just as competition forced Darwin's finches to find new ecological niches to exploit on the Galápagos Islands, so must the later-born siblings be willing to diversify, to depart from the mainstream norms. The later-borns must be open to alternative possibilities, new options. Moreover, the later in the birth sequence the children fall, the more likely that their older siblings will have filled up the more obvious niches. Hence, the later the child comes in ordinal position, the more intense the pressures to diversify, to be sensitive to novel opportunities, to do what no one else has done.

Before further detailing Sulloway's Darwinian argument, I must pause to highlight the interesting parallel between birth order's developmental progression and an analogous transition that occurs during creative problem solving. Back in chapter 2 I noted how when individuals first encounter a particular problem, they determine whether the problem has a straightforward solution. Perhaps there is some easy algorithm that will dispatch the problem in an eye blink. If not, people will rummage around through a collection of heuristics that can help narrow the range of the search to settle on a solution. If even that approach fails, the problem solver may have to regress into primary-process thinking, into trial and error, into remote association and divergent thinking. As one attempted solution after another falls by the wayside, future attempts become ever more haphazard, ever more desperate, ever less justified, increasingly divergent. In a word, repeated failures force the adoption of increasingly *blind* ideational variations.

Sulloway essentially affirms that an analogous process occurs in development. The most obvious adaptive strategy for a child is to live up to parental expectations and to act as a surrogate parent. The child should identify with the parents, conform to their norms and values—do everything possible to become a "chip off the old block." This rule is so obvious as to be almost algorithmic. But if the firstborn has already claimed this family niche, the second-born must identify some other, less obvious and less conventional niche. Yet as each successive child enters the increasingly crowded family ecology, the fewer customary and conforming roles remain. The later-borns have no other option but to diverge ever more, to become increasingly unpredictable in their developmental trajectories. In short, the later-born siblings must engage in ever more blind behavioral variations to maximize adaptive fitness.

This trend toward ever more Darwinian development can help us explain the most important features about the relationship between birth order and achievement, both everyday and exceptional. Firstborns are more likely to do well in school, just as parents expect. In fact, the gifted children in Terman's longitudinal study were predominantly the eldest. And just like these children, firstborns are more likely to get higher degrees and to become professionals, such as doctors, lawyers, and college professors. The firstborns thus make their parents, relatives, and teachers proud. The best of these firstborns, moreover, advance to become presidents of the United States or Nobel Prize-winning scientists. Meanwhile, their younger siblings struggle to find a niche by aspiring to unconventional, high-risk, and often radical careers. The later-borns are overrepresented among those who participate in physically dangerous sports, for example. Of course, the least successful among them may lose out in the competition, eventually descending to the ranks of alcoholics or the homeless. However, the most successful will become revolutionaries who overthrow the tyranny of their oldest siblings or bohemian artists who defy all social and aesthetic norms. If they cannot find a secure niche in the home and in polite society, they will discover a place in anarchist politics or avant-garde culture. The later-borns, thus, exhibit more Darwinian variability in their career paths.

Revolutionaries and Reactionaries

Sulloway did far more than offer unconstrained speculation about the relationship between birth order and receptiveness to revolutionary ideas. To test his developmental theory, he applied quantitative techniques to "121 historical events, which encompass data on 6,566 participants. These 121 events include 28 revolutions in science, 61 reform movements in American history, 31 political revolutions, and the Protestant Reformation" as well as "a database on U.S. Supreme Court voting behavior, which includes biographical information on the 108 justices to date." Hence, despite the fact that Sulloway is a historian of science and began his studies with the proponents and opponents of the Darwinian revolution, his theory and method drove him into social, political, and religious history as well. He thus endeavored to demonstrate that the same theory applies just as well to American civil rights leaders, French revolutionaries, advocates and enemies of the Protestant Reformation, and Supreme Court justices as it does to those who chose to accept or reject the latest scientific advances. In general, firstborns seem most likely to oppose revolutionary ideas, whereas later-borns appear more likely to accept them.

In the case of the Darwinian revolution, for example, later-borns were nearly five times more likely to accept the theory than were firstborns. Indeed, the opposition included firstborns like Louis Agassiz, Élie de Beaumont, John Herschel, Roderick Murchison, William Dwight Dana, and John Stevens Henslow, whereas the proponents included later-borns like Ernst Haeckel, T. H. Huxley, Joseph Dalton Hooker, and George Bentham. Moreover, not only was Darwin himself a later-born, but so was the cofounder of evolutionary theory, Alfred Russell Wallace, who was the eighth of his parents' nine children. In fact, pre-Darwinian advocates of evolutionary ideas also tended to be later-borns, including Benoît de Maillet, Erasmus Darwin, Jean-Baptiste Lamarck, and Étienne Geoffroy Saint-Hilaire.

This is not to say there exist no exceptions to the rule. To Sulloway's credit, he actually named and discussed numerous aberrant cases. For instance, later-born opponents of evolutionary theory included Adam Sedgwick and Richard Owen, while firstborn proponents included Charles Lyell, Asa Gray, and August Weismann. But rather than shrug his shoulders, Sulloway responded by elaborating his theory to the point that the number of exceptions is dramatically reduced. Furthermore, these elaborations are not post hoc, but rather they ensue directly from his Darwinian theory of family niches. In particular, Sulloway scrutinizes the developmental repercussions of innate temperament, the spacing of births, early parental loss and parent-offspring conflict, as well as gender and membership in a minority group. For example, eldest children who do not get along with their parents, for whatever reasons, tend to become functional later-borns. Similarly, but with a different underlying cause, children born with an innate inclination toward shyness and introversion are going to find it difficult to retain dominant status when confronted by a younger sibling who is predisposed toward extroversion.

Sulloway also took great pains to consider the specific historical nature of a particular scientific revolution. To begin with, he showed that the later-born predominance in the early phases of a revolution may be replaced by a firstborn hegemony in the later phases. The firstborns learn how to reassert their authority by deflecting the revolution toward different ends. Sulloway provided detailed quantitative evidence how this usurpation occurred during the French Revolution, the guillotines of the Reign of Terror being the tragic consequence. In addition, Sulloway noted that not all scientific movements have the radical ideological implications of the Darwinian and

Copernican revolutions. Some actually reflect more conservative notions that work in favor of the status quo. A good example is the highly idealistic systems of biological classification, such as that of the Quinarians, which seemed to endorse the belief in an all-powerful, all-knowing Creator who conceived all living forms according to a wonderfully logical and eternal scheme. Advocates of these intellectual movements were more likely to be led by firstborns than by later-borns.

Once more, Sulloway was not content to speculate. Instead, these diverse complicating factors were subjected to scientific scrutiny. The jewel of these empirical analyses is a single mathematical equation that predicts the odds that a scientist in Darwin's time would come out as an evolutionist. Not only does this equation make the correct prediction in 84% of the cases, but additionally birth order comes out as the single most important predictor. The effects of ordinal position are 1,000 times more influential than socio-economic class and 37 times more powerful than national loyalties, for example.

Moreover, those who played leading positions in the emergence of evolutionary theory tended to have the most impressive predicted probabilities. Darwin's predicted likelihood of endorsing evolution was 94%, that for Wallace, 96%. In other words, if the odds are high enough, one might predict that a person will originate a revolutionary theory rather than just support a revolutionary theory someone else proposed. Consistent with this is the predicted probability that Patrick Matthew would support evolutionary theory. Back in 1831, this obscure dilettante with an interest in botany had proposed a theory that was for all scientific purposes equivalent to that of Darwin and Wallace. Darwin himself wrote to Wallace that Matthew "gives *most clearly* but very briefly . . . our view of Natural Selection. It is a most complete case of anticipation." Wallace agreed, saying that "he appears to have completely anticipated the main ideas of the *Origin of Species*." Unfortunately, Matthew published this theory in an appendix of the book *On Naval Timber and Arboriculture*, which did not attract many readers, and even fewer enthusiasts. This was an evolutionist who was clearly ahead of his time. Nevertheless, it must be considered a striking confirmation of Sulloway's developmental model that Matthew possessed a 97% probability of becoming an evolutionist.

These last findings show that Sulloway's is not just a theory of who appreciates revolutionary genius but a theory of the origins of revolutionary genius besides. It is a remarkable testimony to the power of Darwin's theory that it should provide the foundation for explaining not only why some scientists were more receptive to his arguments, but also why it was only an elite triumvirate of intellects who could so much as propose such revolutionary ideas.

Integration

No doubt Sulloway's theory will have to undergo radical transformations as it encounters new facts and new critiques. This is the way of science. As pointed out in chapter 2, evolutionary epistemologies presume that scientific progress is itself Darwinian. Just as life never stops evolving, so do scientific theories undergo an incessant process of formulation, refutation, and modification. But also like organic evolution, the future fate of Sulloway's theory is not easily forecast. As is apparent from the book's dust jacket, Darwinian sympathizers have proclaimed *Born to Rebel* a masterpiece of the highest order. Edward O. Wilson called it "one of the most authoritative and important treatises in the history of the social sciences." Ernst Mayr ventured that "every once in a long while a book is published which changes a whole field of scholarship, perhaps even everybody's thinking. Such a book is *Born to Rebel*." And Sarah Hrdy proclaimed that this "book will have the same kind of long-term impact as Freud's and Darwin's." Other scholars were not nearly so generous, and a few have condemned it to the class of intellectual fashions that will not survive the struggle for continued existence in the history of scientific ideas. A systematic study of the birth orders of Sulloway's adherents and opponents remains to be carried out.

Nonetheless, whatever the ultimate fate of Sulloway's monograph, I believe it provides a useful model of how to resolve some of the controversies that have plagued developmental theories since their inception. Certainly Sulloway did not take an extreme stance on either side of the nature-nurture debate. A later-born himself, he may have been too open ever to have adopted a one-sided stance. Instead, he tried to integrate nature and nurture in a coherent developmental model. Moreover, nature and nurture do not operate in a passively independent fashion, heredity providing this, genetics providing that. On the contrary, in his integrative thinking, the diverse factors, whether genetic or environmental, interact in complex ways, moderating their respective influences. Furthermore, these interactions take place dynamically over time, so that the impact of a factor may change with a change in circumstances. For example, the sudden death of a parent may dramatically influence the degree to which the firstborn must identify with parental authority. Yet this consequence is itself contingent on the family's socioeconomic class as well as the eldest's gender and temperament. The trajectory of talent development is always capacious, as fortuitous events may without warning deflect a youth toward success or failure.

Eventually Sulloway's framework—with all necessary modifications—may be expanded to encompass all of the central facets of talent development. The childhood and adolescent emergence of creative genius will then be described as an evolutionary process, a process of variation and selection. After all, each year millions of human beings are born into the world with a certain set of potential talents and with a specific set of conditions in which those talents will either wither or grow. Each of these humans enters the world with the same ultimate purpose—to find that niche where he or she can be fruitful and multiply. For some individuals, this task is easy, the solution to life's greatest riddle practically dictated to them on their first birthday. These are the bright, extroverted firstborns, especially males from middle-class majority backgrounds who will grow up to become doctors, lawyers, engineers, ministers, and professors. But for many others, discovering the right niche entails a true quest, with many trials and almost as many errors. And each error has some chance of proving fatal. The developmental lineage goes extinct when the youthful talent pursues an irreversible course that leads to a cul-de-sac of lifelong unfulfillment. Perhaps only a small percentage will survive the cruelties of this variation-selection process. Only a lucky elite will find that perfect match between an ever-evolving configuration of interests, abilities, and values and the constantly transforming familial, educational, and occupational niches.

Darwin illustrates well enough the vagaries of evolutionary development. His whole biography is a litany of "what ifs"—any one of which might have deflected his latent talent into oblivion. What if his elder siblings had all died in infancy leaving Charles to assume the place of the first child? What if his mother had not died when he was eight years old? What if he had been more proficient in languages and mathematics or too sickly to enjoy strenuous outdoor activities? What if he had encountered some Cambridge professor of theology who had taken him on as a protégé instead of having his botanical mentor Professor Henslow? Most important, what if Darwin had not become naturalist on the *Beagle*?

Darwin himself recognized the central place that this "chance of a lifetime" had in his personal and professional development. He left England an aimless youth, headed in the direction his father most feared—the life of an idle sportsman. He returned five years later a mature scientist, having "discovered, though unconsciously and insensibly, that the pleasure of observing and reasoning was a much higher one than that of skill and sport." As Darwin continued,

> the voyage of the *Beagle* has been by far the most important event in my life, and has determined my whole career. . . . I have always felt that I owe to the voyage the first real training or education of my mind; I was led to attend closely to several branches of natural history, and thus my powers of observation were improved, though they were always fairly developed. . . . That my mind became developed through my pursuits during the voyage is rendered probable by a remark made

by my father, who was the most acute observer whom I ever saw, of a sceptical disposition, and far from being a believer in phrenology; for on first seeing me after the voyage, he turned round to my sisters, and exclaimed, "Why, the shape of his head is quite altered."

In fact, from this point onward Darwin aspired to make his mark on the world of science, an ambition from which he never wavered. "I am sure that I have never turned one inch out of my course to gain fame," he admitted.

Yet Darwin also marveled that this life-changing experience was by no means inevitable, for "it depended on so small a circumstance as my uncle offering to drive me thirty miles to Shrewsbury, which few uncles would have done, and on such a trifle as the shape of my nose." In this he refers to the fact that it was Darwin's uncle who persuaded his father to let him go, and that Captain FitzRoy of the *Beagle*, a physiognomist, doubted that any one with Darwin's nose "could possess sufficient energy and determination for the voyage." Fortunately for Darwin's hopes, both his father and the captain changed their minds, unleashing a chain of events in the development of Darwin's talent that would eventually alter the course of history.

Naturally, some might argue that Darwin's talent would have realized its potential by some other means. Cousin Galton might have argued such, at least when he wrote *Hereditary Genius*. Yet in terms of a bona fide Darwinian theory of talent development, this does not seem likely. Most biological lineages end with extinction, and most promising talents do the same. In each case, the niches needed to support further evolution vanish at some fatal juncture. Of course, even the biggest alteration in Darwin's developmental trajectory would have left only a modest trace on that of Wallace, the codiscoverer of natural selection. So evolutionary theory might still have appeared, only under a different name. This book would then be discussing (awkwardly) Wallacian perspectives on creativity. Nevertheless, from the standpoint of Charles Darwin—born on 12 February 1809, with a unique configuration of genetic and environmental traits—the outcome would have been tragically different. One of the world's greatest potential talents would have become as extinct as the dodo.

5
~

PRODUCTS

By What Works Shall We Know Them?

~

I f the genius of modern European civilization is largely defined by such creators as Newton, Shakespeare, Michelangelo, and Beethoven, so are these geniuses themselves mostly defined by the creative products on which their respective reputations are founded. Take away the *Principia*, the *Opticks*, and the mathematical essays, and Newton would become just a paranoid and emotionally volatile aficionado of alchemy and esoteric biblical exegesis. If it is ever proven that Shakespeare was not the true author of the plays and poems currently attached to his name, all that would remain would be a meager residual of mundane facts about an obscure Elizabethan actor. If all of Michelangelo's artistic and architectural achievements were destroyed in some tragic holocaust, there would survive only a minor writer of Italian sonnets. And Beethoven, in the absence of his concert, chamber, church, and theater compositions, would become a once promising piano virtuoso sadly reduced by progressive deafness to an impoverished alcoholic.

The genius of Darwin, too, ceases to exist without the *Voyage of the Beagle, Origin of Species, Descent of Man, Insectivorous Plants, Formation of Vegetable Mould,* and his other scientific works. He would be obliged to become that very person his father most feared he would become, a member of the idle well-to-do. Needless to say, from the standpoint of the Galtonian definition of genius, these assertions are all truisms. If genius is defined as an exceptionally high IQ score, then it matters not one iota whether the stratospheric intellect devotes every spare moment to reading cheap detective novels. But if genius is defined in terms of eminence in a domain of creative activity, then there must be some concrete evidence of achievement. Creative products provide just that evidence.

Given the definitive nature of these products, no account of genius can be considered complete without a detailed theoretical analysis of creative productivity. I will begin my analysis with a general treatment of the creative careers from which these products emerge. This first section will apply to all forms of creativity, whether artistic or scientific. However, the following two sections will concentrate on issues pertaining to specific types of creative products. I first look at artistic creativity, with the specific focus on the determinants of artistic style. I then turn to scientific creativity, examining a distinctive phenomenon that almost devastated the life of Charles Darwin. I close with a general discussion of why creative products—even a masterpiece like Darwin's *Origin of Species*—must originate in a Darwinian process.

Productive Careers

The first step toward understanding a creator's productivity is to recognize that it has two separate aspects. First, as pointed out in previous chapters, creative individuals vary in regard to the number of products that can be credited to their names. There are one-idea men and women, and there are the extremely prolific whose life work is truly phenomenal. So we are looking at individual differences, or cross-sectional variation, in the total lifetime output of creative ideas. Second, the career of any given creative genius is by no means a homogeneous entity, but rather it consists of life phases or periods. In other words, creative productivity may wax and wane over the course of the career. Thus arises the issue of longitudinal variation, or developmental changes, within a single career. In Darwin's case, for example, we can ask how Darwin's productivity differed from that of his fellow scientists, and we can ask how his output fluctuated from the time he ended the *Beagle* voyage to the day he last laid down his pen.

Individual Variation

According to Darwin's theory of natural selection, individual differences in adaptive fitness cause individual differences in reproductive success. It turns out that this seemingly simple idea is riddled with all sorts of complexities. One problem is conceptual: It is often difficult to conceive a gauge of fitness that is independent of reproductive success. Thus, evolutionary explanations can sometimes become circular. If fitness is synonymous with the capacity to reproduce, then it cannot serve as a cause of the differential reproductive success of various members of a species. Another problem is empirical: It is not always easy to measure reproductive success. To be sure, we can always count the number of copulations, or the number of offspring born or eggs laid, or the number of progeny that survive to maturity, and so forth. But each potential measure is laden with potential difficulties. For example, in species in which the females have multiple partners during their sexual cycle, clandestine sperm competition and cryptic female choice may decide which male is actually successful. Even in species that form pair bonds, such as birds often do, the females will occasionally cuckold their partners to increase the genetic diversity of their broods. Fortunately, modern techniques of DNA fingerprinting can alleviate many of these ambiguities by helping to identify the paternity of offspring. Nonetheless, these methods are far from error-free, especially when the breeding populations are quite homogeneous genetically.

As already noted, productive success may be considered the sociocultural analogue of reproductive success. Those individuals who make the most contributions to their disciplines are also those who have the greatest claim to the appellation of creative genius. In a sense, eminent creators are those who have proven themselves to be best adapted to their sociocultural milieu. However, the assessment of individual differences in productive success is fraught with all sorts of conceptual and empirical difficulties. Perhaps the biggest problem concerns measurement. What counts as a creative product? Should Newton's substantial but unpublished work on alchemy be counted along with his obviously more accomplished research on mathematics, physics, and celestial mechanics? Or should his alchemical speculations be put in the same class as copulations that yield not a single fertilized ovum?

Even if we concentrate on products that have been exposed to the scrutiny of contemporaries, should we consider all published works or only those that actually had an impact on the field? Often in biological reproduction only a small proportion of the offspring in any given breeding season will be sufficiently fit to produce offspring themselves, either because they fail to reach maturity or because they cannot successfully compete for mates as adults. The sociocultural system is no less cruel in the application of its selectionist winnowings. In the sciences, for example, between one-third and one-half of the articles published in technical journals are apparently ignored by colleagues; the typical article receives absolutely no citations in other publications appearing in the scientific literature. This sociocultural neglect holds even for publications by distinguished individuals. One study scrutinized the total output of 10 highly eminent psychologists, including figures as diverse as Donald Campbell, J. P. Guilford, B. F. Skinner, and Wolfgang Köhler. Fully 44% of their publications received no citations during a five-year period. In other words, nearly half of their output was essentially ignored by the scientific community. An even more drastic selectivity was found in a study of 10 famous composers, which included such notables as Bach, Mozart, and Beethoven. Only 35% of their total output continues to have any active place in the classical repertoire today.

The response I adopt here is to use two different definitions of what counts as a product. The inclusive definition considers any published work as a product, regardless of its reception by contemporaries or future generations. This conception is closest to a purely behavioral definition of the phenomenon. However, we can also consider a more exclusive definition, which takes into consideration the actual impact of the product. By this latter, more sociocultural conception, a scientific article that no one cites or a musical composition that no one performs cannot qualify as a creative product. Because the exclusive definition depends on the reactions of others, such as colleagues, readers, and audiences, this conception is one step removed from objectivity. Indeed, to the extent that these social judgments are unstable, so will the identification of products be unreliable. Nonetheless, the exclusive definition comes closest to fitting our definition of creativity. Products that have had an influence on contemporaries and posterity must be considered adaptive in an certain sense. These are the entities most closely analogous to a biological variant that has managed to survive and reproduce its kind.

Given these definitions, I wish to examine two main features of individual differences in the output of products. I begin by looking at the specific shape of the cross-sectional distribution. Next, I turn to the functional relationship between those products defined inclusively and those defined exclusively.

Normal versus skewed distributions. Darwin was more interested in the existence of variation than in the specific form of that variation. Perhaps this lack of interest reflects his dearth of mathematical acumen. Nonetheless, many researchers before and after 1859 have preoccupied themselves with the specific shape of individual differences. For instance, back in 1835 Lambert Adolphe Jacques Quételet established the importance of the normal distribution—the distribution defined by a bell-shaped "Gaussian" curve. Hence, for a trait like height, most people would exhibit average height. The probability of individuals being taller or shorter than this population mean would at first decline rapidly as the departure from the mean increases. But eventually the likelihood of encountering someone either extremely short or extremely tall will approach the zero point asymptotically. At this outer edge the distribution has tails that approximate the rim of a bell. A distinctive feature of the bell curve is that it is symmetric around the mean or average level of a trait. The probability of finding a person who is one foot taller than average is the same as that for a person who is one foot shorter than average.

Francis Galton, in his 1869 *Hereditary Genius*, extended the bell curve to the distribution of natural ability. The further out an individual stood on the right-hand tail of the normal distribution, the greater that person's claim to genius. Later still, the pioneers in the psychometric measurement of intelligence made the normal curve almost an article of faith. This credo is obvious in the very title of the controversial book *The Bell Curve*, which discusses the origins and consequences of intelligence. Yet the same symmetric distribution has now been used to describe individual differences on virtually any psychological attribute, including creativity. In fact, this probability distribution is currently so ensconced in the behavioral sciences that the overwhelming majority of statistical methods *posit* normal (and multi-normal) distributions as essential preconditions for all inferences!

If the traits on which adaptive fitness is based are normally distributed, it seems reasonable to suppose that reproductive success would itself be normally distributed. Yet in the biological world this is seldom the case. On the contrary, it is commonplace for a very small percentage of the individuals to generate the most substantial percentage of the offspring in a given breeding season. This disparity is especially conspicuous when reproductive opportunities are contingent on the individual's placement in a dominance hierarchy or when they require the possession and successful defense of a suitable territory. Indeed, in some species many members of a single cohort—most commonly males—may not breed at all in their entire lives, while the top, "alpha male" may sire most of the offspring. To illustrate, one inquiry examined the reproductive prowess of a single tomcat with an easily traceable genetic trait. Scrutiny of all the kittens in all the litters produced by all the female cats in the study area revealed that this dominant male fathered more than 95% of the offspring! Hence, the cross-sectional distribution of reproductive success frequently departs substantially from the normal curve. Rather than a symmetrical, bell-shaped curve, the distribution may be highly skewed to the right; the lion's share of offspring is produced by a small percentage of organisms, while the vast majority reproduce themselves but once if they succeed at all.

The same highly skewed distribution is characteristic of productive success. In any given domain of creative activity it is typical to find that around 10% of the creators are responsible for 50% of all the contributions. Stated in terms of the length of the curriculum vitae, only one creator in a hundred will make at least 10 contributions, and only one creator in a thousand will make at least 100 contributions. On the other hand, those creators who make up the bottom half of the population in terms of output are usually responsible for merely around 15% of the total supply of products. Indeed, the most frequent (or modal) level of lifetime output is usually a single product. These one-idea contributors usually constitute more than half of the total number of creators in the field. In contrast, the most productive members of the discipline are at least 100 times more prolific than members of this one-idea group. Actually, these statistics understate the magnitude of the productive elitism, for only those individuals who have generated at least one creative product are included. Needless to say, the population of individuals who have failed to make even a single contribution—whether patent or painting, article or book, poem or composition—is far, far greater. As in many biological populations, many individuals fail to pass this minimal test for creativity, leaving absolutely nothing for posterity to ponder or appreciate.

The skewed distribution of total output has been replicated so consistently that it has been described in terms of two mathematical laws. The simplest principle is the Price law. This affirms that if k represents the number of creators active in a given domain, then $\sqrt{k}$ gives the number of those who can be credited with roughly half of the products in that domain. For example, if there are 100 individuals active in a field, then just 10 of them, or 10%, will be responsible for half of everything published. A more complex mathematical principle is the Lotka law, which states that the number of individuals who contribute exactly n products will be inversely proportional to n^2. In formal terms, if $f(n)$ is the count of the creators who have made n contributions, then $f(n) = c/n^2$, where c is some constant that is contingent on the particular domain of creative activity.

Most of the research on skewed distribution has used an inclusive definition of the creative product. For instance, the investigator might tabulate all of the papers published in a given set of scientific journals or all of the books recorded in the Library of Congress. Nonetheless, the same cross-sectional distribution appears when an exclusive definition is used. For example, all of the works that make up the standard repertoire are the product of approximately 250 classical composers. The square root of this number is 16, when rounded off to the nearest integer. In actual fact, just 16 composers account for half of all the pieces performed. Moreover, the 150 at the bottom of the heap can be credited with only one work each. All of their compositions together represent 6.0% of the repertoire, which is less than Mozart's figure of 6.1%, and only slightly greater than the 5.9% each contributed by Bach and Beethoven.

Given the solidity of this finding, the obvious next question is where this skewed distribution comes from. Why do the top creative geniuses form such a conspicuous elite from the standpoint of productive success? One early suggestion can be dismissed at once, namely that the distribution merely represents the truncated upper tail of the normal curve. At first glance this seems a reasonable explanation. If creative output reflects underlying individual differences in natural ability, and if there exists a minimal level of ability necessary to generate a creative idea (e.g., an IQ of 120), then all of the members of the population with capacities below the threshold level will merely disappear from the tabulations. Unhappily for this explanation, the right-hand tail of the productivity distribution extends out much too far for this to provide a plausible account. To provide a dramatic illustration, if IQ scores were distributed the same way as creative productivity, the current human population could boast a half million intellects with IQs of 340 or higher! This figure easily exceeds by more than 100 points the highest IQ score ever recorded.

This overly simple explanation thus ruled out of court, I can turn to the following three alternative interpretations of the phenomenon:

1. *Cumulative advantage*—Many sociologists of science have argued that the observed individual differences in productivity can be explained according to the reward structures of the scientific community. The creative output of a scientist is rewarded each time a paper is accepted for publication in a major journal and each time a grant proposal is approved by a major funding agency. Because journal editors and program directors must be selective, the odds of success are usually very small. Hence, those scientists who just happen to be successful early in their careers will have their creativity reinforced sooner, giving them an edge over those of their cohorts who at first failed. This process will often be accentuated by the fact that those who are successful earlier will find themselves affiliated with more prestigious institutions that provide more support for scientific research. All of this differential reinforcement can then accumulate over time to generate large inequalities among scientific workers, even when all began their careers with equal creative potential. The rich just get richer while the poor get poorer. The outcome of this process will be the highly skewed distribution observed in the empirical literature. Although this model was first proposed with respect to scientific creativity, it is not hard to extend the same explanation to individual differences in the output of artistic products.

2. *Multiplicative influences*—William Shockley, the Nobel laureate who was not bright enough to make it into the Terman sample, has provided an interpretation that recognizes that many different factors determine creative productivity. Furthermore, these several determinants may participate in a multiplicative rather than additive fashion. That is, the capacity for producing creative ideas may be the product rather than the sum of the various components. Thus, people who

have an insufficiently high intelligence will be uncreative no matter how high they may be on the other participating factors. This multiplicative model has a critical implication with respect to the predicted probability distribution of productivity. If the diverse components are normally distributed in the population, the distribution of their product will not assume the same form. On the contrary, the expected distribution would be "lognormal." This is a distribution that would be normal were the productivity counts subjected to a logarithmic transformation. This asymmetrical distribution is highly skewed right. Most of the cases are collected at the lower end of the distribution, while the upper end of the distribution is characterized by an extremely long tail. This upper tail, in fact, is indistinguishable from that observed for creative output. Thus, according to the multiplicative model, the most prolific creators will be extremely rare.

3. *Combinatorial explosions*—According to the analysis of the creative process discussed in chapter 2, the generation of ideational variants depends on the richness of a person's associative network. The larger the number of concepts in that network, and the more diffuse their interconnections, the greater is the potential supply of recombinations. However, it is necessary to recognize that the number of available ideational variants would not increase as a linear function of the number of ideas that can be freely permuted. On the contrary, the number of possible combinations would increase explosively with increases in the number of elements being combined. As a rough but reasonable approximation, we might suppose that the potential supply of ideational variants increases exponentially with the amount of raw material. Let us further assume that the size of the reservoir of ideas available for recombination is normally distributed in the population. It immediately follows that the cross-sectional distribution of total potential variants would again be a lognormal distribution. Once more we can obtain a highly skewed distribution that permits the emergence of a supremely productive elite.

There is no particular reason why we must adopt one of these explanations to the exclusion of the other two. It is conceivable that all three processes collaborate in the determination of creative output. Even so, the three interpretations have variable implications for a Darwinian conception of creative genius. The combinatorial-explosion account is clearly the one most consistent with Campbell's variation-selection theory of creativity. Moreover, the multiplicative-influences interpretation has obvious affinities with the behavioral-genetic model of emergenesis. It has the additional advantage of being applicable to both productive and reproductive success.

Biological fitness may also be a multiplicative function of a large number of normally distributed traits. This would explain why the cross-sectional distribution of reproductive success tends to exhibit the same skewed form observed for productive success. In fact, both Price and Lotka's laws may apply to the output of progeny. To verify this conjecture, I reanalyzed the data from a 15-year study of 32 male rhesus macaques and found that the six ($\approx\sqrt{32}$) most prominent progenitors sired 48% of the offspring. This is in close agreement with the prediction of the Price law. So both cultural and biological fitness may be governed by a deeper multiplicative process.

In contrast, the cumulative-advantage explanation would appear to sit uneasily with a Darwinian view. In particular, advocates of this theory frequently argue that individual differences are imposed from the outside rather than being intrinsic to the creative person. Variation in associative powers, personal disposition, and early background—such as treated in the prior two chapters—may be simply irrelevant. Instead, the contrasts between genius and nonentity can be ascribed to the capricious influence of luck and timing. Indeed, this notion has been christened the "Ecclesiastes hypothesis" after the biblical passage "The race is not to the swift, nor the battle to the strong, neither bread to the wise, nor yet riches to men of understanding, nor yet favor to men of skill; but time and chance happeneth to them all." Consequently, productive success becomes decoupled from cultural fitness. Such a hypothesis is as anti-Darwinian as would be the analogous claim that variation in reproductive success had absolutely no correspondence with adaptive fitness.

Hence, if cumulative advantage were the only plausible explanation of individual differences in creative output, a Darwinian theory of creative genius would be seriously jeopardized. Even worse, a psychology of creativity would appear to be a meaningless enterprise. The more productive creators would not differ in any important manner from their unsuccessful colleagues. It is fortunate, therefore, that this sociological model fails to accommodate all aspects of the phenomenon. A recent investigation has shown, for example, that this interpretation cannot account for how productivity changes across the career. According to the model, the output in adjacent periods of the career should be more highly correlated than is the output in noncontiguous periods. Instead, individual differences in the output in the several periods that define a career appear to reflect cross-sectional variation in an underlying factor. This latent factor has been styled "creative potential." The particular skewed distribution of this potential may be then explicated in terms of both the multiplicative-influences and combinatorial explosion theories. Thus, there is no need to assume that the distinctive cross-sectional distribution of creative productivity is inconsistent with a Darwinian conception of genius. Nor do we have to dismiss the discussion in chapters 3 and 4 as being irrelevant to a theory of creativity.

Quality versus quantity of output. As noted earlier, reproductive success has more than one operational definition. Although this might seem worrisome, the existence of alternative definitions is only a problem if the various conceptions lead to dramatically different conclusions. Yet the contrary appears to be the case. Those sexually reproducing organisms that copulate more also tend to parent more offspring, and to have more offspring survive to reproduce themselves. So alternative measures all converge on the same basic assessment. But does the same convergence hold in the case of productive success? Do individual differences in the output of works inclusively defined correspond to individual differences in output exclusively defined? Is it true that those who generate the most products are also those who generate the most products that actually exert an influence? And are those who had virtually no impact on the field also those who ventured very little in the first place?

Certainly we can conceive two types of creative careers that strongly contradict the correspondence between inclusive and exclusive definitions. First, there may exist perfectionists who produce very little, but every single product is a masterpiece of the highest order. Second, there may appear mass producers who originate numerous products to no effect, not one of their offerings making any noticeable impression on their colleagues or the world at large. This latter career type is especially problematic, for mass producers would be creative by the inclusive definition but uncreative by the exclusive definition. They are cultural counterparts to a sterile beast who incessantly copulates but still conceives not a single offspring.

Fortunately, study after study has found that those creators who are the most prolific by the inclusive definition are also the most prolific by the exclusive definition. In other words, productive quality of output, or socially certified creativity, is positively correlated with productive quantity, or mere behavioral output regardless of consequence. For example, U.S. Nobel laureates publish two times as many scientific papers as do scientists still worthy enough to make it into *American Men and Women of Science.* The number of citations that a scientist received in the work of fellow scientists is strongly associated with the total output of publications. In fact, the total number of publications predicts the amount of citations received by a scientist's three most acclaimed works. Moreover, this correspondence between quantity and quality holds over the long haul. For instance, the total length of the bibliography of a nineteenth-century scientist predicts how famous he or she is today. Thus, a scientist who was then in the top 10% of the most productive elite has a 50-50 chance of earning an entry in a recent edition of the *Encyclopaedia Britannica.* In contrast, their less prolific colleagues have only three chances out of a hundred of earning that distinction. Mendel could make a lasting impact on science with only a half dozen publications, but cases like his are not frequent enough to undermine the correspondence.

The positive correlation between quantity and quality has a provocative repercussion. If the number of influential works is directly proportional to the total number of works produced, then the creators with the most masterpieces will be those with the most ignored and neglected products! Even the most supreme creative geniuses must have their careers punctuated with wasted efforts. W. H. Auden put it well: "The chances are that, in the course of his lifetime, the major poet will write more bad poems than the minor." This holds for major creators in other domains. In Einstein's crusade to overthrow quantum physics, he often made embarrassing mistakes. Once after an extended debate with Niels Bohr, Einstein conceived a sophisticated argument that he thought would demolish the Copenhagen school. Bohr found a fatal flaw nonetheless: Einstein had neglected to consider the implications of his own theory of relativity. Yet Einstein would defend his mistakes with the maxim "Science can progress on the basis of error as long as it is not trivial."

Naturally, from the Darwinian perspective these results are not surprising. Owing to the harsh struggle for existence, only a small proportion of even a successful organism's progeny will survive to populate the next generation. Many offspring die before even leaving the nest or den, and still more fall victim to predation, disease, starvation, or exposure once they start to fend for themselves in the wild. Even should they become mature adults, they may succumb to the rigors of territorial defense, dominance hierarchies, and mate competition. Yet none of this matters. The more potential descendants generated, the more actual descendants may survive—and that is all that Darwin's theory demands. Adaptive fitness does not signify that every nestling or cub or child will become a sexually active adult. Fitness only permits the organism to make many trials, and many errors, with the implicit hope that at least one variant will carry its genes into the next generation.

One final Darwinian feature of the quantity-quality relationship deserves emphasis. If the creative genius is generating failures as well as successes, this seems to support the assumption that the creative process is to a certain extent blind. Even the greatest creators possess no direct and secure path to truth or beauty. They cannot guarantee that every published idea will survive further evaluation and testing at the hands of audiences or colleagues. The best the creative genius can do is to be as prolific as possible in generating products in the hope that at least some subset will survive the test of time. To be sure, a critic might take the existence of the mass producers and the perfectionists as exceptions to this rule. Perhaps these careers differ in a qualitative manner from those whose successful works are a predictable proportion of their total output. On the one hand, perhaps the mass producers are not really generating variations, but rather they are one-idea individuals applying the same technique or theory over and over. On the other hand, maybe the perfectionists have grasped some special trick that allows them to circumvent the process of trial and error, allowing them to produce masterpiece after masterpiece.

Nonetheless, the existence of mass producers and perfectionists does not really introduce problems for the Darwinian interpretation. After all, the relationship between quantity and quality is far from perfect. As a consequence, there will always exist considerable scatter (or residual errors) around the regression line that predicts quality as a function of quantity. Moreover, in all empirical data sets so far published these departures are distributed around the prediction line in the usual statistical fashion. Most of the errors will be close to the line of best fit, with very few errors far away. There apparently exist no dramatic outliers that would represent the truly problematic cases. Thus the mass producer may be considered a person who was simply unlucky, whereas the perfectionist may be considered a person who was merely lucky. Chance alone will randomly distribute luck both good and bad, and a small percentage of individuals will appear unusually lucky or unlucky. If I repeatedly flip a coin 10 times in a row, I will eventually obtain 10 straight heads or 10 straight tails. But when this happens, those with savvy in probability theory do not suddenly jump to the conclusion that the coin is weighted.

The same pattern applies to reproductive success. Two organisms may have identical adaptive fitness, but one may produce more descendants than the other owing to totally extraneous factors. Just by chance one will become a victim of a predator, an epidemic, a dispute over territory or mate, a flood, or fire, or volcanic eruption. For this reason fitness cannot be equated with reproductive success. If they were really equal, then identical twins would invariably have exactly the same number of offspring, which is no more true in the animal world than it is in the human world. Accordingly, fitness must be defined as a *propensity* to survive and reproduce. Individuals with the identical genetic constitution living in equivalent ecological niches will have the same propensity, but the actual success exhibited by these individuals will be scattered around some mean value that represents the predicted reproductive success. Because an individual's fitness represents solely a probability or likelihood, two individuals with identical outcomes in the struggle for existence may actually have had unequal levels of adaptive fitness. Thus, in organic evolution the linkage between fitness and success is stochastic rather than deterministic.

I realize that the parallel just drawn between natural and cultural selection runs counter to a recurrent myth about creative genius. There exists a strong tendency to idolize historic creators, to see them as infallible in their capacity to generate one magnum opus after another, to deem them all perfectionists. The list of their contributions by the inclusive definition is thought equivalent to the list according to the exclusive definition. In brief, they are all hits and no misses. Yet we must never forget that we inevitably view the achievements of eminent creators through the selective processes of sociocultural evolution. The successful products are what survive, while the unsuccessful products are usually condemned to oblivion. The bad books go out of print while the surviving copies rot in storage rooms. The inferior paintings sit in crates in museum basements. The poor compositions collect dust in obscure musical archives. These are cultural variants that suffered extinction, buried until almost inaccessible beneath cultural strata. But the assiduous biographer, just like the meticulous paleontologist, can often dig up these forgotten creations from the depths of the creator's and history's past.

Darwin himself illustrates what can be dug up with only a little effort. For many Darwinists, he appears to represent the model scientist, the bona fide perfectionist. Hit seemed to follow hit in a most admirable progression. But if we delve carefully into his lifetime output, this idealized portrait begins to reveal many blemishes. He was capable of publishing erroneous interpretations and even silly conjectures. An early paper provided such a completely mistaken explanation for a particular geological formation that it came to cause Darwin considerable embarrassment. Later, despite his extremely detailed work on the cirripedes, he was forced to admit that he had "blundered dreadfully about the cement glands." Later still, he introduced the erroneous theory of pangenesis that contaminated his evolutionary theory with the Lamarckian notion of acquired characteristics. Yet all of these mistakes and numerous others are forgotten and forgiven. His geological paper on Glen Roy is politely ignored by geologists, and his work on the barnacles has been superseded by more accurate monographs. Darwin's theory of pangenesis has been reduced to a tiny footnote in the history of evolutionary theory. What remains in posterity's eyes is a sanitized Darwin whose career seems quite un-Darwinian—no variation and selection, no trial and error, no hits and misses. Yet I hope that this misperception will eventually enter the historical record as just another false idea that did not survive cultural selection. This unjustified glorification of genius must be buried and fossilized along with the dinosaurs.

Developmental Change

Darwin's scientific career was impressively long. While still a teenager attending Edinburgh University, he had read two papers before the local

Plinian Society. At age 22 he began the voyage on the *Beagle*, and soon after his novel observations began to be read before various scientific societies. Shortly after his return to England, he began writing up his findings, and he started collecting notes on the transmutation of species. Before he turned 30 he already had several publications to his credit, beginning the pattern of consistent output that was to continue throughout his life. In the last year of his life, at age 74, he read before the Linnean Society papers on the effects of ammonia carbonate on plant roots and chlorophyll bodies, besides sending a note to *Nature* on the dispersal of freshwater bivalves and writing a preliminary notice to a colleague's paper on Syrian dogs. The day after the latter piece was read before the Zoological Society, Darwin died. All told, Darwin's scientific life lasted well over a half century.

During that long interval he underwent many profound developmental changes. Moreover, as an evolutionist with a deep fascination with development, he could not resist making his own observations on how human beings change across the life span. For instance, he published a pioneer study of the early development of one of his own children. Darwin's writings also contain many insightful statements about adulthood and old age. In the *Origin of Species*, for example, Darwin predicted an antagonistic response from his scientific elders. Specifically, he did not "expect to convince experienced naturalists whose minds are stocked with a multitude of facts all viewed, during a long course of years, from a point of view directly opposite to mine." Instead, Darwin looked "with confidence to the future— to the young and rising naturalists, who will be able to view both sides of the question with impartiality." In private conversations, Darwin expressed this opinion in stronger terms, as is evident from what he once told Lyell, who was a dozen years his senior. "What a good thing it would be," Darwin told his colleague, "if every scientific man was to die when sixty years old, as afterwards he would be sure to oppose all new doctrines." When Lyell finally converted to evolution after having already reached his 70s, he told Darwin that "he hoped that he might be allowed to live."

Almost a century later, Max Planck made a similar claim with respect to the reactions to the new quantum theory: "A new scientific truth does not triumph by convincing its opponents and making them see the light, but rather because its opponents eventually die, and a new generation grows up that is familiar with it." Despite Darwin's patent priority, this proposition is now styled "Planck's principle." Nonetheless, the first empirical test of this developmental hypothesis was based on the reception history of the theory of evolution by natural selection. Not only was Darwin's conjecture proven correct, but other studies have shown that the phenomenon is truly a general one. Older scientists and scholars are somewhat disinclined to accept new ideas. In fact, this age effect seems generally operative in the affairs of everyday life, too, such as in business and farming.

Given his powers of observation, it is unfortunate that Darwin did not offer any definite hypotheses about how creative productivity changes across the career. The only such speculation I can identify is his conclusion that elder scientists are often prone to propose foolish theories. So strong was his belief, in fact, that he promised himself he would not theorize after he had turned 60 years old (a promise he failed to keep). Despite this apparent silence, longitudinal changes in the output of products must be considered by any comprehensive theory of creativity. Below I examine two aspects of the phenomenon: career trajectories and the equal-odds rule.

Career trajectories. Curiously, the first scientist to study the cross-sectional distribution of human characteristics was also the first to investigate the longitudinal fluctuations in the output of creative products. Back in 1835, Quételet looked at the plays produced by the leading dramatists of France and England and tabulated the number of works produced in consecutive age periods. Many other investigators have followed this pioneer effort, making the necessary methodological improvements. This research has established the following four empirical generalizations:

1. The output of creative products tends to increase as a curvilinear, single-peak function of age. Figure 5.1 gives the typical age curve. Needless to say, any particular career will depart noticeably from this idealized trajectory. Physical illness, war, and other extrinsic events can disrupt the creative process. Even so, if tabulations of output are averaged across many careers, so that these random shocks can cancel each other out, the correspondence between this function and the data becomes quite striking. Usually about 95% of the career fluctuations in productivity can be ascribed to this inverted backward-J curve.

2. This trajectory in output is a function of career age rather than chronological age. Thus, late bloomers who delayed launching their careers will have the predicted peak displaced by a proportional amount. By the same token, early bloomers will have their career high points advanced.

3. The specific shape of the curve varies according to the discipline. In domains like pure mathematics and lyric poetry, the curve approaches the peak rather rapidly, and the decline after the optimum level may be dramatic. In fields like geology and philosophy, the rise to the maximum output point is more gradual, and the subsequent descent less precipitous.

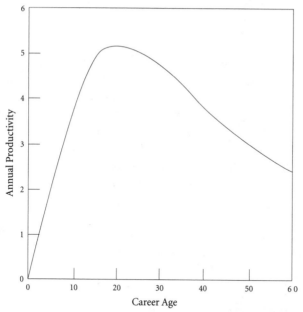

Figure 5.1 Typical curve describing the annual output of creative products
as a function of age according to a Darwinian model of the
creative process.

4. Once allowance is made for these interdisciplinary contrasts, individual differences in lifetime output do not affect the overall shape of the
curve. Instead, this cross-sectional variation determines the overall
height of the curve. The more prolific creators are simply generating
more products per unit of time. As a consequence, two individuals
working within the same field will have their peaks occur at the same
career age, any contrasts in total output notwithstanding.

There have been numerous attempts to offer theoretical explanations for
these empirical results, most of which fail because they cannot accommodate all the facts. Some theories cannot account for individual differences—
a fatal flaw given that such differences produce more variance in output at a
given career age than does career age itself. Other theories have the drawback of assuming that the output of products is a function of chronological
age. And many theories cannot explicitly account for interdisciplinary differences. However, I have developed a theoretical model of creative productivity that handles all four general results, as well as several more detailed
findings. What makes this model especially provocative is that it purports to
operate according to Darwinian principles. That is, it begins with the

assumption that the creative process is described by Donald Campbell's variation-selection theory. Because I have elaborated this explanation into a formal mathematical model, we cannot possibly examine all the specifics. Nevertheless, I will provide a sketch sufficient to illustrate its Darwinian nature.

The model starts with the assumption that creativity employs a combinatorial process. The various cognitive elements are recombined to produce ideational variants. Those conceptual variations that survive certain selection criteria are then retained for further elaboration. Once sufficiently developed, they become finished creative products. This simple, two-stage model has four parameters, two concerning individual differences and two concerning the characteristics of the creative discipline. The first individual-difference parameter is the initial creative potential, which registers the total number of ideational variants a person is capable of generating in an unlimited lifetime. Because this is a combinatorial model, creative potential is assumed to feature a highly skewed cross-sectional distribution. The second individual-difference parameter is the age at career onset, which defines the age at which the variation-selection process begins. Career age is set at zero at the moment the career begins. The two disciplinary parameters are the ideation rate and the elaboration rate. The first defines the rate at which the initial creative potential is transformed into ideational variants, while the second defines the rate at which those variants are elaborated into actual products. These two information-processing parameters are presumed to be contingent on the specific nature of the concepts that characterize the discipline. In some domains the disciplinary concepts are sufficiently finite and well-defined that variations can be produced rather quickly, whereas in other domains the concepts are so numerous and ambiguous that the combinatorial process slows down. Disciplines also differ in what is required to elaborate a variant into a concrete product. Given these parameters, a mathematical model could be derived that yielded an equation stating how creative productivity should change across the career. It was this resulting formula, in fact, that generated figure 5.1.

This Darwinian mathematical model does an excellent job handling all the principal features of the developmental changes in creative output. In particular, it successfully predicts the empirically observed productivity curves, including such detailed features as the asymptotic approach to the zero output level in advanced old age. Its predictions are explicitly expressed in terms of career rather than chronological age. It not only accommodates interdisciplinary differences in career trajectories, but in addition it provides a substantive interpretation for those differences. Indeed, when the ideational and elaboration rates are estimated using career data drawn from various disciplines, the resulting estimates seem to reflect the underlying information-processing needs of each domain. For instance, the ideational and elaboration rates are faster in poetry than they are in philosophy, which accounts for the later career peaks for philosophers relative to poets. Or, bringing the illustration closer to home, these two information-processing rates are more rapid in the mathematical and physical sciences than they are in the biological and earth sciences—Darwin's own professional turf. Finally, individual differences in initial creative potential are incorporated in the required manner: The predicted peak at maximum output appears at the same career age, but the height of the curve is changed throughout the career trajectory. At present, there exists no other model that can accomplish what this Darwinian model can achieve with respect to explaining how creative productivity varies across the life span.

Of the four parameters of this mathematical model, initial creative potential is perhaps the most controversial. All of the other parameters—age at career onset and the two information-processing rates—can be directly defined or estimated. In contrast, the initial potential is a latent variable that can only be inferred from its probable effects. It serves merely as an underlying indicator of a person's capacity for generating creative products under ideal circumstances. Obviously, conditions are seldom ideal, and so the actual lifetime output will rarely match the potential output. Certainly Darwin would have been able to publish far more had he enjoyed good health. He frequently reported losing days, weeks, and even sometimes months to his recurrent and chronic illnesses. Moreover, according to the mathematical model, prolific creators who live to a ripe old age will usually fail to exploit all of their creative potential. They often leave this world with sketchbooks and notebooks crammed with all sorts of ideational variants still awaiting elaboration. Mahler's unfinished Tenth Symphony and Puccini's unfinished opera *Turandot* are just two among innumerable examples. And, needless to say, who can even guess what ideas had not yet so much as popped into their heads?

Despite the fact that initial creative potential is one step removed from overt action, that conceptual distance does not invalidate the scientific utility of this theoretical construct. Indeed, it may not have passed unnoticed that this notion closely parallels the propensity definition of fitness. An organism's fitness is thus defined as its potential for generating a certain number of viable offspring under a given set of circumstances. In a similar fashion, initial creative potential is an estimate of an individual's propensity for conceiving publishable products under certain conditions. Given such-and-such scores on intellectual, personality, and developmental variables, so-and-so's lifetime output should be the value designated by this parameter. But for both biological and cultural offspring, actual success may differ substantially from the predicted success. Thus, initial creative potential serves as a gauge of sociocultural fitness by defining the likelihood that a given person will display Darwinian genius.

Equal-odds rule. Another distinctive aspect of the above model deserves special emphasis. Because it is based on Campbell's theory of the creative process, the variations are assumed to be generated by a blind combinatorial procedure. Good, bad, and indifferent combinations will therefore be randomly distributed across the course of a career. Accordingly, the predicted career trajectory for products under the inclusive definition will be identical to that for products under the exclusive definition. A logical consequence of this parallel distribution is the equal-odds rule. This rule states that the probability of conceiving a truly successful product is a constant function of the total number of works. In other words, if we calculate the ratio of hits to total attempts (i.e., hits and misses), that "quality ratio" should not systematically change as the career progresses. There should be no increase in the hit rate, nor a decrease, nor should the proportion exhibit some curvilinear form. Rather, the quality ratio will fluctuate randomly from year to year, from decade to decade. Note that these expectations closely parallel what would be expected by a purely Mendelian process of genetic variation. Because the independent assortment of genes is blind under the classic model, superior and inferior variants will be randomly interspersed throughout the reproductive life of an organism. The parents have no way of using their knowledge of the fate of their earlier offspring to improve the genotypic fitness of their later offspring.

Empirical data on the longitudinal relationship between quality and quantity are entirely in accord with the Darwinian predictions. Over 160 years ago, Quételet demonstrated the parallel form of the age curves for products of variable cultural impact, and subsequent research has done the same. The peak for producing major works is located in the same age period as the peak for producing minor works. In addition, Quételet's published data have been reanalyzed to show that the quality ratio does not systematically change over the course of the creative year. The proportion of hits to total attempts merely fluctuates randomly from decade to decade. Other investigations have established the equal-odds rule on other samples of creative geniuses, including studies providing longitudinal data on the careers of both scientific and artistic creators. No matter what kind of creativity we examine, the odds of a successful creative product is a constant probability of the total number of products generated.

Additional support for the equal-odds rule comes from research on career landmarks. These are the products that define the three highlights of a creative life: the first major contribution, the best contribution, and the last major contribution. In the case of Darwin, for example, these would be the *Journal of Researches* of the *Beagle* voyage of 1839, the *Origin of Species* of 1859, and *The Formation of Vegetable Mould through the Action of Worms* of 1881. If the equal-odds rule holds, then the model makes some highly specific predictions about how these three landmarks will be distributed across the career. For instance, if major works are most likely to appear when the most works are produced, then the single best work has the highest probability of appearing during the age of peak output. In addition, the longitudinal location of this best work will not be contingent on the creator's total lifetime output but rather on the age of career onset and the particular creative domain. The model makes similarly precise predictions about the location of the first and last career landmarks. For instance, those individuals with higher initial creative potential will have higher overall rates of output throughout the career. As a consequence, their first landmark will appear earlier in their career and the last landmark later in the career. This model even uses the equal-odds rule to derive extremely specific predictions (e.g., that the correlation between the age at first work and the age at last work will have a negative sign after partialling out either age at best work or age at maximum output). These predictions have been tested and verified on data for both scientific and artistic careers. The equal-odds rule thus appears to boast considerable empirical support.

Admittedly, it could be argued that this Darwinian generalization seems inconsistent with Planck's principle. If creators really do become less accepting of new ideas as they get older, wouldn't that affect the odds of producing a major work in the latter part of the career? Not necessarily. Consider two points:

1. Planck's principle applies to the reception of work by others rather than to one's own production of work. Some researchers have argued that the resistance of older scientists to the ideas of their younger colleagues may concern other issues besides cognitive rigidity. One sociologist observed that "as a scientist gets older he is more likely to be restricted to innovation by his substantive and methodological preconceptions and by his other cultural accumulations," but also added that "he is more likely to have high professional standing, to have specialized interests, to be a member or official of an established organization, and to be associated with a 'school.'" Some empirical studies have suggested that these sociological constraints may be more important than age per se.

2. Even if age had a direct effect on the actual products ventured by the creator, it is not immediately obvious that its effect would be to change the quality ratio in the latter part of the career. Perhaps older scientists take fewer risks, so that their output becomes less variable in quality. But that would only mean that the best works produced in old age would be less good *and* the worst works produced in the same period would be less bad.

The ratio of hits to total attempts itself, might remain stable.

Apropos of both points, it behooves us to recognize that Planck's principle does not necessarily reveal the intrusion of some unfortunate evil. From the perspective of historical hindsight, Darwin and Planck were apparently in the right, and so the conservatism of their senior colleagues seems absurd if not outright tragic. But not all new ideas that enter the struggle for sociocultural existence are indeed fit for survival. Many, maybe even most, will fail to survive selection with good cause. The most recent example in the history of science is the advent of cold fusion. This supposed empirical discovery had no theoretical foundation, and thus it provoked considerable controversy. Although I know of no investigation showing that Planck's principle applied to this case, it would not be surprising if the older, better established scientists were more skeptical than their younger colleagues. If so, the senior members of the scientific community got the last laugh when experiment after experiment failed to replicate the original results.

In a sense, this conclusion parallels what Sulloway claimed with respect to birth-order effects. Firstborns appear more likely to reject revolutionary ideas, whereas later-borns seem more likely to accept them. Thus, older siblings essentially begin their careers being older than later-borns at the same nominal career age. Sulloway has actually calculated the equivalence of age and birth order with respect to the reception of Darwin's theory of evolution. "Throughout the debates over evolution, 80-year old laterborns were as open to his theory as were 25-year old firstborns. During the Darwinian revolution, being a laterborn was equivalent to a 55-year dose of the open-mindedness that typically resides in youth." Yet Sulloway also admits that later-borns are more inclined to jump on some passing scientific bandwagon without waiting for the same degree of empirical and logical proof as do the firstborns. Hence, younger colleagues, like the later-borns, may be said to adopt high-risk strategies that may win big, but may lose big as well. In contrast, the older scientists, like the firstborns, have less to gain, and more to lose, by putting their reputations at stake for what may soon appear a mere unfounded fad. What we see here is two alternative strategies for sociocultural survival, each having advantages and disadvantages. The very fact that these two radically different strategies manage to coexist strongly suggests that, in the long run, they have comparable adaptive value from a sociocultural perspective.

Artistic Styles

Darwin underwent many developmental transformations, among them a dramatic narrowing of interests. As he confessed, "later in life I wholly lost, to my great regret, all pleasure from poetry of any kind, including

Shakespeare." Milton, Gray, Byron, Wordsworth, Coleridge, and Shelley all fell from grace in Darwin's heart. At the time he wrote his autobiography Darwin noted that "for many years I cannot endure to read a line of poetry; I have tried lately to read Shakespeare, and found it so intolerably dull that it nauseated me. I have also almost lost my taste for pictures or music." The main aesthetic interest that survived this developmental change was novels, so long as "they do not end unhappily—against which a law ought to be passed." It is interesting that this developmental shift began in his 30s, shortly after he became a full-time scientist. Perhaps his preoccupation with biology became increasingly incompatible with any deep interest in something so blatantly cultural as the arts. When Darwin did touch on aesthetic matters in his writings, he did so from the standpoint of primary Darwinism. *The Descent of Man*, in particular, contains a chapter entitled the "Secondary Sexual Characters of Man" (chapter 19), in which artistic creativity is explicitly tied to sexual selection: "The impassioned orator, bard, or musician, when with his varied tones and cadences he excites the strongest emotions in his hearers, little suspects that he uses the same means by which his half-human ancestors long ago aroused each other's ardent passions, during their courtship and rivalry." Art merely replaces the peacock's tail and the stag's antlers.

Others since Darwin have attempted to provide a basis for artistic creativity in organic evolution. Some have continued his emphasis on sexual selection, an explanation that circumvents the problem of trying to determine its fitness value from the standpoint of natural selection. Others have taken a more difficult route, speculating on how aesthetic expression and appreciation might make a direct contribution to survival. Among the best of the recent attempts is the 1992 book *Homo Aestheticus: Where Art Comes From and Why*. Here Ellen Dissanayake tried to root artistic creativity in more fundamental ceremonial and ritual adaptations of our species.

Rather than discuss in detail such fascinating applications of primary Darwinism, however, I wish here to examine a bold example of secondary Darwinism being applied to a critical facet of artistic genius. This theory was put forward by Colin Martindale, who was interested in solving a special enigma in the arts: Why do styles change? Just as species evolve, so do aesthetic styles change. And as most species face a slow extinction, so do most styles die a leisurely death. The history of European art, for example, is largely characterized as a progression of styles: Romanesque, Gothic, Renaissance, mannerist, baroque, neoclassical, romantic, realist, impressionist, and so forth. Martindale provided a specific illustration drawn from the history of French poetry. Consider the following poetic lines:

1. "Beneath your fair head, a white delicate neck / Inclines and would outshine the brightness of snow."

2. "I love you opposite the seas / Red as the egg when it's green."

The first lines are by the romantic poet André Chénier (1762–94), the second by the surrealist poet André Breton (1896–1966). Clearly, something very striking happened to poetic style in the 134 years that separate their respective births. On the one hand, Chénier's lines use rather straightforward metaphorical imagery. It does not require much of a mental stretch to compare whiteness of feathers to the whiteness of snow. On the other hand, Breton's lines can create real problems for all but the literary aficionado. What can it possibly mean to compare a sea (or myself, or my love) to a green egg when eggs aren't green? Can anyone conjure up a vivid image of a green egg that looks red (or a red egg that looks green)? If Darwin was disgusted by the romantic poets of his day, one could imagine what his response would have been had he lived long enough to read the surrealists.

So what happened to French poetry between Chénier and Breton? What motivated this dramatic stylistic change?

Primordial Cognition and Aesthetic Selection

Martindale began by assuming that creativity operates according to Campbell's model of blind-variation and selective-retention. The main source of ideational variants is primary-process thought, or what Martindale preferred to call primordial cognition, in order to avoid any extraneous psychoanalytic connotations. Martindale explicitly recognized that this process is not an all-or-none affair, but rather it may exhibit degrees. In psychoanalytic terms, we may speak of the depth of the regression into primary-process imagery. In terms of Mednick's theory, the process may rely on ever more remote associations. Moreover, certain constraints must be imposed on these variations. Artistic creations are conceived within a particular stylistic tradition. This tradition has much the same function as the Kuhnian paradigm in science. The style determines the vocabulary, images, techniques, and other features of a work of art, whether it be a poem, play, novel, painting, sculpture, musical composition, or architectural design. An Elizabethan English sonnet, for example, contains a specified number of lines (14), formal structure (three quatrains and a couplet), rhyme scheme (*abab cdcd efef gg*), meter (iambic pentameter), themes (beauty, love, death, the ravages of time), and other features.

If all the artists had to do was produce aesthetic variants on a particular style, artistic creativity would be a relatively simple business. However, selection criteria are also imposed by the external world—the domain of readers, audiences, and patrons. These criteria are of two types. The first type is the cultural analog of natural selection. An artistic product must meet certain practical requirements with respect to political, religious, and economic realities. Art in medieval Europe had to deal with Christian rather than Islamic or Buddhist themes, just as art in the former Soviet Union had to focus on proletarian themes rather than those of bourgeois capitalists. The existence of these standards is not new to Martindale's theory, of course. Marxist theories of art have consistently argued for the "reflection-ist" basis of artistic products. A poem, painting, or composition is merely a reflection of more fundamental material conditions, especially those eco-nomic. Although there exists evidence that the external zeitgeist can deter-mine the content of artistic products, Martindale maintained that this force has rather less relevance as a determinant of aesthetic style. The reason is simple: Fundamental material conditions—the Marxist "means of produc-tion"—change far too slowly.

The second selection criterion has much more power to shape the course of stylistic change. This criterion is the cultural analog of sexual selection. This latter force usually operates in a rather different fashion than natural selection. As already pointed out with respect to the tails of peacocks, sexual selection tends to push the organism toward the possession of ever more exaggerated traits. Indeed, the only constraint on sexual selection is natural selection. Who knows how large and brilliant a peacock's plumage would be if he did not have to concern himself with finding food and avoiding preda-tors? Nonetheless, when Martindale claimed that artistic style is subjected to a selection pressure like that in sexual selection, he was not arguing from the standpoint of primary Darwinism, such as Darwin did in *The Descent of Man*. In fact, there is absolutely nothing "sexual" about this process. Instead, Martindale was affirming that there exists a selection pressure that operates in a parallel fashion to cause the stylistic traits that make up an artistic product to become increasingly exaggerated, perhaps even to a maladaptive degree. In order to appreciate the nature of this second selective force, we must understand what the artistic creator is trying to accomplish.

Arousal Potential and Hedonic Value

To make names for themselves—and perhaps even to attract mates—artists must generate works that command the attention of connoisseurs, critics, audiences, and patrons. The works thus must be interesting, fasci-nating, even shocking—but never boring. Yet this means that artistic cre-ators cannot simply repeat what their predecessors have already expressed. Poets after Shakespeare cannot get away with merely offering paraphrases of his sonnets. Appreciators have habituated to those earlier forms of expres-sion, rendering them passé. So the next generation of artists must offer something to excite the jaded tastes—these creators must grab attention by offering ever more original aesthetic variants. Each generation must thus resort to increasingly outlandish combinations constrained only by the precepts of the given artistic style. To discover these ever more remote associations and divergent ideas requires that the artist regress further and further into primordial cognition or primary-process imagery.

As artists rely on increasingly bizarre associations to create novelty, the received aesthetic style becomes progressively less capable of producing intelligible art. The products become incrementally more obscure and strange, until the style begins to disintegrate. Indeed, the very disintegration of the style becomes a principal way to produce ever more stimulating products. Rather than elaborate the ideational material to make it conform closely to the stylistic constraints, the traditional rules are stretched and broken. Eventually, a generation of artists finds itself in an evolutionary cul-de-sac. Either all the combinatorial variants have been exhausted or else the ones that remain are too esoteric to generate anything more than decadent art. The old style thus dying, the world of artistic creativity can only be saved with the advent of a new style. Owing to the style's novelty, the first artists working in that style can make exciting creations without delving too deeply in primary-process imagery. But successive generations are not so lucky, and the descent into ever remote associative material repeats itself until that new style is also exhausted.

One final aspect of this evolutionary progression deserves mention. Like a true Darwinian theory, the process of change is governed by gradualism. The peacock's glorious tail did not suddenly appear in full splendor. Back at the beginning of the evolutionary emergence of this trait, the male's tail may have differed only slightly from the female's. But once the peahens began selecting mates according to the tail display, the pressure was exerted on each masculine generation to outdo the feathery accomplishments of their predecessors. Moreover, throughout this gradual transformation produced by sexual selection, natural selection was imposing increasingly powerful pressures that put a brake on the process. Certainly a peacock whose plumage was "ahead of its time" would suffer considerable disadvantage in the struggle for existence. Indeed, because the peahen's tastes must coevolve with the peacock's display, it is doubtful that the precocious possession of the current plumage would have been considered sexually attractive. Instead, such excessive displays might have been taken as maladaptive. A peahen would rather not mate with a peacock that seems to carry genes that may harm the reproductive success of her male progeny.

An analogous mechanism holds for aesthetic appreciation. According to one influential theory of artistic perception, the hedonic value of an artwork—its capacity to elicit pleasure—is contingent on its arousal potential, where the latter is determined by such factors as novelty, the ability to invoke surprise, complexity, and ambiguity. Nevertheless, hedonic value is not a positive monotonic function of arousal potential. On the contrary, the relationship is defined by the inverted-U "Wundt curve." Aesthetic products with too little arousal potential will be utterly boring, whereas those with too much will provoke anxiety and hostility. At some optimum point between the two extremes is the level of arousal that ensures the best reception. There actually exists considerable amount of empirical research supporting this optimal arousal theory of aesthetic appreciation. For example, one study looked at the success of all the works that make up the repertoire of classical music. Hedonic value was gauged by the frequency that the composition was likely to be performed, whereas arousal potential was assessed by a computerized content analysis of the composition's melodic originality. In line with theoretical prediction, the popularity of a work was a curvilinear, inverted-U function of its originality.

Armed with this nonlinear relation, it should be apparent why stylistic evolution must advance gradually rather than exhibit quantum leaps. Any artist whose works depart too drastically from the optimum level will find that those products will be poorly received. Thus, the pressure toward constantly more original works is moderated by this counterforce. Were it not for the progressive habituation to the advances of the preceding generation, in fact, there would be no need to arrive at increasingly original aesthetic variants. But audiences, appreciators, and patrons do become habituated. The shocking avant-garde of today converts into the clichéd derrière of tomorrow, forcing each generation to become a little more daring than the previous. As the peacock's features become gradually ever more spectacular, so do artistic products become ever more astonishing.

Theoretical Predictions and Empirical Tests

A commendable feature of Martindale's theory is its capacity for yielding rather specific predictions. For example, the theory predicts that primordial cognition should become increasingly prominent as artists exploit the full potential of a particular style. Once the descent into primordial cognition bottoms out, the style should show signs of disintegration. Nonetheless, after a new stylistic paradigm replaces the old, primordial cognition becomes less necessary. Because the style is itself novel, it is much easier to produce original variants. So the amount of primordial cognition resets roughly to the initial level. Accordingly, primordial cognition should exhibit a cyclical pattern over the course of stylistic evolution. In addition, changes in basic style should also display a cyclical pattern, only the cycles will be the opposite of those for primordial cognition. Finally, the theory predicts that the overall capacity of artistic creations to evoke arousal should increase over historical time. Indeed, it is precisely because a style no longer permits this upward progression in originality that it must yield to a new style.

Besides generating empirically testable predictions from his theory, Martindale did his utmost to test the predictions against empirical data. To begin with, Martindale conducted several inquiries in which judges evaluated aesthetic masterworks on several dimensions. These evaluative dimensions tap such attributes as a work's potential to elicit arousal as well as the degree to which it introduces primordial imagery. He applied this approach to Italian painting from the late Gothic to the rococo period and to European classical music in several nations. In these studies he found that arousal potential tends to increase over time. And primary process oscillates in inverse synchrony with stylistic changes in the art forms.

Moreover, Martindale conducted a laboratory experiment that simulated the key features of literary change according to his Darwinian theory. He put 10 highly creative subjects in a room and asked them to write a series of similes. Each subject was compelled to make each simile more original than the preceding one, while concomitantly obeying certain stylistic restrictions. Martindale spotted patterns that closely paralleled those in actual literature. Regression into primordial cognition deepens as the subjects reach for originality, and eventually a change takes place in how the creators conceive the similes. The only way that novelty can be achieved is through stylistic disintegration, the necessary precursor of a new style. Thus, 10 responses to "A pencil is like_____" proceeded from "a yellow cigarette, spreading its cancer on paper" to "an artist's brush, painting paper" to "God micturating upon the cosmos." This progression is not unlike what transpired in French poetry between Chénier and Breton.

Significantly, in assessing the descent into ever more primordial thought, Martindale did not depend on subjective evaluations. On the contrary, to provide his theory the most objective test possible, Martindale became a pioneer in the computer analysis of literary texts. Besides applicability to the data generated by his laboratory simulation, his computer software can evaluate actual poetry and prose on an immense range of objective attributes. The most critical part of his content-analytical software is his Regressive Imagery Dictionary. This tells the computer what to look for when scoring the amount of primordial cognition evident in a composition. For instance, the lexicon includes words with strongly sexual or sensuous connotations. In addition, Martindale's programs can assess the stimulatory powers of literary text. An example is his Composite Variability Index. This taps such dimensions as word and phrase length, the use of unique words, and the presence of an associatively rich vocabulary or striking or intense semantic usages. Martindale even invented methods by which computers can identify stylistic shifts in literary traditions. One clue is a change in the literary vocabulary, a deviation that a computer can readily detect. Martindale thus escaped from an uncomfortable dependence on the manifestos of writers or the discriminations of critics.

These utterly objective measurements have been applied to a variety of literary creations: English and French poetry, American and Hungarian short stories, and the lyrics of popular music. By subjecting the resulting scores to detailed statistical analyses, Martindale obtained more direct evidence for his theory. As predicted by his evolutionary model, the Composite Variability Index tends to increase steadily over historical time. Also, the index of primordial cognition, based on his Regressive Imagery Dictionary, tends to rise and fall in cycles. And these cycles are inversely synchronized with the introduction of new literary styles.

Besides these quantitative analyses, furthermore, Martindale has discussed how his theory can explicate stylistic evolution in Japanese ukiyo-e prints, Gothic architecture, New England gravestones, American popular music, and other art forms. In addition, Martindale boldly extended his model and methods to domains outside the arts. For example, he developed his theory to account for shifts in scientific paradigms, the scientist's analog of a received style. He then tested this extension through the computerized content analysis of articles in professional psychology journals. The results clearly display the major paradigm changes in the field, such as the advent of behaviorism. Finally, Martindale applied his methods to the primordial imagery in articles appearing in the *Publications of the Modern Language Association* from 1885 to 1985. As predicted, the index of primordial cognition oscillated. More important, the ups and downs corresponded to major shifts in paradigmatic approaches—the onset of "new criticism" and again the inception of structuralism. The computer even detected the psychological antecedents of deconstruction and poststructuralism.

All in all, Martindale's evolutionary theory represents the most precise and comprehensive application of secondary Darwinian theory to the problem of artistic creativity.

Scientific Multiples

Darwin was a very cautious scientist. He knew full well that his evolutionary theory would be highly controversial. The fate of pre-Darwinian evolutionists provided ample evidence of the hostile reception he might likely receive. He realized that his scientific reputation would be destroyed if he offered anything less that the most rigorous and well-documented argument. Hence, even though back in 1842 he had written a long essay containing all the central features of his theory—and he even had a clean copy prepared in 1844 in case he were to die unexpectedly—Darwin did not seek its immediate publication. Instead, he labored away on what was to become a multivolume study—the definitive and utterly convincing demonstration of evolution by natural selection. Only a few of his closest colleagues were kept abreast of his efforts. Friends like the geologist Charles Lyell advised Darwin not to procrastinate too long, for fear that he might be preempted by some other scientist. But he refused to listen. So imagine how Darwin felt when he received a paper from a younger colleague named Alfred Wallace. Darwin sent Wallace's paper to Lyell, adding his own cover letter:

> Your words have come true with a vengeance—that I should be forestalled. You said this, when I explained to you here very briefly my views of "Natural Selection" depending on the struggle for existence. I never saw a more striking coincidence; if Wallace had my MS. sketch written out in 1842, he could not have made a better short abstract! Even his terms now stand as heads of my chapters. Please return me the MS., which he does not say he wishes me to publish, but I shall, of course, at once write and offer to send to any journal. So all my originality, whatever it may amount to, will be smashed, though my book, if it will ever have any value, will not be deteriorated; as all the labour consists in the application of the theory.

Darwin's magnum opus would be reduced to the elaboration of another scientist's theory.

Fortunately, the story has a happy ending. Lyell and Hooker convinced Darwin to contribute to a joint paper read before the Linnean Society on the evening of 1 July 1858. The collaboration consisted of Wallace's essay "On the Tendency of Varieties to depart indefinitely from the Original Type," extracts from Darwin's 1844 sketch, and part of a letter to Asa Gray, dated 5 September 1857, in which Darwin had outlined his ideas. Darwin then worked at great haste to write an "abstract" of his unfinished treatise. In his diary he proudly recorded what happened to the 1,250 copies that came out toward the end of 1859: "The first edition was published on November 24th, and all copies sold the first day."

Not always are these matters settled so amicably. Sometimes similar events incite extremely bitter priority disputes. The controversy between Newton and Leibniz over who invented the calculus was infamously vicious. Eventually priority had to be decided by a special commission of the Royal Society of London, which condemned Leibniz as a plagiarist. Only later was it learned that the draft of the commission's report was written by the society's president, Sir Isaac himself! On other occasions whole nations entered the fray, as happened when both J. C. Adams and Leverrier independently used Newtonian mechanics to predict the existence of a new planet—the one now called Neptune. It became an issue of national pride between British and French patriots who should most properly be credited with the discovery. Even the planet's very name became a matter of nationalistic controversy.

From a Darwinian point of view, these priority disputes seem understandable enough. According to the Galtonian conception of creative genius, reputation is based on productive success. But to be successful means that the creator receives credit for his or her creations. So sometimes rival claimants must fight it out like two rams competing for an ewe. Although it is not accurate to describe Darwin's own reactions in quite this manner, it is obvious that he was not willing to concede victory without some kind of fight. So he did not decline to prepare the joint paper read before the Linnean Society, nor did he waste any time getting his *Origin of Species* to press. In the latter work, moreover, Darwin left no doubt in any reader's mind who had been the first to work out the implications of the theory of evolution by natural selection. Indeed, Lyell actually took Darwin to task for not mentioning Wallace in the summary chapter of the first edition, obliging the author to insert Wallace's name more conspicuously in the second edition. Darwin may not have been vociferously combative in the defense of his turf, but he certainly was not going to forfeit his claim to fame passively.

The priority disputes may make perfectly good sense, but what about the phenomenon that provided the basis for the controversy? Do such events tell us anything crucial about the nature of scientific genius? And are those implications consistent or inconsistent with a Darwinian theory of creativity?

The Traditional Explanation: Sociocultural Determinism

The theory of evolution by natural selection, the invention of the calculus, and the discovery of Neptune are all instances of what have been called "multiples." A multiple occurs when two or more scientists independently make the same discovery. Although it is not a definitional requirement, these independent discoveries are often simultaneous as well. Most dramatically, the multiples may even take place on the same day. One example is what happened to William Lassell, who one night discovered the dark inner "crepe" ring of Saturn. Lassell devoted the early morning hours to verifying the observation. After convincing himself that he had something to enhance his reputation, he sat down to read the morning paper. There he read an article about how George Bond had just made the same discovery, but had been shrewd enough to notify the reporters at once.

Lists of such multiples can get quite extensive. Hundreds of cases have been reported in virtually every domain of science and technology. Table 5.1 provides a partial list of just that subset of those claimed in the domains of evolution and genetics. Because of the frequency of their occurrence and their dramatic nature, multiples have inspired a number of explanations. The oldest and most widely disseminated interpretations have come from

Experimental disproof of spontaneous generation of maggots: Leeuwenhoek and Redi (both 1688).

Hybridization of maize: Cotton (1716) and P. Dudley (1724).

All plant appendages are modified leaves: C. F. Wolff (1759) and Goethe (1790).

Skull composed of modified vertebrae: Goethe (1790) and Oken (1805).

Theory of inheritance of acquired characteristics: E. Darwin (1794) and Lamarck (1809).

Evolution by natural selection: W. C. Wells (1813), P. Matthew (1831), C. Darwin (1844), and A. Wallace (1858).

Segregation in pea hybrids: J. Goss and A. Seton (both 1822).

Cell clump of nucleated protoplasm: Dujardin (1835) and Schleiden (1838).

Spermatozoon, a single cell containing nucleus and cytoplasm: F. Schweigger-Seidel and A. von la Valette St. George (both 1865).

Genetic laws: Mendel (1865) and later de Vries, Correns, and Tschermak (all three 1900).

New phylum Chordata of vertebrates and invertebrates with notochords in at least embryonic stages: Kovalevski (1870s) and Balfour (1880).

Discovery of the centrosome in the ovum: Flemming (1875) and Beneden (1876).

Cell nucleus as basis for inheritance: Hertwig, Strasburger, Kölliker, and A. Weismann (all 1884–85).

Centrosome does not disappear at end of the process of mitosis: T. Boveri and Beneden (both 1887).

Law of numerical equality of paternal and maternal chromosomes at fertilization: T. Boveri and L. Guignard (both 1890).

Double fertilization in angiosperms: S. Nawaschin (1898) and L. Guignard (1899).

Theory that sex controlled within germ cell and not by environment: L. Cuénot and Strasburger (both 1899).

Explanation of xenia in corn as due to double fertilization: de Vries and Correns (both 1899).

Theory of mutations: Korschinsky (1899) and de Vries (1901).

Hardy-Weinberg law in population genetics: G. H. Hardy and W. Weinberg (both 1908).

Artificial transmutation of gene using X rays: Muller and L. J. Stadler (both 1927).

sociologists and anthropologists who believe that such events cast serious doubt on any purely psychological theory of creativity. Rather than being the products of the individual mind, multiples are said to prove that creative ideas are the effects of the zeitgeist, or spirit of the times. At a specific instant in the history of a domain, the time becomes ripe for a given idea. The idea is "in the air" for anyone to pick, making its inception inevitable.

According to the eminent sociologist Robert K. Merton, for example, "discoveries and inventions become virtually inevitable (1) as prerequisite kinds of knowledge accumulate in man's cultural store; (2) as the attention of a sufficient number of investigators is focused on a problem—by emerging social needs, or by developments internal to the particular science, or by both." The simultaneity of so many multiples is taken as especially telling. Thus, Alfred Kroeber, the distinguished anthropologist, was highly impressed by the simultaneous rediscovery of Mendel's genetics by de Vries, Correns, and Tschermak. He concluded, "It was discovered in 1900 because it could have been discovered only then, and because it infallibly must have been discovered then." This idea was not only inevitable, but inevitable at a specific moment in the history of science. Such sociocultural determinism leaves little room for individual genius. For instance, anthropologist Leslie White drew this emphatic conclusion from the multiple invention of the steamboat: "Is great intelligence required to put one and one—a boat and an engine—together? An ape can do this."

Now if the zeitgeist so inevitably determines the output of creative products, a Darwinian theory of genius would seem to lose considerable force. The locus of causal determination has been placed in the larger sociocultural milieu. At best the individual creator becomes the spokesperson for the age, while at worst genius is reduced to a mere epiphenomenon of massive and impersonal forces. The cognitive processes discussed in chapter 2, the personality profiles examined in chapter 3, and the developmental factors reviewed in chapter 4, would all have little or no causal relevance. Indeed, the more Darwinian the process, the less compatible it would be with sociocultural determinism. Serendipity, especially, would be highly suspect. As observed in chapter 2, serendipitous discoveries are the primary source of purely (and undeniably) blind variants in the history of science. Yet how can a discovery happen by accident when all discoveries are inevitable? "Determined chance" constitutes an oxymoron.

One way around this problem is simply to assert that sociocultural determinism applies only to scientific products. Artistic products, on the other hand, may still originate according to Darwinian principles, just as Martindale argued. The foundation for this bifurcation of creativity is the observation that multiples are supposed to characterize scientific but not artistic creativity. As one historian of science put it, "if Michelangelo and Beethoven had not existed, their works would have been replaced by quite different contributions. If Copernicus or Fermi had never existed, essentially the same contributions would have had to come from other people."

Needless to say, if we yield on this point, then the explanatory power of secondary Darwinism is immensely reduced. But this is not the only alternative. Rather than accept the veracity of sociocultural determinism, we can attempt to discredit this explanation sufficiently so that more latitude remains for the operation of Darwinian accounts. Better yet, we might actually be able to establish that the interpretation with the best explanatory comprehensiveness and predictive precision may originate in the Darwinian camp.

Objections to the Zeitgeist Hypothesis

Can we identify any explanatory weaknesses in the doctrine of sociocultural determinism? Is the case on behalf of the zeitgeist as strong as many scholars would have us believe? To respond requires that I carefully consider the following four issues: Generic versus specific categories, independent versus antecedent events, simultaneous discoveries versus rediscoveries, necessary versus necessary and sufficient causes.

Generic versus specific categories. Although the number of multiple discoveries looks rather impressive, the specific cases do not always bear up under scrutiny. Rather, the lists of putative multiples include many clear illustrations of "a failure to distinguish between the genus and the individual." Two supposed duplicates are often not actually identical, but rather an extremely generic category has been superficially imposed on distinct creations. As an example, nuclear magnetic resonance was independently and simultaneously spotted in 1946 by Bloch, Hansen, and Packard at Stanford and by Purcell, Torrey, and Pound at Harvard. This earned Bloch and Purcell a Nobel medal in 1957. Still, although physicists "have come to look at the two experiments as practically identical," said Purcell, "when Hansen first showed up [at our lab] and started talking about it, it was about an hour before either of us understood how the other was trying to explain it." An even greater discrepancy occurs in the case of the steam turbine, which has been credited to four independent inventors. Detailed analysis of each invention has proven that they have quite contrasting forms and operate under rather different physical principles. This conflation of distinct events is often evident in table 5.1 as well: Many of the so-called multiple discoveries actually involved research on organisms literally kingdoms apart. That is, frequently one investigator would make the discovery on plants while another made the "identical" discovery on animals. Only with the historical hindsight of modern genetics does it appear obvious that these processes must be essentially the same.

Evolutionary theory has for some time made the distinction between analogous and homologous characters. The wings of bats and birds are analogous. While superficially similar and functionally equivalent in many respects, these wing structures are highly divergent in details, as befits their rather different evolutionary origins. The wing of a bat, in contrast, is homologous with the hand of a human and the flipper of a seal, the contrary forms and functions notwithstanding. Close examination of many multiples reveals that they actually represent instances of convergent evolution producing analogous rather than homologous creative products. This outcome may hold even when the products defining the multiple appear for all purposes identical. Although instances of exact convergence are extremely rare, such multiples do occur from time to time. For example, the Pelton water wheel was independently conceived of by two different inventors, but from entirely different antecedent inventions. Because of the contrast in evolutionary history, it was Pelton alone who realized the importance of the innovation and thus took the steps necessary to patent and exploit the device. It is interesting that in patent law a new invention can only receive protection so long as it does not constitute an *obvious* development from previous inventions. Yet what may not be obvious in one evolutionary sequence may be quite obvious in an entirely different evolutionary sequence, even when the final product is the same.

Pelton's willingness to profit from his new invention suggests another critical contrast between the products that compose a multiple. What a creator does with an idea is often just as important as originating the idea. One scholar has even argued that a scientist should not be credited with a contribution unless it represents that claimant's "central message." On this basis, Meyer willingly admitted the preeminence of Mendeleyev in advancing the periodic law of the elements. The Russian chemist stood alone among claimants in his willingness to advocate the controversial scheme. Only Mendeleyev elaborated the details. Only he risked making specific predictions that could be put to the test. The history of chemistry would have altered had Mendeleyev not made the periodic law a central message of his career.

The same criterion applies to the Darwin-Wallace multiple. Although the general principles of their original contributions were the same, and the evolutionary origins often similar—such as the common influence of Malthus—the details were often quite different. For example, the artificial selection seen in the breeding of domestic animals had a unique part to play in Darwin's thinking. Furthermore, it was Darwin who made evolutionary theory his central message, expanding its explanatory power to every possible corner of the biological world. It was also Darwin who took the bold step of applying the theory to the evolution of human higher mental powers, something Wallace (an advocate of Spiritualism in later life) was unwilling to do. So central was Darwin's contribution that Wallace was perfectly willing to concede Darwin primary credit for the theory. As Wallace confessed in a letter written a few years after Darwin's death, "I have not the love of *work, experiment* and *detail* that was so pre-eminent in Darwin, and without which anything I could have written would never have convinced the world." Later still, Wallace conferred eponymic status on his deceased colleague by publishing the 1889 book *Darwinism, an Exposition of the Theory of Natural Selection with Some of its Applications.*

It is interesting that Darwin himself insisted on the validity of the central-message criterion even when it operated to his disadvantage. For example, in the *Origin of Species* Darwin had briefly stated an important generalization with respect to comparative embryology, but this discovery was later attributed to others who had published the same idea after him. Rather than express bitterness at being overlooked, Darwin simply noted, "I had materials for a whole chapter on the subject, and I ought to have made the discussion longer; for it is clear that I failed to impress my readers; and he who succeeds in doing so deserves, in my opinion, all the credit."

The distinction between generic and specific categories has another implication that wants highlighting: Perhaps scientific and artistic creativity are not as divergent as seemingly implied by the long lists of multiples. The noted molecular biologist Gunter Stent pointed out that multiples may happen only in the sciences merely because we use extremely inclusive categories to describe discoveries and inventions but highly exclusive categories to describe paintings, plays, and other works of art. Of course, Beethoven's Fifth Symphony was created just once. Yet, by the same token, only Darwin wrote the *Origin of Species*, and probably was the only scientist who could have done so. Not even Wallace claimed that he could have carried the banner of evolutionary theory nearly as well. Indeed, the widespread belief in the abstract nature of the scientific enterprise often makes us overlook the idiosyncratic nature of individual scientists and their products. Ludwig Boltzmann stressed how "a mathematician will recognize Cauchy, Gauss, Jacobi, or Helmholtz, after reading a few pages, just as musicians recognize, from the first few bars, Mozart, Beethoven, or Schubert." Once Newton sent off a response to a mathematical problem that had been posed as a challenge to the international community. Although the solution had been sent anonymously, the recipient at once spotted "the claw of the lion." According to Stent, it is possible to group artistic products into similarly abstract categories and thereby compile long lists of artistic multiples. If Stent's argument is correct, then the occurrence of multiples need not prove that scientific and artistic products ensue from different creative processes. That leaves open the possibility that all forms of creativity may be Darwinian.

Independent versus antecedent events. The long lists of multiples suffer from another liability, namely that the separate contributions fail to satisfy the criterion that the products be independent. Far too often those cited as independent contributors were actually influenced by one or more of the others party to the duplicate invention. McCormick knew about the earlier reaper invented by Patrick Bell. Dollond devised his achromatic lens with knowledge of Hall's previous work. Fulton explicitly built upon the prior efforts of Jouffroy to construct a steam boat; he even was present at the first trials of Symington's ship. In creating the kinetic theory of gases, Rankine was well aware of Waterston's earlier efforts. Lavoisier was found to have repeated experiments done by others, such as Cavendish or Priestley, and then passed on the discoveries as his own. Just recently, a priority dispute between Einstein and Hilbert over the general theory of relativity was finally settled by the discovery of the first set of proofs of Hilbert's paper. This set lacks the central features of the theory—features that were snuck in the "corrections" upon learning of Einstein's critical results through private correspondence. Ironically, because Hilbert's paper was published first, it was Einstein who was most often charged with plagiarism! In any event, these examples show that a large proportion of the multiples that support the zeitgeist doctrine may represent the basic process of antecedence, not independence, and so cannot legitimately count as multiples.

Note that this is one of those realms in which biological and cultural evolution operate in very different ways. With extremely few exceptions, genes can only transfer from organism to organism through direct asexual or sexual reproduction. Genes do not jump across lineages. Thus, if a particular structure appears in different lineages, the inference of independent invention is secure. The eye of the octopus is strikingly similar to that of vertebrates, but there is no doubt that the two ocular systems represent an instance of convergent evolution. There exists no common ancestor of the chordates and the molusks that featured this organ. Memes, in contrast, can easily jump around from head to head, skipping historical periods and whole cultures. For example, Gutenberg's invention of the printing press was partially inspired by his awareness of printing in faraway China. When we consider how ideas may transfer by word of mouth or by now-lost correspondence or artifacts, it is not easy to prove that two scientific multiples are indeed independently invented. Nonetheless, it seems reasonable to suppose that a substantial percentage of the examples given in the published lists actually represent cases of one discovery being antecedent to another. The greater the percentage, the weaker is the case for the traditional interpretation.

Simultaneous discoveries versus rediscoveries. Unlike independence, simultaneity is not an essential requirement for two or more products to be categorized as a multiple. Even so, a clue concerning the nature of the phenomenon may be found in the fact that supposed multiples are seldom simultaneous in any strict sense. In one study of 264 multiples, only 20% took place even within a one-year interval. In contrast, with fully 34% of the multiples, at least a decade elapsed before the duplications ceased. In fact, occasionally hundreds of years will divide the first and last instance of a multiple. Examples include the observation of the transit of Venus across the solar disk by al-Kindi and Horrocks, the statement of the hydrostatic principles by Archimedes and Stevinus, and the discovery of "eustachian" tubes by Alcmaeon and Eustachio.

This frequent temporal hiatus raises two doubts, one empirical and the other theoretical. On the empirical side, the longer the delay separating hypothesized duplicate discoveries, the more hazardous is the supposition that they satisfy the essential criterion of independence. Given the capriciously (and often surreptitiously) mobile nature of memes, it may become increasingly difficult to assume that some informal influence may have causally linked the separate discoveries. Therefore, a more conservative definition of multiples might require simultaneity as well as independence. For instance, the lists may be confined to only those multiples separated by no more than a year. Such a restriction would then delete 80% of the cases, not even counting the deletions due to unacceptably generic categories and well-documented causal link.

On the theoretical side, the very existence of these rediscoveries—even when truly independent—must call into question the explanatory power of sociocultural determinism. For example, if the laws of genetics become unequivocally inevitable at a specific point in history, why were they discovered first in 1865 and then rediscovered in 1900? That implies a lot of slippage in the zeitgeist's deterministic powers. Furthermore, it is begging the question to claim that Mendel was simply "ahead of his time." The times are supposed to define what products can and cannot appear. Because the zeitgeist failed to deny Mendel the discovery, it should become evident that we must segregate the creative product from whatever determines the social acceptance of that product. As William James expressed the contrast, "social evolution is a resultant of the interaction of two wholly distinct factors: the individual, deriving his peculiar gifts from the play of psychological and infra-social forces, but bearing all the power of initiative and origination in his hands; and, second, the social environment, with its power of adopting or rejecting both him and his gifts." The rejection is most likely to take place when, as Stent observed, a discovery's "implications cannot be connected by a series of simple logical steps to canonical, or generally accepted, knowledge." The idea is then premature, reducing the unfortunate anticipator to the status of a precursor genius. This principle may partially explain the failure of Patrick Matthew to make an impression on the naturalists of his time. After all, his book outlining his very Darwinian theory of evolution was published in 1831, the same year that Darwin began his *Beagle* voyage. Given that Darwin would not even arrive at the Galápagos Islands until September of 1835, we might even wonder whether Matthew's theory would have seemed premature to Darwin himself. But by 1859, the body of knowledge that could be marshaled on behalf of evolutionary theory was so massive that Darwin felt obliged to call his *Origin of Species* a mere abstract, despite its being a volume exceeding 400 pages.

Necessary versus necessary and sufficient causes. The occurrence of long-delayed rediscoveries implies that we must take care to distinguish between necessary and sufficient determinants of a creative product. A necessary cause is one that supplies a prerequisite for another event to happen. The calculus presupposes some principle of limits. But this causal claim is too weak to support the inference of determinism. To get a stronger statement, we must argue that the milieu provides necessary and sufficient causes. Such causes don't just allow an effect to take place, but rather they require it to happen, inevitably. Yet the evidence argues against this strong form. Very often a contribution builds upon a cultural substrate that has been around for decades, or even centuries. Martin and Synge shared the 1952 Nobel Prize for chemistry for developing paper chromatography. Yet Martin lessened the achievement by noting "all the ideas are simple and had peoples' minds been directed that way the method would have flourished perhaps a century earlier." The broad applicability of this remark is supported by the many rediscoveries separated by a decade or more. If the earliest contribution is truly identical to the latest, then it must be the case that all the prerequisites had been satisfied years earlier. Hence, the necessary causes were not sufficient causes.

Admittedly, those who believe in the inexorable advance of science might still argue that all discoveries will eventually appear once the requisite groundwork has been laid. Yet to say that something will eventually see the light of day is a far cry from claiming the inevitability of its birth at a precise point in time. Furthermore, even when we can hold that a specific discovery will happen eventually, that does not necessitate that the events will unfold in a predetermined pattern. Not just the timing but the nature of the creative product itself may change. Stent illustrated this point with Watson and Crick's formulation of the structure of deoxyribonucleic acid (DNA):

> If Watson and Crick had not existed, the insights they provided in one single package would have come out much more gradually over a period of many months or years. Dr. B might have seen that DNA is a double-strand helix, and Dr. C might later have recognized the hydrogen bonding between the strands. Dr. D later yet might have proposed

a complementary purine-pyrimidine bonding, with Dr. E in a subsequent paper proposing the specific adenine-thymine and guanine-cytosine replication mechanism of DNA based on the complementary nature of the two strands. All the while Drs. H, I, J, K and L would have been confusing the issue by publishing incorrect structures and proposals.

So rather than have the comprehensive theory propounded in final form in a single *Nature* paper, DNA might have emerged by a far more indeterminate process of conceptual variation and selection. That, of course, is precisely what Darwin's *Origin of Species* did for evolution. Just as the Watson and Crick model would be the starting point for all future work in molecular genetics, so would Darwin's theory mark the point of departure for all further discussion of evolutionary theory.

The Darwinian Interpretation: Individual Indeterminism

Curiously, despite the unfortunate Wallace episode, Darwin himself once recorded dissatisfaction with the traditional explanation. In his autobiography we read:

> It has sometimes been said that the success of the *Origin* proved "that the subject was in the air," or "that men's minds were prepared for it." I do not think that this is strictly true, for I occasionally sounded out not a few naturalists, and never happened to come across a single one who seemed to doubt about the permanence of species. Even Lyell and Hooker, though they would listen with interest to me, never seemed to agree. I tried once or twice to explain to able men what I meant by Natural selection, but signally failed. What I believe was strictly true is that innumerable well-observed facts were stored in the minds of naturalists ready to take their proper places as soon as any theory which would receive them was sufficiently explained.

Thus, at best, the times were ripe for a catalyst that would precipitate the sudden crystallization of diverse facts around a single theory. Even so, the zeitgeist alone was not going to serve that crucial function. The "spirit of the times" merely provided the necessary conditions, while Darwin's genius produced the necessary and sufficient condition, his great book.

Given Darwin's views, he probably would have been quite pleased with the argument that the secondary Darwinian theory of creativity may actually provide a better explanation of multiples. Moreover, it does so with considerable elegance and completeness. The explanation begins with the reiteration that creativity entails a variation-selection mechanism. Various ideas must undergo blind recombination to produce ideational variants.

These variants, in turn, are selected for further elaboration and communication. The communicated ideas then run the gauntlet of subsequent selection processes. A great number of the ideas that enter into the combinatorial processes are provided by the zeitgeist, or sociocultural milieu. That is, they come from the cumulative cultural and intellectual heritage at a particular time in history. Still, other ideas will come directly from nature—such as all the newly acquired knowledge that Darwin obtained on the *Beagle* voyage. The ideas coming from culture and nature together provide the necessary conditions for all possible variants at a given moment in history and within a particular sociocultural system. That means that certain variants will be permissible, whereas others will have to wait until the sociocultural system is infused with the requisite ideas or ideational combinations. Each creative individual incorporates a subset or sample of this total cultural store. The ideational subset is usually defined by the discipline (and allied disciplines) with which each creator is affiliated. Stated in less abstract terms, physicists acquire the concepts and techniques of physics, geologists those of geology, and so forth.

It may seem strange, but this is all we need to explicate the key features of the multiples phenomenon. In particular, from these basic Darwinian principles I can derive precise predictions regarding multiple grades, temporal separation, and multiples participation.

Multiple grades. Some multiples have more participants than others do. Only two mathematicians claimed to have devised the calculus, while four have some claim to discovering the periodic law of the elements. The calculus is a grade-2 multiple, or "doublet," whereas the periodic law is a grade-4 multiple, or quadruplet. It is also apparent from the published lists of multiples that some grades may be more frequent than others. In the broadest terms, the higher the grade, the lower the frequency. The highest grade ever claimed was grade 9, or a nonet, but this is very rare. In contrast, grade-2 multiples are the most common, followed by grade 3, then grade 4, and so on. From the combinatorial theory we can predict the specific shape of the probability distribution. In the first place, because the process is blind, a large number of variants must be generated before a useful variant survives. In other words, the probability of success is relatively small. There are many trials and many errors. Concomitantly, any given discipline will consist of a fairly large number of creators independently subjecting roughly the same subset of ideas to the combinatorial process. Thus, the low probability of success for any one individual is somewhat compensated by the large number of participants. Essentially, this is a form of parallel processing, where each creator is blindly generating ideational combinations, but where the discipline has "safety in numbers." Because of this redundancy, the odds will be enhanced by the fact that many of the potentially useful combinations will be found by at least one member of the field. At the same time, this redundancy will permit a certain number of multiples to emerge, even if the creators are truly working independently of one another. By chance alone, there will appear multiples of grade 2, 3, 4, and so forth up to the sole grade-9 multiple—just as two siblings will on rare occasions look almost identical despite their not being monozygotic twins.

Given these conditions, the predicted probabilities of occurrence for multiple grades must be closely approximated by what is called the Poisson distribution. This distribution accurately describes the occurrence of events when the number of trials is extremely large but the probability of success extremely low. In fact, research has repeatedly shown that this distribution does an excellent job of predicting the observed frequencies of events when those events are so unlikely to happen that they can only happen because there are so many attempts (e.g., the number of Prussian cavalry officers killed by horse kicks in a given period of time). The same predictive success holds for multiples as well. To illustrate, in one investigation I identified 449 doublets, 104 triplets, 18 quadruplets, 7 quintuplets, and 1 octuplet, whereas the model predicts 435, 116, 23, 4, and 0, respectively. Statistical tests demonstrate that the departures between predicted and observed frequencies are so small that they can be safely attributed to statistical error.

It must be noted that the traditional explanation for multiples cannot accommodate these findings. After all, sociocultural determinism maintains that discoveries and inventions are inevitable, or nearly so. As a result, high-grade multiples should not only be extremely common, but they should be more frequent than low-grade multiples, not less so. It is equally important to recognize that the predicted distribution according to the Darwinian model is not contingent on whether there exist a priori constraints on the order in which certain ideational combinations can appear. Monte Carlo simulations have shown that the same monotonically decreasing distribution emerges even if certain combinations must occur before other combinations can appear. Indeed, the provision for such necessary conditions only serves to lower the probability that a successful variant will emerge. Often creators will waste considerable time producing ideational combinations that are useless simply because one essential component is lacking from the given repertoire of ideas undergoing permutation. An excellent illustration is the airplane. Inventors had devised many attempts at heavier-than-air flight that were preposterously (and often fatally) useless because they lacked (a) an understanding of controlled gliding and (b) a motor with a workable power-to-weight ratio. By the time of the more fortunate Wright brothers, Otto Lilienthal had solved the former problem, while inventors of gasoline (rather than steam) engines had solved the latter problem.

Temporal separation. As noted earlier, sociocultural determinists place a great deal of emphasis on the near simultaneity of so many multiples. To have Alexander Graham Bell and Elisha Gray show up at the patent office two hours apart on the same day for the same invention must be more than mere coincidence. Yet a Darwinian critic can also argue that multiples are almost compelled to be simultaneous for the multiple even to happen. What if Lassell had planned to scan Saturn rings one day later? He would have read the morning paper and altered his observatory's schedule. In other words, if the communication system in science were perfect, multiples would have to be simultaneous to occur at all! Because no one deliberately reinvents the wheel, all creators must include among their selection criteria the requirement that they have not heard the idea before. The application of this criterion depends on how rapidly the ideas of other creators are disseminated throughout the discipline.

Probability models have already been constructed that incorporate this communication feature (e.g., by introducing a "contagion" process). As in the similar Poisson model, combinations are randomly generated, but with the addition of one further constraint. The longer the time lapse after the first appearance of a successful combination, the lower the likelihood of a duplicate discovery. Knowledge of the innovation probabilistically but inevitably disseminates so as to preempt others from continuing further on the same project. Models based on this constraint still predict the comparative frequencies of the multiple grades, but at the same time accurately predict how many years will lapse before duplicates can no longer appear. Just as low-grade multiples will be more common than high-grade multiples, so will short temporal separations be more likely than long separations.

Because these more complex stochastic models still operate on an underlying variation-selection mechanism, the Darwinian interpretation would seem to have more explanatory power than sociocultural determinism. This is especially true given how the latter perspective has no a priori means of accommodating multiples with ample temporal separation.

Multiples participation. Just as there exist individual differences in creative productivity, so does there exist cross-sectional variation in how many times a particular scientist has inadvertently duplicated the efforts of some other scientist. The Darwinian explanation can easily explicate these differences. In particular, the model leads to two predictions:

1. The greater the number of scientists working within a given domain, the higher the likelihood that those scientists will participate in one or more multiple discoveries. If there are dozens of creators all subjecting the same subset of ideas to combinatorial variation, then the odds of arriving at a duplicate variant will be very great. In contrast, a scientist who works in isolation, and thus avoids the "hot topics" of the

day, will be less prone to duplicate the variants produced by others.

2. The greater a scientist's lifetime productivity, the higher the likelihood that he or she will participate in one or more multiple discoveries. After all, those who create more ideational variants are more likely to duplicate the variants of others. Merton recognized this same principle when he observed that those of "great scientific genius will have been repeatedly involved in multiples . . . because the genius will have made many discoveries altogether." Indeed, those of "scientific genius are precisely those . . . whose work in the end would be eventually rediscovered. These rediscoveries would be made, not by a single scientist, but by an entire corps of scientists." The single scientific genius is "the functional equivalent of a considerable array of other scientists of varying degrees of talent." Note that because eminence is strongly correlated with total output, the more eminent scientists should tend to participate in more multiples. This might be considered a corollary of this second prediction.

Empirical studies endorse both of these predictions. It must be confessed that these endorsements do not provide unequivocal support for the Darwinian account. The same two predictions might be derived from some other theory. Even so, given this confirmation plus the predictive precision of the stochastic models predicated on Darwinian principles, it would seem that the case on behalf of the traditional zeitgeist interpretation is considerably weakened. The fine structure of multiple discoveries implies that the creative process is far from deterministic. The zeitgeist still plays a role in the Darwinian theory, but a far more restricted one. Essentially, the zeitgeist helps provide the necessary conditions—the memes that feed the combinatorial procedures—and determines the probability that a new ideational variant will be successfully disseminated and will earn acceptance. The creative genius does the rest.

Before leaving this subject of multiples, I would like to touch on one curious issue regarding multiple participation. As pointed out in chapter 1, discoveries and inventions are often given eponymic tags to facilitate professional discussion. This assignment is unproblematic when there is only one claimant. But what happens when there two or more? Several solutions are possible. The names might be hyphenated, as occurred in the James-Lange theory of emotion. Alternatively, the central-message criterion might be used, as happened in the case of Darwin and Wallace. The problem would become especially acute, however, whenever a prolific scientist participated in two or more multiple discoveries. The scientific community would then have a hard time determining which particular discovery is being referred to. In such cases, ironically, it is sometimes the least prolific scientist who attains eponymic status. This possibility was first pointed out by Donald Campbell in his analysis of the eponymic fate of a law "relating the apparent size of an afterimage to the distance of the surface upon which it is projected." This finding came to be known as Emmert's law of 1881 despite the fact that Emmert had several notable anticipators. Although Emmert's discovery came at least a quarter century after the first claim, he had two special advantages for an eponym. First, he wrote the most comprehensive treatment on the subject, making it the central message of a whole article. Second, Emmert "contributed nothing else to the field," making the principle the central and only message of his entire career. By assigning Emmert eponymic status, scientists avoided the confusion that might have arisen from taking a name associated with many more distinct contributions. Campbell speculated that "the names of one-time contributors are more efficient than the names of the great who contribute many principles to science."

This phenomenon illustrates again the sometimes capricious nature of sociocultural evolution. The Galtonian definition of genius is based on reputation, the latter then being founded on the total contributions made during a career. Although fairness would dictate that reputation should be exactly proportional to those contributions, sometimes credit for products is meted out according to criteria that have nothing to do with the actual products generated. The eponymic fate of some multiples illustrates one source of slippage. Anytime there are multiple claimants for a discovery that needs a convenient label, the eponym may be decided according to convenience rather than to deserved priority. The names for memes seem to undergo a selection process that sometimes diverges from the memes themselves. I know no analog of this bifurcation in biological evolution.

Genius and the Masterpiece

The empirical and theoretical discussion of this chapter seems to imply that genius depends immensely, perhaps even predominantly, on chance. Scrutiny of creative careers revealed that creativity (quality) is only a probabilistic function of productivity (quantity). Whether we are speaking of individual differences or longitudinal changes, the equal-odds rule seems to apply. The more shots one attempts, the more hits one can expect—but also the more misses. Likewise in the case of multiple discovery, the odds of a success was deemed so small that the occurrence of multiples was ascribed to mere accident rather than to the inevitable operation of sociocultural determinism. Even the studies of the evolution of artistic style invite the intrusion of chance. As a style is progressively exploited, artistic creators must regress into increasingly Darwinian thought, producing aesthetic combinations that become ever more bizarre, and eventually unintelligible. Stylistic conventions soon break down, rendering the aesthetic products ever more unpredictable in form and content.

Of course, to note that chance participates so conspicuously in the making of the creative product is not tantamount to asserting that genius is random. The effects of chance are constrained by certain behavioral laws that impose order on what would otherwise be chaos. The distribution of lifetime output is successfully predicted by the Lotka and Price laws, just as the career trajectory of creative output is accurately predicted by a relatively simple, single-peaked mathematical function. The distribution of multiple grades and their temporal separation can be closely predicted using precise stochastic models. And the specific trends and cycles in the various components of aesthetic products can be predicted with a respectable degree of precision.

Indeed, we find ourselves in a situation similar to what Darwin described with respect to his own theory: "I am inclined to look at everything as resulting from designed laws, with the details, whether good or bad, left to the working out of what we can call chance." Primary Darwinism describes the general pattern of organic evolution without being able to provide the specifics about the direction that evolution will take for this species or that genus—or even for some definite order, class, or phylum.

After roughly the same manner, we can predict which periods during a creator's career are most likely to produce their most influential work without predicting which specific contribution will enjoy the greatest impact. We can predict when a stylistic change is most likely to appear in a given aesthetic tradition without being able to anticipate which artistic genius will launch the new style. We can predict the probability that a multiple will be grade 3 without knowing which specific discoveries will be made exactly three times. And so forth. The broad outlines of genius and its products can be explained and predicted with commendable confidence, but the minuscule names, dates, and places are left in the whimsical hands of historical chance.

Operants, Reproductive Strategies, and Expertise

The lawful regularities notwithstanding, many behavioral scientists may still believe that creative genius has much more control over fate than Darwinian theory may imply. Certainly in the conception of genius that prevailed during the romantic era, the creator was seen as actively willing masterworks into existence. Although I believe this rhapsodic viewpoint has been rendered untenable by all that has been discussed in the preceding chapters, a more sober and informed challenge can emerge from respected research programs in the behavioral sciences. In particular, three objections can be derived from research on operant conditioning, reproductive strategies, and expertise:

1. Back in the first chapter I briefly noted that creativity may be viewed as a behavior within B. F. Skinner's operant conditioning paradigm. Experimental research has shown how creative behavior can be increased through reinforcement. Although these laboratory studies dealt with psychometric assessments of creativity rather than with the generation of recognized creative products, Skinner himself has argued that such products can be explicated in the same terms. The production of a creative product is an operant that can be reinforced by the reception it receives from colleagues, audiences, or readers. The creation of successful products will be reinforced so that more products will be generated of that type. Unsuccessful products will receive no reinforcement, and perhaps even punishment, diminishing the likelihood of the further production of bad work. Over time, the cumulative record of a creative career should exhibit an increase in the number of hits and a decrease in the number of misses. The genius will have learned how to create masterpieces.

2. In the mathematical models of population biology there frequently appear two central parameters r and K. The first concerns the rate of population increase, whereas the second concerns the carrying capacity of the environment (i.e., the size of the population that can be supported). These two parameters have become terms describing the end points of a continuum connecting alternative reproductive strategies. At one extreme are those species that pursue the r strategy. These species maximize the production of offspring but minimize the parental care devoted to the survival of those offspring. An example is the oyster that can generate 500 million eggs per year but that provides absolutely no parental care to any of those eggs or the larvae that hatch from them. As a consequence, only a tiny percentage of the offspring survive to reproduce themselves. At the other extreme are those species that pursue the K strategy. These species minimize the production of offspring to maximize the parental care that can be devoted to their survival. Good illustrations are the great apes, who may produce only one infant every half decade but will nurse, feed, and train each through the hazardous early years of life. As a result, a much larger percentage of progeny make it to adulthood. If productive success is the sociocultural analog of reproductive success, can this same continuum be applied to productive careers? If so, it would seem that the Darwinian genius depicted in this chapter is engaged in an r-type productive strategy, generating lots of products with scant hope of success. But why can't there exist geniuses operating accord-

ing to a *K*-type productive strategy? Instead of madly dashing off one half-baked idea after another, couldn't the genius carefully polish, revise, and perfect each idea until it is ready to take the world by storm? Indeed, given the time that Darwin devoted to the *Origin*, why can't we infer that he was himself employing a *K*- rather than *r*-type productive strategy?

3. Recent research on expertise would seem to support the argument that *K*-type strategies might be the rule rather than the exception in human achievement. Cognitive psychologists have closely studied expertise in diverse domains, including chess, sports, music performance, medicine, and physics. On the basis of this research, investigators have argued that the capacity to attain world-class skill in any domain is acquired through deliberate practice and training. Once a sufficient level of mastery is acquired, the individual becomes an expert who can display a consistent level of performance. A champion chess player will consistently defeat challengers below a certain rating, just as a violin virtuoso will reliably offer the audience the highest quality performance. Of course, there might occasionally appear off days, injuries, or other disruptive factors. But these will be rare, and when they do appear, they will be explicable. So why can't creativity be considered a form of expertise? There is already ample evidence that it takes considerable time and effort to acquire the wherewithal to become a creative genius. Research on expertise indicates that it takes about a decade of intense daily study to acquire the necessary mastery of a domain, and the same amount of time has been found necessary for the acquisition of whatever is required for world-class creativity. Furthermore, if it is correct to speak of creative expertise, shouldn't we expect the creative expert to exhibit a consistent level of mastery? Why wouldn't the expert creator consistently produce masterpiece after masterpiece? In short, why can't creators use their expertise to adopt a less wasteful *K*-type productive strategy?

The easiest response to these three objections is simply to point to the empirical data. If the creative product is an operant, if the creator can adopt a perfectionist strategy, if creativity is a special case of expertise—then why does the creative career look the way it does? For instance, why does the ratio of hits to total attempts obey the equal-odds rule over the course of the career? How can a creative genius produce an artistic or scientific failure *after* producing a universally recognized masterpiece? Researchers in the areas of operant conditioning, reproductive strategies, and expertise all have their data, and investigators in the area of creative genius have their own data. That these data seem to contradict each other may only serve to affirm that the data relate to highly distinct phenomena. Creative products may not be operants, nor may creators be able to acquire mastery that enables them to adopt a K-type productive strategy. So even the most exalted creative genius is left with no recourse but to fall back on the r-type strategy. Rather than stop here, however, I would like to argue that there exist strong theoretical and empirical reasons for suspecting creative productivity to operate according to different cognitive and behavioral rules.

Environmental Feedback, Configurational Creations, and Human Reason

Consider what would be required for the production of a creative product to be placed in the class of operants. Obviously the operant would have to be a fairly well-defined behavior. The rat in a Skinner box learns to press a lever; a pigeon is conditioned to peck at a disk. Yet the very requirement that a creative product be original seems to militate against finding a precise definition for what counts as a product worthy of reinforcement. The specification is negative rather than positive: Don't do what already has been done, and especially don't repeat yourself. At the same time, the requirement that the product be adaptive imposes another ambiguous criterion. For instance, according to the optimal-arousal theory of aesthetic appreciation, a work of art must elicit just the right amount of excitement to place the audience or spectator at the peak of the inverted-U Wundt curve. Hence, not just any amount of originality will do; it must be precisely the right amount, not too little, and not too much. Is there any other way of finding this peak except via a considerable amount of trial and error? First such-and-such a work bores aficionados silly, while the next work sends them screaming out of the concert hall or art gallery!

To be sure, at this point we might expect that the creator will gradually converge on the optimum. The oscillations in quality will diminish until every single work hits the bull's-eye. Yet there are at least three obstacles that will usually prevent such convergence from taking place.

First, the feedback from the environment is almost invariably inconsistent. It is extremely rare for any creative product to be "universally acclaimed." The critics disagree with the audiences and among themselves, one theater audience gives a standing ovation while another boos, and so forth. Even in the so-called objective sciences, the response from colleagues will seldom form a solid consensus. For example, studies of the peer-review process in professional journals and funding agencies have revealed that the judgments of separate referees agree very little on the merit of submitted manuscripts and grant proposals. The independent assessments are often only "a little better than a dice roll." Nor do matters improve much once a creative product enters the public domain. Citations to new scientific ideas are seldom uniformly positive, and they can often be highly critical. The diverse reactions to Darwin's *Origin of Species* amply illustrate the tremendous evaluative confusion that most creative products must endure. In some respects, the creator would be like a pigeon in a Skinner box who receives both a food pellet and an electric shock upon pecking at the disk. The pigeon, like the creator, would then have to engage in a complex deliberation over the precise magnitude of the cost-benefit ratio.

Second, the reinforcements and punishments are not stable over time. A work might become an instantaneous success, only to be soon dismissed as a mere faddish piece. Another work might lie dormant, its appeal not catching on until years, even decades later—perhaps even posthumously, such as happened to Gregor Mendel. Indeed, one major reason so many scientific multiples are rediscoveries is precisely because the first discovery did not have the impact necessary to preclude future scientists from working on the same problem. Notice, too, that according to Martindale's evolutionary theory, environmental feedback is inherently unstable. Owing to habituation, the target is constantly shifting. What would have been an exciting work had it been published this year might be a boring work if its performance or publication is unexpectedly delayed. Moreover, when a particular style starts to become exhausted, there is little basis for determining the best time to switch styles, or perhaps even which style to switch to.

Third, and perhaps most important, the environmental feedback, even if consistent and stable, normally provides minimal information about the specific basis for success or failure. One reason is that reactions are often global—applause or disapproval, making the best-seller list or going out of print, making it to the Top 40 or not being championed by a single disk jockey. Therefore, the creator often cannot discern what were the attributes of the creative product that led to success or failure. Admittedly, critics may provide detailed assessments, but again, the critics may disagree amongst themselves and with the public at large—and they may even guess wrong about the basis for their own reactions. Making this inference all the more difficult is the fact that most creative products are extremely complex, with multiple dimensions that may assume virtually an infinity of values. A musical composition, for example, may consist of melody, rhythm, harmony, counterpoint, formal structure, instrumentation, and a host of other variables. How is the composer to know which of these factors made a positive contribution to a work's reception and which made a negative contribution?

Indeed, two sets of entirely different empirical studies suggest that it is virtually impossible for a creator to make the inferences necessary for environmental feedback to have any consequence. The first set pertains to the attributes of creative products that render them successes or failures. What this literature demonstrates is that it is extremely difficult to identify those qualities that contribute to the differential impact of products. No matter how many potential predictors are included in the investigation, usually only a small percentage of the variation in impact can be explained—typically just between 1% and 3%. This low predictability holds for both scientific and artistic products, and it depends little on how success is assessed (citation counts, performance frequencies, number of editions, etc.). Of course, we can always suppose that some crucial attributes have been omitted, yet these studies have examined the most obvious candidates and still obtain prediction equations that do only slightly better than tossing a coin. What is more likely happening is that the factors contributing to the products' differential success do not operate according to simple additive and linear functions. Instead, the various components operate in complex multiplicative and curvilinear relationships. What might be a superior melody for one musical form might be inferior for another design. The technique ideal for treating one scientific problem might be the worst possible choice for another. A color just right for this part of a painting will be too dark for another part or too light for yet another. Thus, whether a product is deemed a masterpiece depends on an intricate configuration of attributes all having precisely the right values on innumerable dimensions. In support of this conclusion I can cite one curious empirical fact: The differential success of single creative products tends to be characterized by the same highly skewed distribution that describes individual differences in total output. For instance, the comparative popularity of Shakespeare's 37 plays fits a lognormal distribution, a mere half dozen of his dramas accounting for about a third of the Bard's presence on the stage. This is precisely what would be predicted if dramatic impact were governed by a multiplicative process.

The configurational nature of the creative product brings us to the second set of findings. A sizable empirical literature has emerged on the powers of human reasoning. Although the brain of our species is often hailed as one of the pinnacles of organic evolution, it is not as good at processing information as our self-flattery would have us believe. Instead, study after study has revealed all sorts of quirks and limitations. For example, in situations of uncertainty, people will employ certain heuristics, or rules of thumb, that often derail the ideal course of logical inference (e.g., the availability and representativeness heuristics). Furthermore, these inferential weaknesses are not restricted to average or below-average intellects. Even extremely bright people can display the most incredible inferential errors, restrictions, and biases. These foibles of human thought would surely render more difficult the creators' attempts to extract useful feedback from reactions to their products. One particular finding is especially crucial, namely that the human mind does not easily master complex configurational relationships. Rather, even the best intellects are only able to handle a few dimensions at a time, combining these dimensions in a simple additive and linear fashion. If multiplicative or curvilinear relationships are to be discerned, the number of dimensions must be appreciably reduced.

In light of these results, it seems extremely doubtful that creative individuals have the cognitive apparatus necessary to master the highly specific and intricate configurational relationships. And, needless to say, such mastery is rendered even more unlikely given the inconsistent, unstable, and global nature of the environmental feedback. As a consequence, creatively useful operant conditioning, K-type productivity, and acquired expertise could only occur under five highly restrictive circumstances:

1. The creative products expected in a domain must vary along only a very small number of dimensions. Judging from the research, the number of variables probably should not exceed about a half dozen (i.e., the "magic number" 7 ± 2). This is probably fewer available dimensions than required to write a song or a haiku, even less a symphony or a novel.

2. The causal connections between those few dimensions and the impact of the product must all be linear and additive. If there exist any curvilinear or multiplicative functions, the number of dimensions must be correspondingly reduced so as not to overtax the creator's inferences.

3. A properly weighted combination of these factors must predict almost perfectly the quality of the creative product. There exists no appreciable error term, or stochastic component, in the hypothesized equation's power to predict the reactions of others. Human beings do not easily perceive patterns when relationships are obscured by noise (or random exceptions). Even fairly substantial correlations between two variables can look chaotic to all but the most discerning eye.

4. The feedback from audiences, readers, colleagues, etc., must be consistent, stable, and highly specific to the particular strengths and weaknesses of a product. This means not only that each evaluation source must provide highly detailed assessments but also that all evaluators must concur on those details in an unchanging manner throughout the creator's career.

5. The creator must be sufficiently productive to have ample opportunity to learn which attributes will predict success. The number of trial-and-error episodes must proportionately increase with (a) the number of dimensions on which products may vary, (b) the complexity of the predictive relationships, (c) the amount of stochastic error in predicting reception from values on the relevant attributes, and (d) the inconsistency, instability, and/or undifferentiated nature of the environmental feedback. Those fields of creativity that do not support prolific output—owing to the magnitude of each creative product—

will not provide sufficient trials for a creator to exhibit an upward trajectory on some implicit learning curve.

It is arguable whether there exists any domain of genius-grade creativity
that dependably satisfies all of these criteria, even if only for the length of a
single career. Perhaps only artifacts produced in highly stable and coherent
craft traditions would regularly qualify. As a general rule, therefore, creative
products in the arts and sciences probably cannot be treated as operants,
nor as intellectual offspring easily susceptible to K-type strategies, nor as
repeated performances of some creative expertise. This is not to say that
creative individuals cannot learn to make their products meet certain minimum standards, whether for publication, exhibition, or performance. On
the contrary, that capacity is in all likelihood mastered very early in the creator's career, by the time the first work is published, exhibited, or performed. In addition, short of serious mental deterioration—such as sadly
happened to Robert Schumann when he began to succumb to mental illness—that baseline level of professional competence will probably stay with
creators for the rest of their lives. Hence, what is at issue here is not whether
an expert creator has some knowledge and skill unavailable to a mere novice
that enables the former to generate consistently competent work. Rather,
the crucial question is whether domain expertise has the power to secure a
predictable success for almost every product offered to the world. According
to the argument here, and in line with the empirical data on actual careers,
even a genius cannot escape the Darwinian reality that a creative life consists of hits and misses.

But what about Darwin's *Origin of Species?* Did that masterpiece manage
somehow to bypass all the trial and error implied by our Darwinian theory
of creativity? Must we conclude that Darwin himself was not a Darwinian
genius? I do not think so. In the two decades it took Darwin to produce
his masterpiece, he was in fact engaged in a long and difficult variation-
selection process. This is quite evident from his notebooks and correspondence. He was fully aware of many of the objections that would be raised
against his theory, especially since many of these were earlier inveighed
against the works of Lamarck and other predecessors. He would offer tentative solutions, bounce them off others, test them against other ideas or facts,
and reject, modify, or accept these hypotheses as the feedback dictated. He
would also encounter new objections that demanded additional sequences
of hypothesis and refutation. By the time fate called his hand in 1858, he had
worked out most of the principal difficulties with his theory, so that only a
few loose ends remained, such as the evolution of the complex eye.

Looking at the entire picture, the development of the *Origin of Species*
does not seem to differ in any substantial manner from the drawn-out

variation-selection process that underlies the production of other master-works. In examining the unedited notebooks or sketchbooks of others that led to the emergence of some acclaimed product, we can see the same chaos of trial and error. For example, Picasso's *Guernica*—perhaps his greatest painting—clearly originated in this fashion. This master's accumulated expertise notwithstanding, Picasso's sketchbooks are replete with false starts and wild experiments. The amount of time and effort consumed in these sketches amply exceeded what Picasso expended on the painting itself. Furthermore, this behind-the-scenes procedure of variation-selection still can't guarantee productive success. An already accomplished creator may devote years to cultivating a hoped-for magnum opus, only to discover that the labors proved largely if not entirely futile. A case in point is Einstein's unified field theory, which emerged stillborn, long after he had eminently demonstrated his ability to generate ideas that could revolutionize physics.

Successful or unsuccessful, why can't we still view this covert variation-selection process as an instance of a K-type productive strategy? After all, Darwin himself referred explicitly to the *Origin of Species* as his child—a child that took him as much time to raise as one of his biological offspring (and more personal care). Yet I would maintain that any resemblance is purely superficial. With the possible exception of some extremely poor parents of the human race, species that adopt the K-type reproductive strategy do not engage in such a pervasive trial-and-error process of parenting. For instance, birds know precisely what to do to raise their young, and they do it. It is part of their inherited expertise. Birds don't randomly try out different foods, feeding techniques, nesting materials, predator-defense strategies, or other behaviors associated with parental care. Variation in parenting is almost entirely cross-sectional (across parents) rather than taking place during each reproductive career (within parents). Hence, we can still claim that Darwin was generating ideas according to an r-type strategy, but he was subjecting them to the most rigorous standards of scientific selection before being willing to make those ideas public. This arduous and private selection process could not assure him of cultural triumph, but it could at least lessen the chance of immediate failure. The *Origin of Species* was the culmination of a doubly Darwinian process—Darwin applying creative Darwinism.

6

~

GROUPS

The Right Place and the Right Time?

~

Judging from its title, the *On Origin of Species by Means of Natural Selection* deals with groups—with collections of interbreeding organisms called species. Yet the clear focus of his evolutionary theory is the survival and reproduction of individuals. A species prospers and differentiates or declines and faces extinction, according to the reproductive success of the single creatures that constitute that group. So, only when the last passenger pigeon died in the Cincinnati Zoo on 1 September 1914 did the species *Ectopistes migratorius* become officially classified as extinct. This individualistic emphasis is one of the triumphs of Darwinian theory, because the evolution of all life-forms could be reduced to the repercussions of billions of organisms all separately engaged in their own singular struggles for existence. No grand plan, no overriding coordination of all the striving beings great and small, is required to obtain the most complex adaptations, nor even the most finely tuned social and ecological systems.

Yet this same individualism is also something of a liability. As observed in chapter 1, Darwinism has often encountered difficulties when obliged to deal with group phenomena. The altruism of the social insects was then offered as an example. Although the concepts of kin selection and inclusive fitness seem to have successfully subsumed this particular phenomenon under the individualistic framework of Darwinism, other group processes and events appear much more resistant. This difficulty is especially paramount in the case of the human species. From social Darwinism to modern sociobiology, the application (or extrapolation) of Darwin's ideas to human groups has often evoked as much controversy and rejection as praise and acceptance.

Of course, because genius appears to be such an individual phenomenon, it would seem that these theoretical difficulties would not have relevance for a Darwinian theory of creativity. As long as we have established sound theories about the creative genius, why is it necessary to worry about groups at all? The reasons are twofold. First, it is often claimed on evolutionary grounds that certain human groups differ in their per capita output of genius. Such claims oblige us to devote some discussion to three social categories that have a critical place in the history of evolutionary theory: race, culture, and gender. Second, and far more critical, it can be argued that we can comprehend the evolutionary origins of genius only by examining human social and cultural behavior. This compels us to look at the relationship between sociocultural evolution and individual creativity.

Race

Race has got to be one of the most problematic concepts in the evolutionary sciences. In Darwin's time, the term was often used in a scientific sense to denote subspecies. This usage is quite conspicuous in Darwin's early 1844 *Essay* on his evolutionary theory, albeit by 1859 he had largely switched to the term *variety*. Moreover, back in those days it seemed quite natural to speak of human races in the same way. The classification of human beings into different races even became an important scientific enterprise among physical anthropologists of the nineteenth and early twentieth centuries. Although such racial taxonomies may not be inherently dangerous, they soon became so when they became intermixed with Darwinian theory. This hazard is immediately apparent in Galton's *Hereditary Genius.* Darwin's cousin made the seemingly objective observation that some nationalities produced disproportionately more geniuses than did other nationalities. Rather than conclude that his reference books exhibited some ethnocentric bias, Galton inferred that these contrasts reflected the relative natural ability of various races of *Homo sapiens.* In drawing this inference, of course, he was being consistent with his own theory about the tight relationship between inherited genius and reputation. Just as important, this conclusion allowed Galton to embed his analysis in a larger Darwinian context. The "inferior races" are those that are "less evolved" than the "superior races." The former represent more primitive versions of the human species, varieties doomed to lose out in the never-ending struggle for existence.

The upshot of this thinking is a chapter that cannot help but make Galton's admirers wince. Titled "The Comparative Worth of Different Races," this chapter provided quantitative rankings of different racial groups. It is here that we find his statement that "the average intellectual standard of the negro race is some two grades below our own." In contrast, judging from the golden age that graced Attica in ancient times, Galton inferred that "the average ability of the Athenian race is, on the lowest possible estimate, very nearly two grades higher than our own—that is, about as much as our race is above that of the African Negro." Given this preoccupation with racial superiority, it surprises us not in the least that the following chapter discusses how to improve the genetic quality of the human race through selective breeding. Galton, in fact, was one of the early pioneers in eugenics, the movement to take active steps to encourage the best specimens of the species to be fruitful and multiply. Tragically, by the time of Nazi Germany, this movement had become twisted into an active campaign to remove undesirable genetic material from the population through sterilization and genocide.

I hasten to point out that Galton was by no means unique in generating such ideas on race. Similar notions are conspicuous in many of the writings of the early evolutionists—most notably Herbert Spencer—and Darwin himself was not immune from such thinking. In the 1871 *Descent of Man*, Darwin often cited with approval his cousin's racial beliefs. Darwin even used the notion of an evolution-based racial hierarchy to identify the so-called savage as the "missing link" between the anthropoid apes and civilized humans. Of the major figures in these early years, only Alfred Wallace had relatively egalitarian views about racial differences. In fact, because Wallace refused to use "primitive races" as the transitional forms linking the apes with white Europeans, he experienced more difficulty trying to understand how natural selection could account for the evolution of the human brain. If the brain of a nearly naked jungle dweller matches that of the most sophisticated (and well-attired) urbanite, then it seemed to Wallace, at least, that evolutionary theory has got some real explaining to do. In any event, it was because of this issue that Wallace actually concluded that the human central nervous system must have arisen by some other means. Wallace's adherence to this view certainly did not endear him to Darwin, Galton, and other early evolutionists.

A Modern Theory

Although the association between Darwinism and racial hierarchies has waned in the twentieth century, and especially since World War II, the affinity still reappears from time to time. The most recent episode involves the theory advanced by J. Philippe Rushton in the 1980s. Rushton began by reviewing what he considered to be secure empirical differences between three main racial groups: Mongoloids, Caucasoids, and Negroids. These differences concerned intelligence (cranial capacity, brain weight, and test scores), maturation rate (gestation time, skeletal development, age of walking, age of first intercourse, age of first pregnancy, and longevity), personality and temperament (activity level, aggressiveness, anxiety, dominance, extroversion, impulsivity, and sociability), sexuality (multiple birthing, genitalia size, secondary sex characters, intercourse frequencies, and permissive attitudes), and social organization (marital stability, mental health, and law abidingness). He then claimed that in every case the order of the three groups was the same, with the mean value for Caucasoids falling between that of the Mongoloids and the Negroids.

Rushton next linked these intergroup contrasts with what would be anticipated according to r/K reproductive strategies—the idea that I introduced in the preceding chapter. Mongoloids fall on the K end of the spectrum, whereas Negroids fall on the r end, with Caucasoids again in the middle. Thus, K strategists would have the characteristics favoring a low rate of reproduction but with low offspring mortality, whereas the r strategists would have the characteristics favoring a high rate of reproduction but with high offspring mortality. According to Rushton, these racial differences reflect the rather contrasting ecological circumstances in which the three races evolved. In general, environments favoring r strategies (or r selection) are highly unstable, whereas those favoring K strategies (or K selection) are highly stable. Especially critical are the disparate environments of the Mongoloids and Negroids, the former emerging near the subarctic climates, the latter in the vicinity of the equator.

Although Rushton's evolutionary theory does not explicitly address the origins of genius, its relevance ensues immediately from two sources. First, given the greater importance of competent and foresightful child care, K strategists are predicted to have higher IQ scores than r strategists. Therefore, if we adopt the psychometric definition of genius, the former group should have more individuals with high-IQs than the latter, and hence more geniuses, as defined by IQ tests. Second, and more crucial, other scholars have explicitly linked these same three racial categories, in the same hierarchical ordering, to their relative contributions to human civilization. Hence, the r/K reproductive strategies would seem to provide the theoretical basis for explaining racial differences in Galtonian genius.

I have tried to be as objective as possible in presenting this theory, which is not easy to do. Rushton's views have stimulated considerable controversy, and the feedback from the public and fellow academics has been mostly hostile. Independent of whether the theory fits the scientific facts, it is certainly true that Rushton's ideas are not consonant with the prevailing political zeitgeist. Indeed, some scholars might criticize me for giving so much space to what they consider a highly racist theory. Nonetheless, it is naive to think that a politically unpalatable theory will necessarily vanish just because it is ignored. To disallow rational discussion may serve only to feed white supremacist and conspiracist groups. Moreover, Rushton is a competent, dedicated, and responsible researcher who has tried to make it quite clear what his theory does *not* claim with respect to prejudice, civil rights, and economic opportunities. Most important, Rushton's theory probably embodies the most responsible and thorough attempt to explicate supposed racial differences in intellectual ability according to Darwinian concepts. If this is the best available theory, and if this theory fails to hold up to scientific scrutiny, then other theories of this type may not be very promising from a scientific perspective.

A Brief Critique

Many respected scientists have criticized such evolutionary theories on scientific grounds alone. One crucial complaint regards the use of reproductive strategies as the basis for explanation. Many would argue that the r/K theory has enough empirical and theoretical problems that it may not offer a sufficiently strong foundation for differentiating the characteristics that supposedly describe the three groups and their environments. The same theory can even be used to suggest very different interpretations for the same phenomena. For instance, it has been put forward that the reproductive strategy adopted by an individual may be a function of environmental cues that prevail during childhood. In particular, if the father is absent from the home, the child may adopt an r strategy as an adult; but the same child might pursue a K strategy under more auspicious circumstances. Father absence then would function as a developmental cue because it has implications for whether the child is more likely to grow up in an r- or K-selected environment. Father absence is associated with instability, father presence with stability. Other consequences of reproductive strategy then follow suit. Under this scheme, the strategy is not a permanent feature of a particular race but rather reflects the developmental impact of an ecological setting for a specific generation. Observed differences in group means in intelligence may then merely reflect temporary contrasts in the modal environments in which different races typically find themselves.

But besides this specialized criticism, there are four others that may apply to all attempts to explain racial differences in biological terms. First, race is such a nebulous concept that it might prove too ambiguous to provide the basis for a scientific theory. This complaint is especially potent for categories as inclusive as Mongoloid, Caucasoid, and Negroid (which necessarily include representatives who have occupied a tremendous diversity of habitats). Second, the individual variation within each group may be so vast, and thus the overlap in characteristics between groups so substantial, that the theory may not be accounting for a very conspicuous phenomenon, if the phenomenon exists at all. Third, given the racial prejudice that plagues many people—including scientists—it is often risky to place a great deal of scientific confidence in many of the empirical findings regarding supposed group differences. Nor must prejudices be blatant or overt to contaminate results, because biases can impact research by more subtle means. Fourth, it is always difficult to prove, beyond the shadow of a doubt, that a particular group difference in a psychological attribute has biological origins. Many supposed differences may instead reflect environmental or cultural differences, and therefore characteristics that can change without any alteration of the gene pool.

Admittedly, at this point none of these four criticisms is decisive. Further scientific research might even prove Rushton's theory to have captured some genuine truth. I am only claiming that there are considerable grounds for skepticism—for withholding judgment until these various concerns can be ameliorated in a scientifically satisfactory manner. For me, at least, the fourth criticism carries special weight. Human beings may be so much creatures of culture that cultural characteristics play the predominant part in a people's participation in world civilization. A "superior race" in one era may, for cultural causes, see its grandeur quickly extinguished, just as an "inferior race" in another period may find itself just as suddenly propelled by another cultural agency to history's foremost ranks. Take the Arabic peoples as a case in point. The Arabs lived for ages in a cultural backwater of the Fertile Crescent, only their poetry showing any major mark of distinction. Within a century of their conversion to the Islamic faith, the Arabs began producing landmarks in science, philosophy, literature, art, and music. Yet after only about a half millennium, the Arabs found themselves quickly losing ground to other nationalities within Islamic civilization, including the Persians and Turks. Even the most massive and intrusive program of eugenics could not produce effects this profound in so short a time.

I can do better than to cite just a single example.

Culture

One of the classics in the study of creative genius is the 1944 book *Configurations of Culture Growth* by Alfred Kroeber, the eminent American anthropologist. In many respects, this work is comparable in importance to Galton's *Hereditary Genius*. In fact, a glance through both volumes reveals many curious similarities: Both books contain chapters that examine the main domains of human achievement, and both adopt a quasi-Baconian (inductive) method of providing detailed lists of geniuses from various nationalities and historical eras. Yet on closer inspection some critical differences also appear: Galton lists his geniuses in alphabetical order so as to emphasize family pedigrees, whereas Kroeber arranges his geniuses in chronological order so as to stress historical contiguity; Galton gives his chapters titles that imply a focus on individuals ("Literary Men," "Men of Science," "Musicians," "Painters," etc.), whereas Kroeber labels his chapters to underline the achievements of more impersonal cultural groups ("Science," "Painting," "Literature," "Music," etc.); and Galton's data show a strong bias toward the geniuses of European civilization, whereas Kroeber gives ample attention to the monumental attainments of Islamic, Indian, Chinese, Japanese, Native American, and other world civilizations.

These contrasts are more than superficial, for Kroeber had explicitly sought to disprove Galton's biological theory of genius. As a cultural anthropologist, Kroeber believed that genius was a sociocultural phenomenon rather than the consequence of genetically endowed "natural ability." Significantly, Kroeber had been the student of the German-educated Franz Boas. The latter took such an effective stand against theories of racial superiority that the Nazis publicly burned his most influential book and rescinded his Ph.D. from Kiel University. Of course, by the time Kroeber was writing *Configurations*, Nazi racial theories had already become a eugenic monster.

In any case, Kroeber compiled chronology after chronology showing that genius tends to cluster into cultural configurations. No matter what the particular domain studied, great creators group together into a temporal pattern of golden and silver ages separated by dark ages in which creativity sometimes seems to vanish altogether. For instance, Kroeber presented data showing that scientific genius in England falls into two clusters. The first group contained such figures as Gilbert, Napier, Harvey, Wallis, Hooke, Boyle, Barrow, Mercator, Halley, and the great Newton—individuals all born within one century of each other. The second group began after a relative lull of several generations and included such notables as Cavendish, Hutton, Rumford, Davy, Dalton, Faraday, Joule, Kelvin, and Maxwell—again, all born no more than a century apart. It is this second cluster, of course, that contained the major players in the classic era of Darwinian theory: Lyell, Charles Darwin, Hooker, Wallace, Galton, and T. H. Huxley, all born within a quarter century of each other.

To be sure, Galton was also aware of this clustering phenomenon. For example, Galton recognized the golden age of Greece, but he attributed this event to the racial superiority of the Athenian nation. The decline, in particular, could be ascribed to the adoption of degenerate practices—namely miscegenation with inferior stock. Yet Kroeber recognized the inadequacy of Galton's interpretation. The glory that was Greece rose and fell too quickly to be ascribed to changes in the Greek gene pool. Human populations are big enough that it would require rather impractical eugenic interventions to make substantial and rapid alterations in gene frequencies. But if Galton's misplaced primary Darwinism failed to explain these cultural configurations, what can? Kroeber himself did not offer much of an answer. He merely made some vague speculations about the emergence, growth, culmination, and exhaustion of cultural patterns. Is it possible to do better than this?

It has been argued recently that the transhistorical clustering of genius may still reflect a Darwinian process. But the process is secondary rather than primary. In chapter 2 I examined Campbell's variation-selection theory of creativity, and in the following chapters I discussed how both individual differences and personal development may correspond to what we would predict if creativity were indeed described by this Darwinian process. In the same way, the ups and downs in the appearance of creative genius may correspond to underlying changes in the sociocultural milieu that affect the appearance of such Darwinian personalities. That is, some environmental factors may enhance the emergence and manifestation of individuals capable of the unrestrained generation of ideational variations, whereas other factors may inhibit the realization of such Darwinian potential. To see the value of this interpretation, let us review the conditions that nurture the creativity of groups at particular times and places. This "Darwinian zeitgeist" is composed of domain activity, intellectual receptiveness, ethnic diversity, and political openness.

Domain Activity

To say that creative genius groups into configurations is actually to assert that two distinct phenomena hold. First, because the creators fall into contiguous generations, all except those at the very beginning of the configuration will have predecessors who lived one or more generations before. Second, because many creators will fall in the same generation, they will rub shoulders with contemporaries of genius. These two phenomena need to be examined separately.

Predecessors. Generational time-series analyses have consistently shown that the number of eminent creators in one generation is a positive function of the number in the preceding generation who are active in the same or affiliated domains. This aggregate-level relationship has its counterparts on the individual level. Creative talent is nourished by the presence of role models and mentors. In both the arts and sciences, the more eminent geniuses tended to have studied under more different mentors and to have been influenced by a greater variety of predecessors. Charles Darwin is an example. Among his teachers were such scientific luminaries as Alexander Monro and Adam Sedgwick, and among the predecessors who had some impact on his thinking were such scientific notables as James Hutton, Lamarck, C. K. Sprengel, Malthus, Alexander von Humboldt, K. E. von Baer, Geoffroy Saint-Hilaire, J. F. Herschel, and Charles Lyell (but, oddly, not Erasmus Darwin, his grandfather). Certainly, like Newton before him, Darwin stood on the shoulders of many different giants.

In chapter 4 I observed how creativity is favored by an intellect that has been enriched with diverse experiences and perspectives. And in chapter 3 I noted that creativity is associated with a mind that exhibits a variety of interests and knowledge. Having several mentors, role models, and other influential predecessors is an obvious means to attain these desired qualities. Indeed, it was precisely because Darwin was obliged to assimilate key findings in a number of domains—geology, zoology, botany, embryology, economics, anthropology, and even animal breeding—that he possessed the wherewithal to compose his grand synthesis of 1859. In contrast, Patrick Matthew's 1831 version of evolutionary theory, although in an abstract sense identical to Darwin's, was far more narrow in its conceptual underpinnings. Lacking the needed integrative power, Matthew's work could not make a truly convincing case. For Darwin alone was the argument comprehensive and persuasive.

One remaining aspect of such predecessor influences attracts special note. We learned about Planck's principle in chapter 5—the tendency for older scientists to become more resistant to innovative ideas. It would seem that this tendency might interfere with a scientist's ability to effectively mentor the younger generation of scientific talent. Such scientists will likely be less receptive to the divergent ideas of their students. There actually exists empirical evidence to this effect, not only in the sciences but also in the arts. The most distinguished scientific and artistic creators have generally studied under teachers and masters who were closer to their own creative primes.

There are exceptions, of course, but those exceptions often have a twist that reaffirms the rule. When the young Beethoven studied under the great Haydn, the latter was already an elder statesman in the music world. Certain creative conflicts were the inevitable consequence. Most notably, when Beethoven thought himself ready to publish his Opus 1, a set of three piano trios, Haydn tried to dissuade him from including the Trio in C Minor, the third in the set. Haydn thought it was far too daring and that his pupil would be ill-advised to include such a work that would only damage his reputation. The master's opinions notwithstanding, Beethoven believed this trio to be the highlight of his current efforts. It must be counted fortunate that Beethoven ignored Haydn's advice, for posterity agrees with the student rather than the master. It should not astonish us to learn that Beethoven felt himself obliged to take secret lessons from other composers younger than Haydn, such as Antonio Salieri, who was then at the peak of his career. Beethoven thereby obtained both diversity and youth in mentorship, enabling him to grow into a revolutionary musical genius.

Contemporaries. Darwin had more than predecessors. Despite his quiet life in Down, he was surrounded by contemporaries who claimed notable distinction in the biological sciences. These illustrious scientists were his friends, associates, colleagues, and correspondents, as well as rivals and competitors. A partial list alone must include such figures as Lyell, Owen, J. D. Hooker, Asa Gray, F. Müller, Wallace, Galton, T. H. Huxley, Lubbock, Haeckel, and even, later in life, his son and collaborator Francis Darwin. Empirical research has demonstrated that eminent scientists are historically more likely to appear in times when they can form relationships with other scientists making contributions to the same and affiliated domains. The same pattern holds for the arts as well, and hence this simultaneous clustering of genius constitutes a universal pattern. No matter what the domain of achievement, genius of the highest quality tends to be contemporaneous with genius of a lesser rank, and even with the more obscure also-rans and nonentities. It is almost as if the equal-odds rule discussed in the preceding chapter holds not just for creative products but for productive creators besides. Increase the total number of individuals in a particular generation who are struggling to make it big, and the odds are increased that one of the genuine giants will emerge.

Naturally, if creativity in one generation is stimulated by creativity in the prior generation, we should predict that creative genius would be concurrent with other exemplars of the phenomenon. But something more than this spurious effect is operating. Even after statistical adjustment is made for the impact of predecessors, the heights attained by a creator are raised by the immersion in an environment that permits an abundance of professional contacts and networks. Thus, the favorable effect of such surroundings must be granted its own distinct interpretation.

Now some portion of this contemporaneous effect probably has nothing to do with Darwinian processes. For example, creators must have audiences or followings, and very often they are made up primarily of fellow creators. This is especially obvious in the case of scientific creativity, given that the readership for the technical literature is made up almost entirely of scientists in the same specialty. Yet the same necessity often arises in the arts as well. The poet W. H. Auden once expressed this dependence in a humorous fashion: "The ideal audience the poet imagines consists of the beautiful who go to bed with him, the powerful who invite him to dinner and tell him secrets of state, and his fellow-poets. The actual audience he gets consists of myopic schoolteachers, pimply young men who eat in cafeterias, and his fellow-poets. This means that, in fact, he writes for his fellow-poets." It is highly unlikely that high-caliber genius can emerge as a mere "voice crying out in the wilderness." Without the presence of kindred spirits, the unheard creators would most likely sink into silence. In support of this conclusion, research has shown that individuals whose creativity emerges in comparative isolation are more prone to suffer truncated careers.

Of course, this aspect of the phenomenon might be made to fit a Darwinian perspective. We could argue that it is the contemporaries who ultimately decide whether a given creative product has met the test of adaptiveness. The creator produces the originality, and fellow creators determine if that originality constitutes genuine creativity. Some proponents of Darwinian views have taken this very position. For instance, Aharon Kantorovich asserted the following in his book *Scientific Discovery*:

> No scientist can know that he has made discovery before he has submitted it to the scientific community. An essential part of the process of discovery is the processing of the proposed hypothesis by the scientific community. Only when this processing is terminated with acceptance, is the process of discovery terminated. Hence, . . . *the discoverer is the whole scientific community*, rather than the scientist(s) who proposed the hypothesis.

Yet Kantorovich goes beyond this claim to assert that the scientific community is engaged not just in selection but in variation besides. Campbell's blind-variation process occurs not merely within individual minds. An analogous process takes place in the intellectual exchange of scientists working within a given discipline. That is,

> when a scientist proposes an idea to the scientific community, he is not anymore in control over the idea, which is processed by the community synchronically and diachronically. The end product may solve a problem the originator of the idea has not dreamt about; in suggesting the idea, the originator was "blind" to the problem that is eventually solved in the process he initiated.

An instance of this phenomenon is what happened to Max Planck's quantum hypothesis. Originally designed to solve a rather narrow problem in physics (blackbody radiation), it was unexpectedly used by Einstein to explicate the photoelectric effect. That success inspired further applications that led to the quantum revolution, a revolution that went well beyond what Planck had envisioned—and much further even than Einstein thought justified. Of course, a similar cascade of collective variations occurred in the case of Darwin's theory.

David Hull has taken the Darwinian argument in yet another direction in his *Science as a Process: An Evolutionary Account of the Social and Conceptual Development of Science.* Hull noted that in the modern scientific enterprise, the active researchers are engaged simultaneously in competitive and in cooperative activities. There is competition to make and get credit for discoveries, but there is also cooperation among scientists who belong to the same school or research team. In the latter case, collaborators and colleagues act to optimize their "conceptual inclusive fitness." The rivalry between scientific groups is similar to that between ant colonies or lion prides or primate troops. The upshot of this dynamic interplay is a group-level variation-and-selection process that drives scientific discovery while at the same time imposing the checks and balances needed for scientific progress. After all, rival groups have strong incentives to prove competing hypotheses wrong, and such will likely happen if a hypothesis is actually incorrect.

But aside from all these interpersonal and sociological processes, immersion in an environment of intellectual and cultural ferment is also more likely to fuel the variation-selection process *within* the mind of a creative genius. The intellect of any creator is richly endowed with associative material belonging to a certain domain. At the same time, the creative person is open to new experiences, ever ready to exploit the chaos of ideas in that milieu. The interaction between the internal meanderings of the creative intellect and this external influx should excite the associative activity. Not only will solutions more likely be primed for old problems, but in addition new problems will be stimulated into being. In the absence of this incessant influx, the creative mind will more quickly run dry. As Sir Joshua Reynolds noted in his *Discourses on Art,* "The greatest natural genius cannot subsist on its own stock: he who resolves never to ransack any mind but his own, will be soon reduced, from mere barrenness, to the poorest of all imitations; he will be obliged to imitate himself, and to repeat what he has before often repeated. When we know the subject designed by such men, it will never be difficult to guess what kind of work is to be produced." Pablo Picasso amply illustrated the value of having a mind always open to the ideas and images of other artists. He borrowed, stole, and assimilated his way into the most incredibly prodigious and varied body of work of any artist in the twentieth century. Over a career nearly three-quarters of a century long, he produced more than 20,000 works of art in a myriad of media and styles. Hence, being surrounded by the ideas generated by contemporary creators may inspire the best creators to attain heights well above what they could possibly achieve in isolation. Individual genius through social and cultural interaction becomes intensified.

There is some indirect evidence for this conjecture. In chapter 5 I mentioned the Price law. What exactly does it mean to assert that half of all work in a field comes from the square root of the total number of workers? If there are only 10 creators active in a domain, about 3, or 30%, will account for half of the output; if 100 workers, then 10, or 10%; and if there are 10,000, then 100, or just 1%, will claim credit for half of the contributions. Hence, according to the Price law, as the number of creators in a domain increases, the most prominent producers must become even more prolific. The 3 out of 10 do not have to produce as much to account for half of all products as would the 100 out of 10,000 (remembering that I am considering only creators who have generated at least one product). This intensified productivity of the elite suggests that the creative process within the top geniuses is further fired by a cornucopia of creative contemporaries.

Intellectual Receptiveness

Charles Darwin did not live in a milieu of homogeneous beliefs. He was not living during the European Middle Ages, when heretical views could get you burned at the stake. On the contrary, the intellectual revolution launched by René Descartes continued to have reverberations throughout the Western world. New schools of thought emerged and proliferated. During the course of Darwin's career, John Stuart Mill and Herbert Spencer were extending the British empiricist tradition in new directions, Comte was introducing positivism in France, and the philosophical successors of Kant and Hegel were proliferating and diversifying in Germany. In the latter group was Karl Marx, who had been living in England since 1849.

To be sure, Darwin was by no means involved in these philosophical movements, even as a passive observer. He even complained about his inability to follow deep philosophical arguments. Even so, that is not the relevant consideration here. Darwin had only to realize that intellectual hegemonies were continuing to break down. If truth and beauty, good and evil are all matters for active debate, why should the Genesis stories continue to hold their privileged position with respect to the origin of species? Darwin was not a philosopher, nor even much of a free thinker outside his scientific work. In religion, he confessed being an agnostic while denying that he was an atheist. But the zeitgeist did help instill in him a persistent skepticism about the claims of authority and tradition. This attitude enabled him to venture ideas that others of his time and station would never dare.

Mao Ze-dong once said, "Letting a hundred flowers blossom and a hundred schools of thought contend is the policy for promoting the progress of the arts and the sciences." If Mao was correct, then Darwin's case would be far from unique. In actual fact, empirical research shows that Mao's policy would have been a wise one if faithfully executed. When a civilization is characterized by conspicuous ideological diversity—the presence of numerous rival philosophical schools—then creativity tends to increase, even in those domains that have relatively little to do with intellectual trends.

This may partially explain why economic prosperity is often seen as a powerful group factor underlying creative genius. According to one econometrics text, "art and literature flourish in a rising economy, but they wither and perish in one that declines." Although there can be no doubt that a strong economic foundation is required for many forms of creativity—most notably monumental architecture—many creative activities really do not demand substantial material support. Poetry is a case in point, and much great poetry has initially been privately printed (Whitman's *Leaves of Grass*) or even just circulated in manuscript form (Shakespeare's sonnets). As a consequence, it may be that the economy also operates via some other factor. On the one hand, rapid economic growth may cause sufficient social change to loosen the bonds imposed by tradition and thus prepare the way for an intellectual renaissance. On the other hand, economic stagnation and depression often augments tendencies toward authoritarianism, dogmatism, and rigidity, thereby undermining the intellectual receptiveness required for the emergence of creative genius.

Ethnic Diversity

I noted back in chapter 4 that immigrants often seem to have the inside track on the path to creative genius. This tendency was even observed by Galton in *Hereditary Genius* (albeit he had an alternative, genetic interpretation). In particular, Galton observed that "it is very remarkable how large a proportion of the eminent men of all countries bear foreign names, and are the children of political refugees—men well qualified to introduce a valuable strain of blood." Speaking at a more sociological level, Robert Park pointed to the importance of population shifts in the making of history: "Every advance in culture, it has been said, commences with a new period of migration and movement of populations."

It is critical to realize that it is not just the immigrants who can benefit from these population shifts. The native citizens may have their creativity stimulated as well. For example, one quantitative study examined the entire history of Japanese civilization. This culture was deliberately selected because it has been highly variable in its openness to outside influences. During some points foreign ideas and people were vigorously suppressed, while during others Japan would open wide its gates to the outside world. Significantly, those periods in which Japan was receptive to alien influx were soon followed by periods of augmented creative activity. Furthermore, the foreign influence could take several forms, including study abroad, mentorship under a foreign master, or the immigration of individuals from the outside. Whatever the specific means, the native Japanese themselves experienced the enhanced odds of exhibiting creative genius.

These historiometric results probably do not reflect anything idiosyncratic about the Japanese civilization. For example, scrutiny of Nobel laureates reveals that an extremely high percentage had studied abroad sometime during the course of their career development. In addition, these findings are compatible with laboratory experiments that show how exposure to discrepant or dissenting viewpoints can stimulate divergent thought processes. It is as if the mere exposure to different lifestyles and divergent values enables individuals to expand the range and originality of their ideational variations. The awareness of cultural variety helps set the mind free.

Darwin was not an immigrant, nor did he study abroad, nor did he work with a foreign teacher. Yet he was a world traveler at one crucial juncture in his formative years. He had visited strange places, and he had exchanged gestures and vocal utterances with non-European peoples. As is readily apparent from his diaries, letters, and, of course, *The Voyage of the Beagle*, Darwin's capacity for displaying Darwinian genius was irreversibly broadened and enriched by these experiences.

Political Openness

Many of the foregoing circumstances are themselves highly contingent on the prevailing political zeitgeist. The history of Japanese civilization again offers an illustration. The degree of openness to foreign influences was often a matter of explicit government policies rather than of personal choice. At times travel abroad was severely restricted and advocates of alien ideas were subjected to official persecution. The same contingency holds for ethnic diversity within a culture. Oppression of the minority by the majority can completely undo any potential advantage of ethnic marginality. Thus, Jews could rise above historical obscurity only in those nations where they enjoyed at least the basic freedoms. There were fewer Jews in Switzerland than in Russia. Yet the former are 83 times more likely to pick up a Nobel Prize in science than are the latter, on a per capita basis. That contrast may bespeak the comparative status of Jews in the two societies.

As a consequence, often the only way a minority can realize its creative potential is to break the chains imposed by the majority. Suppressed nationalities seldom make monumental contributions to human civilization. This conclusion is expressed by the Danilevsky law: "In order for the civilization of a potentially creative group to be conceived and developed, the group and its subgroups must be politically independent." In fact, empirical research shows that political fragmentation—the division of a multiethnic civilization into many sovereign states—has a positive impact on the amount of creativity displayed. This effect operates both directly, through the encouragement of cultural cross-fertilization, and indirectly, through its influence on intellectual openness, which tends to expand under such conditions.

Conversely, the expansion of empires into "universal states" often proceeds at the expense of the cultural vitality of the enslaved peoples. Imperial Russia's effort to "Russify" its subject nationalities—and the Soviet empire's revised attempts to the same end—are prototypical. For this reason, revolts and rebellions against the culturally oppressive imperial state can stir up the intellectual and aesthetic broth, exposing developing talents to new alternatives, perspectives, and traditions. Therefore, a couple of decades after civil disturbances, the world frequently sees a new golden age of creative activity. This influx in the next generation occurs across all major creative domains. Hence, many nationalities achieve a climax of creativity shortly after their liberation from foreign rule. The golden age of Greece followed upon the heels of the Persian Wars, which conclusively fixed Greek freedom. The peoples of the Netherlands did not come fully into their own until they had declared their independence from Spain; the Dutch nation then became home to Vondel, Rembrandt, Huygens, and Spinoza.

Speaking in general terms, any political circumstance that increases the intermixture of cultural and intellectual material will likely encourage the emergence of individuals capable of more original ideational variations. Yet political circumstances can also discourage the appearance of Darwinian genius. Aversive events are many, but probably the most powerful is war. As one historian noted, "Warfare usually tends to produce cultural and intellectual sterility." This negative effect holds for every form of creativity, even for technology.

I realize that the latter claim may seem surprising, given how many innovations have emerged during wartime. Thus World War II saw the appearance or development of radar, ballistic missiles, jet airplanes, and the atom bomb. Yet we necessarily overlook all of the other inventions that had their evolution delayed because of the severe restrictions imposed by national priorities. When all research must be dedicated to the "war effort," there leaves little latitude for the unrestrained production of technological variations. Indeed, the overall effect of war is to narrow the focus of a nation's creativity, channeling that creativity into just a few urgent and obvious directions. The individualism and the freedom of the creative genius becomes subordinated to the collective emergency. The only exceptions occur when the conflict does not represent an immediate threat to the nation. According to empirical research, imperialistic wars fought abroad to consolidate power in the colonies have no detrimental influence on creativity at home.

This last observation applies perfectly to Darwin's own situation. Darwin could not have picked a better time to live in Great Britain. After the defeat of Napoleon in 1815 when Darwin was only six years old, the British nation entered a period of military security lasting nearly a century. During this interval it never felt itself immediately threatened by a foreign power. "All of the military and naval operations of the British Empire took place away from the British Isles," notes one military encyclopedia. Until Darwin's death, only the faraway Crimean War did so much as disturb the economy of the homeland. And even that conflict terminated three years before Darwin published the *Origin of Species*.

Gender

Galton's *Hereditary Genius* did not have a great deal to say about gender differences in outstanding creativity. But it is evident from even the most casual reading that Galton shared the views of his Victorian contemporaries: Women were the inferior sex. This fact is quite evident in the very notation he devised to indicate family pedigrees. The code went as follows: father *F* and mother *f*, brother *B* and sister *b*, uncle *U* and aunt *u*—and so forth for other relatives. In every case, the male gets its term's first letter capitalized, while the female gets the male's letter in lowercase. Moreover, it is apparent from Galton's lists of eminent pedigrees that women do not fare well. Only in the chapter "Literary Men" do they have any conspicuous representation (e.g., the Brontë sisters).

Unfortunately, we cannot completely fault Galton for the minimal presence of women in the annals of history. In the diverse histories of cultural attainments, the names are overwhelmingly male. In Western civilization, for example, women make up only around 3% of the most illustrious figures of history. And many of these females entered the records in part by birthright or marriage. Elizabeth I of England, Christina of Sweden, Catherine the Great of Russia, Maria Theresa of Austria are examples. Furthermore, in specific areas the female presence may sink to one-third of that percentage. In the annals of science, fewer than 1% of all notables are female. Names like Hypatia, Caroline Herschel, Marie Curie, and Barbara McClintock are but drops in a sea of male scientists. In classical music, the percentage of female luminaries may shrink to near zero. For every Hildegard von Bingen, Fanny Mendelssohn, Clara Schumann, Amy Beech, Nadia Boulanger, Ruth Crawford Seeger, and Thea Musgrave, there are dozens of male composers more famous. Until recently, creative writing was the only area in which women could really shine. Among the giants of world literature, about 1 in 10 are female. Even so, perhaps only in Japanese literature can we say that a female author has won the highest of reputations. In Japan, Murasaki Shikibu authored the world's first novel, *Tale of Genji*, securing herself a status comparing favorably with that of William Shakespeare in England.

So what are we to make of these facts? In line with what we have discussed regarding race and culture, there are two principal explanations. At one extreme, the low proportion of female genius may be ascribed to the organic evolution of our species. At the other extreme, this same historical datum may be merely the upshot of sociocultural evolution, with no biological underpinnings whatsoever.

Sexual Dimorphism and Selection

From the standpoint of Galton's theory, the answer to our inquiry would be clear: If natural ability almost invariably results in acclaim, women must have less natural ability. The dearth of female genius would merely reflect an inferiority in intellect, motivation, and other qualities that contribute to posthumous reputation. Furthermore, it would be no hard task to argue that this lower inherent genius has some evolutionary foundation. After all, sexual dimorphism is as apparent in *Homo sapiens* as it is in many other vertebrate species. Moreover, as Darwin pointed out in his discussion of sexual selection, this dimorphism often operates so that the males embody the most extreme, and hence, presumably, the more evolved, forms. If men exhibit more brawn, it seemed logical to suppose that they would display more brains as well. Supposedly, runs the argument, it takes less intellect to take care of domestic chores than it does to hunt down the big game.

The empirical evidence for this thesis is extremely weak, however. Although much effort has been expended on proving that women's brains are inferior to men's, the results here are even more controversial than is the case for racial differences. Even more important, it is extremely difficult to prove that women score lower on IQ tests or some other measure of intelligence. In fact, by some criteria, such as scholastic performance, women often do better than men.

These difficulties have led some primary Darwinists to adopt a different line of attack in their efforts to prove female inferiority. The average woman may be as smart as the average man, they will argue, but men are said to exhibit much more variability. The direct repercussion would be that the brightest man would be brighter than the brightest woman, and that more men than women would boast genius-level IQs. The women would be left with the consolation prize of knowing that the least intelligent male may be less intelligent than the least intelligent female, and that there would be more very unintelligent males than very unintelligent females. This alternative formula also has roots in Darwin's theory of sexual selection, by which he had suggested that the males exhibited more variability than females. Indeed, when Darwin sought to establish this thesis, he placed more emphasis on data drawn from human beings than from any other species.

Yet this tactic has its own set of problems. One difficulty is that it is not completely clear why men should be more variable than women. Darwin himself was hard-pressed for an explanation, and subsequent researchers may not have done much better. Another difficulty involves the empirical evidence: Although men have sometimes been shown to display more variation than women on certain relevant traits, including intellectual abilities, the data are not entirely convincing. The statistics often admit multiple interpretations, not all of which suggest biological differences—such as differences in educational experiences. And recall what I noted in chapter 1: The highest IQ recorded in the *Guinness Book of Records* is held by a woman, not a man.

Not surprisingly, feminists often conclude that these Darwinist explanations are little more than theoretically cloaked attempts to defend male social supremacy. As such, these speculations fall in the same camp as the attempts to conceive racial hierarchies in Darwinian terms. It must be considered more than mere coincidence that the primary advocates of these theories are men, and that somehow the arguments tend to emerge with the men ranked superior to women in areas of real import. This is true even when Darwinian concepts are applied to the animal world.

Take the brilliant plumage of the peacock, for example. A great deal of emphasis is placed on the superiority of the male accouterments relative to the female's drab feathers. Yet we tend to forget that sexual selection is a two-way street in which male and female must coevolve. While the peacock is evolving elaborately colored and configured displays, the peahen must be evolving ever more sophisticated powers of perceptual discrimination in order to make fine distinctions between rival mates. In other words, we could turn the argument on its head and claim that the male may get all the looks while the female gets all the brains. Whether this is true is not the real issue. The point is that Darwinian interpretations can be used to compose a wide variety of "just-so" stories. This latitude can too easily serve merely as a Rorschach test in which theorists inadvertently project their gender prejudices on the social world.

In fact, it is actually possible to use Darwin's idea of sexual selection to argue that both men and women might evolve the same capacity for creative genius. At the close of chapter 3, I briefly discussed Geoffrey Miller's recent attempt to explain the origins of creativity in terms of the evolution of the protean mind. The ability to be unpredictable, to be surprising, has assets in a complex social world in which the capability to outsmart rivals has clear-cut adaptive advantages. But Miller has argued that the same ability may reach even greater heights of creative expression when it becomes a criterion for mate selection. Both men and women could try to attract mates by demonstrating creative behaviors, whether it be through singing or dancing, toolmaking or basket weaving. Even more crucial was the advent of the human capacity for language, for then courtship could take place on a more intellectual plane. Flirtatious displays of humor and wit, wisdom and creativity could be conveyed in verbal terms. Lovers could woo each other with poems and songs as well as gifts and adornments. This beautiful feature of human courtship is wonderfully illustrated in Murasaki's *Tale of Genji*, which recounts the amorous adventures of the title character—adventures ever punctuated by the exchange of verse between male and female. And who has not admired Elizabeth Barrett's famous sonnet for Robert Browning that begins "How do I love thee? Let me count the ways"? Indeed, who among my readers, no matter what the gender, has not written a love poem?

Miller believes that sexual selection for these creative skills could have instigated a runaway evolutionary process that favored the emergence of the human brain. This is a crucial possibility, because sexual selection is as strong a force for forest dwellers as it is for denizens of the city. The desire to win an attractive mate is a cross-cultural and transhistorical universal for all peoples that have survived eons of natural selection. Hence, Miller's evolutionary mechanism would resolve Wallace's doubts about whether Darwinism can account for the origins of the human intellect. Perhaps sexual selection rather than natural selection deserves most of the credit.

It needs emphasis that, under this scenario, mate choice is working on both the male and the female simultaneously and equally, because these assets are of comparable value to the reproductive success of their offspring. So men and women concurrently evolve the capacity for creativity. Figuratively speaking, both males and females acquire brilliant intellectual plumage. Yet this coevolution does not really conflict with the classic model of sexual selection as applied to the peacock and peahen. Natural selection prevents the peahen from competing with the peacock in the same terms. So there exists an asymmetry in the evolutionary pressures in this case that presumably would not hold in the case of creative intelligence. In fact, the augmented intellectual abilities of both genders would quickly become preadaptations (or exaptations) that would later be co-opted for purposes besides winning mates. The most prominent spin-off would be the rapid evolution of human culture, which provided a totally new basis for adaptations.

The above is not to say that that argument is necessarily correct. I offer it merely to show how Darwinian theory can be used to argue for innate gender equality in creative genius. Presumably, this equality could ensue from different selection processes than those that produce human sexual dimorphism. Accordingly, the even handed evolution of creativity could have occurred at the same time that evolution was supporting gender differences on other attributes, such as innate contrasts in physical aggressiveness. Hence, until we can scientifically separate the sound theories from the silly stories, it may be ill-advised to conclude that women got left behind in the biological origins of genius.

Gender Socialization and Stereotypes

The advent of human culture was clearly an epochal event in the evolution of our species. From that time forward, organic evolution would become increasingly less important than cultural evolution in the development of adaptations. Therefore, it could very well be that the low representation of women in the annals of creative genius is the consequence of cultural rather than biological forces. Consider the following four observations:

1. Parents raise children differently according to gender. In most literate societies across the globe, boys are socialized toward independence and achievement, whereas girls are trained to center their lives around family and relationships. Accordingly, many women of enormous talent do not even consider the prospect of life goals outside the home. This response is most notable when a family has both boys and girls, in which case the parents will usually channel limited resources toward their sons. Daughters are expected to rely on catching a prosperous mate. A longitudinal study of Mills College graduates showed this bias: Those women "who were successful in careers at age 43 were, with few exceptions, those who did not have brothers." Similar results held for eminent female mathematicians. It is telling that these gender-differentiated child-rearing practices can vary substantially across cultures and families. Such variation suggests that these behaviors may be culturally rather than biologically based.

2. Marriage and family have terrific costs for anyone who wishes to pursue the path to genius. Francis Bacon warned with respect to ambitious males: "He that hath wife and children hath given hostages to fortune; for they are impediments to great enterprises, either of virtue or mischief. Certainly the best works, and of greatest merit for the public, have proceeded from the unmarried or childless men, which, both in affection and means, have married and endowed the public." If Bacon advises ambitious men to shy away from domestic commitments, how much more this advice applies to women who are socialized to view family matters as a far more serious responsibility. Just contemplate the number of female creators who felt obliged to avoid such distractions. A partial list would include Jane Austen, Emily and Charlotte Brontë, Emily Dickinson, George Eliot, Barbara McClin-

tock, Georgia O'Keeffe, and Virginia Woolf. Nor are these eminent women's lives atypical. Women who win an entry in *Who's Who* are four times more likely than similarly illustrious men to be unmarried. Moreover, those successful women who somehow fit marriage in their lives are three times more likely to be childless in comparison to equally successful married men. Hence, a woman with husband and children suffers a handicap not experienced by an equally capable man with wife and children. Only the woman has so often had to make such a discrete choice between reproductive success and pro- ductive success—between contributing to the gene pool or adding something to the meme pool.

3. If the preceding two factors have not diverted an aspiring woman from her quest, active sex discrimination may yet obstruct her path to creative genius. Sometimes discrimination takes the form of subtle but prejudiced judgments: The assets of women may be undervalued in comparison with those of equally capable men. Other times the discrimination is blatant: Men who control the gateways to success often deliberately deny women access. Marie Curie was not elected to the French Academy of Sciences, notwithstanding two Nobel Prizes, and lacked a regular academic position until she was allowed to suc- ceed her husband, Pierre. This male dominance of resources alone could explain why women have the best prospects of success in litera- ture. A talented woman doesn't require a well-equipped laboratory, a full orchestra, or a large block of marble to write a masterpiece of fiction or poetry. A writing desk and a brain will do. Anne Sexton wrote prizewinning poetry in the corner of her dining room, taking advantage of whatever moments she could steal from raising two chil- dren and housekeeping. Moreover, female authors can more easily bypass male prejudices by adopting a male nom de plume, like the women who wrote pseudonymously as George Sand and George Eliot. As a last resort, pieces can always appear anonymously. In *A Room of One's Own*, Virginia Woolf said, "I would venture to guess that Anon, who wrote so many poems without signing them, was often a woman."

4. The most ubiquitous factor may be the gender-germane zeitgeist of a particular civilization at a given time. For instance, some religious and philosophical systems are not sympathetic to female attainments. Whenever one of these systems monopolizes the zeitgeist, women suffer accordingly. The history of Japanese culture provides yet another illustration. Just as Japan has fluctuated greatly in its open- ness to foreign ideas, so has the prominence of Confucian ideology fluctuated. Confucianism advocates extremely hierarchical views

about sex roles, placing the woman irrevocably subordinate to the man. In line with this bias, the ups and downs in women's achievements in Japanese history roughly correspond to the shifts in the prevalence of Confucian ideology. Nor is Confucianism the only cultural culprit in Japanese history. Sometimes the prevailing culture does not disfavor female attainments directly, but rather it discourages women by emphasizing those activities where they have fewer opportunities to enter the competition. To be specific, those periods of Japanese culture in which the machismo cult of the warrior flourished tended to be the very periods in which literary creativity languished. This inverse relation harmed women more than men, for the latter could pursue alternative paths. Women could not become samurai warriors. I must underscore a key aspect about these historical trends in Japanese history: The shifts could be rapid, even volatile. The fluctuations in the emergence of female genius occurred far too quickly to be attributed to some inexplicable change in the genetic makeup of the Japanese people.

This is by no means a complete inventory of the various cultural factors involved. But these points should suffice to render us wary of all attempts to minimize female genius through the application of primary Darwinism. The true source of the documented disparities may eventually be found in the rather different evolutionary forces that have shaped human culture. If so, as those forces change, so may the presence of female genius become ever more conspicuous. This assertion is not purely hypothetical, for the overwhelming power of culture is again quite amply demonstrated in the history of Japanese civilization. When all cultural factors converged to the detriment of women, female genius literally vanished from the annals of Japanese creativity. Yet when the factors smiled on their gender, women would reach the supreme heights of creative achievement. The Heian period of medieval Japan was just such a golden age. Female literary genius was prominent in both quantity and quality, as is obvious from the official anthologies that were filled with poems by female hands. This momentous era of female genius reached its acme with the *Pillow Book* of Sei Shonagon and, of course, the *Tale of Genji* by Murasaki Shikibu.

Cultural Evolution and Genius

It should now be clear that of the three social groups just discussed— race, culture, and gender—it is culture that may assume the largest place in a Darwinian theory of creativity. What is often attributed to race or gender may be more rightly subsumed under the operations of cultural processes.

Culture rather than the genes may determine whether a genius will be black or white, male or female. Moreover, as cultural entities transform over time, so will the opportunities for humanity's various groups. This latter assertion now compels us to discuss how the evolution of cultures may help explain the origins of genius. In general, there are two distinct approaches to this issue, the Spencerian and the Darwinian.

Spencerian Progress

The emphasis on culture would seem, to many, to destroy the very foundation of racial and gender hierarchies. If differences among the races or the sexes can be ascribed to cultural factors, then racial and gender contrasts are as malleable as cultures are changeable. Racism and sexism would thus lose much if not most of their putative biological basis. However, this apparent obliteration of distinctions is insufficient, for doctrines of racial superiority can still assume a more surreptitious guise. Rather than ranking races, those who are so inclined can rank cultures instead. Ethnocentrism then takes over the function racism once fulfilled.

Early theories of cultural evolution exemplify this trend. These speculations were inspired by the widespread belief that organic evolution was a progressive phenomenon. Lower forms evolved into higher forms, starting with the simple unicellular organisms and culminating in *Homo sapiens*. By the same token, cultures were said to display a history of advancement, beginning with "primitive" tribal peoples and gradually progressing toward the peak of the "advanced" civilized nations. Herbert Spencer was an emphatic proponent of this view. All forms of evolution entailed the combined process of differentiation and integration. Species and cultures both advance by means of the organized division of labor. That is, progress consists in the formation of specialized subunits coordinated by some structural and functional system. From the single-celled protozoan emerged the complex human being, replete with thousands of distinct cell types, and everything beautifully coordinated by the central nervous system. Likewise, from the "savage" and homogeneous "hordes" in which everyone struggled to scratch out a bare existence, there evolved intricate social systems in which citizens differentiated into thousands of different occupations, all wonderfully integrated by the benevolent designs of government.

The earliest versions of these theories were highly speculative and subjective, making the ethnocentric biases more transparent. Modern theories of cultural evolution have become more sophisticated in at least three ways. First, the older theories tended to be unilinear, meaning that all cultures were thought to go through the same sequence of changes. But eventually evolutionary theorists realized that such a fixed progression was most implausible. After all, organic evolution did not adopt a single path; human beings do not have insects in their ancestry (nor insects humans in theirs). Second, modern advocates have tried to avoid using criteria of evolutionary advance that are obviously linked to the distinctive characteristics of one particular culture (namely, the theorist's own). For example, rather than judge a culture according to whether its religious beliefs and practices approximate those of the Christian faith, the evolutionist might apply a more abstract criterion, like the extent to which a culture has successfully harnessed all the available resources in its environment. Third, some investigators have applied scientific techniques to the Spencerian ranking of cultures. By replacing subjective and qualitative judgments with objective and quantitative assessments, the researchers hope to avoid the pitfalls that have ensnared earlier advocates of Spencerian evolution.

Let me discuss an evolutionary inquiry that illustrates these improvements. The study has the additional advantage of having implications for understanding the cultural emergence of creative genius. At the same time, the investigation shows that even contemporary approaches to Spencerian evolution are not completely free from the potential charge of implicit ethnocentric bias.

Scale analysis and evolutionary sequences. Robert Carneiro's goal was to rate cultures along an evolutionary scale. He adopted an explicitly Spencerian conception of evolution in which "simplicity precedes complexity." Stated less simply, Carneiro defined evolution as "a change from a state of relatively indefinite, incoherent homogeneity to a state of relatively definite, coherent heterogeneity, through continuous differentiations and integrations." The objective and quantitative manifestation of this phenomenon would be the accumulation of certain critical traits. These traits would represent the acquisition of increased complexity with respect to economic, political, religious, social, military, legal, technological, and artistic systems. Furthermore, these traits will not just appear randomly, but rather some traits will occur earlier in the evolution of a culture. There must appear special religious practitioners, such as shamans, before there can evolve temples, and the latter in turn must emerge before there can be a temple that exacts tithes. Given this necessary ordering, Carneiro argued that a sound scientific test of the validity of evolutionary sequences would be to perform a scale analysis. This is a statistical technique that can determine whether a set of discrete traits form an ordered sequence in a consistent manner across a set of cases. So Carneiro applied this method to 100 world cultures that were assessed on 354 distinct traits. These traits concerned subsistence; settlements; architecture; economics; social organization and stratification; political organization; law and judicial process; warfare; religion; ceramics and art; tools, utensils, and textiles; metalworking; watercraft and navigation; and special knowledge and practices. The statistical analysis revealed that 90% of these traits formed a recurrent evolutionary scale. To validate the evolutionary sequence on transhistorical rather than cross-cultural data, Carneiro examined the history of a single culture, namely Anglo-Saxon England. He found that the same broad pattern observed across the 100 cultures reappeared within the evolution of a single culture.

This investigation has three features that require emphasis. First, Carneiro had no interest in documenting a unilateral form of cultural evolution. On the contrary, he believed that the set of cultural traits consisted of subsets that evolved in comparative independence. Thus, economic traits would show a fixed sequence, and so would the political traits, but the temporal shuffling of the two sets of traits was open to a certain amount of variation. One culture might have its economic system evolve the fastest, while another culture might have its political system be the most advanced. Second, Carneiro avoided imposing some a priori criterion other than the Spencerian principle of complexity. He did not assume that political advancement was less important than economic advancement, for example. He simply let the cultures themselves dictate the criteria on which they would be judged. Third, by letting a computer program rather than his subjective judgment do the trait scalings, Carneiro was less likely to make ratings that would exhibit some ethnocentric bias. This superior objectivity was apparent in the outcome. The 10 most complex societies on the basis of all 354 traits were as follows: the New Kingdom of Egypt, the Roman Empire, the Assyrian Empire, the Aztecs, China under the Han dynasty, the Incas, the Kingdom of León, the Vikings, the Dahomey, and the Ashanti. Hence, all major racial groups are represented in this list of the top 10.

All this is not to say that Carneiro's Spencerian rankings are flawless. Some serious objections can easily be raised, as I will discuss in a moment. But before doing so, I would first like to make explicit the connection between these evolutionary scales and creative genius. Many of the scaled cultural traits have a direct connection with creativity. Consider the following: craft specialization, craft production for exchange, full-time craft specialists, monumental stone architecture, full-time painters or sculptors, and full-time architects or engineers. Not only do these traits concern manifestations of cultural creativity, but in addition they form a temporal sequence (albeit the last two appear roughly simultaneously). The sequence essentially represents the emergence of professional artists from the ranks of less dedicated artisans. In addition, these creativity traits exhibit an ordinal relationship with other cultural traits. A society must attain a certain degree of political and economic complexity before there can appear full-time painters, sculptors, architects, or engineers. Yet we have already seen in earlier chapters that the attainment of creative greatness requires a lifetime of effort—the work of amateurs will not measure up. Therefore, the scaling of these traits tells us how far a culture must evolve before there can appear creative genius in these domains.

Although these results suggest that creative genius is the upshot of Spencerian evolution, there is another other side of this evolutionary phenomenon.

Societal complexity and cultural creativity. Not all anthropologists were sympathetic to the efforts of cultural evolutionists to revive a Spencerian perspective. Many followed in the footsteps of Franz Boas, Kroeber's teacher. Boas was as opposed to the evolutionary sequences of the cultural anthropologists as he was to the racial doctrines of the physical anthropologists. Human cultures may be too complex, too diverse, to submit easily to such grandiose schemes. Even objective and quantitative techniques may not circumvent more fundamental sources of potential bias. In the case of the Carneiro study, for example, the societal ratings are only as good as the traits that were fed into the statistical hopper. Although 90% of the 354 traits were highly scalable, what about the three dozen traits that were not? Even worse, how do we know that there do not exist another few hundred traits that were left out simply because they were not the kinds of activities that attracted the interest of Western-culture ethnographers? Might it be possible that cultural traits have been lost as well as gained over the course of evolution?

Rousseau and other French philosophes often saw the primitive as a "noble savage" who possessed virtues lost during the advance of civilization. The same pattern of decline has even been suggested to characterize the development of literate peoples. "As civilisation advances, poetry almost necessarily declines," said the British historian Thomas Macaulay. Indeed, Kroeber's scrutiny of cultural configurations proved that creativity can decay as well as grow. When a culture enters the stage of decadence, creative genius begins to disappear, and even the achievements of the past may be lost. The Dark Ages in Europe was not just a period in which no luminary shined. This was also the era in which most of the accomplishments of Greco-Roman genius sank slowly into oblivion.

Note, too, that an analogous issue frequently arises in discussions of organic evolution. By what right do human beings crown themselves as the zenith of evolutionary progress? Are we better adapted to our environments than the cockroach or rat? How do our brains really compare with those of dolphins? Have we nothing but gains to report in our emergence from the early primates, or have there been losses as well? Can we say that we are more or less evolved now that we have lost our fur and tails and prehensile toes? Some biologists argue that it is difficult if not impossible to determine the comparative "advancement" of different species. By definition, all extant species are equally evolved, because all have been around the same number of years since the first primordial life-forms. By the same logic we might say that all human cultures are equally evolved.

Rather than speculate on this matter any further, let me report the results of another cross-cultural investigation that casts a contrary light on Carneiro's societal rankings. In chapter 5 I reviewed Colin Martindale's research testing his Darwinian model of stylistic change in the arts. A critical aspect of these tests was his use of computerized content analysis to score literary texts on primary-process (or primordial) thought. This technique can be applied to any verbal material that has been written down, including folktales transcribed from oral traditions. Martindale was specifically interested in applying his method to the folktales of 45 preliterate societies. The resulting measures of primary-process imagery were then correlated with a second set of measures regarding sociocultural complexity. The latter indicators were based on technology, the number of craft specialties, subsistence level, economic institutionalization, social stratification, political complexity, demographic level, and religious level. An overall composite measure was also applied. The amount of primary-process thought was *negatively* correlated with the degree of societal complexity for all the separate measures and for the global composite indicator. Apparently, as a culture evolves, primary-process thinking declines.

Now Martindale's initial purpose for conducting this investigation was to test theories of the "primitive mentality" as proposed by Lévy-Bruhl and Cassirer. Primary-process thought was taken as an index of prelogical or dedifferentiated thought. Yet I can just as well put a different spin on this empirical finding. As discussed in earlier chapters, the primary process has long been associated with the capacity for creativity. Creative genius, in fact, must have more of this capacity than do noncreative personalities. Consider this in relationship with Carneiro's observation that as a society evolves artistic creativity becomes concentrated in the hands of relatively few full-time practitioners. Together these two trends suggest that cultural evolution has costs as well as benefits. The average person is reduced to the status of the noncreative, while a select minority reaches the rank of creative genius. This transformation is quite compatible with what many anthropologists are fond of pointing out, namely that modern Western conceptions of genius are not universal. In many "primitive" societies creativity is an activity of an entire community rather than the specialty of an elite. Almost everyone sings and dances, paints and carves, tells jokes and makes up stories. The universality of creative expression is precisely what Darwin predicted in his own theory of the origins of artistic creativity.

The contrast could not be greater with what we see in civilized society, with its active creators, passive aficionados, and inert masses. Unfortunately, whether this can be considered a cultural ascent or descent is increasingly left to civilized peoples to decide.

Darwinian Change

Charles Darwin certainly shared Herbert Spencer's belief in progress. This optimistic conception was a conspicuous part of the overall intellectual zeitgeist of the Victorian era. But Darwin also realized that evolution is not invariably upward in its trajectory. Species can degenerate as well as advance. Of all naturalists, Darwin was keenly aware of this fact. He devoted eight years to the study of barnacles—species that have lost almost all of the motor and sensory adaptations of their crustacean ancestors. Some parasitic forms have even become mere gonads extracting nutriment from other marine invertebrates. In the final analysis, the sole aspiration of life is not abstract progress but rather concrete reproductive success. And the latter goal can sometimes be better achieved through increased simplicity than augmented complexity. Adaptations do not always move toward more highly differentiated structures and functions. Indeed, phylogeny can sometimes invert ontogeny, making evolution run backwards.

Besides, Darwin was most interested in proving that species evolve and in providing a theoretical foundation for such evolution. If otherwise, his 1859 book might have been titled differently. Rather than use the neutral designation "origin," he might have said that the volume discussed the advancement, betterment, improvement, elevation, upgrading, or progression of species. Most subsequent developments in primary Darwinism have followed Darwin's example. And from a purely scientific perspective, Darwinian theories of evolutionary change have proven far more fruitful than Spencerian theories of evolutionary progress.

Fortunately, many applications of secondary Darwinism to the phenomenon of cultural evolution have shared this emphasis, concentrating on how cultures change rather than how they advance. The lead for these successful applications was taken from population genetics, which neither presumes nor strives to prove that evolution is progressive. The more modest goal is simply to describe how the frequencies of various genes (or more strictly speaking, alleles) change as a function of mutation, recombination, selection, genetic drift, chromosomal linkage, and other potential forces operating on a reproducing population. In a similar fashion, the corresponding theories of cultural evolution describe how the frequencies of various cultural traits (memes or culturgens) change as a function of sometimes analogous factors impinging on a cultural group.

Using roughly the same mathematical apparatus, these secondary theories have demonstrated how much more complex human behavior can become when it is a function of two distinct evolutionary processes, one organic and the other cultural. Not only can culture provide a potent ecological niche that shapes the course of biological evolution, but in addition cultural evolution can encourage the emergence of traits that would be discouraged under primary Darwinism. The most notable instance is altruistic behavior that goes well beyond the limits of kin selection. Moreover, models of cultural evolution have provided a rigorous basis for explaining otherwise inexplicable cultural phenomena. Most fascinating is the occurrence of cultural behaviors that parallel what occurs under runaway sexual selection. A dramatic example is how the growing of huge yams became an indicator of male prestige on the Micronesian island of Pohnpei. Not only could these yams surpass three feet in diameter and nine feet in length, but their cultivation often required considerable sacrifice, families sometimes going hungry even when the edible yams were ready to harvest.

But from the standpoint of a Darwinian theory of creativity, these powerful and impressive theories of cultural evolution lack one thing: They seem to have no place for genius. Outstanding creators are neither posited in their models nor do these models attempt to account for the emergence of genius as a cultural trait. In this respect, these Darwinian accounts are no different than the Spencerian, which also ignore the role of creative genius in cultural evolution. The only substantial difference is that the Spencerian theorists can often be more emphatic about proclaiming the irrelevance of genius in the origination of even landmark creative ideas. One such theorist is the prominent cultural evolutionist Leslie White. In the previous chapter I quoted White's assertion that even an ape could invent a steamboat (at least if the ape lived in the appropriate cultural world). Speaking even more boldly, White contended that "a consideration of many significant inventions and discoveries does not lead to the conclusion that great ability, native or acquired, is always necessary. On the contrary, many seem to need only mediocre talents at best." Although Darwinians will not assert anything so baldly dismissive, these theorists still find it quite possible to omit genius from their analyses. To the best of my knowledge, there exists only one minor exception to this generalization—an exception that seems to have left no impact on subsequent theories of cultural evolution.

Admittedly, the omission of creative genius is not grievous given the theoretical goals of these Darwinian treatments. As observed earlier, according to the data collected with respect to Spencerian evolution, the role of the creative genius is not a cross-cultural universal. Instead, such an elite position does not appear until the division of labor within a cultural group supports a sufficient level of specialization. According to Carneiro's data, Anglo-Saxon culture in medieval England had reached the stage that it had full-time craft specialists and craft production for exchange, but it could not yet boast full-time painters, sculptors, architects, and engineers—clear societal prerequisites for the appearance of genius. Quite the contrary, it was not until three centuries after the Norman Conquest of the Anglo-Saxons that England produced its first universally recognized creator, Geoffrey Chaucer, the author of *The Canterbury Tales*. Hence, it seems understandable that cultural evolutionists might propose theories with the widest possible scope rather than confine their models to just a subset of humanity.

Nevertheless, I believe the current chapter will be incomplete without at least some discussion of this issue. To what extent can Darwinian theories of cultural change help us comprehend the appearance of genius? It is impossible for me to provide a complete answer to this question. As far as I know, the issue has never been formally addressed in this literature, and the techniques researchers employ are well outside my own area of expertise. So may it suffice merely to point to three factors that might be worth consideration in any comprehensive theory. These are social learning, niche exploitation, and group competition.

Social learning. Genes pass from generation to generation via reproduction. Memes, in contrast, are transferred through imitation and instruction. As noted in chapter 1, this is a crucial divergence. In organic evolution, offspring can usually obtain their genes from only one source, their parents. Unfortunately, there is no choice in the matter. A child may not want to inherit her father's funny nose or her mother's unruly hair, but if she did, she did. In cultural evolution, on the other hand, there are more options. If a child admires his father's friendliness and his mother's conscientiousness, he can pick and choose what to emulate and what not. Indeed, to a certain extent children and adolescents can model themselves after anyone they want—grandparents, teachers, peers, celebrities, and heroes of the past. They can even identify themselves with whole groups rather than just single individuals, and thereby imitate idealized or abstract roles and norms. The young can go so far as to emulate behaviors so maladaptive that their very repetition sabotages any prospects for reproductive success. The most clear-cut illustration is the Werther effect, a phenomenon named after the character in a Goethe novel whose fictional suicide inspired copycat suicides throughout Europe. Research on contemporary populations has demonstrated that real celebrity suicides have had the same consequence. Such evidence shows, dramatically, that some cultural influences can seemingly usurp powerful biological imperatives.

Complicating matters yet further is the fact that any given individual or group is a repository of thousands of traits. People differ in the ways they talk and dress, their interests and hobbies, their values and beliefs, their ambitions and plans. Even when we focus on a very narrow aspect of a person's activities, the number of separate characteristics open to social learning is quite large. Take a young aspiring painter. Such a youth not only has hundreds of predecessors and contemporaries available for emulation, but each of those potential models represents an impressive variety of skills, techniques, themes, approaches, media, and even worldviews. So the young artist may admire A's color, B's line, C's brushwork, D's formal organization, E's use of light, F's sculptural sense, G's thematic content, and so on. So who should be imitated? Does the young talent pick just A because color is of primary concern, or does the artist pick and choose the best from each, and on that basis try to synthesize a new artistic style?

One problem with current Darwinian theories of cultural evolution is that they fail to capture the potential richness of human social learning. Instead, the focus is on how an individual selects from a handful of alternative behavioral variants (or cultural alleles). One solution is to select that variant with the highest frequency in the population—the "when in Rome do as the Romans do" criterion. If a lot of people behave a certain way, they must have learned that such behavior was adaptive. An alternative solution is perhaps even more influential: Imitate the variants displayed by the powerful or successful. Whatever actions enabled the rich and famous to get where they are should prove the most adaptive. Yet not only does this not always work, as the Werther effect demonstrates, but also there are still too many potential models and traits to choose from. As a consequence, additional criteria are often imposed to restrict the social variations open to personal selection. Models for emulation may have to share roughly the same demographic characteristics, such as ethnicity, gender, age, and class. Or a person may take the extreme step of focusing on just one available model, as when a son decides he wants to be just like his father.

When we turn to the problem of creative genius, we see immediately why this becomes a critical issue. As noted earlier, the most eminent creators are more likely to admire a larger number of predecessors and to allow their thoughts to be shaped by more contemporaries. They have worked under more mentors or teachers as well. They seem to have employed the strategy of adopting what looks good and rejecting what seems bad. But this same richness of inputs obliges the creator to attempt to put it all together, to synthesize the diverse influences into a single coherent perspective or approach. If that synthesis fails, then the person may succumb to an eclecticism that is at best eccentric, and at worst debilitating. Einstein's scientific career provides an excellent example of the optimal solution. Einstein held several of his predecessors in great esteem—such as Newton, Faraday, and Maxwell. Much of his career may be seen as an attempt to integrate the divergent perspectives of these masters. Thus, the primary impetus behind the special theory of relativity was the recognition of a fundamental inconsistency between Newtonian mechanics and Maxwellian electromagnetic theory.

From what we know about the creative personality, it is easy to see how a creator can adopt this inclusive approach to social learning. The more eminent creators tend to have wider interests and are open to more varied influences. They have a high tolerance of ambiguity and a strong appreciation for complexity. They are nonconforming and independent minded. Creative geniuses are thus ideally suited to embrace a more diversified array of models and mentors. They have the capacity to expose themselves to a full range of cultural variants available in their milieu, and then to put together that unique subset that contributes most to the development of their talent.

Two processes discussed earlier suggest that this approach to social learning might have rather broad utility.

First, in chapter 2 I outlined Epstein's generativity theory, a formal model of creative insight based on Darwinian operant conditioning. According to this model, an organism when confronted with a problem situation tries to retrieve the solution that has worked in the past. But when the problem is more difficult—novel and complex—the organism must descend through a hierarchy of potential solutions, each becoming increasingly improbable. Most critical, when no complete solution presents itself on the basis of already realized solutions to similar problems, the organism must recombine potentially relevant operants until a solution is found. The successful solution will be some permutation of the components of prior solutions to other problems of roughly the same class.

Social learning can operate the same way. When an individual wishes to learn the most adaptive behavior in a given circumstance, it is hard to imagine a better strategy than to imitate those who have proven themselves successful under the same or similar conditions. If that does not work, then the person can begin to loosen both the criteria of problem similarity and the standards of model success. If that procedure still does not guide the individual to an adaptive response, the best approach may be to try out various combinations of behaviors exhibited by a wide range of models. The various behavioral components undergo permutation in a strict Darwinian fashion. If A's color scheme does not work with B's forms to convey a given artistic idea, perhaps C's sense of structural organization will work with D's distinctive palette. Thus, by fragmenting available models into specific behavioral variants, an individual can improve the chances of arriving at an optimal solution.

Second, when discussing objections to Rushton's theory of racial differences, I mentioned an alternative position on the distinction between r and K reproductive strategies. Individuals may adopt one or another strategy according to the circumstances that prevailed during their childhood. It might also be possible that the prevailing environment during early development determines the manner in which a person engages in social learning. Individuals who grow up in highly stable circumstances can probably do no better than to model themselves after their parents, teachers, and other successful "elders." Presumably, a sociocultural system will be stable because it is well adapted to its ecological conditions. Therefore, the behaviors of these models will closely reveal what it takes to become well adjusted in the world. Moreover, there should be no need to diversify the range of models emulated. Indeed, it would be highly likely that the range of behavioral variants will be sharply restricted anyway.

But what happens if the milieu is highly unstable? This instability would presumably occur when there is some incompatibility between the culture and its environment. A significant percentage of even mature individuals would then exhibit maladaptive behaviors. As a consequence, it may not be advisable to copy the behavioral variants of a select group of elders. On the contrary, members of the older generation may betray maladaptive (outdated or obsolete) behaviors. In addition, as increasingly more group members engaged in trial-and-error learning (operant conditioning) to deal with life problems for which the traditional culture offers no viable solution, the number of behavioral variants available for imitation would increase. Under these unstable circumstances, it might behoove one to adopt a more inclusive and opportunistic approach to social learning. To maximize adaptive success during development, the youth should expand the range of potential models, assimilating behavioral variants piecemeal rather than as wholes. The upshot is the emergence of an individual who picks and chooses from among the behavioral offerings just that subset of those with the highest odds of contributing to adjustment in the new sociocultural world.

This milieu-contingent approach to social learning helps us better appreciate some of the distinctive features of creative development. Creative genius is more likely to appear in unstable and diversified home environments, even those that have encountered traumatic experiences. And creative genius is more likely to emerge in a sociocultural milieu that is culturally and intellectually heterogeneous, as well as politically unstable or fragmented. In short, the genius grows up in ambiguous surroundings. Nobody knows all the answers; not one soul is perfectly adjusted. Such a world forces creative talents to fend for themselves among the varied alternatives. The most adaptive response, then, is to expand the number and variety of models and mentors and from that rich input derive one's unique genius.

But why wouldn't all members of a cultural group become geniuses once a system begins to strain under environmental maladaptation? There may be two main reasons. First, the signs of societal maladjustment may be unevenly distributed across various subgroups of the system. Children from groups first experiencing the increasing sociocultural malaise will also be those to first develop the more inclusive approach to social learning. This may be another reason immigrant or minority populations so often provide reservoirs of future genius. Marginal groups may suffer first and so benefit first. Second, the ability to emulate multiple and varied models may depend on several individual-difference variables with a genetic foundation. Insofar as intelligence determines the capacity to process complex information, this would certainly constitute one such factor. It is no small cognitive task to discriminate the assets of various available behavioral variants and then to integrate them into a new coherent behavior. Whatever the specific genetic traits entailed, only a small proportion of the youth encountering societal anomalies may be able to respond in the constructive manner required for the emergence of genius. Those who fail may instead join fringe groups that display antisocial behaviors.

Niche exploitation. It was the genius of Darwin to realize how much evolution depended on the ample supply of diverse ecological niches. If different variants of a species have different reproductive fitness in the various available niches, the result after many generations will be the emergence of distinct species, each specialized to exploit a particular niche. Again, this was what so impressed Darwin about the finches of the Galápagos Islands. Because human beings have created culture, our species was able to take this process of adaptive radiation to ever higher levels of evolutionary achievement. No species has adapted itself to as many diverse ecological niches as has *Homo sapiens*—from the equator to the Arctic Circle, from ocean shore to mountain peak, from rain forest to desert. Furthermore, it is not just the diversity of occupied niches that is impressive but also the speed with which humans occupy them. Cultural evolution can occur at a pace that organic evolution can seldom match. It can take many generations for a favorable genetic mutation to work its way to the status of the predominant characteristic of a population. Yet a culture can transform very quickly, in a generation or less. When the Europeans introduced the horse into North America, it took the Native Americans of the Great Plains very little time to evolve a new culture in which the horse played a central role.

Yet cultural evolution has done much more than provide an accelerated means to exploit niches in the environment. Culture also evolves new niches, niches within the society itself. That is, niches can be internal (societal), not just external (ecological). Here Spencer captured a profound reality. Increased division of labor is a ubiquitous aspect of much cultural change. Very early in cultural evolution a society begins to acquire religious and political leaders, as well as creators specializing in specific crafts and performing arts. For most of the world's cultures, the number of available roles has become very large indeed. This means that human beings must often find their distinctive niche in their social world. According to Sulloway's theory discussed in chapter 4, this process of niche finding begins in the family, as each successive child must carve out its own identity vis-à-vis its siblings. The process then continues in school, and later in the larger competitive world of young adulthood.

Moreover, the individual has more options than merely to fill already established niches. People can always strive to carve out a new niche—a niche never before exploited in that culture. This process must be a powerful one, because it may be by this very means that Spencerian evolution takes place. The society differentiates, becomes more heterogeneous, because human beings are often driven to create social functions in which they can maximize their adaptive fitness. This operation began when the first human being was widely recognized as having more spiritual powers than other tribal members and thus became the group's shaman. It continued when the first warrior convinced his peers that his military prowess gave his opinions privileged status in group decisions about war. And, of course, this opportunistic process continues today, as new occupations, legal and illegal, proliferate at a dizzying pace.

Given how quickly the human race populated the world's open niches, I believe the capacity for niche-finding and niche-filling behavior emerged early in the evolution of our species. At first the capacity was specifically dedicated to the isolation of new ecological niches, and it was later transferred to the creation of societal niches. This transferal from external to internal niches could take place once the population reached sufficient size and the means of subsistence became sufficiently productive. Under such conditions, not everyone had to be a hunter and gatherer. As the division of labor expanded into ever more specialized occupations, a society would eventually reach the point where it could support full-time artisans. As the latter prospered, these roles would evolve to those of genuine artists. In a short time, the way would be prepared for someone to claim the status of creative genius, first in the arts and later in the sciences. Even the most exalted geniuses, under this view, are only doing what everyone else is trying to do: find a place for themselves in the natural and social world into which they were born.

But how does one create a new niche for oneself? Perhaps the answer comes from the inclusive form of social learning discussed earlier. Obviously a person who emulates only one model has little choice but to follow in that model's footsteps. This is not a workable means to develop new roles. Yet increase the number of models, and the individual acquires the capacity to synthesize a new role from various dissociated parts of other roles. This process would enable a culture to adapt more successfully to new ecological opportunities. As new environmental niches open up, new social roles can spontaneously generate to exploit those niches. Those new social roles may then inspire the formation of new societal niches, which then invites the creation of roles to match. Hence, there could exist some selection pressure for individuals to learn to adopt a more flexible approach to social learning. To the extent that this more flexible approach requires the attributes of a creative personality, these selection pressures would then provide a basis for the emergence of the creative genius—someone who is the master of synthesizing new wholes from parts of the old.

Group competition. So far I have adopted an individualistic analysis. In social learning, individuals select models to maximize their adaptive fitness in a changing environment. In niche exploitation, individuals are on the lookout for spots in their natural and social worlds where they can create for themselves a new role—again with the aim of increasing personal adaptive fitness. But we also have to recognize that in the social animals, groups may also have to compete for available resources. In fact, many species have evolved such group-level behaviors as territorial defense and lethal warfare. This type of behavior, of course, is especially prominent in human societies. Warfare is among the oldest of all behaviors in our species, and in most instances such conflicts are driven by the quest for greater group territory, wealth, and power. It is also evident that this intergroup competition can become maladaptive from the standpoint of individual survival. Such competition can behave like a runaway process, advancing far beyond the initial provision of benefits that might accrue to the group members. An obvious example is arms races that accelerate to the point that the participating nations become economically handicapped. Needless to say, these races may also escalate into all-out conflicts in which life, and not just wealth, becomes the sacrifice.

This group competition puts a premium on societal creativity, a necessity most clearly illustrated in the case of technological advance. The group that can more rapidly identify new environmental niches to exploit will gain power more rapidly than its neighbors. That power may come from population growth (e.g., the discovery of new foods), the acquisition of material goods (e.g., new metals for weapons), or some other technological source. In short, the group that demonstrates more technological creativity will increase in strength relative to its rivals. Thus, group selection operating on alternative cultural systems should support the emergence of a milieu more favorable to the emergence of creativity. If this cultural milieu endured for a long enough time, it could actively shape the course of humanity's organic evolution. The genetic variants that enhanced individual creativity would coevolve with cultural traits that could exploit this creativity for group survival.

I use the term *group selection* advisedly. Although such a selection mechanism might seem incompatible with the individualistic tenor of primary Darwinism, its potential participation here would seem to have more justification. To begin with, as applied to organic evolution, group selection is often evoked to explain the origin of behaviors that are plainly maladaptive at the individual level—such as altruistic behavior. Yet it is less obvious that creativity would have similarly negative repercussions for reproductive success. On the contrary, both in this chapter and in chapters 2 and 3 I noted some of the ways creative behavior might actually have adaptive consequences. Group selection could then reinforce individual selection. Furthermore, in the present case we are applying group selection to a cultural entity rather than to biological subpopulations of species. Cultures operate far more like closed systems, with definite boundaries that severely limit the exchange of members. These boundaries are defined by language, religion, political ideology, customs and mores, modes of artistic expression, and so forth. Such features should allow the effects of group selection to strengthen the other selection forces operating solely at the individual level. Darwin himself argued, in chapter 5 of his *Descent of Man*, that competition between human groups, beginning at the tribal level, could help explain the huge gap in intellectual capacity and inventiveness that separates *Homo sapiens* from its nearest evolutionary relatives.

Another idea drawn from primary Darwinism indicates how this group-selection process might become accentuated: the Red Queen hypothesis. This peculiar term came from the passage in Lewis Carroll's *Through the Looking Glass* when the Red Queen remarks "Now, *here*, you see, it takes all the running *you* can do, to keep in the same place." This process applies to the coevolution of competing species, such as predator and prey, host and parasite, or two species occupying identical niches. Adaptations that enhance the fitness of one species will automatically lower the adaptive fitness of the rival species. This puts increased pressure on the latter species to catch up or face extinction. Often this can become a virtual runaway arms race, as evinced by the huge canines of the saber-toothed cat versus the immense tusks of the mastodon—plus the massive size of both. The irony, of course, is that each species often ends up no better than before. The evolutionary gain is not in getting ahead but rather in avoiding getting behind. Yet since extinction is an even worse outcome, interspecies competition can favor the emergence of mechanisms that can accelerate the evolutionary process. Whichever species evolves the fastest may win, or at least not lose.

It has been suggested, for example, that this phenomenon underlies the appearance of sexual reproduction. Although it can be shown that sex actually has many adaptive drawbacks in comparison with asexual reproduction, sexual behavior is actually rather commonplace throughout the plant and animal kingdoms. By the production of genetic variation, sexual reproduction can accelerate evolution, enabling a species to keep up with its competitors. Conceivably, the Red Queen hypothesis applies to cultural evolution as well. The combinatory powers of the creative mind permit human groups to discover new technological variants so that the culture will not fall far behind the achievements of its neighbors.

The foregoing arguments presume that group competition can select for technological innovation. Yet I do not want to leave the impression that creativity was exclusively dedicated to the discovery of new technologies. More intangible or symbolic forms of creativity may be just as important, if not more so. For instance, the success of any society depends to a large extent on how strongly its members identify with the cultural qualities that uniquely distinguish the group. It is difficult to defend self-perceived inferiority in the face of another group's self-proclaimed superiority. A Cheyenne must be proud of being a Cheyenne, just as a Chinese must be proud of being a Chinese.

A large part of this pride is founded on the cultural creativity of a group's members. A people must feel that their accomplishments are the best, at least in those domains that the culture values. In preliterate societies, this ethnocentric cohesion may be found in the myths told around the fire, in the skills displayed by their artisans, in songs and dances that decorate their ceremonies. In urban cultures, this source of esprit de corps is even more conspicuous. The English may claim that Shakespeare is the greatest writer who ever lived; the Germans, Goethe; the Italians, Dante; the Spanish, Cervantes; and so forth through the list of the world's tongues. This form of group identification is seen in the pride people feel when someone from their country receives the Nobel Prize. At the same time, this group competition over cultural superiority can sometimes inflate to jingoistic proportions. An example was given in chapter 5, when I mentioned how the multiple discovery of Neptune led to a vicious controversy over whether the true discoverer was an Englishman or a Frenchman.

So, perhaps by some group-selection process, most cultures have developed means by which they can actively encourage at least some degree of creativity in its members. This would imply that creativity should be strongly associated with nationalism, with the rise of new cultures. Earlier in this chapter we saw that this was in fact true. This is the import of Danilevsky's law, and the same point was made by Kroeber in his *Configurations of Culture Growth*. Once a people begin to acquire an awareness of themselves as a distinct culture, they begin to take steps to accentuate their uniqueness and superiority. This process often begins with the production of great epics, such as Homer's *Iliad*, Virgil's *Aeneid*, and the anonymous *El Cid*, *La chanson de Roland*, and *Das Niebelungenlied*. But however the process starts, it soon expands to most other forms of creativity. Within a few generations, the people have a body of creative achievements that can provide the strongest possible cultural basis for group strength.

It was not irrelevant to the rise of Adolf Hitler that he placed so much stress on the monumental achievements of German genius. In his *Mein Kampf* Hitler emphasized that the Aryan race provided the "culture makers," in contrast to the Jews, who he thought represented the "culture destroyers." When Hitler made his pilgrimage to Bayreuth to hear Wagner's *Der Ring des Nibelungen*, he was proclaiming to all Germanic peoples the superiority of their race. Is it any wonder, then, that Wagner's music could not be heard in Israel for decades after the Holocaust? Wagner, although deceased before Hitler was even born, was expropriated as an integral part of the conspicuous cultural matrix that secured the Jews' oppression throughout German-occupied Europe. Nor was Hitler introducing a novel motive for war. From Alexander the Great and Julius Caesar to Hernando Cortés and Napoleon, ethnic superiority has been transported on the backs of invading armies. Even so-called barbarian conquerors, such as Genghis Khan, believed they were destroying decadent cultures that had lost the virtues of the nomadic life. This inverted form of ethnocentric conquest has been such a potent force in human affairs that Ibn Khaldun, the great Islamic thinker, made it the central basis for his cyclical theory of historical change.

There is one last feature of this hypothesized process that needs some treatment. Up to this point I have outlined a process of group competition that may operate equally in both preliterate and urban cultures. All kinds of human social systems should experience some evolutionary pressure to support the emergence of creative activity among its members. At the same time, as was already noted, creative genius is more likely to originate in the more complex societies. A true Spencerian evolutionist might attribute this to cultural progress. However, another, more obvious factor may be far more crucial: Population growth. In Carneiro's scheme of culture scaling, for example, many of the items used to rank world cultures concern the size of the social group. Usually before craft specialization can emerge, there first must appear communities of 100 or more. The culture normally must reach the point at which it has towns of 2,000 or more before artisans are employed by religious or political authorities to glorify their regimes. Full-time painters, sculptors, architects, and engineers do not emerge until cities approaching 10,000 citizens exist. And as Galton observed in *Hereditary Genius*, Athens had grown to the population of at least 90,000 free-born citizens by the time it began to produce figures of the caliber of Socrates, Plato, and Phidias. Many empirical investigations have actually demonstrated that the single most powerful predictor of a society's creative output is its population size.

Increased population nurtures the birth of creative genius in three ways. First, and in the Spencerian fashion of interpretation, a larger population means that social roles can differentiate further. Artisans can specialize into particular crafts, for example, only when a people can afford to have more than one artisan. Second, as a population expands, ever increasing demands are placed on technology to exploit the environment more fully. As Malthus demonstrated in his famous 1798 essay, human beings can quickly outstrip the capacity of a particular ecological niche to maintain them. Hence, the industrial and agricultural revolutions of modern Europe were in large part propelled by the need to provide food and shelter to a rapidly growing population. The steam engine, for instance, emerged as a response to the increased need for coal in Great Britain. Third, and most important in my view, is the fact that an enlarged population means increased variation on those attributes necessary for supreme genius to emerge. Intelligence offers a prime example. If we describe intelligence in terms of a hypothetical distribution with a mean of 100 and a standard deviation of 16, then what happens as population size increases? There would have to be at least 100 people in all to produce one person with an IQ above 140, around 10,000 to get someone with an IQ above 150, about 30,000 for the emergence of an individual with an IQ exceeding 160, and one million to find someone whose intelligence exceeds 170. Thus, the larger the population, the more extreme the highest levels of intelligence possible in the population. With a country the size of the United States, the country could produce a denizen, Marilyn vos Savant, with the IQ of 228.

To be sure, a population of, say, 30,000 could boast about 300 citizens with a genius-level intellect. But this cannot easily translate into a golden age of creativity. Consider the following five complications:

1. Only adults can make creative contributions, and so the required population figure must be scaled upward proportionately. The exact magnitude of this adjustment is contingent on the group's age stratification, but the adjustment will always be substantial.
2. If women and ethnic minorities are excluded from the race, the estimated population must be scaled up still more. It was partly for this reason that Galton did not count the approximately 40,000 slaves when he estimated the magnitude of Athenian genius.
3. A society will include many roles, not all of which will entail creativity. Some roles will be drawn from the available pool of elevated intellect. When one very bright Athenian named Pericles decided to enter politics, that meant there was one less brain available for Greek philosophy, drama, or sculpture.
4. There must probably exist a certain critical mass of potential genius before that potential can be actualized as observable creativity. This

requirement was implicit in our earlier discussion of Kroeberian cultural configurations. The creators usually need other creators to learn from and other creators to respond to their ideas.

5. Intelligence is only one of many cognitive and personality factors that contribute to the manifestation of genius. To the extent that extreme values on many different attributes are required, it will take a very large population to provide everything necessary for the emergence of supreme genius. Indeed, to the degree that creativity is an emergenic trait (as hinted in chapter 4), the required size of the population must be multiplied all the more. Only a minuscule percentage of the gene pool would inherit everything it takes to become a genius.

In light of the above considerations, I believe population growth may constitute the single most critical factor separating the creativity of preliterate cultures from that of the so-called civilized societies. To be sure, population is most unlikely to be the sole determinant. Certainly, considerable advantage accrues to cultures that have developed a form of written communication, which enables the accumulation of memes in public and private libraries. The blooming of the European Renaissance would have been rendered far more improbable had the Greco-Roman world only survived through some pale oral tradition. And by his own admission, Darwin's achievements would have been minimal indeed had he been denied access to his notes, books, and journals. Even so, neither literacy nor any other technological innovation can have much impact on the appearance of genius without a sufficiently ample reservoir of human resources. So in that sense, population growth alone may be the sine qua non of group creativity. No Darwin could have been born among a tribe consisting of a mere few hundred people, no matter how culturally rich the milieu.

Prospects for a Darwinian Synthesis

This has been by far the most difficult chapter to write. And for many readers it may also count as the least successful, convincing, or impartial. As mentioned at the chapter's outset, Darwinian theory has always encountered its biggest problems dealing with groups, and especially with such human social categories as race, culture, and gender. Often primary Darwinism has taken explanatory precedence over secondary Darwinian accounts, even when the latter may ultimately have more scientific value. Aggravating matters yet further, incautious applications of primary Darwinism often provoke needless controversies that undermine the overall credibility of Darwinian models. I am not among those who believe there should be a moratorium on such discussion, nor do I maintain that all Darwinians engaging in these discussions are racist and sexist. Instead, I only urge heightened scientific modesty and social sensitivity. If one is grappling with a controversial issue that can easily be distorted by the oversimplifications of the print and electronic media, then theorists must assume an even more responsible role. This has to be done for the theorists' own sake and for the sake of the further advancement of Darwinian science.

Part of that enhanced scientific responsibility must include superior sophistication in theory construction. Thanks to population genetics and other analytical methods, primary Darwinism has become an impressive theoretical enterprise. Moreover, several venturesome pioneers have helped extend these powerful techniques to the realm of cultural evolution. Especially noteworthy has been the development of the dual-inheritance theories. These presume that human behavior is the joint manifestation of both genes and memes, simultaneously coevolving in complex interactions across the history of our species. By integrating primary and secondary processes into a single explanatory framework, these models have the potential of moving us beyond the rather simplistic debates that have so far plagued this field. Just as modern behavioral genetics has elevated scientific deliberations beyond the now old-fashioned nature-versus-nurture debate, so should these dual-inheritance theories improve the arguments over the amount of creativity displayed in various human groups.

To be sure, I said earlier that these evolutionary theories may have to undergo considerable development before they can fully account for the origins of genius. Their focus has been on individuals as largely passive receptacles of memes—so-called beanbag models—rather than as genuine agents of cultural change. Creators generate *new* memes rather than merely serving as repositories of received memes. Nonetheless, such limitations may not be intrinsic to these models but rather may only reflect the current state of the art. The evolution of scientific theories tends to be Spencerian, increasing in complexity with the differentiation of new concepts and the integration of those concepts into ever more encompassing systems. In the future, dual-inheritance models may advance to the stage where they will not merely account for the origins of genius but will also provide an objective perspective on how creativity might vary across groups defined by race, culture, or gender. At that point, the relative contributions of primary and secondary Darwinian processes will be discerned with a scientific sophistication that should transport the whole discussion beyond the realm of politically charged debates. Chapters such as this one can then be written with less hesitation and ambivalence.

7

~

DARWINIAN GENIUS

The Future of an Idea

~

Darwin's ideas about evolution themselves slowly evolved over more than two decades—from his original insight of 1838 to the 1859 publication of the *Origin of Species*. Even after the publication of that landmark work, his ideas continued to evolve, seeking out new intellectual niches in which to extend the explanatory power of the unguided mechanism of variation and selection. His work on human evolution and sexual selection, the expression of emotions, the fertilization of orchids, the insectivorous plants and the climbing plants, and many other subjects all emerged through a kind of adaptive radiation. Even after his death his ideas did not become extinct, but rather they thrived and expanded, assuming the many varied forms of contemporary primary Darwinism, from molecular evolution to sociobiology. Moreover, his contributions soon began to prove productive in their secondary form. Whether one considers the immune system, neurological development, operant conditioning, genetic programming, or evolutionary epistemology, Darwinism has proven itself to be a powerful scientific force. No idea in the sciences boasts such universal application in the world of self-organizing systems. Darwinism has generated memes that have permeated almost every corner of the intellectual universe. To be sure, some Darwinian lineages have gone extinct, social Darwinism among them. Yet new variations continue to emerge, waiting for the next round of scientific selection.

The thesis of this book constitutes another such ideational variant. Published and thrust before the world, it must survive the often cruel winnowing process of the scientific enterprise. These selection pressures will determine the fate of the whole and of each part. To facilitate this next stage in this Darwinian proceeding, I would like to complete two final tasks. First, I wish to recapitulate the central ideas contained in this book. Second, I would like to evaluate these ideas from three separate perspectives.

Recapitulation

Darwin claimed that the *Origin of Species* was "one long argument from the beginning to the end." In a far more modest way, the same may be said of this book. For here I have systematically argued how Darwinism can enhance our appreciation of the creative genius. The first chapter began this task by defining the nature of both creativity and genius. After showing how Darwin himself exemplified the Galtonian definition of creative genius, the chapter surveyed the explanatory framework that would find applications throughout the rest of the book. Especially critical was the introduction of the distinction between the two classes of Darwinism—primary and secondary. The first deals strictly with organic evolution—with the origin of species—whereas the latter treats more inclusively all biological, behavioral, cognitive, and cultural phenomena that operate by a closely analogous variation-selection process.

Chapter 2 then looked at the cognitive processes underlying creativity. In particular, Donald Campbell's blind-variation-and-selective-retention model offered the foundation for explaining (a) introspective reports of creative individuals, (b) laboratory experiments on creative insight and imagination, and (c) computer models of creativity. After dealing with some of the common objections raised against this secondary Darwinian interpretation, I grappled for the first time with an issue that recurs throughout the book: How can primary Darwinism provide for the evolutionary emergence of the genius demanded by the secondary Darwinian model?

Chapter 3 turned to the discussion of individual differences. People vary in their capacity to engage in the Darwinian thought described in chapter 2. According to Darwinian theory, these differences should be associated with variation on those intellectual and personality traits that support engagement in variation-selection processes. After scrutinizing cognitive differences in the capacity to produce remote associations and divergent thinking, the chapter switched to the personality profile of creative genius. Special attention was devoted to the relation between genius and madness, including a discussion of how primary Darwinism might support the evolutionary emergence of a Darwinian personality.

Chapter 4 next took the main thesis of chapter 3 one step further. If creative thought presupposes a creative person, then how does the latter individual emerge from the masses? This developmental question obliged us to confront one of the most thorny problems in the behavioral sciences—the nature-nurture issue. Three potential answers were then addressed: environmentalism, hereditarianism, and evolutionism. The latter suggested a more comprehensive Darwinian perspective on creative development.

Chapter 5 then moved away from the scrutiny of the creative person. Instead, the focus was on the creative product. The analysis began with the general question of how the output of products varies across and within creative careers, with particular importance assigned to the equal-odds rule. Discussion then moved to two more specialized topics: stylistic changes in the arts and multiple discoveries in science. The two phenomena were successfully explained in terms of the provided Darwinian perspective. In fact, for both cases, Darwinism yielded specific predictions that have survived direct empirical tests. The chapter closed with a detailed treatment of why the creative genius must usually adopt an r-type rather than K-type strategy when generating creative products.

Chapter 6 dramatically altered the unit of analysis from single products to whole social groups. Specific attention was paid to race, culture, and gender, with the goal of suggesting that secondary Darwinism may provide a superior account to the usual primary Darwinian explanations. Then considerable time was spent discussing the connection between cultural evolution and the creative genius. Both Spencerian and Darwinian theories were examined, with some attempt at a conceptual integration that preserves whatever may be valid in both theoretical positions. The suggested synthesis indicates some of the distinctive features of cultural evolution that may have encouraged the emergence and distribution of exceptional creativity.

Evaluation

Did the book succeed in making a convincing case on behalf of a Darwinian theory of creativity? I believe that this question may best be answered by looking at the current presentation from three distinct perspectives. First, do Darwinian theories and models have sufficient explanatory scope to accommodate the myriad facets of creative behavior? Second, to what extent do Darwinian concepts and principles demonstrate genuine utility in the treatment of these diverse substantive issues? Third, can these Darwinian ideas truly aid our comprehension of the specific manifestations of creative genius observed in the historical record?

Explanatory Scope

No doubt a huge part of the success of Darwin's evolutionary theory was the range of his explanatory system. Virtually every aspect of life could be provided a scientific interpretation. By the same token, it should be apparent from the above recapitulation that Darwinian theories can facilitate our understanding of the most prominent aspects of creative genius: cognitive processes in animals, humans, and computers; individual differences in intellect and personality; the genetic and environmental influences on creative development; creative products in both the arts and the sciences; and social groups, especially cultures and their evolution. These topics and their diverse subtopics cover all of the central features of the phenomenon.

Admittedly, someone might always suggest that a particular subject has been overlooked. For instance, what is the relationship, if any, between creative genius and hemispheric differentiation or handedness? Is it accidental or telling that the evolution of a brain capable of creativity was roughly concomitant with the increased specialization of the right and left hemispheres? And what about drugs and alcohol? Can ingestion of such chemicals make a direct contribution to creative thought? Did the appearance of mind-altering substances in various cultures accelerate or retard the emergence of creativity? These and other more narrow questions are left as projects for future researchers who wish to elaborate and extend the Darwinian framework.

Naturally, substantive issues such as these are much less problematic than another unanswered question that has cropped up in almost every chapter: What is the ultimate evolutionary basis for the emergence of creative genius? This recurrent issue has been addressed from both primary and secondary Darwinian perspectives. It has been analyzed as a consequence of natural selection, and as a repercussion of sexual selection. And although I have scrutinized the direct adaptive value of creativity, I have also examined the possibility that creative behavior emerged out of some preadaptation, such as proteanism. Indeed, I have even suggested that creative genius might not be under any selection whatsoever, owing to its rarity and emergenic source—factors that allow its emergence only in large populations. In short, it should be obvious that we still do not hold a single convincing Darwinian explanation for why creative genius should emerge during the organic and cultural evolution of our species.

Even so, I believe it is a remarkable feature of Darwinism that it can be such a fertile source of hypotheses regarding the origins of genius. Later theoretical developments and empirical findings may narrow the range of permissible accounts until a single explanation emerges supreme. But whatever interpretation finally wins out, the best bet is that it will remain Darwinian.

Explanatory Utility

The previous discussion highlights another crucial feature of this book's presentation. In treating the core topics regarding creativity, I have exploited some of the central concepts of Darwinian theory, both primary and secondary. These concepts include genetic mutation and recombination, natural and sexual selection, inclusive fitness, preadaptation, ecological niches and adaptive radiation, r/K reproductive strategies, the Red Queen, and much, much more. These theoretical ideas were not introduced just to impose crude analogies over a rather dissimilar phenomenon. Instead, at every step I have tried to make the case that creative genius is Darwinian to its very core. For example, I have shown that the blindness of scientific and artistic variations is an inherent consequence of the psychological and social processes by which creative products emerge. This is not a false analogy artificially manufactured to make the creativity look more Darwinian than it really is.

Nonetheless, I must admit one major liability in these extensive applications of Darwinian theory. When it comes to explaining creative genius, it would be false to claim that there exists a single explanatory system. Rather, I have had to speak of Darwinian theories and models, using the plural throughout. In lieu of a grand theory by some Darwinian Newton, we possess a family of explanations put forward by Campbell, Epstein, James, Eysenck, Galton, Sulloway, Martindale, Kantorovich, and many others, including myself. Not only do these accounts often differ in terms of the core concepts and definitions, but in addition they are often applied to different aspects of the phenomenon. At present, we lack a distinct theoretical system that will accommodate all creative activities in a coherent fashion. Darwinian perspectives on creative genius must still be unified into another "modern synthesis" that can subsume the diversity of the more specialized models we currently possess.

Hence, explanatory scope has been purchased at the expense of theoretical unity. Even so, the cost is not too dear. After all, there is nothing fundamentally incompatible about most of these separate models. The future should therefore see the arrival of some behavioral scientist—surely a Darwinian creative genius—who will be able to synthesize this conceptual diversity into a comprehensive and precise explanatory framework.

Explanatory Specificity

Darwin's revolutionary theory was designed mainly to explain the general features of organic evolution. Nonetheless, its applicability to the peculiarities of particular species was always made clear. The *Origin of Species* is rich in details about the traits and behaviors of specific animals and plants—characteristics that often made sense only after being embedded in primary Darwinian theory. In fact, Darwin's careful attention to these minutiae of living systems helped give his treatment its clear superiority over the presentations of rival claimants. Unlike Patrick Matthew and Alfred Wallace, Darwin both sketched the big picture and filled in the most minute details.

In the same fashion, I have tried in this book to do more than merely show how Darwinian theory might explicate the abstract aspects of creative phenomena. On the contrary, I have also provided ample illustrations drawn from the careers of noted creators in the arts and sciences. And among the scientific geniuses, Charles Darwin himself has been the single most prolific source of concrete examples. Drawing from his life and work, we have seen something of his thinking habits, character, personal growth, productive output, and sociocultural milieu. In these observations, we have witnessed how Darwin often exemplifies some of the main attributes of Darwinian genius, such as his multiple discovery shared with Alfred Russell Wallace. Rather than just show that this event illustrated a more general phenomenon—that of scientific multiples—I also demonstrated that this whole class of events can be best explicated from a Darwinian perspective. Thus, the current theory can provide an explanatory system for more fully understanding the life of that very creative genius who inspired the theory itself.

Naturally, I hope that the arguments and illustrations that fill this book will enable it to survive the forthcoming rigors of sociocultural selection. Yet like Darwin in 1859, I remain confident about the long-term prospects of this explanatory system. It remains my personal conviction that Darwinism offers the most powerful and distinctive perspective on creativity. By some self-confirming twist of fate, Darwinian theories can account not just for the origins of genius but for the origin of the *Origin of Species* besides.

Notes

~

The documentation for all research and quotations are presented in the order they appear in the main text. The references are organized by chapter and, within each chapter, by consecutive section. The paragraphs are separated by primary headings. Quotations are identified by initial words.

Preface

"She has been" Hyman 1963, 373.

Chapter 1

"Universal History" Carlyle 1841, 1. Cultural growth: Kroeber 1944; see also Gray 1958, 1966; Sorokin and Merton 1935; cf. Barber 1981. **Genius.** "The true Genius" Johnson 1781, 5. **Intelligence.** IQ definition: Terman 1925; Hollingworth 1926, 1942. Mensa: Serebriakoff 1985. Highest IQ: McFarlan 1989. Terman's children as adults: Oden 1968; Terman and Oden 1959. Shockley: Eysenck 1995, 65. Minimal correlation with success: Bayer and Folger 1966; Bloom 1963; Cole and Cole 1973, 69–70; Helson and Crutchfield 1970; Jones 1964. **Eminence.** "the opinion of" Galton 1892/1972, 77. Transhistorical stability of eminence: Simonton 1991c; see also Helmreich, Spence, and Thorbecke 1981; Over 1982b; Rosengren 1985; Simonton 1998b; cf. Lang and Lang 1988. "worldly renown" Dante c. 1307/1952, 69. Cross-cultural consensus: Simonton 1991c, 1996b, 1998a. African Americans: Simonton 1998a. Unrecognized genius: Lenneberg 1980. Relative eminence of composers: Farnsworth 1969. Capriciousness of fame: Kasof 1995; Lehman 1943; Martindale 1995b; Mills 1942; Simonton 1984e, 1987c. "Some are born" Shakespeare 1601/1952, 13. "fame" Simonton 1984c, 23. **Creativity.** Adaptive science: e.g., Thagard 1992. Adaptive art: e.g., Meyer 1956; Peckham 1967. Symphonic success: Simonton 1995a. Alternative measures: Hocevar and Bachelor 1989. Social definition of creativity: Amabile 1982; Csikszentmihály 1990; Simonton 1988b. Eminence and creative productivity: Albert 1975; Cole and Cole 1967; Feist 1993; Simonton 1977a, 1991a, 1991b, 1992b; Wispé 1965. Classical repertoire: Moles 1958/1968. Scientific citations: Cole and Cole 1973; Rushton 1984; Simonton 1984f 1992b, cf. Lindsey 1989; Moravcsik and Murugesan 1975. Citations and Nobel Prize: Ashton and Oppenheim 1978.

Charles Darwin. "much slower" Darwin 1892/1958, 6. "as a very ordinary" and "singularly incapable" Darwin 1892/1958, 9. "I have no great quickness" Darwin 1892/1958, 54–55. IQ: Cox 1926. 100 most influential people: Hart 1987. "books that changed the world" Downs 1956. *Great Books of the Western World*: Hutchins 1952. Eponyms: Hendrickson 1988. Darwinism: see, e.g., Dennett 1995. **Primary Darwinism.** General introduction: Ridley 1993a. *Hereditary Genius*: Galton 1869. **Sexual selection.** Darwin 1871/1952a; see also Andersson 1994. **The "modern synthesis."** Huxley 1942. Blending inheritance: Fisher 1930. Mendelianism: cf. Olby 1979. Mutations: de Vries 1905. Population genetics: e.g., Crow 1986. Genetic drift: Wright 1970. Runaway sexual selection: Fisher 1930. **Sociobiology.** Cooperation: Dugatkin 1997. Reciprocal altruism: Trivers 1971; see also Ridley 1997. Group selection: Wilson 1980; Wilson and Sober 1996. Altruism in social insects: Hamilton 1972. Sociobiology: Wilson 1975; see also Buss 1990, 1995. Criticisms: e.g., Howard, Blumstein, and Schwartz 1987; Nisbett 1990; Travis and Yeager 1991. **Secondary Darwinism.** For a more comprehensive survey of theories: Cziko 1995; see also Dennett 1995. **Biological phenomena.** Antibody formation: Söderqvist 1994. "Darwinism of the synapses" Changeux 1985. "Neural Darwinism" Edelman 1987. "blooming" and "pruning" Greenough and Black 1992. "Darwin machine" Calvin 1987, 1990. **Behavioral phenomena.** Operant conditioning: Catania 1992; Epstein 1991. Applications: Skinner 1972. Creativity: Skinner 1972. Reinforcement of creative behavior: Eisenberger and Cameron 1996; cf. Amabile 1996. **Cultural phenomena.** Cultural evolution: e.g., Cavalli-Sforza and Feldman 1981; see also Campbell 1965; for recent review see Janicki and Krebs 1998. "tunes, ideas, catch-phrases" and "just as genes propagate" Dawkins 1989, 192. Two evolutions compared: Hull 1988, chap. 11. Dual-inheritance: Lumsden and Wilson 1981; Boyd and Richerson 1985; recent review in Janicki and Krebs 1998.

Darwinian Genius. Internal variation-selection: Campbell 1965; Dennett 1995. Shakespeare's English: Macrone 1990. "Ode to Shakespeare" Giles 1923/1965, 418. "nothing in biology" Sober 1994, 490.

Chapter 2

Two evolutionary epistemologies: Bradie 1995. Primary evolutionary epistemology: Barkow, Cosmides, and Tooby 1992; Pinker 1997. "biologizing of Kant" Bradie 1995, 455. Secondary evolutionary epistemology: Campbell 1974; Stein and Lipton 1989; Toulmin 1981. Adaptations as knowledge: Plotkin 1993. Science as a variation-selection process: Hull 1988; Kantorovich 1993; R. J. Richards 1981; Shrader 1980; e.g., Parshall 1988. "The growth of our knowledge" Popper 1979, 261. Blind-variation and selective-retention: Campbell 1960; see also Staw 1990.

Biographical Illustrations. "it takes two" Hadamard 1945, 30. "when it was only" Dryden 1664/1926, 1. "the world little knows" Beveridge 1957, 79. "have lots of ideas" Root-Bernstein, Bernstein, and Garnier 1993, 339. "I cannot remember" Darwin 1892/1958, 55–56. **Associative Richness.** Ideational recombination: e.g., Barlow and Prinz 1997; Barnett 1953; Hadamard 1945; Mednick 1962. "a powerfully developed" and "more is required" Mach 1896, 167. "Instead of thoughts" James 1880, 456. "Ideas rose in crowds" Poincaré 1921, 387. "the hooked atoms" to "their mutual impacts" Poincaré 1921, 393. Theoretical discussion: Findlay and Lumsden 1988. **Mental Imagery.** "must have a vivid" Planck 1949, 109. "imagination is more important" Jeffares and Grray 1997, 237, "combinatory play" to "conventional words" Hadamard 1945, 142–43. "as to words" Hadamard 1945, 82. "It is a serious" Hadamard 1945, 69. "as the notes" Hadamard 1945, 69. "I turned my chair" Findlay 1948, 37. Janusian and homospatial thinking: Rothenberg 1979. "actively conceiving two or more discrete" Rothenberg 1979, 69. "actively conceiving two or more opposite" Rothenberg 1979, 55. Einstein and Bohr: Rothenberg 1987. "One of the" Bohr 1967, 328. **Intuitive Cognition.** Imageless thought quotes: Roe 1952, 144. "necessary to construct" to "unknown to us" Hadamard 1945, 28–29. Incubation and illumination: Wallas 1926. "I turned my" Poincaré 1921, 388. "a manifest sign" Poincaré 1921, 389. "the sterile combinations" Poincaré 1921, 386. "Among the great" Poincaré 1921, 392. "a sudden illumination" Poincaré 1921, 392. "The role of the preliminary" Poincaré 1921, 393–94. "While thought continues" Spencer 1904, 465. **Serendipitous Discovery.** "I can remember" Darwin 1892/1958, 43. "were always" Cannon 1940, 204. Serendipity: Austin 1978; Cannon 1940; Mach 1896; Shapiro 1986. Serendipity as blind variation: Kantorovich and Ne'eman 1989. "mere floating" Ghiselin 1952, 147. Kuhnian theory: Kuhn 1970; cf. Friman et al. 1993; Robins and Craik 1994. Pseudoserendipity: Roberts 1989; see also Díaz de Chumaceiro 1995. "were seen numbers" Mach 1896, 167. "I think that" Hyman 1963, 373. "instinct for arresting" Darwin 1892/1958, 101.

Experimental Investigations. Introspection and higher mental processes: Nisbett and Wilson 1977. "It is my design" Poe 1846/1884, 160. "most writers" Poe 1846/1884, 159. Coleridge: Schneider 1953; see also Perkins 1981. **Animal studies.** Chimps: Köhler 1925. Pigeons: Epstein 1990. "to get pigeons" Epstein 1990, 116–17. "At first the pigeon" Epstein 1990, 120. "principle of resurgence" Epstein 1990, 128. **Human studies.** Two-strings problem: Maier 1931. Insight studies: Sternberg and Davidson 1995. Compatible interpretations: Mandler 1995; Martindale 1995a; Seifert et al. 1995; Smith 1995. "finally, two days ago" Hadamard 1945, 15. Arousal and association probabilities: Martindale 1995a; Simonton 1980a; see also Krampen 1997. **Imagery.** Creative cognition approach: Smith, Ward, and Finke 1995. Geneplore model: Finke, Ward, and Smith 1992. Homospatial experiments: Rothenberg 1986; Sobel and Rothenberg 1980; see also Proctor 1993. "I was struck by" Chipp 1968, 429. **Intuition.** Primary process: Freud 1908/1959; Gedo 1997; Ochse 1989; Suler 1980. Implicit learning and memory: Reber 1993. Implicit grammars: e.g., Saffran et al. 1997. Conditioning without awareness: e.g., Krosnick et al. 1992; Verplanck 1955. Unconscious priming: Bowers, Farvolden, and Mermigis 1995; Bowers, Regehr, and Balthazard 1990; see also Erdley and D'Agostino 1989. Spreading activation: Findlay and Lumsden 1988; Martindale 1995a. Tip-of-the-tongue: Brown 1991; Brown and McNeill 1966. Thinking aloud and insight: Schooler and Melcher 1995; see also Simonton 1975b, 1980a. Unjustified hunches: Platt and Baker 1931. Feeling of knowing: Smith 1995. Complexity of the unconsciousness: Epstein 1994; Kihlstrom 1987.

Discovery Programs. "required to handle" Simon 1973, 479. "On eight occasions" Simon 1986, 7. Balmer's formula: Qin and Simon 1990, 305. "interested in how" and "in order to follow" Qin and Simon 1990, 283. **The computer models.** Discovery programs: Langley et al. 1987. Program names: Shrager and Langley 1990. BACON: Bradshaw, Langley, and Simon 1983. KEKADA: Kulkarni and Simon 1988. **The criticisms.** Faraday: Tweney 1990. Imagery program: Cheng and Simon 1995. Problem finding: Csikszentmihályi 1988; Getzels and Csikszentmihályi 1976; Jay and Perkins 1997; Okuda, Runco, and Berger 1991; Rostan 1994. "The formulation of a problem" Einstein and Infeld 1938, 95. Aesthetics in science: Dirac 1963; Hardy 1969; Wechsler 1978. "that I had only" Helmholtz 1898, 282. Additional critique: Sternberg 1989. **Genetic Algorithms.** BIG BLUE: Newborn 1996. Connectionist models, creativity, and Darwinism: Martindale 1995a; cf. Johnson-Laird 1993. Computer simulations of organic evolution: Dawkins 1986; Levy 1992. Genetic algorithms: Holland 1975. Technological achievements: Holland 1992. Genetic programming: Koza 1992.

Kepler's third law: Koza 1992, 255–58. Shakespeare quotation: Dawkins 1986. Creative achievements: Koza 1992, 1994. Role of mutation: Bäck 1996. DNA computers: Adleman 1994.

Variational Blindness. Directed mutations: Lenski and Mittler 1993. Objections: Dasgupta 1996; Perkins 1994; Sternberg 1998; Weber 1992; cf. Ceiko 1998: Perkins 1998. Goal orientation: Gruber 1989. **Creative rationality.** Rational constraints: Finke 1995; Simonton in press-a. Regression in service of the ego: Kris 1952; see also Gedo 1997. Degrees of primary process: Martindale 1975, 1990. "Freud's concept" and "if you are" Epstein 1990, 129. Heuristics: Newell and Simon 1972. **Creative volition.** General discussion: Simonton 1995a. Darwin's evolution: Gruber 1974. Expertise acquisition: Ericsson 1996. "chance favours" Beveridge 1957, 46. Zeigarnik effect: Seifert et al. 1995. Ten-year rule: Gardner 1993. "it would be an error" Jevons 1900, 577. "One phenomenon" to "sudden awakening" Hadamard 1945, 8. "Just at this time" Poincaré 1921, 387–88. *"The bath, the bed"* Boden 1991, 15. "I have written" Martindale 1995a, 251. "One can hardly reject" Nietzsche 1927, 896–897. Punctuated equilibrium: Eldredge and Gould 1972. "Many species once" Ridley 1993a, 522. Continuity: Ridley 1993a.

Evolutionary Origins. Internal trial and error: Campbell 1965; Dennett 1995. "just so" stories: Rose and Lauder 1996. Diversity of patented inventions: Basalla 1988, 2.

Chapter 3

"those qualities" to "the men who achieve" Galton 1892/1972, 77–78. Individual differences in output: Dennis 1954a, 1954b; Lotka 1926; Price 1963, 1976; Shockley 1957; Simon 1955. Productivity-eminence relationship: Albert 1975; Feist 1993; Raskin 1936; Simonton 1977b, 1991a, 1991b, 1992b; Wispé 1965. Behavioral definition of genius: Albert 1975. Gray: Dennis 1954a. Correlates of creativity: Barron and Harrington 1981; Hayes 1989a; Martindale 1989; MacKinnon 1978. Normal vs. revolutionary science: Kuhn 1970. Artistic styles: Hasenfus, Martindale, and Birnbaum 1983.

Intellect. IQ and creativity: Barron and Harrington 1981; Cox 1926; Haensly and Reynolds 1989; Hattie and Rogers 1988; Simonton 1976a, 1991d; Sternberg 1985; Walberg, Rasher, and Parkerson 1980. Threshold and triangular distribution: Guilford 1967; Simonton 1994. **Remote Association.** Associational theory: Mednick 1962. Figure 3.1 greatly modified from Simonton 1988d, 47. Associates of "foot" and "command" Eysenck 1995, 99. RAT: Mednick 1962. Evaluation: Ochse and Lill 1990. Primary process and synesthesia: Dailey, Martindale, and Borkum 1997. Intuitive vs. analytic genius: Simonton 1980b, 1988d. Figure 3.2 modified from Simonton 1988d. Evidence: Simonton 1975b, 1980a. Scientific creativity and remote associates: Gough 1976; see also Upmanyu, Bhardwaj, and Singh 1996. Optimal level: e.g., Simonton 1980d. **Divergent Thinking.** Convergent vs. divergent thought: Guilford 1967. Measures: Wallach and Kogan 1965. Validation: Crammond 1994; Runco 1992; Torrance 1988. Art vs. science: Hudson 1966; see also Runco 1986. Domain-specific: Baer 1993, 1994; see also Okuda, Runco, and Berger 1991. Word-association tests: e.g., Gough 1976. Sequences of divergent responses: Christensen, Guilford, and Wilson 1957;

Derks 1987; Derks and Hervas 1988; Meadow and Parnes 1959; Parnes 1961.

Character. Creativity as disposition: e.g., Gough 1979. **Personality.** General reviews: Barron and Harrington 1981; Cattell and Butcher 1968; Martindale 1989, 1995a; Specific studies: e.g., Charlton and Bakan 1988–89; Barron 1963a, 1963b, 1969; Cattell 1963; Chambers 1964; Crutchfield 1962; Helson and Crutchfield 1970; McCrae 1987; MacKinnon 1978; Manis 1951; Matthews et al. 1980; Raskin 1936; Roe 1952; Root-Bernstein, Bernstein, and Garnier 1993, 1995; Simonton 1976a, 1976e, 1991d; Taylor et al. 1984; White 1931. "I had, as a very young boy" to "a wish to travel" Darwin 1892/1958, 8–10. "His wide interest" Darwin 1892/1958, 84. "It's dogged" Sulloway 1996, 145. **Primary Darwinian traits.** Traits of greatness: Cox 1926; Simonton 1991d, 1994. **Secondary Darwinian traits.** "fifteen months" Darwin 1892/1958, 2–3. "The greater the attentional" Mendelsohn 1976, 396. Multiple projects: Gruber 1989; Hargens 1978; Root-Bernstein, Bernstein, and Garnier 1993; Simon 1974; Taylor et al. 1984. Network of enterprises: Gruber 1989; see also Root-Bernstein, Bernstein, and Garnier 1995. "I have always" Darwin 1892/1958, 53. "a first principle" Skinner 1959. Long hours: Boyce, Shaughnessy, and Pecker 1985; Chambers 1964; Hargens 1978; Manis 1951. "a mind forever" Jeans 1942, 716. Brainstorming: Bouchard and Hare 1970; Diehl and Stroebe 1987; Dillon, Graham, and Aidells 1972; Dunnette, Campbell, and Jaastad 1963. "I am a horse" Sorokin 1963, 274. "We are all agreed" Cropper 1970, 57. "essential tension" Kuhn 1977, 343. **Psychopathology.** "Those who have become" Andreasen and Canter 1974, 123. "no great genius" Seneca 1932, 285. "*First, and most*" Babcock 1895, 752. Psychoanalytic view: Gedo 1997. Humanistic psychologists: Maslow 1972; May 1975; Rogers 1954. **Empirical findings.** Table 3.1 from many sources, especially: Arieti 1976; Babcock 1895; Goodwin and Jamison 1990, chap. 14; Prentky 1980; Rothenberg 1990. Darwin's illness: Bowlby 1990. Historiometric studies: Ellis 1926; Juda 1949; Ludwig 1995; Martindale 1972; Post 1994, 1996. Leaders vs. creators: Goertzel, Goertzel, and Goertzel 1978; Walker, Koestner, and Hum 1995. "Perhaps no person can" Macaulay 1825/1900, 9. Fractal self-similarity: Ludwig 1998. Psychiatric studies: Andreasen 1987; Andreasen and Canter 1974; Jamison 1989, 1993. Criticisms: Rothenberg 1990. IPAR studies: MacKinnon 1978. Creative writers: Barron 1969. Corroborative study: Rust, Golombok, and Abram 1989. "What garlic is" Esar 1949/1989, 174. "Great Wits are sure" Dryden 1681, 6. Ego-strength: Barron 1969. Schizophrenic poets: Rothenberg 1990. Possible causal models: Brod 1997; Eisenman 1997; Ludwig 1995; R. Richards 1981. Eminence, stress, and disorder: Schaller 1997; see also Simonton 1994. **Theoretical interpretation.** See Eysenck 1993, 1994, 1995, 1997. Psychoticism and creativity: Aguilar-Alonso 1996; Eysenck 1994; Götz and Götz 1979a, 1979b; Pearson 1983; Rushton 1990; Stavridou and Furnham 1996; Woody and Claridge 1977. Eminent philosophers: Simonton 1976e. "I arrived at" Forbes 1967, 735. Schumann: Slater and Meyer 1959; Weisberg 1994. Darwin on Henslow: Darwin 1892/1958, 22–23.

Evolution. Iceland: Karlson 1970. Corroborative genetic studies: Juda 1949; Heston 1966; McNeil 1971; Myerson and Boyle 1941; Richards et al. 1988. "the result of a balance" Huxley et al. 1964, 220. Cultural unpredictability: Hammer and Zubin 1968. Proteanism and creativity: Miller 1997. Protean behavior: Driver and Humphries 1988.

Chapter 4

"You care for nothing" Darwin 1892/1958, 9. "If you can find" Darwin 1892/1958, 27. "MY DEAR ADÈLE" Cox 1926, 42. Galton's IQ: Terman 1917. "The Child is father" Wordsworth 1807/1928, 79.

Nature and Nurture. "genius must be born" Dryden 1693/1885, 60. "could add the names" Galton 1892/1972, 261. "I do not think" Galton 1892/1972, p. 3. "inclined to agree" Hyman 1963, 339. Replications: Bramwell 1948; Simonton 1983c; Woods 1906. Early critic: Candolle 1873. "The phrase 'nature and nurture'" Galton 1874, 12. **Environmentalism.** Review: Simonton 1987a. **Enrichment.** Homes of gifted: Schaefer and Anastasi 1968; Terman 1925; Holahan and Sears 1995; Winner 1996. Homes of geniuses: Goertzel and Goertzel 1962; Goertzel, Goertzel, and Goertzel 1978; Moulin 1955; Simonton 1986b; Walberg, Rasher, and Parkerson 1980. Scientific vs. artistic backgrounds: Schaefer and Anatasi 1968; see also Terman 1954. "to have fathers" Schaefer and Anatasi 1968, 47. **Adversity.** Terman's gifted: Terman 1925; Holahan and Sears 1995. "There's only one" Ferris 1977, 49. Disabilities: Goertzel and Goertzel 1962. Illness: Roe 1952. Economic difficulties: Berry 1981; Goertzel and Goertzel 1962. Table 4.1 from several sources, including: Eisenstadt et al. 1989; Goertzel, Goertzel, and Goertzel 1978; Illingworth and Illingworth 1969, 34–35; Silverman 1974; Woodward 1974. 699 eminent: Eisenstadt 1978. 301 geniuses: Albert 1971. Follow-up study: Walberg, Rasher, and Parkerson 1980; cf. Goertzel, Goertzel, and Goertzel 1978. Scientists: Berry 1981; Eiduson 1962; Roe 1952; Silverman 1974; cf. Woodward 1974. 64 scientists: Roe 1952. Mathematicians: Roe 1952. Writers: Brown 1968; cf. Martindale 1972. Prime ministers: Berrington 1974; Rentchnik 1989. Bereavement syndrome: Eisenstadt 1978. Robust personality: Simonton 1994; Therivel 1993. Divergent development: Simonton 1994. Juvenile delinquents and psychiatric patients: Eisenstadt 1978; cf. Brown 1968. "can be an impetus" Eisenstadt 1978, 220. "My mother died" Darwin 1892/1958, 5–6. Literary vs. physics laureates: Berry 1981; see also Raskin 1936. **Education.** Termites' education: Terman 1925; Burks, Jensen, and Terman 1930; Holahan and Sears 1995; Terman and Oden 1947. "it is, in fact" Schlipp 1951, 17. "One had to cram" Hoffman 1972, 31. "came as a tremendous surprise" Seelig 1958, 28. "during my second year" Darwin 1892/1958, 15. FRS: Hudson 1958. Science vs. art: Goertzel, Goertzel, and Goertzel 1978; Raskin 1936; Grades and success: Baird 1968; Bednar and Parker 1965; Bretz 1989; Cohen 1984; Dye and Reck 1989; Gaston 1973, 51; Guilford 1959; MacKinnon 1960; McClelland 1973; Nicholson 1915; Razik 1967; Samson et al. 1984; Taylor 1963; Taylor, Smith, and Ghiselin 1963. Negative attitudes: Goertzel, Goertzel, and Goertzel 1978. "The idea that it is" Brittain 1948, 7. Curvilinear relation: Simonton 1983b, 1984c; see also Eisenman 1970. "I consider that" Hilts 1975, 45. "I have never let" Harnsberger 1972, 553. Voracious reading: Chambers 1964; Goertzel, Goertzel, and Goertzel 1978; Simonton 1984c. "I shall not become" Hoffman 1972, 55. **Marginality.** Termite ethnicity: Terman 1925; Holahan and Sears 1995. "One of the consequences" Park 1928, 881. Creative minority: Toynbee 1946. "persons who have been" Campbell 1960, 391. Immigrants among famous moderns: Goertzel, Goertzel, and Goertzel 1978; see also Helson and Crutchfield 1970. Jewish eminence: Arieti 1976, 325–26; Hayes 1989b, table 4; Veblen 1919. Jewish laureates: Berry 1981. Bilingualism: Carringer 1974; Lambert, Tucker, and d'Anglejan 1973;

Landry 1972; Lopez, Esquivel, and Houtz 1993. Hybridization: Harrison 1993. U.S. science and religious affiliation: Lehman and Witty 1931; see also Helson and Crutchfield 1970. Marginality in science: Hudson and Jacot 1986. "All decisive advances" Koestler 1964, 230. "it has often happened" Bartlett 1958, 58. "almost always the men" Kuhn 1970, 90. X-ray astronomy: Simonton 1984d; cf. Gieryn and Hirsh 1983. Continental drift: Stewart 1986. "But I never" to "So much the better" Asimov 1982, 423. **Modern behavioral genetics.** Identical twins: Lykken 1982. Twins in old age: McClearn et al. 1997. Heritability coefficients: Bouchard 1994; Bouchard et al. 1990; Plomin, Owen, and McGuffin 1994. Religiosity: Waller et al. 1990. Shared versus nonshared environment: Plomin and Rende 1990. Minimal role of parents: Scarr and McCartney 1983. "the self-perceived ability" Lykken 1982, 370. "probably depends on" Lykken 1982, 370. Emergenesis: Lykken 1982; Lykken et al. 1992; Simonton in press-b. **Genetic origins of genius.** Genetic effects on environment: Plomin and Bergeman 1991; Scarr and McCartney 1983. Home demands of child prodigies: Feldman and Goldsmith 1986; Winner 1996. Intelligence and age at reproduction: Rushton 1995. Age of parents at birth of their celebrated child: Bowerman 1947; Ellis 1926; Galton 1874; Raskin 1936; Simonton 1992c; Visher 1947. Shared environment effects: Coon and Carey 1989; Waller and Shaver 1994. Gauss: Lykken 1982. Creativity emergenic: Waller et al. 1993. Genius rate: Galton 1869. **Evolutionism.** 64 scientists: Roe 1952. Half or more of great scientists: Chambers 1964; Eiduson 1962; Helmreich et al. 1980; Rubin 1970; Terry 1989. Citation rates: Helmreich et al. 1980. Creativity ratings: Helson and Crutchfield 1970. Nobel Prize: Clark and Rice 1982. *A Study of British Genius* (2d ed.): Ellis 1926. Composers: Schubert, Wagner, and Schubert 1977. National politics: Newman and Taylor 1994; Wagner and Schubert 1977; Zweigenhaft 1975. Twentieth-century celebrities: Goertzel, Goertzel, and Goertzel 1978. Writers: Bliss 1970. Revolutionaries: Stewart 1977, 1991; Walberg, Rasher, and Parkerson 1980; cf. Hudson 1990; Rejai 1979. Artists: Eisenman 1964. Some birth-order theories: Harris 1964; Watkins 1992; Zajonc 1976, 1983.

Openness and Birth Order. "a scientific mistake" to "What metaphysical jargon" Sulloway 1996, 14. "How extremely stupid" Sulloway 1990, 18. **Sibling Rivalries and Family Niches.** Birth order and achievement: Albert 1980, 1994; Altus 1966; Feldman and Goldsmith 1986; Schachter 1963; Terman 1925; West 1960. Dangerous sports: Nisbett 1968. Alcoholism: Blane and Barry 1973. **Revolutionaries and Reactionaries.** "121 historical events" to "a database" Sulloway 1996, 376; see also Sulloway in press. "gives *most clearly*" and "he appears to have" Eiseley 1961, 126–27.

Integration. Sulloway's critics: e.g., Falbo 1997; Harris 1998; Modell 1997; Townsend 1997. Chance and development: Bandura 1982. Impact of voyage: Sulloway 1985. "discovered, though unconsciously" and "the voyage of the" Darwin 1892/1958, 28–30. "I am sure" Darwin 1892/1958, 32. "it depended on" Darwin 1892/1958, 28. "could possess" Darwin 1892/1958, 27. Talent extinction: e.g., Montour 1977.

Chapter 5

Individual Variation. Conceptual problems: Mills and Beatty 1979. Citation rates: Cole and Cole 1972; Price 1965; Redner 1998. 10 psychologists: Simonton 1985.

10 composers: Simonton 1977a. **Normal versus skewed distributions.** Normal curve: Quételet 1835/1968; Galton 1869. The bell curve: Herrnstein and Murray 1994; cf. Burt 1963. Creativity and the normal curve: Nicholls 1972. Reproductive success: e.g., D'Amato 1988; Dunbar and Dunbar 1977; Inoue et al. 1993; Kuester, Paul, and Arnemann 1995. No young: e.g., Oring, Colwell, and Reed 1991; Huck, Lisk, and McKay 1988. Tomcat: Ponteir and Natoli 1996; see also Dixson, Bossi, and Wickings 1993. Productivity differences: Allison 1980; Dennis 1955, 1954c; Shockley 1957. No work at all: Bloom 1963. Price law: Price 1963, chap. 3. Lotka law: Lotka 1926. Relation between the laws: Allison et al. 1976. Inclusive definition: Cole and Cole 1972; Green 1981; Oromaner 1977. Classical composers: Moles 1958/1968; Simonton 1984d. Normal curve: Dennis 1954c. Objection: Simon 1954. IQ 340: Simonton 1994. Cumulative advantage: Allison, Long, and Krauze 1982; Allison and Stewart 1974. Research institutions: Allison and Long 1987, 1990; Crane 1965; Simonton 1992b. Multiplicative factors: Burt 1943; Shockley 1957; see also Eysenck 1995; Sternberg and Lubart 1995. Combinatorial explosion: Barlow and Prinz 1997; Eysenck 1995; Simonton 1988d. Skewed distribution of reproductive success: Oring, Colwell, and Reed, 1991; Smith 1993. Rhesus macaques: Smith 1993. Ecclesiastes hypothesis: Turner and Chubin 1976, 1979. Evidence against cumulative advantage: Simonton 1997a. Correlations among career periods: Christensen and Jacomb 1992; Cole 1979; Dennis 1954b. **Quality versus quantity of output.** Perfectionists vs. mass producers: Cole and Cole 1973. Quantity/quality relationship: Crandall 1978; Davis 1987; Dennis 1954a; Simonton 1984c, 1985. Laureates: Zuckerman 1977; cf. Helson and Crutchfield 1970. Publication and citation: Davis 1987; Cole and Cole 1973; Helmreich et al. 1980; Simonton 1984f, 1992b. Three most cited works: Cole and Cole 1973. Nineteenth-century scientists: Dennis 1954a; cf. Dennis 1954c. "The chances are" Bennet 1980, 15. Propensity definition of fitness: Mills and Beatty 1979. "blundered dreadfully" Darwin 1892/1958,172. **Developmental Change.** "expect to convince" to "question with impartiality" Darwin 1860/1952b, 240. "What a good thing" and "he hoped that" Hyman 1963, 375–76. "A new scientific truth" Planck 1949, 33–34. Reception of Darwin's theory: Hull, Tessner, and Diamond 1978; Sulloway 1996; cf. Levin, Stephan, and Walker 1995. Other studies: Diamond 1980; Messerli 1988; Oromaner 1977; Stewart 1986; Sulloway 1996; Whaples 1991. General effect: Green, Rich, and Nesman 1985; Vroom and Pahl 1971. **Career trajectories.** Early studies: Dennis 1956, 1966; Lehman 1953, 1962; Quételet 1835/1968; Raskin 1936. General reviews of literature: Simonton 1988a, 1997a. Figure 5.1: modified from Simonton 1984b. Extrinsic events: Roe 1965; Simonton 1977a, 1985, 1988a. Variance explained: Simonton 1984b, 1989a. Chronological vs. career age: Simonton 1984b, 1988a, 1997a; see also Bayer and Dutton 1977; Hargens 1978; Lyons 1968. Disciplinary contrasts: Adams 1946; Cole 1979; Dennis 1966; Lehman 1953; Levin and Stephan 1989, 1991; Manniche and Falk 1957; Moulin 1955; Simonton 1975a, 1991a; Stephan and Levin 1992, 1993. Individual differences: Christensen and Jacomb 1992; Horner, Rushton, and Vernon 1986; Raskin 1936; Simonton 1991a, 1991b; Zusne 1976. Theories: Lehman 1953; Simonton 1988a. Cross-sectional variation: Over 1982a, 1982c. Chronological age: Lehman 1953; McCrae, Arenberg, and Costa 1987. Darwinian model: Simonton 1984b, 1993, 1997a. *Equal-odds rule.* The principle: Simonton 1994; cf. Simonton 1988a. Empirical support: Davis 1987; Over 1988, 1989, 1990; Quételet 1835/1968; Simonton 1977b, 1984c,

1985, 1988b; Weisberg 1994. Reanalysis: Simonton 1997a. Career landmarks: Pressey and Combs 1943; Raskin 1936; Zhao 1984; Zhao and Jiang 1986; Zusne 1976. Predictions and empirical tests: Simonton 1991a, 1991b, 1997a. "as a scientist" and "he is more likely" Barber 1961, 601. Evidence: Messerli 1988; Stewart 1986. Cold fusion: Huizenga 1993. "Throughout the debates" Sulloway 1996, 36.

Artistic Styles. "later in life" Darwin 1892/1958, 10. "for many years" to "they do not end" Darwin 1892/1958, 53–54. "The impassioned orator" Darwin 1871/1952a, 571. Art's adaptive inutility: Pinker 1997, chap. 8. Overview of Darwinian aesthetics: Thornhill 1998. "Beneath your fair" Martindale 1975, 71, italics removed. "I love you opposite" Martindale 1975, 88. **Primordial Cognition and Aesthetic Selection.** Martindale's theory: 1975, 1984b, 1986a, 1990. Elizabethan sonnet: Simonton 1989b, 1990. Zeitgeist and art: Cerulo 1984; Dressler and Robbins 1975; Lomax 1968; Martindale 1975; Simonton 1983a, 1986a, 1986e. **Arousal Potential and Hedonic Value.** Optimal arousal theory: Berlyne 1971. Empirical support for inverted-U curve: Berlyne 1974; Kammann 1966; Simonton 1980d, 1987b; Steck and Machotka 1975; Vitz 1964; cf. Martindale and Moore 1989; Simonton 1980c. **Theoretical Predictions and Empirical Tests.** General review: Martindale 1990. Italian painting: Martindale 1986b. Classical music: Martindale and Uemura 1983. Simulation: Martindale 1973. "a yellow cigarette" to "upon the cosmos" Martindale 1990, 348. Literature: Martindale 1975, 1984a, 1990. Further extensions: Martindale 1990.

Scientific Multiples. "Your words have come" Darwin 1892/1958, 196. "The first edition" Darwin 1892/1958, 218. **The Traditional Explanation: Sociocultural Determinism.** Advocates: Boring 1963; Brannigan 1981; Kroeber 1917; Lamb and Easton 1984; Merton 1961a, 1961b; Ogburn and Thomas 1922. Published lists: Kroeber 1917; Ogburn and Thomas 1922. Priority disputes: Merton 1968. "discoveries and inventions become" Merton 1961a, 306. "It was discovered" Kroeber 1917, 199. "Is great intelligence" White 1949, 212. "if Michelangelo" Price 1963, 69. **Generic versus specific categories.** "a failure to" Schmookler 1966, 191. "have come to look" and "when Hansen" Zuckerman 1977, 203. Pelton water wheels and steam turbines: Constant 1978. Patent law: Burge 1984. Central message: Patinkin 1983. "I have not" Darwin 1892/1958, 201. "I had materials" Darwin 1892/1958, 46. Scientific idiosyncrasies: Holton 1971–72. "a mathematician will" Koestler 1964, 265. Artistic multiples: Stent 1972. **Independent versus antecedent events.** Einstein-Hilbert: Corry, Renn, and Stachel 1997. **Simultaneous discoveries versus rediscoveries.** 264 multiples: Merton 1961b. "social evolution is a resultant" James 1880, 448. "implications cannot be" Stent 1972, 84. **Necessary versus necessary and sufficient causes.** "all the ideas" Daintith, Mitchell, and Tootill 1981, 531. "If Watson and Crick" Stent 1972, 90. **The Darwinian Interpretation: Individual Indeterminism.** "It has sometimes been said" Darwin 1892/1958, 45. **Multiple grades.** Merton 1961b; Simonton 1978. Monotonic decline: Kroeber 1917; Merton 1961b; Ogburn and Thomas 1922; Simonton 1979. Poisson distribution: Price 1963; Simonton 1978, 1986d. Illustration of model fit: Simonton 1979; see also Simonton 1986f. Probability models: Brannigan and Wanner 1983a, 1983b; Price 1963; Schmookler 1966; Simonton 1978, 1979, 1986f. Monte Carlo simulations: Simonton 1986c. **Temporal separation.** Communication models: Brannigan and Wanner 1983b; Simonton 1986c, 1986d, 1986f. **Multiples participation.** "great scientific genius" to "degrees of talent" Merton 1961b, 484. Empirical support: Hagstrom 1974; Simonton 1979, 1988d. "relating the apparent" Campbell and Tauscher 1966, 58. "contributed nothing" Campbell and Tauscher 1966, 61. "the names of one-time" Campbell and Tauscher 1966, 62.

Genius and the Masterpiece. "I am inclined" Darwin 1892/1958, 249. **Operants, Reproductive Strategies, and Expertise.** Creative products as operants: Skinner 1972; see also Ohlsson 1992. r and K strategies: Pianka 1970; Wilson 1975. Expertise: Ericsson 1996; Ericsson and Charnes 1994; Ericsson, Krampe, and Tesch-Römer 1993. Creative expertise: Simonton 1996a. Ten-years and expertise: Chase and Simon 1973. Ten-years and creativity: Hayes 1989b; Simon 1986; Simonton 1991b. **Environmental Feedback, Configurational Creations, and Human Reason.** Peer review: Cicchetti 1991. "a little better than a dice roll" Lindsey 1988. Critical citations: Moravcsik and Murugesan 1975. Predicting success of creative products: Martindale et al. 1988; Shadish 1989; Simonton 1980d, 1986a, 1989b, 1990. Skewed distribution: Simonton 1997a. Shakespeare's plays: Simonton 1986e. Foibles of human reason: Bruner, Goodnow, and Austin 1956; Faust 1984; Fiske and Taylor 1991; Kahneman, Slovic, and Tversky 1982; Meehl 1954; Tweney, Doherty, and Mynatt 1981. Magic number: Miller 1956. Guernica: Arnheim 1962; Weisberg 1992. Darwin's ideational evolution: Gruber 1974.

Chapter 6

Essay of 1844 C. Darwin 1844/1963.

Race. "the average intellectual" Galton 1892/1972, 394. "the average ability" Galton 1892/1972, 397. Race rankings: Rushton 1985, 1988, 1995; see also Lynn 1991a. Race and civilization: Lynn 1991b. Discussion: Gross 1990. Father absence: Draper and Belsky 1990. Criticisms: Anderson 1991; Weizmann et al. 1990; Zuckerman 1990, 1991; and comments on Lynn 1991a; cf. Rushton 1991a, 1991b. See also: Gould 1981; Hertz 1970; Tobias 1970.

Culture. Galton vs. Kroeber: Simonton 1988c. Configurations: Kroeber 1944; see also Cattell 1903; Rainoff 1929; Schneider 1937; Simonton 1975d, 1988c, 1992a, 1996b; Sorokin and Merton 1935. Dysgenic decline: Galton 1869; see also Lynn 1996. Original suggestion: Simonton 1988b, 1988d. **Predecessors.** Generation time-series analyses: Sheldon 1979, 1980; Simonton 1975d, 1976d, 1988c, 1997b. Role models and mentors: Goldstein 1979; Simonton 1977b, 1984a, 1992c; Walberg, Rasher, and Parkerson 1980; Wispé 1965. Mentor age: Simonton 1984a, 1992b. **Contemporaries.** Studies: Simonton 1975c, 1975d, 1984a, 1988c, 1992b, 1992c, 1997b. "The ideal audience" Auden 1948, 176. Career length: Simonton 1992c. "No scientist can know" Kantorovich 1993, 194–95. "when a scientist" Kantorovich 1993, 198. Research groups: Dunbar 1995. Hull's theory: Hull 1988. "The greatest natural" Reynolds 1769–90/1966, 90. Evidence for increased elitism: Zhao and Jiang 1985. **Intellectual Receptiveness.** "Letting a hundred" *Who Said* 1991, 314. Research: Simonton 1976b, 1976c. "art and literature" Davis 1941, 572. Economic prosperity: Kavolis 1964; Kuo 1986. Economic decline: Doty, Peterson, and Winter 1991; Sales 1973. **Ethnic Diversity.** "it is very remarkable" Galton 1892/1972, 413. "Every advance" Park 1928, 881. Japanese culture: Simonton 1997b. Nobel laureates: Moulin 1955; see also Ellis 1926. Laboratory experiments: Nemeth 1986; Nemeth and Kwan 1985, 1987; Nemeth and Wachtler 1983. **Political**

openness. Swiss vs. Russian Jews: Berry 1981. Suppressed nationalities: Kroeber 1944. "In order for civilization" Sorokin 1947/1969, 543. Political fragmentation: Naroll et al. 1971; Simonton 1975d, 1976e. Fragmentation and openness: Simonton 1976c. Universal states: Toynbee 1946. Disturbances: Simonton 1975d; cf. Kavolis 1966. "Warfare usually" Norling 1970, 248. Empirical evidence: Price 1978; Simonton 1980b, 1983a. Narrowing influence: Simonton 1976f. "All of the military" Dupuy and Dupuy 1993.

Gender. Overview: Eccles 1985; Ochse 1991. Famous women in the West: Cattell 1903; Eisenstadt 1978. Female scientists: Simonton 1991a; cf. Cole 1987. Female composers: Simonton 1991b. Female writers: Cattell 1903; Cox 1926; Simonton 1992a. **Sexual Dimorphism and Selection.** Darwinist theories: Shields 1975. General critique: Fausto-Sterling 1997. Sexual selection and creativity: Miller 1998. Physical aggressiveness: Hyde 1986. **Gender Socialization and Stereotypes.** Socialization practices: Barry, Bacon, and Child 1957. Mills College: Helson 1990. "who were successful in" Helson 1990, 49. Brothers: Helson 1980. "He that hath wife" Bacon 1597/1942, 29. Marriage and family: Hayes 1989b, 312–13; see also Goertzel, Goertzel, and Goertzel 1978; Hargens, McCann, and Reskin 1978; Kyvik 1990; McCurdy 1960; McDowell 1982; Stohs 1992; Tomlinson-Keasey 1990. Prejudiced judgments: Fidell 1970; Glick, Zion, and Nelson 1988. "I would venture" Woolf 1929, 51. Females in Japan: Simonton 1992a.

Spencerian Progress. Classic presentation: Spencer 1967. Modern: e.g., Adams 1988; Service 1975; White 1949. **Scale analysis and evolutionary sequences.** Cited study: Carneiro 1970; see also Lomax and Arensberg 1971; Lomax with Berkowitz 1972. "simplicity precedes complexity" and "a change from a state" Carneiro 1970, 835. **Societal complexity and cultural creativity.** "As civilisation advances" Macaulay 1825/1900, 7. Cultural decline: Kroeber 1944; see also Sorokin and Merton 1935; Simonton 1996b; Spengler 1926–28/1945; Yuasa 1974. Biological advance: Capitanio and Leger 1979; Yarczower and Hazlett 1977. Sociocultural advance: Granovetter 1979; Nolan 1982. Primary-process study: Martindale 1976. Primitive mentality: Cassirer 1925/1955; Lévy-Bruhl 1978. Creativity in preliterate societies: e.g., Brenneis 1990; Dissanayake 1992. **Darwinian Change.** Cultural evolution: Boyd and Richerson 1985; Cavalli-Sforza and Feldman 1981; Lumsden and Wilson 1981; for review see Janicki and Krebs 1998. Altruism and yams: Boyd and Richerson 1985. "a consideration" White 1949, 212; see also Schneider 1937. Lone exception: Findlay and Lumsden 1988. **Social learning.** Social learning theory: Bandura 1977. Group identification: Harris 1995. Werther effect: Phillips 1974; Stack 1987. Darwinian theory: Boyd and Richerson 1985. **Niche exploitation.** See, e.g., Campbell 1965. **Group competition.** Competition for niches: Colinvaux 1980. Arms races: Richardson 1960a, 1960b. Coevolution: Lumsden and Wilson 1981. Group selection: Wilson 1980. Red Queen: Ridley 1993b. "Now, *here*, you see" *Oxford University Press Dictionary of Quotations* 1985, 130. Social integration: Kavolis 1963, 1964, 1966; Sorokin 1937–41. Ibn Khaldun c. 1377/1967. Population and creativity: Fowler 1987. Simonton 1981, 1992a; Taagepera and Colby 1979. Population and technology: Simon and Sullivan 1989; Taagepera 1979. Population and IQ: Simonton 1994, 219. Population and achievement: Charness and Gerchak 1996.

Chapter 7

Darwin's ideational evolution: Gruber 1974, 1989; Sulloway 1985. Evolution of Darwinism: Depew and Weber 1995.

Recapitulation. "one long argument" Hyman 1963, 401.

Explanatory Scope. Hemispheric differentiation: Ehrenwald 1984; Katz 1997; McManus and Bryden 1991; cf. Efron 1990; Hines 1991; Hoppe and Kyle 1990. Handedness: McManus and Bryden 1991; O'Boyle and Benbow 1990. Evolution of laterality: Bradshaw 1988; Corballis 1989. Alcohol and creativity: Brunke and Gilbert 1992; Ludwig 1990; cf. Davis 1986; Lester 1991. Drugs and creativity: Berlin et al. 1955; Harman et al. 1966; Janiger and de Rios 1989.

References

~

Adams, C. W. (1946). The age at which scientists do their best work. *Isis, 36,* 166–69.

Adams, R. N. (1988). *The eighth day: Social evolution as the self-organization of energy.* Austin: University of Texas Press.

Adleman, L. M. (1994). Molecular computation of solutions to combinatorial problems. *Science, 266,* 1021–24.

Aguilar-Alonso, A. (1996). Personality and creativity. *Personality and Individual Differences, 21,* 959–69.

Albert, R. S. (1971). Cognitive development and parental loss among the gifted, the exceptionally gifted and the creative. *Psychological Reports, 29,* 19–26.

———. (1975). Toward a behavioral definition of genius. *American Psychologist, 30,* 140–51.

———. (1980). Family positions and the attainment of eminence: A study of special family positions and special family experiences. *Gifted Child Quarterly, 24,* 87–95.

———. (1994). The achievement of eminence: A longitudinal study of exceptionally gifted boys and their families. In R. F. Subotnik and K. D. Arnold (Eds.), *Beyond Terman: Contemporary longitudinal studies of giftedness and talent* (pp. 282–315). Norwood, N.J.: Ablex.

Allison, P. D. (1980). Inequality and scientific productivity. *Social Studies of Science, 10,* 163–79.

———, and Long, J. S. (1987). Interuniversity mobility of academic scientists. *American Sociological Review, 52,* 643–52.

———, and Long, J. S. (1990). Departmental effects on scientific productivity. *American Sociological Review, 55,* 469–78.

———, Long, J. S., and Krauze, T. K. (1982). Cumulative advantage and inequality in science. *American Sociological Review, 47,* 615–25.

———, Price, D. S., Griffith, B. C., Moravcsik, M. J., and Stewart, J. A. (1976). Lotka's law: A problem in its interpretation and application. *Social Studies of Science, 6,* 269–76.

———, and Stewart, J. A. (1974). Productivity differences among scientists: Evidence for accumulative advantage. *American Sociological Review, 39,* 596–606.

Altus, W. D. (1966). Birth order and its sequelae. *Science, 151,* 44–48.

Amabile, T. M. (1982). Social psychology of creativity: A consensual assessment technique. *Journal of Personality and Social Psychology, 43,* 997–1013.

———. (1996). *Creativity in context.* Boulder, Colo.: Westview.

Anderson, J. L. (1991). Rushton's racial comparisons: An ecological critique of theory and method. *Canadian Psychology, 32,* 51–60.

Andersson, M. (1994). *Sexual selection.* Princeton, N.J.: Princeton University Press.

Andreasen, N. C. (1987). Creativity and mental illness: Prevalence rates in writers and their first-degree relatives. *American Journal of Psychiatry, 144,* 1288–92.

Andreasen, N. C., and Canter, A. (1974). The creative writer: Psychiatric symptoms and family history. *Comprehensive Psychiatry, 15*, 123–31.

Arieti, S. (1976). *Creativity: The magic synthesis.* New York: Basic Books.

Arnheim, R. (1962). *Picasso's Guernica: The genesis of a painting.* Berkeley: University of California Press.

Ashton, S. V., and Oppenheim, C. (1978). A method of predicting Nobel prizewinners in chemistry. *Social Studies of Science, 8*, 341–48.

Asimov, I. (1982). *Biographical encyclopedia of science and technology* (2d rev. ed.). New York: Doubleday.

Auden, W. H. (1948). Squares and oblongs. In R. Arnheim, W. H. Auden, K. Shapiro, and D. A. Stauffer (Eds.), *Poets at work: Essays based on the modern poetry collection at the Lockwood Memorial Library, University of Buffalo* (pp. 163–81). New York: Harcourt, Brace.

Austin, J. H. (1978). *Chase, chance, and creativity: The lucky art of novelty.* New York: Columbia University Press.

Babcock, W. L. (1895). On the morbid heredity and predisposition to insanity of the man of genius. *Journal of Nervous and Mental Disease, 20*, 749–769.

Bäck, T. (1996). *Evolutionary algorithms in theory and practice.* Oxford: Oxford University Press.

Bacon, F. (1942). *Essays and the New Atlantis.* Roslyn, N.Y.: Black. (Original works published 1597 and 1620.)

Baer, J. (1993). *Creativity and divergent thinking: A task-specific approach.* Hillsdale, N.J.: Erlbaum.

———. (1994). Divergent thinking is not a general trait: A multidomain training experiment. *Creativity Research Journal, 7*, 35–46.

Baird, L. L. (1968). The achievement of bright and average students. *Educational and Psychological Measurement, 28*, 891–99.

Bandura, A. (1977). *Social learning theory.* Englewood Cliffs, N.J.: Prentice-Hall.

———. (1982). The psychology of chance encounters in life paths. *American Psychologist, 37*, 747–55.

Barber, B. (1961). Resistance by scientists to scientific discovery. *Science, 134*, 596–602.

Barber, R. J. (1981). Comments on the quantitative study of creativity in Western civilization. *American Anthropologist, 83*, 143–44.

Barkow, J. H., Cosmides, L., and Tooby, J. (Eds.). (1992). *The adapted mind: Evolutionary psychology and the generation of culture.* New York: Oxford University Press.

Barlow, L. W., and Prinz, J. J. (1997). Mundane creativity in perceptual symbol systems. In T. B. Ward, S. M. Smith, and J. Vaid (Eds.), *Creative thought: An investigation of conceptual structures and processes* (pp. 267–307). Washington, D.C.: American Psychological Association.

Barnett, H. G. (1953). *Innovation: The basis of cultural change.* New York: McGraw-Hill.

Barron, F. X. (1963a). *Creativity and psychological health: Origins of personal vitality and creative freedom.* Princeton, N.J.: Van Nostrand.

————. (1963b). The needs for order and for disorder as motives in creative activity. In C. W. Taylor and F. X. Barron (Eds.), *Scientific creativity: Its recognition and development* (pp. 153–60). New York: Wiley.

————. (1969). *Creative person and creative process.* New York: Holt, Rinehart and Winston.

Barron, F., and Harrington, D. M. (1981). Creativity, intelligence, and personality. *Annual Review of Psychology, 32,* 439–76.

Barry, H., Bacon, M. K., and Child, I. L. (1957). A cross-cultural survey of some sex differences in socialization. *Journal of Abnormal and Social Psychology, 55,* 327–32.

Bartlett, F. (1958). *Thinking: An experimental and social study.* New York: Basic Books.

Basalla, G. (1988). *The evolution of technology.* Cambridge: Cambridge University Press.

Bayer, A. E., and Dutton, J. E. (1977). Career age and research—Professional activities of academic scientists: Tests of alternative non-linear models and some implications for higher education faculty policies. *Journal of Higher Education, 48,* 259–82.

Bayer, A. E., and Folger, J. (1966). Some correlates of a citation measure of productivity in science. *Sociology of Education, 39,* 381–90.

Bednar, R. L., and Parker, C. A. (1965). The creative development and growth of exceptional college students. *Journal of Educational Research, 59,* 133–36.

Bennet, W. (1980, January–February). Providing for posterity. *Harvard Magazine,* pp. 13–16.

Berlin, L., Guthrie, T., Weider, A., Goodell, H., and Wolff, H. G. (1955). The effects of mescaline and lysergic acid on cerebral processes pertinent to creative activity. *Journal of Nervous and Mental Disease, 122,* 487–91.

Berlyne, D. (1971). *Aesthetics and psychobiology.* New York: Appleton-Century-Crofts.

Berlyne, D. E. (Ed.). (1974). *Studies in the new experimental aesthetics.* Washington, D.C.: Hemisphere.

Berrington, H. (1974). Review article: The Fiery Chariot: Prime ministers and the search for love. *British Journal of Political Science, 4,* 345–69.

Berry, C. (1981). The Nobel scientists and the origins of scientific achievement. *British Journal of Sociology, 32,* 381–91.

Beveridge, W. I. B. (1957). *The art of scientific investigation* (3d ed.). New York: Vintage.

Blane, H. T., and Barry, H. (1973). Birth order and alcoholism: A review. *Quarterly Journal of Studies on Alcohol, 34,* 837–52.

Bliss, W. D. (1970). Birth order of creative writers. *Journal of Individual Psychology, 26,* 200–202.

Bloom, B. S. (1963). Report on creativity research by the examiner's office of the University of Chicago. In C. W. Taylor and F. X. Barron (Eds.), *Scientific creativity: Its recognition and development* (pp. 251–64). New York: Wiley.

Boden, M. A. (1991). *The creative mind: Myths and mechanisms.* New York: Basic Books.

Bohr, H. (1967). My father. In S. Rozental (Ed.), *Niels Bohr: His life and work as seen by his friends and colleagues* (pp. 325–35). Amsterdam: North-Holland Publishing.

Boring, E. G. (1963). *History, psychology, and science.* (R. I. Watson and D. T. Campbell, Eds.), New York: Wiley.

Bouchard, T. J., Jr. (1994). Genes, environment, and personality. *Science, 264,* 1700–1701.

Bouchard, T. J., Jr., and Hare, M. (1970). Size, performance, and potential in brainstorming groups. *Journal of Applied Psychology, 54,* 51–55.

Bouchard, T. J., Lykken, D. T., McGue, M., Segal, N. L., and Tellegen, A. (1990). Sources of human psychological differences: The Minnesota study of twins reared apart. *Science, 250,* 223–228.

Bowerman, W. G. (1947). *Studies in genius.* New York: Philosophical Library.

Bowers, K. S., Farvolden, P., and Mermigis, L. (1995). Intuitive antecedents of insight. In S. M. Smith, T. B. Ward, and R. A. Finke (Eds.), *The creative cognition approach* (pp. 27–51). Cambridge, Mass.: MIT Press.

Bowers, K. S., Regehr, G., and Balthazard, C. (1990). Intuition in the context of discovery. *Cognitive Psychology, 22,* 72–110.

Bowlby, J. (1990). *Charles Darwin: A new life.* New York: Norton.

Boyce, R., Shaughnessy, P., and Pecker, G. (1985). Women and publishing in psychology. *American Psychologist, 40,* 577–78.

Boyd, R., and Richerson, P. J. (1985). *Culture and the evolutionary process.* Chicago: University of Chicago Press.

Bradie, M. (1995). Epistemology from an evolutionary point of view. In E. Sober (Ed.), *Conceptual issues in evolutionary biology* (2d ed., pp. 454–475). Cambridge, Mass.: MIT Press.

Bradshaw, G. F., Langley, P. W., and Simon, H. A. (1983). Studying scientific discovery by computer simulation. *Science, 222,* 971–75.

Bradshaw, J. L. (1988). The evolution of human lateral asymmetries: New evidence and second thoughts. *Journal of Human Evolution, 17,* 615–37.

Bramwell, B. S. (1948). Galton's "Hereditary Genius" and the three following generations since 1869. *Eugenics Review, 39,* 146–53.

Brannigan, A. (1981). *The social basis of scientific discoveries.* Cambridge: Cambridge University Press.

Brannigan, A., and Wanner, R. A. (1983a). Historical distributions of multiple discoveries and theories of scientific change. *Social Studies of Science, 13,* 417–35.

———.(1983b). Multiple discoveries in science: A test of the communication theory. *Canadian Journal of Sociology, 8,* 135–51.

Brenneis, D. (1990). Musical imaginations: Comparative perspectives on musical creativity. In M. A. Runco and R. S. Albert (Eds.), *Theories of creativity* (pp. 170–89). Newbury Park, Calif.: Sage.

Bretz, R. D., Jr. (1989). College grade point average as a predictor of adult success: A meta-analysis and some additional evidence. *Public Personnel Management, 18,* 11–22.

Brittain, V. (1948). *On being an author.* New York: Macmillan.

Brod, J. H. (1997). Creativity and schizotypy. In G. Claridge (Ed.), *Schizotypy: Impli-*

cations for illness and health (pp. 274–98). Oxford: Oxford University Press.

Brown, A. S. (1991). A review of the tip-of-the-tongue experience. *Psychological Bulletin, 109,* 204–23.

Brown, F. (1968). Bereavement and lack of a parent in childhood. In E. Miller (Ed.), *Foundations of child psychiatry* (pp. 435–55). Oxford: Pergamon.

Brown, R. W., and McNeill, D. (1966). The "tip of the tongue" phenomenon. *Journal of Verbal Learning and Verbal Behavior, 5,* 325–37.

Bruner, J. S., Goodnow, J. J., and Austin, G. A. (1956). *A study of thinking.* New York: Wiley.

Brunke, M., and Gilbert, M. (1992). Alcohol and creative writing. *Psychological Reports, 71,* 651–58.

Burge, D. A. (1984). *Patent and trademark practices* (2d ed.). New York: Wiley.

Burks, B. S., Jensen, D. W., and Terman, L. M. (1930). *The promise of youth: Follow-up studies of a thousand gifted children.* Stanford, Calif.: Stanford University Press.

Burt, C. (1943). Ability and income. *British Journal of Educational Psychology, 12,* 83–98.

———. (1963). Is intelligence distributed normally? *British Journal of Statistical Psychology, 16,* 175–90.

Buss, D. M. (1990). Evolutionary social psychology: Prospects and pitfalls. *Motivation and Emotion, 14,* 265–86.

———. (1995). Evolutionary psychology: A new paradigm for psychological science. *Psychological Inquiry, 6,* 1–30.

Calvin, W. H. (1987). The brain as a Darwin machine. *Nature, 330,* 33–34.

———. (1990). *The ascent of mind: Ice age climates and the evolution of intelligence.* New York: Bantam.

Campbell, D. T. (1960). Blind variation and selective retention in creative thought as in other knowledge processes. *Psychological Review, 67,* 380–400.

———. (1965). Variation and selective retention in socio-cultural evolution. In H. R. Barringer, G. I. Blanksten, and R. W. Mack (Eds.), *Social change in developing areas* (pp. 19–49). Cambridge, Mass.: Schenkman.

———. (1974). Evolutionary epistemology. In P. A. Schlipp (Ed.), *The philosophy of Karl Popper* (pp. 413–63). La Salle, Ill.: Open Court.

Campbell, D. T., and Tauscher, H. (1966). Schopenhauer, Séguin, Lubinoff, and Zehender as anticipators of Emmert's law: With comments on the uses of eponymy. *Journal of the History of the Behavioral Sciences, 2,* 58–63.

Candolle, A. de (1873). *Histoire des sciences et des savants depuis deux siècles.* Geneva: Georg.

Cannon, W. B. (1940). The role of chance in discovery. *Scientific Monthly, 50,* 204–9.

Capitanio, J. P., and Leger, D. W. (1979). Evolutionary scales lack utility: A reply to Yarczower and Hazlett. *Psychological Bulletin, 86,* 876–79.

Carlyle, T. (1841). *On heroes, hero-worship, and the heroic.* London: Fraser.

Carneiro, R. L. (1970). Scale analysis, evolutionary sequences, and the rating of cultures. In R. Naroll and R. Cohn (Eds.), *A handbook of method in cultural anthropology* (pp. 834–71). New York: Natural History Press.

Carringer, D. C. (1974). Creative thinking abilities in Mexican youth. *Journal of Cross-Cultural Psychology, 5,* 492–504.

Cassirer, E. (1955). *The philosophy of symbolic forms* (Vol. 2). New Haven, Conn.: Yale University Press. (Original work published 1925.)

Catania, A. C. (1992). B. F. Skinner, organism. *American Psychologist, 47*, 1521–30.

Cattell, J. M. (1903). A statistical study of eminent men. *Popular Science Monthly, 62*, 359–77.

Cattell, R. B. (1963). The personality and motivation of the researcher from measurements of contemporaries and from biography. In C. W. Taylor and F. Barron (Eds.), *Scientific creativity: Its recognition and development* (pp. 119–31). New York: Wiley.

Cattell, R. B., and Butcher, H. J. (1968). *The prediction of achievement and creativity.* Indianapolis: Bobbs-Merrill.

Cavalli-Sforza, L. L., and Feldman, M. W. (1981). *Cultural transmission and evolution: A quantitative approach.* Princeton, N.J.: Princeton University Press.

Cerulo, K. A. (1984). Social disruption and its effects on music: An empirical analysis. *Social Forces, 62*, 885–904.

Chambers, J. A. (1964). Relating personality and biographical factors to scientific creativity. *Psychological Monographs: General and Applied, 78* (Whole No. 584), 1–20.

Changeux, J.-P. (1985). *Neuronal man: The biology of mind.* New York: Oxford University Press.

Charlton, S., and Bakan, P. (1988–89). Cognitive complexity and creativity. *Imagination, Cognition and Personality, 8*, 315–22.

Charness, N., and Gerchak, Y. (1996). Participation rates and maximal performance: A log-linear explanation for group differences, such as Russian and male dominance in chess. *Psychological Science, 7*, 46–51.

Chase, W. G., and Simon, H. A. (1973). Perception in chess. *Cognitive Psychology, 4*, 55–81.

Cheng, P. C.-H., and Simon, H. A. (1995). Scientific discovery and creative reasoning with diagrams. In S. M. Smith, T. B. Ward, and R. A. Finke (Eds.), *The creative cognition approach* (pp. 205–28). Cambridge, Mass.: MIT Press.

Chipp, H. B. (Ed.). (1968). *Theories of modern art.* Berkeley: University of California Press.

Christensen, H., and Jacomb, P. A. (1992). The lifetime productivity of eminent Australian academics. *International Journal of Geriatric Psychiatry, 7*, 681–86.

Christensen, P. R., Guilford, J. P., and Wilson, R. C. (1957). Relations of creative responses to working time and instructions. *Journal of Experimental Psychology, 53*, 82–88.

Cicchetti, D. V. (1991). The reliability of peer review for manuscript and grant submissions: A cross-disciplinary investigation. *Behavioral and Brain Sciences, 14*, 119–86.

Clark, R. D., and Rice, G. A. (1982). Family constellations and eminence: The birth orders of Nobel Prize winners. *Journal of Psychology, 110*, 281–87.

Cohen, P. A. (1984). College grades and adult achievement: A research synthesis. *Research in Higher Education, 20*, 281–93.

Cole, J., and Cole, S. (1972). The Ortega hypothesis. *Science, 178*, 368–75.

Cole, J. R. (1987). Women in science. In D. N. Jackson and J. P. Rushton (Eds.), *Scientific excellence: Origins and assessment* (pp. 359–75). Beverly Hills, Calif.: Sage.

Cole, S. (1979). Age and scientific performance. *American Journal of Sociology, 84*, 958–77.

Cole, S., and Cole, J. R. (1967). Scientific output and recognition: A study in the operation of the reward system in science. *American Sociological Review, 32*, 377–90.

———. (1973). *Social stratification in science.* Chicago: University of Chicago Press.

Colinvaux, P. (1980). *Fates of nations: A biological theory of history.* New York: Simon & Schuster.

Constant, E. W., II (1978). On the diversity of co-evolution of technological multiples: Steam turbines and Pelton water wheels. *Social Studies of Science, 8*, 183–210.

Coon, H., and Carey, G. (1989). Genetic and environmental determinants of musical ability in twins. *Behavior Genetics, 19*, 183–93.

Corballis, M. C. (1989). Laterality and human evolution. *Psychological Review, 96*, 492–505.

Corry, L., and Renn, J., and Stachel, J. (1997). Belated decision in the Hilbert-Einstein priority dispute. *Science, 278*, 1270–73.

Cox, C. (1926). *The early mental traits of three hundred geniuses.* Stanford, Calif.: Stanford University Press.

Crammond, B. (1994). The Torrance Tests of Creative Thinking: From design through establishment of predictive validity. In R. F. Subotnik and K. D. Arnold (Eds.), *Beyond Terman: Contemporary longitudinal studies of giftedness and talent* (pp. 229–54). Norwood, N.J.: Ablex.

Crandall, R. (1978). The relationship between quantity and quality of publications. *Personality and Social Psychology Bulletin, 4*, 379–80.

Crane, D. (1965). Scientists at major and minor universities: A study of productivity and recognition. *American Sociological Review, 30*, 699–714.

Cropper, W. H. (1970). *The quantum physicists.* New York: Oxford University Press.

Crow, J. F. (1986). *Basic concepts in population, quantitative, and evolutionary genetics.* New York: Freeman.

Crutchfield, R. (1962). Conformity and creative thinking. In H. E. Gruber, G. Terrell, and M. Wertheimer (Eds.), *Contemporary approaches to creative thinking* (pp. 120–40). New York: Atherton Press.

Csikszentmihályi, M. (1988). Motivation and creativity: Toward a synthesis of structural and energistic approaches to cognition. *New Ideas in Psychology, 6*, 159–76.

———. (1990). The domain of creativity. In M. A. Runco and R. S. Albert (Eds.), *Theories of creativity* (pp. 190–212). Newbury Park, Calif: Sage.

Cziko, G. (1995). *Without miracles: Universal selection theory and the second Darwinian revolution.* Cambridge, Mass.: MIT Press.

Cziko, G. A. (1998). From blind to creative: In defense of Donald Campbell's selectionist theory of human creativity. *Journal of Creative Behavior, 32*, 192–208.

Dailey, A., Martindale, C., and Borkum, J. (1997). Creativity, synesthesia, and physiognomic perception. *Creativity Research Journal, 10*, 1–8.

Daintith, J., Mitchell, S., and Tootill, E. (Eds.). (1981). *A biographical encyclopedia of scientists* (Vol. 1). New York: Facts on File.

D'Amato, F. R. (1988). Effects of male social status on reproductive success and on behavior in mice (*Mus musculus*). *Journal of Comparative Psychology, 102*, 146–51.

Dante Alighieri. (1952). Divine comedy (C. E. Norton, Trans.). In R. M. Hutchins (Ed.), *Great books of the Western world* (Vol. 21). Chicago: Encyclopaedia Britannica.

Darwin, C. (1952a). The descent of man and selection in relation to sex. In R. M. Hutchins (Ed.), *Great books of the Western world* (Vol. 49, pp. 253–600). Chicago: Encyclopaedia Britannica. (Original work published 1871.)

Darwin, C. (1952b). On the origin of species by means of natural selection. In R. M. Hutchins (Ed.), *Great books of the Western world* (Vol. 49, pp. 1–251). Chicago: Encyclopaedia Britannica. (Original second edition published 1860.)

Darwin, C. (1963). The essay of 1844. In S. E. Hyman (Ed.), *Darwin for today: The essence of his works* (pp. 81–223). New York: Viking Press. (Original work written 1844)

Darwin, F. (Ed.). (1958). *The autobiography of Charles Darwin and selected letters.* New York: Dover. (Original work published 1892.)

Dasgupta, S. (1996). *Technology and creativity.* New York: Oxford University Press.

Davis, H. T. (1941). *The analysis of economic time series.* Bloomington, Ind.: Principia Press.

Davis, R. A. (1987). Creativity in neurological publications. *Neurosurgery, 20,* 652–63.

Davis, W. M. (1986). Premature mortality among prominent American authors noted for alcohol abuse. *Drug and Alcohol Dependence, 18,* 133–38.

Dawkins, R. (1986). *The blind watchmaker.* New York: Norton.

———. (1989). *The selfish gene* (rev. ed.). Oxford: Oxford University Press.

Dennett, D. C. (1995). *Darwin's dangerous idea: Evolution and the meanings of life.* New York: Simon & Schuster.

Dennis, W. (1954a). Bibliographies of eminent scientists. *Scientific Monthly, 79,* 180–83.

———. (1954b). Predicting scientific productivity in later maturity from records of earlier decades. *Journal of Gerontology, 9,* 465–67.

———. (1954c). Productivity among American psychologists. *American Psychologist, 9,* 191–94.

———. (1955). Variations in productivity among creative workers. *Scientific Monthly, 80,* 277–78.

———. (1956). Age and productivity among scientists. *Science, 123,* 724–25.

———. (1966). Creative productivity between the ages of 20 and 80 years. *Journal of Gerontology, 21,* 1–8.

Depew, D. J., and Weber, B. H. (1995). *Darwinism evolving: Systems dynamics and the genealogy of natural selection.* Cambridge, Mass.: MIT Press.

Derks, P., and Hervas, D. (1988). Creativity in humor production: Quantity and quality in divergent thinking. *Bulletin of the Psychonomic Society, 26,* 37–39.

Derks, P. L. (1987). Humor production: An examination of three models of creativity. *Journal of Creative Behavior, 21,* 325–26.

Diamond, A. M., Jr. (1980). Age and the acceptance of cliometrics. *Journal of Economic History, 40,* 838–41.

Díaz de Chumaceiro, C. L. (1995). Serendipity or pseudoserendipity? Unexpected versus desired results. *Journal of Creative Behavior, 29,* 143–47.

Diehl, M., and Stroebe, W. (1987). Productivity loss in brainstorming groups: Toward the solution of a riddle. *Journal of Personality and Social Psychology, 53,* 497–509.

Dillon, P. C., Graham, W. K., and Aidells, A. L. (1972). Brainstorming on a "hot" problem: Effects of training and practice on individual and group performance. *Journal of Applied Psychology, 56,* 487–90.

Dirac, P. A. M. (1963). The physicist's picture of nature. *Scientific American, 208* (5), 45–53.

Dissanayake, E. (1992). *Homo aestheticus: Where art comes from and why.* New York: Free Press.

Dixson, A. F., Bossi, T., and Wickings, E. J. (1993). Male dominance and genetically determined reproductive success in the mandrill (*Mandrillus sphinx*). *Primates, 34,* 525–32.

Doty, R. M., Peterson, B. E., and Winter, D. G. (1991). Threat and authoritarianism in the United States, 1978–1987. *Journal of Personality and Social Psychology, 61,* 629–40.

Downs, R. B. (1956). *Books that changed the world.* New York: Mentor.

Draper, P., and Belsky, J. (1990). Personality development in evolutionary perspective. *Journal of Personality, 58,* 141–61.

Dressler, W. W., and Robbins, M. C. (1975). Art styles, social stratification, and cognition: An analysis of Greek vase painting. *American Ethnologist, 2,* 427–34.

Driver, P. M., and Humphries, N. (1988). *Protean behavior: The biology of unpredictability.* Oxford: Oxford University Press.

Dryden, J. (1681). *Absalom and Achitophel: A poem.* London: Davis.

———. (1885). Epistle to Congreve. In W. Scott and G. Saintsbury (Eds.), *The works of John Dryden* (Vol. 11, pp. 57–60). Edinburgh: Paterson. (Original work published 1693.)

———. (1926). Epistle dedicatory of *The Rival Ladies.* In W. P. Ker (Ed.), *Essays of John Dryden* (Vol. 1, pp. 1–9). Oxford: Clarendon Press. (Original essay published 1664.)

Dugatkin, L. A. (1997). *Cooperation among animals: An evolutionary perspective.* New York: Oxford University Press.

Dunbar, K. (1995). How scientists really reason: Scientific reasoning in real-world laboratories. In R. J. Sternberg and J. E. Davidson (Eds.), *The nature of insight* (pp. 365–96). Cambridge, Mass.: MIT Press.

Dunbar, R. I., and Dunbar, E. P. (1977). Dominance and reproductive success among female gelada baboons. *Nature, 266,* 351–52.

Dunnette, M. D., Campbell, J., and Jaastad, K. (1963). The effect of group participation on brainstorming effectiveness for two industrial samples. *Journal of Applied Psychology, 47,* 30–37.

Dupuy, R. E., and Dupuy, T. N. (1993). *The Harper encyclopedia of military history: From 3500 B.C. to the present* (4th ed.). New York: HarperCollins.

Dye, D. A., and Reck, M. (1989). College grade point average as a predictor of adult success: A reply. *Public Personnel Management, 18,* 235–41.

Eccles, J. S. (1985). Why doesn't Jane run? Sex differences in educational and occupational patterns. In F. D. Horowitz and M. O'Brien (Eds.), *The gifted and talented: Developmental perspectives* (pp. 251–95). Washington, D.C.: American Psychological Association.

Edelman, G. M. (1987). *Neural Darwinism: The theory of neuronal group selection.* New York: Basic Books.

Efron, R. (1990). *The decline and fall of hemispheric specialization.* Hillsdale, N.J.: Erlbaum.

Ehrenwald, J. (1984). *The anatomy of genius: Split brains and global minds.* New York: Human Sciences.

Eiduson, B. T. (1962). *Scientists: Their psychological world.* New York: Basic Books.

Einstein, A., and Infeld, L. (1938). *The evolution of physics: The growth of ideas from early concepts to relativity and quanta.* New York: Simon & Schuster.

Eiseley, L. (1961). *Darwin's century: Evolution and the men who discovered it.* New York: Anchor.

Eisenberger, R., and Cameron, J. (1996). Detrimental effects of reward: Reality or myth? *American Psychologist, 51,* 1153–66.

Eisenman, R. (1964). Birth order and artistic creativity. *Journal of Individual Psychology, 20,* 183–85.

———. (1970). Creativity change in student nurses: A cross-sectional and longitudinal study. *Developmental Psychology, 3,* 320–25.

———. (1997). Mental illness, deviance, and creativity. In M. A. Runco (Ed.), *The creativity research handbook* (Vol. 1, pp. 295–311). Cresskill, N.J.: Hampton Press.

Eisenstadt, J. M. (1978). Parental loss and genius. *American Psychologist, 33,* 211–223.

Eisenstadt, J. M., Haynal, A., Rentchnick, P., and De Senarclens, P. (1989). *Parental loss and achievement.* Madison, Conn.: International Universities Press.

Eldredge, N., and Gould, S. J. (1972). Punctuated equilibria: An alternative to phyletic gradualism. In T. J. M. Schopf (Ed.), *Models in paleobiology* (pp. 82–115). San Francisco: Freeman, Cooper.

Ellis, H. (1926). *A study of British genius* (Rev. ed.). Boston: Houghton Mifflin.

Epstein, R. (1990). Generativity theory and creativity. In M. Runco and R. Albert (Eds.), *Theories of creativity* (pp. 116–40). Newbury Park, Calif.: Sage.

———. (1991). Skinner, creativity, and the problem of spontaneous behavior. *Psychological Science, 2,* 362–70.

Epstein, S. (1994). Integration of the cognitive and the psychodynamic unconscious. *American Psychologist, 49,* 709–24.

Erdley, C. A., and D'Agostino, P. R. (1989). Cognitive and affective components of automatic priming effects. *Journal of Personality and Social Psychology, 54,* 741–47.

Ericsson, K. A. (Ed.). (1996). *The road to expert performance: Empirical evidence from the arts and sciences, sports, and games.* Mahwah, N.J.: Erlbaum.

Ericsson, K. A., and Charness, N. (1994). Expert performance: Its structure and acquisition. *American Psychologist, 49,* 725–47.

Ericsson, K. A., Krampe, R. T., and Tesch-Römer, C. (1993). The role of deliberate practice in the acquisition of expert performance. *Psychological Review, 100,* 363–406.

Esar, E. (Ed.). (1989). *The dictionary of humorous quotations.* New York: Dorset Press. (Original work published 1949.)

Eysenck, H. J. (1993). Creativity and personality: Suggestions for a theory. *Psychological Inquiry, 4*, 147–48.

———. (1994). Creativity and personality: Word association, origence, and psychoticism. *Creativity Research Journal, 7*, 209–16.

———. (1995). *Genius: The natural history of creativity.* Cambridge: Cambridge University Press.

———. (1997). Creativity and personality. In M. A. Runco (Ed.), *The creativity research handbook* (Vol. 1, pp. 41–66). Cresskill, N.J.: Hampton Press.

Falbo, T. (1997). To rebel or not to rebel? Is this the birth order question? [Review of the book *Born to Rebel.*] *Contemporary Psychology, 42*, 938–39.

Farnsworth, P. R. (1969). *The social psychology of music* (2d ed.). Ames: Iowa State University Press.

Faust, D. (1984). *Limits of scientific reasoning.* Minneapolis: University of Minnesota Press.

Fausto-Sterling, A. (1997). Beyond difference: A biologist's perspective. *Journal of Social Issues, 53*, 233–58.

Feist, G. J. (1993). A structural model of scientific eminence. *Psychological Science, 4*, 366–71.

Feldman, D. H., and Goldsmith, L. T. (1986). *Nature's gambit: Child prodigies and the development of human potential.* New York: Basic Books.

Ferris, P. (1977). *Dylan Thomas.* London: Hodder & Stoughton.

Fidell, L. S. (1970). Empirical verification of sex discrimination in hiring practices in psychology. *American Psychologist, 25*, 1094–98.

Findlay, A. (1948). *A hundred years of chemistry* (2d ed.). London: Duckworth.

Findlay, C. S., and Lumsden, C. J. (1988). The creative mind: Toward an evolutionary theory of discovery and innovation. *Journal of Biological and Social Structures, 11*, 3–55.

Finke, R. A. (1995). Creative realism. In S. M. Smith, T. B. Ward, and R. A. Finke (Eds.), *The creative cognition approach* (pp. 303–26). Cambridge, Mass.: MIT Press.

Finke, R. A., Ward, T. B., and Smith, S. M. (1992). *Creative cognition: Theory, research, applications.* Cambridge, Mass.: MIT Press.

Fisher, R. A. (1930). *The genetical theory of natural selection.* Oxford: Oxford University Press.

Fiske, S. T., and Taylor, S. E. (1991). *Social cognition* (2d ed.). New York: McGraw-Hill.

Forbes, E. (Ed.). (1967). *Thayer's life of Beethoven* (Rev. ed.). Princeton, N.J.: Princeton University Press.

Fowler, R. G. (1987). Toward a quantitative theory of intellectual discovery (especially in physics). *Journal of Scientific Exploration, 1*, 11–20.

Freud, S. (1959). Creative writers and day-dreaming. In J. Strachey (Ed. and Trans.), *Standard edition of the complete psychological works of Sigmund Freud* (Vol. 9, pp. 141–53). London: Hogarth Press. (Original work published 1908.)

Friman, P. C., Allen, K. D., Kerwin, M. L. E., and Larzelere, R. (1993). Changes in modern psychology: A citation analysis of the Kuhnian displacement thesis. *American Psychologist, 48*, 658–64.

Galton, F. (1869). *Hereditary genius: An inquiry into its laws and consequences.* London: Macmillan.

————. (1874). *English men of science: Their nature and nurture.* London: Macmillan.

————. (1972). *Hereditary genius: An inquiry into its laws and consequences* (2d ed.). Gloucester, Mass.: Smith. (Original work published 1892.)

Gardner, H. (1993). *Creating minds: An anatomy of creativity seen through the lives of Freud, Einstein, Picasso, Stravinsky, Eliot, Graham, and Gandhi.* New York: Basic Books.

Gaston, J. (1973). *Originality and competition in science.* Chicago: University of Chicago Press.

Gedo, J. E. (1997). Psychoanalytic theories of creativity. In M. A. Runco (Ed.), *The creativity research handbook* (Vol. 1, pp. 29–39). Cresskill, N.J.: Hampton Press.

Getzels, J., and Csikszentmihalyi, M. (1976). *The creative vision: A longitudinal study of problem finding in art.* New York: Wiley.

Ghiselin, B. (Ed.). (1952). *The creative process: A symposium.* Berkeley: University of California Press.

Gieryn, T. F., and Hirsh, R. F. (1983). Marginality and innovation in science. *Social Studies of Science, 13*, 87–106.

Giles, H. A. (Ed.). (1965). *Gems of Chinese literature.* New York: Dover. (Original work published 1923.)

Glick, P., Zion, C., and Nelson, C. (1988). What mediates sex discrimination in hiring decisions? *Journal of Personality and Social Psychology, 50*, 178–86.

Goertzel, M. G., Goertzel, V., and Goertzel, T. G. (1978). *Three hundred eminent personalities: A psychosocial analysis of the famous.* San Francisco: Jossey-Bass.

Goertzel, V., and Goertzel, M. G. (1962). *Cradles of eminence.* Boston: Little, Brown.

Goldstein, E. (1979). Effect of same-sex and cross-sex role models on the subsequent academic productivity of scholars. *American Psychologist, 34*, 407–10.

Goodwin, F. K., and Jamison, K. R. (1990). *Manic-depressive illness.* New York: Oxford University Press.

Götz, K. O., and Götz, K. (1979a). Personality characteristics of professional artists. *Perceptual and Motor Skills, 49*, 327–34.

————. (1979b). Personality characteristics of successful artists. *Perceptual and Motor Skills, 49*, 919–24.

Gough, H. G. (1976). Studying creativity by means of word association tests. *Journal of Applied Psychology, 61*, 348–53.

Gough, H. G. (1979). A creative personality scale for the Adjective Check List. *Journal of Personality and Social Psychology, 37*, 1398–1405.

Gould, S. J. (1981). *The mismeasure of man.* New York: Norton.

Granovetter, M. (1979). The idea of "advancement" in theories of social evolution and development. *American Journal of Sociology, 85*, 489–515.

Gray, C. E. (1958). An analysis of Graeco-Roman development: The epicyclical evolution of Graeco-Roman civilization. *American Anthropologist, 60*, 13–31.

————. (1966). A measurement of creativity in Western civilization. *American Anthropologist, 68*, 1384–1417.

Green, G. S. (1981). A test of the Ortega hypothesis in criminology. *Criminology, 19*, 45–52.

Green, S., Rich, T., and Nesman, E. (1985). A cross-cultural look at the relationship between age and innovative behavior. *International Journal of Aging and Human Development, 21*, 255–66.

Greenough, W. T., and Black, J. E. (1992). Induction of brain structure by experience. In M. Gunnar and C. Nelson (Eds.), *Developmental behavioral neurosciences Vol. 24. Minnesota symposia on child development* (pp. 155–200). Hillsdale, N.J.: Erlbaum.

Gross, B. (1990). The case of Philippe Rushton. *Academic Question, 3* (4), 35–46.

Gruber, H. E. (1974). *Darwin on man: A psychological study of scientific creativity.* New York: Dutton.

———. (1989). The evolving systems approach to creative work. In D. B. Wallace and H. E. Gruber (Eds.), *Creative people at work: Twelve cognitive case studies* (pp. 3–24). New York: Oxford University Press.

Guilford, J. P. (1959). Traits of creativity. In H. H. Anderson (Ed.), *Creativity and its cultivation* (pp. 142–61). New York: Harper.

———. (1967). *The nature of human intelligence.* New York: McGraw-Hill.

Hadamard, J. (1945). *The psychology of invention in the mathematical field.* Princeton, N.J.: Princeton University Press.

Haensly, P. A., and Reynolds, C. R. (1989). Creativity and intelligence. In J. A. Glover, R. R. Ronning, and C. R. Reynolds (Eds.), *Handbook of creativity* (pp. 111–32). New York: Plenum Press.

Hagstrom, W. O. (1974). Competition in science. *American Sociological Review, 39*, 1–18.

Hamilton, W. D. (1972). Altruism and related phenomena, mainly in the social insects. *Annual Review of Ecology and Systematics, 3*, 193–232.

Hammer, M., and Zubin, J. (1968). Evolution, culture, and psychopathology. *Journal of General Psychology, 78*, 151–64.

Hardy, G. H. (1969). *A mathematician's apology.* Cambridge: Cambridge University Press. (Original work published 1940.)

Hargens, L. L. (1978). Relations between work habits, research technologies, and eminence in science. *Sociology of Work and Occupations, 5*, 97–112.

Hargens, L. L., McCann, J. C., and Reskin, B. F. (1978). Productivity and reproductivity: Fertility and professional achievement among research scientists. *Social Forces, 57*, 154–63.

Harman, W. W., McKim, R. H., Mogar, R. E., Fadiman, J., and Stolaroff, M. J. (1966). Psychedelic agents in creative problem-solving: A pilot study. *Psychological Reports, 19*, 211–27.

Harnsberger, C. T. (Ed.). (1972). *Everyone's Mark Twain.* New York: Barnes.

Harris, I. D. (1964). *The promised seed: A comparative study of eminent first and later sons.* New York: Free Press.

Harris, J. R. (1995). Where is the child's environment? A group socialization theory of development. *Psychological Review, 102*, 458–89.

———. (1998). *The nurture assumption: Why children turn out the way they do.* New York: Free Press.

Harrison, R. G. (Ed.). (1993). *Hybrid zones and the evolutionary process.* New York: Oxford University Press.

Hart, M. H. (1987). *The 100: A ranking of the most influential persons in history.* Secaucus, N.J.: Citadel Press.

Hasenfus, N., Martindale, C., and Birnbaum, D. (1983). Psychological reality of cross-media artistic styles. *Journal of Experimental Psychology: Human Perception and Performance, 9,* 841–63.

Hattie, J., and Rogers, H. J. (1988). Factor models for assessing the relation between creativity and intelligence. *Journal of Educational Psychology, 78,* 482–85.

Hayes, J. R. (1989a). Cognitive processes in creativity. In J. A. Glover, R. R. Ronning, and C. R. Reynolds (Eds.), *Handbook of creativity* (pp. 135–45). New York: Plenum Press.

———. (1989b). *The complete problem solver* (2d ed.). Hillsdale, N.J.: Erlbaum.

Helmholtz, H. von (1898). An autobiographical sketch. In *Popular lectures on scientific subjects, second series* (E. Atkinson, Trans., pp. 266–91). New York: Longmans, Green.

Helmreich, R. L., Spence, J. T., Beane, W. E., Lucker, G. W., and Matthews, K. A. (1980). Making it in academic psychology: Demographic and personality correlates of attainment. *Journal of Personality and Social Psychology, 39,* 896–908.

Helmreich, R. L., Spence, J. T., and Thorbecke, W. L. (1981). On the stability of productivity and recognition. *Personality and Social Psychology Bulletin, 7,* 516–22.

Helson, R. (1980). The creative woman mathematician. In L. H. Fox, L. Brody, and D. Tobin (Eds.), *Women and the mathematical mystique* (pp. 23–54). Baltimore, Md.: Johns Hopkins University Press.

———. (1990). Creativity in women: Outer and inner views over time. In M. A. Runco and R. S. Albert (Eds.), *Theories of creativity* (pp. 46–58). Newbury Park, Calif.: Sage.

Helson, R., and Crutchfield, R. S. (1970). Mathematicians: The creative researcher and the average Ph.D. *Journal of Consulting and Clinical Psychology, 34,* 250–57.

Hendrickson, R. (1988). *The dictionary of eponyms: Names that became words.* New York: Dorset Press.

Herrnstein, R. J., and Murray, C. (1994). *The bell curve: Intelligence and class structure in American life.* New York: Free Press.

Hertz, F. (1970). *Race and civilization* (A. S. Levetus and W. Entz, Trans.). New York: Ktav Publishing House. (Original work published 1928.)

Heston, L. L. (1966). Psychiatric disorders in foster home reared children of schizophrenic mothers. *British Journal of Psychiatry, 112,* 819–25.

Hilts, V. L. (1975). A guide to Francis Galton's *English Men of Science. Transactions of the American Philosophical Society, 65,* Pt. 5, 1–85.

Hines, T. (1991). The myth of right hemisphere creativity. *Journal of Creative Behavior, 25,* 223–27.

Hocevar, D., and Bachelor, P. (1989). A taxonomy and critique of measurements used in the study of creativity. In J. A. Glover, R. R. Ronning, and C. R. Reynolds (Eds.), *Handbook of creativity* (pp. 53–75). New York: Plenum Press.

Hoffman, B. (1972). *Albert Einstein: Creator and rebel.* New York: Plume.

Holahan, C. K, and Sears, R. R. (1995). *The gifted group in later maturity.* Stanford, Calif.: Stanford University Press.

Holland, J. (1975). *Natural and artificial systems.* Ann Arbor, Mich.: University of Michigan Press.

Holland, J. H. (1992). Genetic algorithms. *Scientific American, 267*(1), 66–72.

Hollingworth, L. S. (1942). *Children beyond 180 IQ: Origin and development.* Yonkers-on-Hudson, N.Y.: World Book.

Hollingworth, L. S. (1926). *Gifted children: Their nature and nurture.* New York: Macmillan.

Holton, G. (1971–72). On trying to understand the scientific genius. *American Scholar, 41,* 95–110.

Hoppe, K. D., and Kyle, N. L. (1990). Dual brain, creativity, and health. *Creativity Research Journal, 3,* 150–57.

Horner, K. L., Rushton, J. P., and Vernon, P. A. (1986). Relation between aging and research productivity of academic psychologists. *Psychology and Aging, 1,* 319–24.

Howard, J. A., Blumstein, P., and Schwartz, P. (1987). Social or evolutionary theories? Some observations on preferences in human mate selection. *Journal of Personality and Social Psychology, 53,* 194–200.

Huck, U. W., Lisk, R. D., and McKay, M. V. (1988). Social dominance and reproductive success in pregnant and lactating golden hamsters (*Mesocricetus auratus*) under seminatural conditions. *Physiology and Behavior, 44,* 313–19.

Hudson, L. (1958). Undergraduate academic record of Fellows of the Royal Society. *Nature, 182,* 1326.

———. (1966). *Contrary imaginations.* Baltimore, Md.: Penguin.

Hudson, L., and Jacot, B. (1986). The outsider in science. In C. Bagley and G. K. Verma (Eds.), *Personality, cognition and values* (pp. 3–23). London: Macmillan.

Hudson, V. M. (1990). Birth order of world leaders: An exploratory analysis of effects on personality and behavior. *Political Psychology, 11,* 583–601.

Huizenga, J. R. (1993). *Cold fusion: The scientific fiasco of the century.* Oxford: Oxford University Press.

Hull, D. L. (1988). *Science as a process: An evolutionary account of the social and conceptual development of science.* Chicago: University of Chicago Press.

Hull, D. L., Tessner, P. D., and Diamond, A. M. (1978). Planck's principle: Do younger scientists accept new scientific ideas with greater alacrity than older scientists? *Science, 202,* 717–23.

Hutchins, R. M. (Ed.) (1952). *Great books of the Western world.* Chicago: Encyclopaedia Britannica.

Huxley, J. (1942). *Evolution: The modern synthesis.* London: Allen & Unwin.

Huxley, J., Mayr, E., Osmond, H., and Hoffer, A. (1964). Schizophrenia as a genetic morphism. *Nature, 204,* 220–21.

Hyde, J. S. (1986). Gender differences in aggression. In J. S. Hyde and M. C. Linn (Eds.), *The psychology of gender: Advances through meta-analysis* (pp. 51–66). Baltimore, Md.: Johns Hopkins University Press.

Hyman, S. E. (Ed.). (1963). *Darwin for today: The essence of his works.* New York: Viking.

Ibn Khaldun. (1967). *The Muqaddimah* (F. Rosenthal, Trans., 2d ed.). Princeton, N.J.: Princeton University Press. (Original work published c. 1377.)

Illingworth, R. S., and Illingworth, C. M. (1969). *Lessons from childhood.* Edinburgh: Livingston.

Inoue, M., Mitsunaga, F., Nozaki, M., Ohsawa, H., et al. (1993). Male dominance rank and reproductive success in an enclosed group of Japanese macaques: With special reference to post-conception mating. *Primates, 34,* 503–11.

James, W. (1880). Great men, great thoughts, and the environment. *Atlantic Monthly, 46,* 441–59.

Jamison, K. R. (1989). Mood disorders and patterns of creativity in British writers and artists. *Psychiatry, 52,* 125–34.

Jamison, K. R. (1993). *Touched with fire: Manic-depressive illness and the artistic temperament.* New York: Free Press.

Janicki, M. G., and Krebs, D. L. (1998). Evolutionary approaches to culture. In C. B. Crawford and D. Krebs (Eds.), *Handbook of evolutionary psychology: Ideas, issues, and applications* (pp. 163–207). Mahwah, N.J.: Erlbaum.

Janiger, O., and de Rios, M. D. (1989). LSD and creativity. *Journal of Psychoactive Drugs, 21,* 129–34.

Jay, E. S., and Perkins, D. N. (1997). Problem finding: The search for mechanism. In M. A. Runco (Ed.), *The creativity research handbook* (Vol. 1, pp. 257–93). Cresskill, N.J.: Hampton Press.

Jeans, J. (1942). Newton and the science of to-day. *Nature, 150,* 710–715.

Jeffares, A. N., & Gray, M. (Eds.) (1997). *A dictionary of quotations.* New York: Barnes & Noble.

Jevons, W. S. (1900). *The principles of science: A treatise on logic and scientific method* (2d ed.). London: Macmillan. (Original work published 1877.)

Johnson, S. (1781). *The lives of the most eminent English poets* (Vol. 1). London: Bathurst.

Johnson-Laird, P. N. (1993). *Human and machine thinking.* Hillsdale, N.J.: Erlbaum.

Jones, F. E. (1964). Predictor variables for creativity in industrial science. *Journal of Applied Psychology, 48,* 134–36.

Juda, A. (1949). The relationship between highest mental capacity and psychic abnormalities. *American Journal of Psychiatry, 106,* 296–307.

Kahneman, D., Slovic, P., and Tversky, A. (Eds.). (1982). *Judgment under uncertainty: Heuristics and biases.* Cambridge: Cambridge University Press.

Kammann, R. (1966). Verbal complexity and preferences in poetry. *Journal of Verbal Learning and Verbal Behavior, 5,* 536–40.

Kantorovich, A. (1993). *Scientific discovery: Logic and tinkering.* Albany, N.Y.: State University of New York Press.

Kantorovich, A., and Ne'eman, Y. (1989). Serendipity as a source of evolutionary progress in science. *Studies in History and Philosophy of Science, 20,* 505–29.

Karlson, J. I. (1970). Genetic association of giftedness and creativity with schizophrenia. *Hereditas, 66,* 177–82.

Kasof, J. (1995). Explaining creativity: The attributional perspective. *Creativity Research Journal, 8,* 311–66.

Katz, A. N. (1997). Creativity and the cerebral hemispheres. In M. A. Runco (Ed.),

The creativity research handbook (Vol. 1, pp. 203–26). Cresskill, N.J.: Hampton Press.

Kavolis, V. (1963). Political dynamics and artistic creativity. *Sociology and Social Research, 49,* 412–24.

———. (1964). Economic correlates of artistic creativity. *American Journal of Sociology, 70,* 332–41.

———. (1966). Community dynamics and artistic creativity. *American Sociological Review, 31,* 208–17.

Kihlstrom, J. F. (1987). The cognitive unconscious. *Science, 237,* 1445–52.

Koestler, A. (1964). *The act of creation.* New York: Macmillan.

Köhler, W. (1925). *The mentality of apes* (E. Winter, Trans.). New York: Harcourt, Brace.

Koza, J. R. (1992). *Genetic programming: On the programming of computers by means of natural selection.* Cambridge, Mass.: MIT Press.

———. (1994). *Genetic programming II: Automatic discovery of reusable programs.* Cambridge, Mass.: MIT Press.

Krampen, G. (1997). Promotion of creativity (divergent productions) and convergent productions by systematic-relaxation exercises: Empirical evidence from five experimental studies with children, young adults, and elderly. *European Journal of Personality, 11,* 83–99.

Kris, E. (1952). *Psychoanalytic explorations in art.* New York: International Universities Press.

Kroeber, A. L. (1917). The superorganic. *American Anthropologist, 19,* 163–214.

———. (1944). *Configurations of culture growth.* Berkeley: University of California Press.

Krosnick, J. A., Betz, A. L., Jussim, L. J., and Lynn, A. R. (1992). Subliminal conditioning of attitudes. *Personality and Social Psychology Bulletin, 18,* 152–62.

Kuester, J., Paul, A., and Arnemann, J. (1995). Age-related and individual differences of reproductive success in male and female Barbary macaques (*Macaca sylvanus*). *Primates, 36,* 461–76.

Kuhn, T. S. (1970). *The structure of scientific revolutions* (2d ed.). Chicago: University of Chicago Press.

———. (1977). *The essential tension.* Chicago: University of Chicago Press.

Kulkarni, D., and Simon, H. A. (1988). The process of scientific discovery: The strategy of experimentation. *Cognitive Science, 12,* 139–75.

Kuo, Y. (1986). The growth and decline of Chinese philosophical genius. *Chinese Journal of Psychology, 28,* 81–91.

Kyvik, S. (1990). Motherhood and scientific productivity. *Social Studies of Science, 20,* 149–60.

Lamb, D., and Easton, S. M. (1984). *Multiple discovery: The pattern of scientific progress.* Trowbridge, England: Avebury.

Lambert, W. E., Tucker, G. R., and d'Anglejan, A. (1973). Cognitive and attitudinal consequences of bilingual schooling: The St. Lambert project through grade five. *Journal of Educational Psychology, 65,* 141–59.

Landry, R. G. (1972). The enhancement of figural creativity through second language learning at the elementary school level. *Foreign Language Annals, 4,* 111–15.

Lang, G. E., and Lang, K. (1988). Recognition and renown: The survival of artistic reputation. *American Journal of Sociology, 94,* 79–109.

Langley, P., Simon, H. A., Bradshaw, G. L., and Zythow, J. M. (1987). *Scientific discovery.* Cambridge, Mass.: MIT Press.

Lehman, H. C. (1943). The longevity of the eminent. *Science, 98,* 270–73.

———. (1953). *Age and achievement.* Princeton, N.J.: Princeton University Press.

———. (1962). More about age and achievement. *Gerontologist, 2,* 141–48.

Lehman, H. C., and Witty, P. A. (1931). Scientific eminence and church membership. *Scientific Monthly, 33,* 544–49.

Lenneberg, H. (1980). The myth of the unappreciated (musical) genius. *Musical Quarterly, 54* 219–31.

Lenski, R. E., and Mittler, J. E. (1993). The directed mutation controversy and neo-Darwinism. *Science, 259,* 188–94.

Lester, D. (1991). Premature mortality associated with alcoholism and suicide in American writers. *Perceptual and Motor Skills, 73,* 162.

Levin, S. G., and Stephan, P. E. (1989). Age and research productivity of academic scientists. *Research in Higher Education, 30,* 531–49.

———. (1991). Research productivity over the life cycle: Evidence for academic scientists. *American Economic Review, 81,* 114–32.

Levin, S. G., Stephan, P. E., and Walker, M. B. (1995). Planck's principle revisited—A note. *Social Studies of Science, 25,* 35–55.

Levy, S. (1992). *Artificial life: The quest for a new creation.* New York: Pantheon Books.

Lévy-Bruhl, L. (1978). *Primitive mentality* (L. A. Clare, Trans.). New York: AMS Press.

Lindsey, D. (1988). Assessing precision in the manuscript review process: A little better than a dice roll. *Scientometrics, 14,* 75–82.

———. (1989). Using citation counts as a measure of quality in science: Measuring what's measurable rather than what's valid. *Scientometrics, 15,* 189–203.

Lomax, A. (Ed.). (1968). *Folk song style and culture.* Washington, D.C.: American Association for the Advancement of Science.

Lomax, A., and Arensberg, C. M. (1971). A worldwide evolutionary classification of cultures by subsistence systems. *Current Anthropology, 18,* 659–701.

Lomax, A., with Berkowitz, N. (1972). The evolutionary taxonomy of culture. *Science, 177,* 228–39.

Lombroso, C. (1891). *The man of genius.* London: Scott.

Lopez, E. C., Esquivel, G. B., and Houtz, J. C. (1993). The creative skills of culturally and linguistically diverse gifted students. *Creativity Research Journal, 6,* 401–12.

Lotka, A. J. (1926). The frequency distribution of scientific productivity. *Journal of the Washington Academy of Sciences, 16,* 317–23.

Ludwig, A. M. (1990). Alcohol input and creative output. *British Journal of Addiction, 85,* 953–63.

———. (1995). *The price of greatness: Resolving the creativity and madness controversy.* New York: Guilford Press.

———. (1998). Method and madness in the arts and sciences. *Creativity Research Journal, 11,* 93–101.

Lumsden, C. J., and Wilson, E. O. (1981). *Genes, mind, and culture: The coevolutionary process.* Cambridge, Mass.: Harvard University Press.

Lykken, D. T. (1982). Research with twins: The concept of emergenesis. *Psychophysiology, 19,* 361–73.

Lykken, D. T., McGue, M., Tellegen, A., and Bouchard, T. J., Jr. (1992). Emergenesis: Genetic traits that may not run in families. *American Psychologist, 47,* 1565–77.

Lynn, R. (1991a). The evolution of racial differences in intelligence. *Mankind Quarterly, 32,* 99–121.

———. (1991b). Race differences in intelligence: A global perspective. *Mankind Quarterly, 31,* 254–96.

———. (1996). *Dysgenics: Genetic deterioration in modern populations.* Westport, Conn.: Praeger.

Lyons, J. (1968). Chronological age, professional age, and eminence in psychology. *American Psychologist, 23,* 371–74.

Macaulay, T. B. (1900). Milton. In I. Gollancz (Ed.), *Critical and historical essays* (Vol. 1, pp. 3–66). London: Dent. (Original work published 1825.)

Mach, E. (1896). On the part played by accident in invention and discovery. *Monist, 6,* 161–75.

MacKinnon, D. W. (1960). The highly effective individual. *Teachers College Record, 61,* 367–78.

———. (1978). *In search of human effectiveness.* Buffalo, N.Y.: Creative Education Foundation.

Macrone, M. (1990). *Brush up your Shakespeare!.* New York: Harper & Row.

Maier, N. R. (1931). Reasoning in humans: II. The solution of a problem and its appearance in consciousness. *Journal of Comparative and Physiological Psychology, 12,* 181–94.

Mandler, G. (1995). Origins and consequences of novelty. In S. M. Smith, T. B. Ward, and R. A. Finke (Eds.), *The creative cognition approach* (pp. 9–25). Cambridge, Mass.: MIT Press.

Manis, J. G. (1951). Some academic influences upon publication productivity. *Social Forces, 29,* 267–72.

Manniche, E., and Falk, G. (1957). Age and the Nobel prize. *Behavioral Science, 2,* 301–7.

Martindale, C. (1972). Father absence, psychopathology, and poetic eminence. *Psychological Reports, 31,* 843–47.

———. (1973). An experimental simulation of literary change. *Journal of Personality and Social Psychology, 25,* 319–26.

———. (1975). *Romantic progression: The psychology of literary history.* Washington, D.C.: Hemisphere.

———. (1976). Primitive mentality and the relationship between art and society. *Scientific Aesthetics, 1,* 5–18.

———. (1984a). Evolutionary trends in poetic style: The case of English metaphysical poetry. *Computers and the Humanities, 18,* 3–21.

———. (1984b). The evolution of aesthetic taste. In K. J. Gergen and M. M. Gergen (Eds.), *Historical social psychology* (pp. 347–70). Hillsdale, N.J.: Erlbaum.

———. (1986a). Aesthetic evolution. *Poetics, 15,* 439–73.

———. (1986b). The evolution of Italian painting: A quantitative investigation of trends in style and content from late Gothic to the Rococo period. *Leonardo, 19,* 217–222.

———. (1989). Personality, situation, and creativity. In J. A. Glover, R. R. Ronning, and C. R. Reynolds (Eds.), *Handbook of creativity* (pp. 211–32). New York: Plenum Press.

———. (1990). *The clockwork muse: The predictability of artistic styles.* New York: Basic Books.

———. (1995a). Creativity and connectionism. In S. M. Smith, T. B. Ward, and R. A. Finke (Eds.), *The creative cognition approach* (pp. 249–68). Cambridge, Mass.: MIT Press.

———. (1995b). Fame more fickle than fortune: On the distribution of literary eminence. *Poetics, 23,* 219–34.

Martindale, C., Brewer, W. F., Helson, R., Rosenberg, S., Simonton, D. K., Keeley, A., Leigh, J., and Ohtsuka, K. (1988). Structure, theme, style, and reader response in Hungarian and American short stories. In C. Martindale (Ed.), *Psychological approaches to the study of literary narratives* (pp. 267–89). Hamburg: Buske.

Martindale, C., and Moore, K. (1989). Relationship of musical preference to collative, ecological, and psychophysical variables. *Music Perception, 6,* 431–46.

Martindale, C., and Uemura, A. (1983). Stylistic evolution in European music. *Leonardo, 16,* 225–28.

Maslow, A. H. (1972). A holistic approach to creativity. In C. W. Taylor (Ed.), *Climate for creativity* (pp. 287–93). New York: Pergamon Press.

Matthews, K. A., Helmreich, R. L., Beane, W. E., and Lucker, G. W. (1980). Pattern A, achievement striving, and scientific merit: Does Pattern A help or hinder? *Journal of Personality and Social Psychology, 39,* 962–67.

May, R. (1975). *The courage to create.* New York: Norton.

McClearn, G. E., Johansson, B., Berg, S., Pedersen, N. L., Ahern, F., Petrill, S. A., and Plomin, R. (1997). Substantial genetic influence on cognitive abilities in twins 80 or more years old. *Science, 276,* 1560–63.

McClelland, D. C. (1973). Testing for competence rather than for "intelligence." *American Psychologist, 28,* 1–14.

McCrae, R. R. (1987). Creativity, divergent thinking, and openness to experience. *Journal of Personality and Social Psychology, 52,* 1258–65.

McCrae, R. R., Arenberg, D., and Costa, P. T. (1987). Declines in divergent thinking with age: Cross-sectional, longitudinal, and cross-sequential analyses. *Psychology and Aging, 2,* 130–36.

McCurdy, H. G. (1960). The childhood pattern of genius. *Horizon, 2,* 33–38.

McDowell, J. M. (1982). Obsolescence of knowledge and career publication profiles: Some evidence of differences among fields in costs of interrupted careers. *American Economic Review, 72,* 752–68.

McFarlan, D. (Ed.). (1989). *Guinness book of world records.* New York: Bantam.

McManus, I. C., and Bryden, M. P. (1991). Geschwind's theory of cerebral lateralization: Developing a formal, causal model. *Psychological Bulletin, 110,* 237–53.

McNeil, T. F. (1971). Prebirth and postbirth influence on the relationship between creative ability and recorded mental illness. *Journal of Psychology, 39,* 391–406.

Meadow, A., and Parnes, S. J. (1959). Evaluation of training in creative problem solving. *Journal of Applied Psychology, 43*, 189–94.

Mednick, S. A. (1962). The associative basis of the creative process. *Psychological Review, 69*, 220–32.

Meehl, P. (1954). *Clinical versus statistical prediction: A theoretical analysis and a review of the evidence.* Minneapolis: University of Minnesota Press.

Mendelsohn, G. A. (1976). Associative and attentional processes in creative performance. *Journal of Personality, 44*, 341–69.

Merton, R. K. (1961a). The role of genius in scientific advance. *New Scientist, 12*, 306–8.

———. (1961b). Singletons and multiples in scientific discovery: A chapter in the sociology of science. *Proceedings of the American Philosophical Society, 105*, 470–86.

———. (1968). The Matthew effect in science. *Science, 159*, 56–63.

Messerli, P. (1988). Age differences in the reception of new scientific theories: The case of plate tectonics theory. *Social Studies of Science, 18*, 91–112.

Meyer, L. B. (1956). *Emotion and meaning in music.* Chicago: University of Chicago Press.

Miller, G. A. (1956). The magical number seven, plus or minus two: Some limits on our capacity for processing information. *Psychological Review, 63*, 81–97.

Miller, G. F. (1997). Protean primates: The evolution of adaptive unpredictability in competition and courtship. In A. Whiten and R. Byrne (Eds.), *Machiavellian intelligence II* (pp. 312–40). Cambridge: Cambridge University Press.

———. (1998). How mate choice shaped human nature: A review of sexual selection and human evolution. In C. B. Crawford and D. Krebs (Eds.), *Handbook of evolutionary psychology: Ideas, issues, and applications* (pp. 87–129). Mahwah, N.J.: Erlbaum.

Mills, C. A. (1942). What price glory? *Science, 96*, 380–87.

Mills, S. K., and Beatty, J. H. (1979). The propensity interpretation of fitness. *Philosophy of Science, 46*, 263–86.

Modell, J. (1997). [Review of the book *Born to Rebel.*] *Science, 275*, 624–625.

Moles, A. (1968). *Information theory and esthetic perception* (J. E. Cohen, Trans.). Urbana: University of Illinois Press. (Original work published 1958.)

Montour, K. (1977). William James Sidis, the broken twig. *American Psychologist 32*, 265–79.

Moravcsik, M. J., and Murugesan, P. (1975). Some results on the function and quality of citations. *Social Studies of Science, 5*, 86–92.

Moulin, L. (1955). The Nobel Prizes for the sciences from 1901–1950: An essay in sociological analysis. *British Journal of Sociology, 6*, 246–263.

Myerson, A., and Boyle, R. D. (1941). The incidence of manic-depression psychosis in certain socially important families: Preliminary report. *American Journal of Psychiatry, 98*, 11–21.

Naroll, R., Benjamin, E. C., Fohl, F. K., Fried, M. J., Hildreth, R. E., and Schaefer, J. M. (1971). Creativity: A cross-historical pilot survey. *Journal of Cross-Cultural Psychology, 2*, 181–88.

Nemeth, C. J. (1986). Differential contributions of majority and minority influence. *Psychological Review, 93*, 23–32.

Nemeth, C. J., and Kwan, J. (1985). Originality of word associations as a function of majority vs. minority influence. *Social Psychology Quarterly, 48*, 277–282.

———. (1987). Minority influence, divergent thinking and detection of correct solutions. *Journal of Applied Social Psychology, 17*, 788–99.

Nemeth, C. J., and Wachtler, J. (1983). Creative problem solving as a result of majority vs. minority influence. *European Journal of Social Psychology, 13*, 45–55.

Newborn, M. (1996). *Kasparov versus Deep Blue: Computer chess comes of age.* New York: Springer-Verlag.

Newell, A., and Simon, H. A. (1972). *Human problem solving.* Englewood Cliffs, N.J.: Prentice-Hall.

Newman, J., and Taylor, A. (1994). Family training for political leadership: Birth order of United States state governors and Australian prime ministers. *Political Psychology, 15*, 435–42.

Nicholls, J. G. (1972). Creativity in the person who will never produce anything original and useful: The concept of creativity as a normally distributed trait. *American Psychologist, 27*, 717–27.

Nicholson, F. W. (1915). Success in college and in later life. *School and Society, 2*, 229–32.

Nietzsche, F. W. (1927). *The philosophy of Nietzsche* (Trans. Clifton Fadimen). New York: Modern Library.

Nisbett, R. E. (1968). Birth order and participation in dangerous sports. *Journal of Personality and Social Psychology, 8*, 351–53.

———. (1990). Evolutionary psychology, biology, and cultural evolution. *Motivation and Emotion, 14*, 255–63.

Nisbett, R. E., and Wilson, T. D. (1977). Telling more than we can know: Verbal reports on mental processes. *Psychological Review, 84*, 231–59.

Nolan, P. D. (1982). Energy, information, and sociocultural "advancement." *American Journal of Sociology, 87*, 942–46.

Norling, B. (1970). *Timeless problems in history.* Notre Dame, Ind.: Notre Dame Press.

O'Boyle, M. W., and Benbow, C. P. (1990). Handedness and its relationship to ability and talent. In S. Coren (Ed.), *Left-handedness: Behavioral implications and anomalies* (pp. 343–72). Amsterdam: Elsevier.

Ochse, R. (1989). A new look at primary process thinking and its relation to inspiration. *New Ideas in Psychology, 7*, 315–30.

———. (1991). Why there were relatively few eminent women creators. *Journal of Creative Behavior, 25*, 334–43.

Ochse, R., and Lill, B. van. (1990). A critical appraisal of the theoretical validity of the Mednick Remote Association Test. *South African Journal of Psychology, 20*, 195–99.

Oden, M. H. (1968). The fulfillment of promise: 40-year follow-up of the Terman gifted group. *Genetic Psychology Monographs, 77*, 3–93.

Ogburn, W. K., and Thomas, D. (1922). Are inventions inevitable? A note on social evolution. *Political Science Quarterly, 37*, 83–93.

Ohlsson, S. (1992). The learning curve for writing books: Evidence from Professor Asimov. *Psychological Science, 3*, 380–382.

Okuda, S. M., Runco, M. A., and Berger, D. E. (1991). Creativity and the finding and solving of real-world problems. *Journal of Psychoeducational Assessment, 9,* 45–53.

Olby, R. (1979). Mendel no Mendelian? *History of Science, 17,* 53–72.

Oring, L. W., Colwell, M. A., and Reed, J. M. (1991). Lifetime reproductive success in the spotted sandpiper (*Actitis macularia*): Sex differences and variance components. *Behavioral Ecology and Sociobiology, 28,* 425–32.

Oromaner, M. (1977). Professional age and the reception of sociological publications: A test of the Zuckerman-Merton hypothesis. *Social Studies of Science, 7,* 381–88.

Over, R. (1982a). Does research productivity decline with age? *Higher Education, 11,* 511–20.

———. (1982b). The durability of scientific reputation. *Journal of the History of the Behavioral Sciences, 18,* 53–61.

———. (1982c). Is age a good predictor of research productivity? *Australian Psychologist, 17,* 129–39.

———. (1988). Does scholarly impact decline with age? *Scientometrics, 13,* 215–23.

———. (1989). Age and scholarly impact. *Psychology and Aging, 4,* 222–25.

———. (1990). The scholarly impact of articles published by men and women in psychology journals. *Scientometrics, 18,* 71–80.

The Oxford University Press dictionary of quotations (2d ed.). (1985). New York: Crescent Books. (Original work published 1953.)

Park, R. E. (1928). Human migration and the marginal man. *American Journal of Sociology, 33,* 881–93.

Parnes, S. J. (1961). Effects of extended effort in creative problem solving. *Journal of Educational Psychology, 52,* 117–22.

Parshall, K. H. (1988). The art of algebra from al-Khwarizmi to Viète: A study in the natural selection of ideas. *History of Science, 26,* 129–64.

Patinkin, D. (1983). Multiple discoveries and the central message. *American Journal of Sociology, 89,* 306–23.

Pearson, P. (1983). Personality characteristics of cartoonists. *Personality and Individual Differences, 4,* 227–228.

Peckham, M. (1967). *Man's rage for chaos: Biology, behavior, and the arts.* New York: Schocken Books.

Perkins, D. N. (1981). *The mind's best work.* Cambridge, Mass.: Harvard University Press.

———. (1994). Creativity: Beyond the Darwinian paradigm. In M. A. Boden (Ed.), *Dimensions of creativity* (pp. 119–42). Cambridge, Mass.: MIT Press.

———.(1998). In the country of the blind: An appreciation of Donald Campbell's vision of creative thought. *Journal of Creative Behavior, 32,* 177–91.

Phillips, D. P. (1974). Influence of suggestion on suicide: Substantive and theoretical implications of the Werther effect. *American Sociological Review, 39,* 340–54.

Pianka, E. R. (1970). On *r*- and *K*-selection. *American Naturalist, 104,* 592–97.

Pinker, S. (1997). *How the mind works.* New York: Norton.

Planck, M. (1949). *Scientific autobiography and other papers* (F. Gaynor, Trans.). New York: Philosophical Library.

Platt, W., and Baker, R. A. (1931). The relation of the scientific "hunch" to research. *Journal of Chemical Education, 8,* 1969–2002.

Plomin, R., and Bergeman, C. S. (1991). The nature of nurture: Genetic influence on environmental measures. *Behavioral and Brain Sciences, 14,* 373–86.

Plomin, R., Owen, M. J., and McGuffin, P. (1994). The genetic basis of complex human behaviors. *Science, 264,* 1733–39.

Plomin, R., and Rende, R. (1990). Human behavioral genetics. *Annual Review of Psychology, 42,* 161–90.

Plotkin, H. C. (1993). *Darwin machines and the nature of knowledge.* Cambridge, Mass.: Harvard University Press.

Poe, E. A. (1884). The philosophy of composition. In *The works of Edgar Allan Poe* (Vol. 5, pp. 157–174). London: Routledge. (Original work published 1846.)

Poincaré, H. (1921). *The foundations of science: Science and hypothesis, the value of science, science and method* (G. B. Halstead, Trans.). New York: Science Press.

Ponteir, D., and Natoli, E. (1996). Male reproductive success in the domestic cat (*Felis catus L.*): A case history. *Behavioural Processes, 37,* 85–88.

Popper, K. (1979). *Objective knowledge: An evolutionary approach* (Rev. ed.). Oxford: Clarendon Press.

Post, F. (1994). Creativity and psychopathology: A study of 291 world-famous men. *British Journal of Psychiatry, 165,* 22–34.

Post, F. (1996). Verbal creativity, depression and alcoholism: An investigation of one hundred American and British writers. *British Journal of Psychiatry, 168,* 545–555.

Prentky, R. A. (1980). *Creativity and psychopathology: A neurocognitive perspective.* New York: Praeger.

Pressey, S. L., and Combs, A. (1943). Acceleration and age of productivity. *Educational Research Bulletin, 22,* 191–96.

Price, D. (1963). *Little science, big science.* New York: Columbia University Press.

———. (1965). Networks of scientific papers. *Science, 149,* 510–15.

———. (1976). A general theory of bibliometric and other cumulative advantage processes. *Journal of the American Society for Information Science, 27,* 292–306.

———. (1978). Ups and downs in the pulse of science and technology. In J. Gaston (Ed.), *The sociology of science* (pp. 162–71). San Francisco: Jossey-Bass.

Proctor, R. A. (1993). Computer stimulated associations. *Creativity Research Journal, 6,* 391–400.

Qin, Y., and Simon, H. A. (1990). Laboratory replication of scientific discovery processes. *Cognitive Science, 14,* 281–312.

Quetelet, A. (1968). *A treatise on man and the development of his faculties.* New York: Franklin. (Reprint of 1842 Edinburgh translation of 1835 French original.)

Rainoff, T. J. (1929). Wave-like fluctuations of creative productivity in the development of West-European physics in the eighteenth and nineteenth centuries. *Isis, 12,* 287–319.

Raskin, E. A. (1936). Comparison of scientific and literary ability: A biographical study of eminent scientists and men of letters of the nineteenth century. *Journal of Abnormal and Social Psychology, 31,* 20–35.

Razik, T. A. (1967). Psychometric measurement of creativity. In R. L. Mooney and T.

A. Razik (Eds.), *Explorations in creativity* (pp. 301–9). New York: Harper and Row.

Reber, A. S. (1993). *Implicit learning and tacit knowledge: An essay on the cognitive unconscious.* Oxford: Oxford University Press.

Redner, S. (1998). How popular is your paper? An empirical study of the citation distribution. *European Physical Journal B, 4,* 131–34.

Rejai, M. (1979). *Leaders of revolution.* Beverly Hills, Calif.: Sage.

Rentchnick, P. (1989). Orphans and the will for power. In M. Eisenstadt, A. Haynal, P. Rentchnick, and P. De Senarclens, *Parental loss and achievement* (pp. 35–69). Madison, Conn.: International Universities Press.

Reynolds, J. (1966). *Discourses on art.* New York: Collier. (Original work published 1769–90.)

Richards, R. (1981). Relationships between creativity and psychopathology: An evaluation and interpretation of the evidence. *Genetic Psychology Monographs, 103,* 261–324.

Richards, R., Kinney, D. K., Lunde, I., Benet, M., and Merzel, A. P. C. (1988). Creativity in manic-depressives, cyclothymes, their normal relatives, and control subjects. *Journal of Abnormal Psychology, 97,* 281–88.

Richards, R. J. (1981). Natural selection and other models in the historiography of science. In M. B. Brewer and B. E. Collins (Eds.), *Scientific inquiry and the social sciences* (pp. 37–78). San Francisco: Jossey-Bass.

Richardson, L. F. (1960a). *Arms and insecurity: A mathematical study of the causes and origins of war.* Pittsburgh, Pa.: Boxwood Press.

———. (1960b). In Q. Wright and C. C. Lienau (Eds.), *Statistics of deadly quarrels* Chicago: Quadrangle Books.

Ridley, M. (1993a). *Evolution.* Oxford: Blackwell.

———. (1993b). *The Red Queen: Sex and the evolution of human nature.* New York: Viking.

———. (1997). *The origins of virtue: Human instincts and the evolution of cooperation.* New York: Viking.

Roberts, R. M. (1989). *Serendipity: Accidental discoveries in science.* New York: Wiley.

Robins, R. W., and Craik, K. H. (1994). A more appropriate test of the Kuhnian displacement thesis. *American Psychologist, 49,* 815–16.

Roe, A. (1952). *The making of a scientist.* New York: Dodd, Mead.

———. (1965). Changes in scientific activities with age. *Science, 150,* 113–18.

Rogers, C. R. (1954). Toward a theory of creativity. *ETC: A Review of General Semantics, 11,* 249–60.

Root-Bernstein, R. S., Bernstein, M., and Garnier, H. (1993). Identification of scientists making long-term, high-impact contributions, with notes on their methods of working. *Creativity Research Journal, 6,* 329–43.

———. (1995). Correlations between avocations, scientific style, work habits, and professional impact of scientists. *Creativity Research Journal, 8,* 115–37.

Rose, M. R., and Lauder, G. V. (Eds.). (1996). *Adaptation.* San Diego, Calif.: Academic Press.

Rosengren, K. E. (1985). Time and literary fame. *Poetics, 14,* 157–72.

Rostan, S. M. (1994). Problem finding, problem solving, and cognitive controls: An empirical investigation of critically acclaimed productivity. *Creativity Research Journal, 7,* 97–110.

Rothenberg, A. (1979). *The emerging goddess: The creative process in art, science, and other fields.* Chicago: University of Chicago Press.

———. (1986). Artistic creation as stimulated by superimposed versus combined-composite visual images. *Journal of Personality and Social Psychology, 50,* 370–81.

———. (1987). Einstein, Bohr, and creative thinking in science. *History of Science, 25,* 147–66.

———. (1990). *Creativity and madness: New findings and old stereotypes.* Baltimore, Md.: Johns Hopkins University Press.

Rubin, Z. (1970). The birth-order of birth-order researchers. *Developmental Psychology, 3,* 269–70.

Runco, M. A. (1986). Divergent thinking and creative performance in gifted and nongifted children. *Educational and Psychological Measurement, 46,* 375–84.

———. (1992). Children's divergent thinking and creative ideation. *Developmental Review, 12,* 233–64.

Rushton, J. P. (1984). Evaluating research eminence in psychology: The construct validity of citation counts. *Bulletin of the British Psychological Society, 37,* 33–36.

———. (1985). Differential K theory: The sociobiology of individual and group differences. *Personality and Individual Differences, 6,* 441–52.

———. (1988). Race differences in behaviour: A review and evolutionary analysis. *Personality and Individual Differences, 9,* 1009–24.

———. (1990). Creativity, intelligence, and psychoticism. *Personality and Individual Differences, 11,* 1291–98.

———. (1991a). Do r-K strategies underlie human race differences? A reply to Weizmann et al. *Canadian Psychology, 32,* 29–42.

———. (1991b). Racial differences: A reply to Zuckerman. *American Psychologist, 46,* 983–87.

———. (1995). *Race, evolution, and behavior: A life history perspective.* New Brunswick, N.J.: Transaction Publishers.

Rust, J., Golombok, S., and Abram, M. (1989). Creativity and schizotypal thinking. *Journal of Genetic Psychology, 150,* 225–27.

Saffran, J. R., Newport, E. L., Aslin, R. N., Tunick, R. A., and Barrueco, S. (1997). Incidental language learning: Listening (and learning) out of the corner of your ear. *Psychological Science, 8,* 101–5.

Sales, S. M. (1973). Threat as a factor in authoritarianism: An analysis of archival data. *Journal of Personality and Social Psychology, 28,* 44–57.

Samson, G. E., Graue, M. E., Weinstein, T., and Walberg, H. J. (1984). Academic and occupational performance: A quantitative synthesis. *American Educational Research Journal, 21,* 311–21.

Scarr, S., and McCartney, K. (1983). How people make their own environments: A theory of genotype ——► environmental effects. *Child Development, 54,* 424–35.

Schachter, S. (1963). Birth order, eminence, and higher education. *American Sociological Review, 28,* 757–68.

Schaefer, C. E., and Anastasi, A. (1968). A biographical inventory for identifying creativity in adolescent boys. *Journal of Applied Psychology, 58*, 42–48.

Schaller, M. (1997). The psychological consequences of fame: Three tests of the self-consciousness hypothesis. *Journal of Personality, 65*, 291–309.

Schlipp, P. A. (Ed.). (1951). *Albert Einstein: Philosopher-scientist.* New York: Harper.

Schmookler, J. (1966). *Invention and economic growth.* Cambridge, Mass.: Harvard University Press.

Schneider, E. (1953). *Coleridge, opium, and Kubla Khan.* Chicago: University of Chicago Press.

Schneider, J. (1937). The cultural situation as a condition for the achievement of fame. *American Sociological Review, 2*, 480–91.

Schooler, J. W., and Melcher, J. (1995). The ineffability of insight. In S. M. Smith, T. B. Ward, and R. A. Finke (Eds.), *The creative cognition approach* (pp. 97–133). Cambridge, Mass.: MIT Press.

Schubert, D. S. P., Wagner, M. E., and Schubert, H. J. P. (1977). Family constellation and creativity: Firstborn predominance among classical music composers. *Journal of Psychology, 95*, 147–49.

Seelig, C. (1958). *Albert Einstein: A documentary biography* (M. Savill, Trans.). London: Staples Press.

Seifert, C. M., Meyer, D. E., Davidson, N., Patalano, A. L., and Yaniv, I. (1995). Demystification of cognitive insight: Opportunistic assimilation and the prepared-mind perspective. In R. J. Sternberg and J. E. Davidson (Eds.), *The nature of insight* (pp. 65–124). Cambridge, Mass.: MIT Press.

Seneca. (1932). On tranquillity of mind. In *Moral essays* (J. W. Basore, Trans., Vol. 2, pp. 203–85). Cambridge, Mass.: Harvard University Press.

Serebriakoff, V. (1985). *Mensa: The society for the highly intelligent.* London: Constable.

Service, E. R. (1915). *Origins of the state and civilization: The process of cultural evolution.* New York: Norton.

Shadish, W. R., Jr. (1989). The perception and evaluation of quality in science. In B. Gholson, W. R. Shadish, Jr., R. A. Neimeyer, and A. C. Houts (Eds.), *The psychology of science: Contributions to metascience* (pp. 383–426). Cambridge: Cambridge University Press.

Shakespeare, W. (1952). Twelfth night; or, what you will. In R. M. Hutchins (Ed.), *Great books of the Western world* (Vol. 27, pp. 1–28). Chicago: Encyclopaedia Britannica. (Original work written 1601)

Shapiro, G. (1986). *A skeleton in the darkroom: Stories of serendipity in science.* San Francisco: Harper & Row.

Sheldon, J. C. (1979). Hierarchical cybernets: A model for the dynamics of high level learning and cultural change. *Cybernetica, 22*, 179–202.

———. (1980). A cybernetic theory of physical science professions: The causes of periodic normal and revolutionary science between 1000 and 1870 AD. *Scientometrics, 2*, 147–67.

Shields, S. A. (1975). Functionalism, Darwinism, and the psychology of women: A study in social myth. *American Psychologist, 30*, 739–54.

Shockley, W. (1957). On the statistics of individual variations of productivity in research laboratories. *Proceedings of the Institute of Radio Engineers, 45,* 279–90.

Shrader, D. (1980). The evolutionary development of science. *Review of Metaphysics, 34,* 273–96.

Shrager, J., and Langley, P. (Eds.). (1990). *Computational models of scientific discovery and theory formation.* San Mateo, Calif.: Kaufmann.

Silverman, S. M. (1974). Parental loss and scientists. *Science Studies, 4,* 259–64.

Simon, H. A. (1954). Productivity among American psychologists: An explanation. *American Psychologist, 9,* 804–5.

———. (1955). On a class of skew distribution functions. *Biometrika, 42,* 425–40.

———. (1973). Does scientific discovery have a logic? *Philosophy of Science, 40,* 471–80.

———. (1986). What we know about the creative process. In R. L. Kuhn (Ed.), *Frontiers in creative and innovative management* (pp. 3–20). Cambridge, Mass.: Ballinger.

Simon, J. L., and Sullivan, R. J. (1989). Population size, knowledge stock, and other determinants of agricultural publication and patenting: England, 1541–1850. *Explorations in Economic History, 26,* 21–44.

Simon, R. J. (1974). The work habits of eminent scientists. *Sociology of Work and Occupations, 1,* 327–35.

Simonton, D. K. (1975a). Age and literary creativity: A cross-cultural and transhistorical survey. *Journal of Cross-Cultural Psychology, 6,* 259–77.

———. (1975b). Creativity, task complexity, and intuitive versus analytical problem solving. *Psychological Reports, 37,* 351–54.

———. (1975c). Interdisciplinary creativity over historical time: A correlational analysis of generational fluctuations. *Social Behavior and Personality, 3,* 181–88.

———. (1975d). Sociocultural context of individual creativity: A transhistorical time-series analysis. *Journal of Personality and Social Psychology, 32,* 1119–33.

———. (1976a). Biographical determinants of achieved eminence: A multivariate approach to the Cox data. *Journal of Personality and Social Psychology, 33,* 218–26.

———. (1976b). Do Sorokin's data support his theory?: A study of generational fluctuations in philosophical beliefs. *Journal for the Scientific Study of Religion, 15,* 187–98.

———. (1976c). Ideological diversity and creativity: A re-evaluation of a hypothesis. *Social Behavior and Personality, 4,* 203–7.

———. (1976d). Interdisciplinary and military determinants of scientific productivity: A cross-lagged correlation analysis. *Journal of Vocational Behavior, 9,* 53–62.

———. (1976e). Philosophical eminence, beliefs, and zeitgeist: An individual-generational analysis. *Journal of Personality and Social Psychology, 34,* 630–40.

———. (1976f). The sociopolitical context of philosophical beliefs: A transhistorical causal analysis. *Social Forces, 54,* 513–23.

———. (1977a). Creative productivity, age, and stress: A biographical time-series analysis of 10 classical composers. *Journal of Personality and Social Psychology, 35,* 791–804.

———. (1977b). Eminence, creativity, and geographic marginality: A recursive structural equation model. *Journal of Personality and Social Psychology, 35,* 805–16.

————. (1978). Independent discovery in science and technology: A closer look at the Poisson distribution. *Social Studies of Science, 8*, 521–32.

————. (1979). Multiple discovery and invention: Zeitgeist, genius, or chance? *Journal of Personality and Social Psychology, 37*, 1603–16.

————. (1980a). Intuition and analysis: A predictive and explanatory model. *Genetic Psychology Monographs, 102*, 3–60.

————. (1980b). Techno-scientific activity and war: A yearly time-series analysis, 1500–1903 A.D. *Scientometrics, 2*, 251–55.

————. (1980c). Thematic fame and melodic originality in classical music: A multivariate computer-content analysis. *Journal of Personality, 48*, 206–19.

————. (1980d). Thematic fame, melodic originality, and musical zeitgeist: A biographical and transhistorical content analysis. *Journal of Personality and Social Psychology, 38*, 972–83.

————. (1981). Creativity in Western civilization: Extrinsic and intrinsic causes. *American Anthropologist, 83*, 628–30.

————. (1983a). Dramatic greatness and content: A quantitative study of 81 Athenian and Shakespearean plays. *Empirical Studies of the Arts, 1*, 109–23.

————. (1983b). Formal education, eminence, and dogmatism: The curvilinear relationship. *Journal of Creative Behavior, 17*, 149–62.

————. (1983c). Intergenerational transfer of individual differences in hereditary monarchs: Genes, role-modeling, cohort, or sociocultural effects? *Journal of Personality and Social Psychology, 44*, 354–64.

————. (1984a). Artistic creativity and interpersonal relationships across and within generations. *Journal of Personality and Social Psychology, 46*, 1273–86.

————. (1984b). Creative productivity and age: A mathematical model based on a two-step cognitive process. *Developmental Review, 4*, 77–111.

————. (1984c). *Genius, creativity, and leadership: Historiometric inquiries.* Cambridge, Mass.: Harvard University Press.

————. (1984d). Is the marginality effect all that marginal? *Social Studies of Science, 14*, 621–22.

————. (1984e). Leaders as eponyms: Individual and situational determinants of monarchal eminence. *Journal of Personality, 52*, 1–21.

————. (1984f). Scientific eminence historical and contemporary: A measurement assessment. *Scientometrics, 6*, 169–82.

————. (1985). Quality, quantity, and age: The careers of 10 distinguished psychologists. *International Journal of Aging and Human Development, 21*, 241–54.

————. (1986a). Aesthetic success in classical music: A computer analysis of 1935 compositions. *Empirical Studies of the Arts, 4*, 1–17.

————. (1986b). Biographical typicality, eminence, and achievement style. *Journal of Creative Behavior, 20*, 14–22.

————. (1986c). Multiple discovery: Some Monte Carlo simulations and Gedanken experiments. *Scientometrics, 9*, 269–80.

————. (1986d). Multiples, Poisson distributions, and chance: An analysis of the Brannigan-Wanner model. *Scientometrics, 9*, 127–37.

————. (1986e). Popularity, content, and context in 37 Shakespeare plays. *Poetics, 15*, 493–510.

———. (1986f). Stochastic models of multiple discovery. *Czechoslovak Journal of Physics, B 36,* 138–41.

———. (1987a). Developmental antecedents of achieved eminence. *Annals of Child Development, 5,* 131–69.

———. (1987b). Musical aesthetics and creativity in Beethoven: A computer analysis of 105 compositions. *Empirical Studies of the Arts, 5,* 87–104.

———. (1987c). *Why presidents succeed: A political psychology of leadership.* New Haven, Conn.: Yale University Press.

———. (1988a). Age and outstanding achievement: What do we know after a century of research? *Psychological Bulletin, 104,* 251–67.

———. (1988b). Creativity, leadership, and chance. In R. J. Sternberg (Ed.), *The nature of creativity: Contemporary psychological perspectives* (pp. 386–426). New York: Cambridge University Press.

———. (1988c). Galtonian genius, Kroeberian configurations, and emulation: A generational time-series analysis of Chinese civilization. *Journal of Personality and Social Psychology, 55,* 230–38.

———. (1988d). *Scientific genius: A psychology of science.* Cambridge: Cambridge University Press.

———. (1989a). Age and creative productivity: Nonlinear estimation of an information-processing model. *International Journal of Aging and Human Development, 29,* 23–37.

———. (1989b). Shakespeare's sonnets: A case of and for single-case historiometry. *Journal of Personality, 57,* 695–721.

———. (1990). Lexical choices and aesthetic success: A computer content analysis of 154 Shakespeare sonnets. *Computers and the Humanities, 24,* 251–64.

———. (1991a). Career landmarks in science: Individual differences and interdisciplinary contrasts. *Developmental Psychology, 27,* 119–30.

———. (1991b). Emergence and realization of genius: The lives and works of 120 classical composers. *Journal of Personality and Social Psychology, 61,* 829–40.

———. (1991c). Latent-variable models of posthumous reputation: A quest for Galton's *G. Journal of Personality and Social Psychology, 60,* 607–19.

———. (1991d). Personality correlates of exceptional personal influence: A note on Thorndike's (1950) creators and leaders. *Creativity Research Journal, 4,* 67–78.

———. (1992a). Gender and genius in Japan: Feminine eminence in masculine culture. *Sex Roles, 27,* 101–19.

———. (1992b). Leaders of American psychology, 1879–1967: Career development, creative output, and professional achievement. *Journal of Personality and Social Psychology, 62,* 5–17.

———. (1992c). The social context of career success and course for 2,026 scientists and inventors. *Personality and Social Psychology Bulletin, 18,* 452–63.

———. (1993). Genius and chance: A Darwinian perspective. In J. Brockman (Ed.), *Creativity: The Reality Club IV* (pp. 176–201). New York: Simon & Schuster.

———. (1994). *Greatness: Who makes history and why.* New York: Guilford Press.

———. (1995a). Drawing inferences from symphonic programs: Musical attributes versus listener attributions. *Music Perception, 12,* 307–22.

————. (1995b). Foresight in insight? A Darwinian answer. In R. J. Sternberg and J. E. Davidson (Eds.), *The nature of insight* (pp. 465–94). Cambridge, Mass.: MIT Press.

————. (1996a). Creative expertise: A life-span developmental perspective. In K. A. Ericsson (Ed.), *The road to expert performance: Empirical evidence from the arts and sciences, sports, and games* (pp. 227–53). Mahwah, N.J.: Erlbaum.

————. (1996b). Individual genius and cultural configurations: The case of Japanese civilization. *Journal of Cross-Cultural Psychology, 27,* 354–75.

————. (1997a). Creative productivity: A predictive and explanatory model of career trajectories and landmarks. *Psychological Review,* 104, 66–89.

————. (1997b). Foreign influence and national achievement: The impact of open milieus on Japanese civilization. *Journal of Personality and Social Psychology, 72,* 86–97.

————. (1998a). Achieved eminence in minority and majority cultures: Convergence versus divergence in the assessments of 294 African Americans. *Journal of Personality and Social Psychology, 74,* 804–17.

————. (1998b). Fickle fashion versus immortal fame: Transhistorical assessments of creative products in the opera house. *Journal of Personality and Social Psychology, 75,* 198–210.

————. (in press-a). Creativity as variation and selection: Some critical constraints. In M. Runco (Ed.), *Critical creativity.* Cresskill, N.J.: Hampton Press.

————. (in press-b). Talent and its development: An emergenic and epigenetic model. *Psychological Review.*

Skinner, B. F. (1959). A case study in scientific method. In S. Koch (Ed.), *Psychology: A study of a science* (Vol. 2, pp. 359–79). New York: McGraw-Hill.

————. (1972). *Cumulative record: A selection of papers* (3d ed.). New York: Appleton-Century-Crofts.

Slater, E., and Meyer, A. (1959). Contributions to a pathography of the musician: 1. Robert Schumann. *Confinia Psychiatrica, 2,* 65–94.

Smith, D. G. (1993). A 15-year study of the association between dominance rank and reproductive success of male rhesus macaques. *Primates, 34,* 471–80.

Smith, S. M. (1995). Fixation, incubation, and insight in memory and creative thinking. In S. M. Smith, T. B. Ward, and R. A. Finke (Eds.), *The creative cognition approach* (pp. 136–56). Cambridge, Mass.: MIT Press.

Smith, S. M., Ward, T. B., and Finke, R. A. (Eds.). (1995). *The creative cognition approach.* Cambridge, Mass.: MIT Press.

Sobel, R. S., and Rothenberg, A. (1980). Artistic creation as stimulated by superimposed versus separated visual images. *Journal of Personality and Social Psychology, 39,* 953–61.

Sober, E. (1994). Models of cultural evolution. In E. Sober (Ed.), *Conceptual issues in evolutionary biology* (2d ed., pp. 477–92). Cambridge, Mass.: MIT Press.

Söderqvist, T. (1994). Darwinian overtones: Niels K. Jerne and the origin of the selection theory of antibody formation. *Journal of the History of Biology, 27,* 481–529.

Sorokin, P. A. (1937–41). *Social and cultural dynamics* (4 vols.). New York: American Book.

————. (1963). *A long journey: The autobiography of Pitirim A. Sorokin*. New Haven, Conn.: College and University Press.

————. (1969). *Society, culture, and personality*. New York: Cooper Square. (Original work published 1947.)

Sorokin, P. A., and Merton, R. K. (1935). The course of Arabian intellectual development, 700–1300 A.D. *Isis, 22*, 516–24.

Spencer, H. (1904). *An autobiography* (Vol. 1). New York: Appleton.

————. (1967). *The evolution of society: Selections from Herbert Spencer's Principles of Sociology* (Ed. R. L. Carneiro). Chicago: University of Chicago Press.

Spengler, O. (1945). *The decline of the West* (C. F. Atkinson, Trans.). New York: Knopf. (Original work published 1926–1928.)

Stack, S. (1987). Celebrities and suicide: A taxonomy and analysis, 1948–1983. *American Sociological Review, 52*, 401–12.

Stavridou, A., and Furnham, A. (1996). The relationship between psychoticism, trait-creativity and the attentional mechanism of cognitive inhibition. *Personality and Individual Differences, 21*, 143–53.

Staw, B. (1990). An evolutionary approach to creativity and innovation. In M. W. West and J. L. Farr (Eds.), *Innovation and creativity at work: Psychological and organizational strategies* (pp. 287–308). New York: Wiley.

Steck, L., and Machotka, P. (1975). Preference for musical complexity: Effects of context. *Journal of Experimental Psychology: Human Perception and Performance, 104*, 170–74.

Stein, E., and Lipton, P. (1989). Where guesses come from: Evolutionary epistemology and the anomaly of guided vision. *Biology and Philosophy, 4*, 33–56.

Stent, G. S. (1972). Prematurity and uniqueness in scientific discovery. *Scientific American, 227*, 84–93.

Stephan, P. E., and Levin, S. G. (1992). *Striking the mother lode in science: The importance of age, place, and time*. New York: Oxford University Press.

————. (1993). Age and the Nobel Prize revisited. *Scientometrics, 28*, 387–99.

Sternberg, R. J. (1985). *Beyond IQ: A triarchic theory of human intelligence*. New York: Cambridge University Press.

————. (1989). Computational models of scientific discovery: Do they compute? [Review of Scientific discovery: Computational explorations of the creative process.] *Contemporary Psychology, 34*, 895–97.

————. (1998). Cognitive mechanisms in human creativity: Is variation blind or sighted? *Journal of Creative Behavior, 32*, 159–176.

Sternberg, R. J., and Davidson, J. E. (Eds.). (1995). *The nature of insight*. Cambridge, Mass.: MIT Press.

Sternberg, R. J., and Lubart, T. I. (1995). *Defying the crowd: Cultivating creativity in a culture of conformity*. New York: Free Press.

Stewart, J. A. (1986). Drifting continents and colliding interests: A quantitative application of the interests perspective. *Social Studies of Science, 16*, 261–79.

Stewart, L. H. (1977). Birth order and political leadership. In M. G. Hermann (Ed.), *The psychological examination of political leaders* (pp. 205–36). New York: Free Press.

———. (1991). The world cycle of leadership. *Journal of Analytical Psychology, 36,* 449–59.

Stohs, J. H. (1992). Career patterns and family status of women and men artists. *Career Development Quarterly, 40,* 223–33.

Suler, J. R. (1980). Primary process thinking and creativity. *Psychological Bulletin, 88,* 144–65.

Sulloway, F. J. (1985). Darwin's early intellectual development: An overview of the *Beagle* voyage (1831–1836). In D. Kohn (Ed.), *The Darwinian heritage* (pp. 121–54). Princeton, N.J.: Princeton University Press.

———. (1996). *Born to rebel: Birth order, family dynamics, and creative lives.* New York: Pantheon.

———. (in press). Birth order, sibling competition, and human behavior. In P. S. Davies and H. R. Holcomb III (Eds.), *The evolution of minds: Psychological and philosophical perspectives.* Dordrecht, Netherlands: Kluwer Academic Publishers.

Taagepera, R. (1979). People, skills, and resources: An interaction model for world population growth. *Technological Forecasting and Social Change, 13,* 13–30.

Taagepera, R., and Colby, B. N. (1979). Growth of Western civilization: Epicyclical or exponential? *American Anthropologist, 81,* 907–12.

Taylor, D. W. (1963). Variables related to creativity and productivity among men in two research laboratories. In C. W. Taylor and F. X. Barron (Eds.), *Scientific creativity: Its recognition and development* (pp. 228–50). New York: Wiley.

Taylor, C. W., Smith, W. R., and Ghiselin, B. (1963). The creative and other contributions of one sample of research scientists. In C. W. Taylor and F. X. Barron (Eds.), *Scientific creativity: Its recognition and development* (pp. 53–76). New York: Wiley.

Taylor, M. S., Locke, E. A., Lee, C., and Gist, M. E. (1984). Type A behavior and faculty research productivity: What are the mechanisms? *Organizational Behavior and Human Performance, 34,* 402–418.

Terman, L. M. (1917). The intelligence quotient of Francis Galton in childhood. *American Journal of Psychology, 28,* 209–15.

———. (1925). *Mental and physical traits of a thousand gifted children.* Stanford, Calif.: Stanford University Press.

———. (1954). Scientists and nonscientists in a group of 800 gifted men. *Psychological Monographs: General and Applied, 68* (Whole No. 378), 1–44.

Terman, L. M., and Oden, M. H. (1947). *The gifted child grows up.* Stanford, Calif.: Stanford University Press.

———. (1959). *The gifted group at mid-life.* Stanford, Calif.: Stanford University Press.

Terry, W. S. (1989). Birth order and prominence in the history of psychology. *Psychological Record, 39,* 333–37.

Thagard, P. (1992). *Conceptual revolutions.* Princeton, N.J.: Princeton University Press.

Therivel, W. (1993). The challenged personality as a precondition for sustained creativity. *Creativity Research Journal, 6,* 413–24.

Thornhill, R. (1998). Darwinian aesthetics. In C. B. Crawford and D. Krebs (Eds.),

Handbook of evolutionary psychology: Ideas, issues, and applications (pp. 543–72). Mahwah, N.J.: Erlbaum.

Tobias, P. V. (1970). Brain-size, gray matter, and race—Fact or fiction. *American Journal of Physical Anthropology, 32,* 3–25.

Tomlinson-Keasey, C. (1990). The working lives of Terman's gifted women. In H. Y. Grossman and N. L. Chester (Eds.), *The experience and meaning of work in women's lives* (pp. 213–39). Hillsdale, N.J.: Erlbaum.

Torrance, E. P. (1988). The nature of creativity as manifest in 15 testings. In R. J. Sternberg (Ed.), *The nature of creativity* (pp. 43–75). New York: Cambridge University Press.

Toulmin, S. (1981). Evolution, adaptation, and human understanding. In M. B. Brewer and B. E. Collins (Eds.), *Scientific inquiry and the social sciences* (pp. 18–36). San Francisco: Jossey-Bass.

Townsend, F. (1997). Rebelling against *Born to Rebel. Journal of Social and Evolutionary Systems, 20,* 191–204.

Toynbee, A. J. (1946). *A study of history* (abridged by D. C. Somervell, 2 vols.). New York: Oxford University Press.

Travis, C. B., and Yeager, C. P. (1991). Sexual selection, parental investment, and sexism. *Journal of Social Issues, 47,* 117–29.

Trivers, R. L. (1971). The evolution of reciprocal altruism. *Quarterly Review of Biology, 46,* 35–57.

Turner, S. P., and Chubin, D. E. (1976). Another appraisal of Ortega, the Coles, and science policy: The Ecclesiastes hypothesis. *Social Science Information, 15,* 657–62.

Turner, S. P., and Chubin, D. E. (1979). Chance and eminence in science: Ecclesiastes II. *Social Science Information, 18,* 437–49.

Tweney, R. D. (1990). Five questions for computationalists. In J. Shrager and P. Langley (Eds.), *Computational models of scientific discovery and theory information* (pp. 471–84). San Mateo, Calif.: Kaufmann.

Tweney, R. D., Doherty, M. E., and Mynatt, C. R. (Eds.). (1981). *On scientific thinking.* New York: Columbia University Press.

Upmanyu, V. V., Bhardwaj, S., and Singh, S. (1996). Word-association emotional indicators: Associations with anxiety, psychoticism, extraversion, and creativity. *Journal of Social Psychology, 136,* 521–29.

Veblen, T. (1919). The intellectual preeminence of Jews in modern Europe. *Political Science Quarterly, 34,* 33–42.

Verplanck, W. S. (1955). The control of the content of conversation: Reinforcement of statements of opinion. *Journal of Abnormal and Social Psychology, 51,* 668–76.

Visher, S. S. (1947). Starred scientists: A study of their ages. *American Scientist, 35,* 543, 570, 572, 574, 576, 578, 580.

Vitz, P. C. (1964). Preferences for rates of information presented by sequences of tones. *Journal of Experimental Psychology, 68,* 176–83.

Vries, H. de (1905). *Species and varieties: Their origin by mutation* (Ed. D. T. MacDougal). Chicago: Open Court.

Vroom, V. H., and Pahl, B. (1971). Relationship between age and risk taking among managers. *Journal of Applied Psychology, 55,* 399–405.

Wagner, M. E., and Schubert, H. J. P. (1977). Sibship variables and United States presidents. *Journal of Individual Psychology, 33,* 78–85.

Walberg, H. J., Rasher, S. P., and Parkerson, J. (1980). Childhood and eminence. *Journal of Creative Behavior, 13,* 225–31.

Walker, A. M., Koestner, R., and Hum, A. (1995). Personality correlates of depressive style in autobiographies of creative achievers. *Journal of Creative Behavior, 29,* 75–94.

Wallach, M. A., and Kogan, N. (1965). *Modes of thinking in young children.* New York: Holt, Rinehart, and Winston.

Wallas, G. (1926). *The art of thought.* New York: Harcourt, Brace.

Waller, N. G., Bouchard, T. J., Jr., Lykken, D. T., Tellegen, A., and Blacker, D. M. (1993). Creativity, heritability, familiality: Which word does not belong? *Psychological Inquiry, 4,* 235–37.

Waller, N. G., Kojetin, B. A., Bouchard, T. J., Jr., Lykken, D. T., and Tellegen, A. (1990). Genetic and environmental influences on religious interests, attitudes, and values: A study of twins reared apart and together. *Psychological Science, 1,* 138–42.

Waller, N. G., and Shaver, P. R. (1994). The importance of nongenetic influences on romantic love styles: A twin-family study. *Psychological Science, 5,* 268–74.

Watkins, C. E., Jr. (1992). Birth-order research and Adler's theory: A critical review. *Individual Psychology, 48,* 357–68.

Weber, R. J. (1992). *Forks, phonographs, and hot air balloons: A field guide to inventive thinking.* New York: Oxford University Press.

Wechsler, J. (Ed.). (1978). *On aesthetics in science.* Cambridge, Mass.: MIT Press.

Weisberg, R. W. (1992). *Creativity: Beyond the myth of genius.* New York: Freeman.

———. (1994). Genius and madness? A quasi-experimental test of the hypothesis that manic-depression increases creativity. *Psychological Science, 5,* 361–67.

Weizmann, F., Wiener, N. I., Wiesenthal, D. L., and Ziegler, M. (1990). Differential K theory and racial hierarchies. *Canadian Psychology, 31,* 1–13.

West, S. S. (1960). Sibling configurations of scientists. *American Journal of Sociology, 66,* 268–74.

Whaples, R. (1991). A quantitative history of the *Journal of Economic History* and the cliometric revolution. *Journal of Economic History, 51,* 289–301.

White, L. (1949). *The science of culture.* New York: Farrar, Straus.

White, R. K. (1931). The versatility of genius. *Journal of Social Psychology, 2,* 460–89.

Who said what when: A chronological dictionary of quotations. (1991). New York: Hippocrene Books.

Wilson, D. S. (1980). *The natural selection of populations and communities.* Menlo Park, Calif.: Benjamin-Cummings.

Wilson, D. S., and Sober, E. (1996). Reintroducing group selection to the human behavioral sciences. *Behavioral and Brain Sciences, 17,* 585–654.

Wilson, E. O. (1975). *Sociobiology: The new synthesis.* Cambridge, Mass.: Harvard University Press.

Winner, E. (1996). *Gifted children: Myths and realities.* New York: Basic Books.

Wispé, L. G. (1965). Some social and psychological correlates of eminence in psychology. *Journal of the History of the Behavioral Sciences, 7,* 88–98.

Woods, F. A. (1906). *Mental and moral heredity in royalty.* New York: Holt.

Woodward, W. R. (1974). Scientific genius and loss of a parent. *Science Studies, 4,* 265–77.

Woody, E., and Claridge, G. (1977). Psychoticism and thinking. *British Journal of Social and Clinical Psychology, 16,* 241–48.

Woolf, V. (1929). *A room of one's own.* New York: Harcourt, Brace and World.

Wordsworth, W. (1928). *The poetical works of Wordsworth: With introductions and notes* (T. Hutchinson, Ed.). London: Oxford University Press. (Original work published 1807.)

Wright, S. (1970). Random drift and the shifting balance theory of evolution. In K. Kojima (Ed.), *Mathematical topics in population genetics* (pp. 1–31). Berlin: Springer-Verlag.

Yarczower, M., and Hazlett, L. (1977). Evolutionary scales and anagenesis. *Psychological Bulletin, 84,* 1088–97.

Yuasa, M. (1974). The shifting center of scientific activity in the West: From the sixteenth to the twentieth century. In N. Shigeru, D. L. Swain, and Y. Eri (Eds.), *Science and society in modern Japan* (pp. 81–103). Tokyo: University of Tokyo Press.

Zajonc, R. B. (1976). Family configuration and intelligence. *Science, 192,* 227–35.

———. (1983). Validating the confluence model. *Psychological Bulletin, 93,* 457–80.

Zhao, H. (1984). An intelligence constant of scientific work. *Scientometrics, 6,* 9–17.

Zhao, H., and Jiang, G. (1985). Shifting of world's scientific center and scientists' social ages. *Scientometrics, 8,* 59–80.

———. (1986). Life-span and precocity of scientists. *Scientometrics, 9,* 27–36.

Zuckerman, H. (1977). *Scientific elite.* New York: Free Press.

Zuckerman, M. (1990). Some dubious premises in research and theory on racial differences: Scientific, social, and ethical issues. *American Psychologist, 45,* 1297–1303.

———. (1991). Truth and consequences: Responses to Rushton and Kendler. *American Psychologist, 46,* 984–86.

Zusne, L. (1976). Age and achievement in psychology: The harmonic mean as a model. *American Psychologist, 31,* 805–7.

Zweigenhaft, R. L. (1975). Birth order, approval-seeking, and membership in Congress. *Journal of Individual Psychology, 31,* 205–10.

Index

~